T0271815

The Transformation of a
Peasant Economy

Communities, Contexts and Cultures
Leicester Studies in English Local History

General Editor
Charles Phythian-Adams

The Transformation of a Peasant Economy

Townspeople and villagers
in the Lutterworth area
1500–1700

JOHN GOODACRE

Routledge
Taylor & Francis Group

LONDON AND NEW YORK

First published 1994 by Scolar Press

Published 2017 by Routledge
2 Park Square, Milton Park, Abingdon, Oxon OX14 4RN
711 Third Avenue, New York, NY 10017, USA

Routledge is an imprint of the Taylor & Francis Group, an informa business

The author and publishers gratefully acknowledge the financial support given to this publication by the Marc Fitch Fund.

British Library Cataloguing-in-Publication data

Goodacre, John
    Transformation of a Peasant Economy:
    Townspeople and Villagers in the
    Lutterworth Area, 1500–1700. –
    (Communities, Contexts & Cultures:
    Leicester Studies in English Local
    History)
    I. Title II. Series
    942.544

ISBN 13: 978-1-85928-073-7 (hbk)

Typeset in 10 point Garamond by Bournemouth Colour Graphics, Parkstone.

Illustration 1. Lutterworth Thursday market in 1992, dating back to the market charter of 1214. View looking South down the High Street, shewing the Hind (and the sign of the Denbigh) on the western side. Until recently the market stalls lined the High Street and the present Market Place was occupied by island premises (including the King's Head) which had encroached on what was presumably the original mediaeval market-place.

Photograph: John Goodacre

For J. H. M. G.,
father, farmer and lord of the manor

In memory of H. G. G.

ENVOY

Pray with me, God speed the Plough.

Thy Friend, if thou be so to
the Publique and the Poore,

John Moore.

A Scripture-Word against Inclosure; viz: Such as doe Un-People Townes, and Un-Corne Fields. As also, Against all such, that daub over this black Sinne with untempered morter. By John Moore, Minister of the Church at *Knaptoft* in *Leicester-shire.* (1656), Advertisement

Contents

List of Illustrations, Maps and Figures

Illustrations

Maps

Figures

List of Tables

List of Weights and Measures

Number

One hundred		
(great or long hundred)	=	six score (120)
One score	=	twenty
One dozen	=	twelve

Length

One statute mile	=	1,760 yards
One yard	=	3 feet
One foot	=	12 inches

Weight

One ton	=	2,240 pounds (lbs)
One quarter	=	28 lbs
One stone	=	14 lbs

Grain and corn (by volume)

One quarter	=	8 strikes
(One bushel	=	2 strikes)

Wool

One tod	weighs 28 pounds

Money

One pound (£1)	=	20 shillings
One shilling (1/-)	=	12 pence
One penny (1d.)	=	2 halfpence
One halfpenny ($\frac{1}{2}$ d.)	=	2 farthings

Land measures

Yard land	unit of open-field farm holding
Acre (strip or 'land')	unit of land in open fields
Acre (measure)	local customary land measure
One statute acre	= 4,840 square yards

Other measures

Kid	furze or gorse gathered for fuel
Lease	yarn
Load	coals

Dates

As New Year began on Lady Day (the 25th of March), dates from the 1st of January to that day are given with the year in the transitional form (as 1633/4).

Orthography

Contemporary spelling, but not punctuation or capitalization, has been modernized, with the exception of surnames and book titles, and of a few other instances where it contributes to the meaning.

Glossary

Unfamiliar terms or familiar words used as special terms are indexed. They are explained in context, usually at the first occurrence, marked by double quotation marks.

Prosopography

The names of local people are given where they are referred to elsewhere and their entries in the index may include explanatory details.

General Editor's Foreword

The title of this series, *Communities, Contexts and Cultures*, expresses succinctly the scope of its coverage. Contributions to it are concerned above all with the full-length elucidation, for any historical period, of English local societies, their composition over the generations, their cultures, and their distinctive topographical settings. As such, the series reflects the current shift of academic local historical emphasis, away from the investigation of the single local community and the search for a taxonomy of communities – important as those preoccupations nevertheless remain for the discipline and, indeed, for the series – towards a wider view. This embraces broadly definable *collectivities* of communities that are grouped together at a variety of levels of formal or informal association and interaction: as the societal components of either historically determined territories or of geographically specific landscapes; as points of conjuncture within regional or local economic networks; as linked together by generations of blood-related 'core' families; or as sharing some cultural trait – like dialect – that, in broad terms, is spatially delimited.

These then are but some of the new and exciting ways in which local history is beginning to open up and, indeed, to sophisticate more general perceptions concerning the evolving structure of what is usually termed British 'society'. For the analysis of that has been left too long in the hands of those whose interests are primarily with such abstract matters as the history of the State, the national economy or the so-called 'class-system'. In reality, if 'society' is defined as a spatially dense system of interrelationships between people, involving personal transactions or shared affinities of all kinds, then 'society' only has meaningful existence at ground level and, for the great majority of people before modern methods of communication helped to distance such interrelationships, especially within specifically restrained regional contexts. Above that 'real' level, indeed, it may be more appropriate to think, not about such concepts as 'society' at all, but rather about national forms of social organization, whether these be constitutional, legal, religious, economic, cultural or whatever. Within this overall context local societies, and the local economies that colour their basic characters, therefore demand to be understood for what they are: as existing simultaneously in their own terms as integral parts of the wider whole.

One of the current roles of the English local historian, then, is to reintegrate from below the study of the English past: to repair that which has been thematically torn asunder by the ever-more specialized historical methodologies of the last academic generation or so. Necessary as has been the refinement of such specialisms, sometimes they have resulted in gross intellectual distortions. For present purposes, the most damaging has been the originally unintended severance of agrarian history from urban history – both of which began simply as broad 'fields' of study only to become instead closed quasi-disciplines in their own rights. Yet a continuing distinction between the studies of town and country is becoming rapidly more difficult to sustain. From the viewpoint of the town alone, for example, an urban society itself will not necessarily be confined by the technical limits of the built-up area, since some nearby rural settlements rather than others may be regarded as 'urban' extensions of it due to exceptionally dense marriage connections, occupational specialisms, or daily employment opportunities. Equally, an urban workforce can be profitably studied as integral to, and as sharing together with the inhabitants of the surrounding countryside, a predominant industrial culture – as Dr David Hey has demonstrated so successfully for the metal-workers of Hallamshire during the years around 1700 in the previous volume of this very series. Finally, and especially at the entry-point to the urban hierarchy, townspeople may be seen, as in the present volume, to be reactive to, and even the initiators of, long-term fluctuations in the supply and marketing of agricultural products in their immediate rural neighbourhoods.

It is, then, the constant interaction between countryside and market town that rightly lies at the heart of this pioneering study, the first of its kind to probe with clinical logic and almost surgical finesse into the wider ramifications of that interplay. By consistently relating the economic mechanisms of the agricultural working world in all their local diversity to urban societal developments, Dr John Goodacre here makes a number of quite fundamental contributions to both agrarian history and urban history simultaneously. In doing so, he throws up additionally a major incidental finding as to the existence of what seems to have been, or to have become, a clearly defined economic 'edge' to his area in relation to its northern neighbourly equivalent. Above all, by tracing the emergence of his local economy with such learning and sensitivity, Dr Goodacre is able to pinpoint, for the first time with any precision for any region, the part played locally in, and hence the local timing of, a crucial change in the overall system of socio-economic organization: the eventually nationwide shift from a customary to a commercial economy. It would be difficult to imagine a more 'relevant' or more crucial historical contribution to our understanding of the current 'culture' of the market and how that first developed. To have been marginally associated with the development of this important work in one shadowy advisory capacity or another over the 20 years or so of its gestation, therefore, has been both a pleasure and a privilege.

Charles Phythian-Adams
Head of the Department of English Local History
University of Leicester

Preface

I was brought up in one of the villages in the Lutterworth area. Some of my earliest memories are of "going to Lutterworth", weekly trips to the town for shopping and other family business, and I have always been fascinated by the many ways in which it serves as the local centre. Our branch of the family came to Leicestershire from Kent during the Civil War and in the eighteenth century raised themselves in three generations from husbandman, through grazing yeoman farmer, to landowning gentleman. While never staying in the same place they always kept within the area and one generation lived in Lutterworth, where the family attorney's practice blossomed into the town's first bank. Following my grandfather's lead, and armed with his copy of the relevant volume of *The History and Antiquities of the County of Leicester* by that tireless Georgian antiquary John Nichols, I set about studying the records of our family and the village that became the centre of the family's estates. The achievement of Professor Hoskins's local history of the Leicestershire village of Wigston magna, published as *The Midland Peasant*, was an encouragement to address wider questions. My legal training taught me not to expect my father's lordship of the manor of our village to retain any present significance beyond such trifles as the statutory right to appoint a gamekeeper; but what puzzled me was that even at the enclosure of its common fields in the mid-seventeenth century, which I was able to reconstruct from our copies of the award and our title deeds, no manorial influence appeared to be at work. I realized that such questions could not be tackled in the context of one village in isolation and here too the records often suggested connexions of all kinds with the town. Reading my grandfather's book on Lutterworth, which he subtitled *The Story of John Wycliffe's Town*, I was struck not so much by the worldwide fame of the town for having been the death place of "the Morning Star of the Reformation" as by the fact that the townspeople, villagers and traders who frequent the Thursday market in the draughty Market Place at the top of the steep High Street are persisting in a pattern of activity datable back nearly eight centuries, to a royal market charter of 1214 (see Illustration 1).[1]

The countryside around is typical of the 'Land of the Ridge and Furrow' and still bears traces of the generations of labour that went into working the open fields. Although it straddles the Midland watershed it is not spectacular; it was once described for me by the Automobile Association as 'flat, undulating country of no particular interest'. In a modest way, however, Lutterworth can be said to dominate the southern uplands of Leicestershire

from its situation along the top of an east–west ridge. Certainly from the
south, where the ridge slopes down fairly quickly to the River Swift just
outside the town, it is conspicuous on the skyline from far off. 'The town of
Lutterworth', to quote another local antiquary, Sir Thomas Cave of Stanford
on Avon, 'is situated on a pretty eminence, the church appearing over the
houses in a very agreeable manner'. He was writing in the eighteenth
century; how very much more striking it must have been in the bare
landscape of the open fields, 'which before', according to Nichols,
'presented to the eye of the traveller a cheerless aspect'. William Burton, in
his pioneering book *The Description of Leicester Shire, Containing Matters
of Antiquitye, Historye, Armorye, and Genealogy*, first published in 1622,
noted that the parish church of St Mary was 'a very fair and large Church,
with an high and neat spire Steeple'. Before it fell in the Great Storm of 1703
not only did this landmark 'give a grandeur and dignity to the town it
belonged to, but even guided the steps of wandering travellers', perhaps
reminding them that it was "Wycliffe's town" that they were approaching.
But what of the local inhabitants of all kinds who resorted to Lutterworth
habitually as their market town? What did they think of on the road there
when first catching sight of the spire?[2]

My preoccupation with the interrelationship between the town and its
area has prompted me to unravel some of the ways in which villagers and
townspeople made it function as an urban centre. Even though the records
of its administration as a town are not plentiful, an excellent starting point
presented itself in the form of a detailed terrier of the town and fields written
at the beginning of the sixteenth century,[3] which is echoed by a survey made
a century later. As for the seventeenth-century enclosures, the pamphlet
controversy between two local parsons is also a double treasure. Of the
veritable snowstorm of literature that flew off English presses during the Civil
War period these are some of the few writings to contain detailed local
evidence. Among classically educated Englishmen, too, there was usually a
measure of cultural blindness to such a basic activity as open-field husbandry.
Just as depictions of the countryside could pass straight from fashionable
gardens with Italianate parterres and ordered orchards surrounding a house
to wild landscapes of a suspiciously Tuscan character so farming manuals
tended to start from Roman authorities like Columella, Varro or Virgil and to
pass over open fields by recommending enclosed grounds as generally
preferable.[4] Here, however, were two local men whose clerical education
rendered them almost excessively articulate concerning the issues of the day;
yet they could at the same time cut through the usual citations of biblical
authority for their views and the age-old commonplace which contrasts the
honest toil of the ploughman with the idleness of the shepherd,[5] so as to
argue in practical husbandry terms from the experiences of their parishioners
and neighbours, and indeed from their own experience as owners and

occupiers of farms. Otherwise, apart from the fame deriving from Wycliffe, which cannot be said to have had any direct effect on the character of Lutterworth before the nineteenth century,[6] this town was an ordinary market town and its very lack of singularity makes it an ideal subject for a detailed study.

I wish to record my gratitude to my family and my friends and to the staff and generations of students at the Department of English Local History at Leicester University. Furthermore I value the encouragement I have received over the years from Dr Joan Thirsk, Professor Alan Everitt, Professor Rodney Hilton and my brother Hugh Goodacre. Above all Professor Charles Phythian-Adams has been unfailingly generous with criticism and detailed advice at every stage of my work.

John Goodacre

Introduction

The realization of how important it is to understand peasant society has not only resulted in studies dealing with contemporary problems of the third world: it has also encouraged the re-assessment of various periods of change in history. If peasant society is treated as a monolithic, timeless concept, a definition of it that can be applied in both fields becomes too general to be of use.[1] One result is that English historians disagree about the precise period when the peasantry of this country is supposed to have come to an end. Here the peasantry is taken to mean occupiers of land holdings engaged as family units in the agricultural production by which they subsist, grouped into communities so as to share a degree of collective rights in the land and common possessions, supporting labourers and craftsmen from within their own ranks and also, by means of exactions and market involvement, supporting from out of their surplus production the superstructures of landlords, church, state and towns.[2] In England a peasantry of this kind seems not to have survived the Agricultural Revolution which underpinned the Industrial Revolution. Even before then, however, in the pre-industrial period, it is obvious that peasant society shewed considerable diversity and underwent great change. In 1500, for instance, the majority of the population of lowland England belonged to agrarian communities whose chief activity was production aimed at satisfying their own subsistence needs while the primary unit of local jurisdiction and regulation was still the manor, although the classic form of a village subject to a single manor was the exception rather than the rule.[3] By 1700, in total contrast, agricultural production had been enormously increased through both regional specialization and its corollary, the adoption of improved farming techniques. The parish had become the basic unit of local government, with duties and rights defined by the succession of acts that dealt with the relief and settlement of the poor. Meanwhile manorial constraints, in regions like the Midlands at least, had been broken open, allowing the growth of a consumer economy which already exhibited the advantages and disadvantages of what had become a system of more or less free trading across the country.

No doubt the various changes that made up this "transformation" developed at different times during these two centuries and at different rates. The overall increase in the population and the quickening of internal trade, for instance, may have been gradual, but more important changes, such as the spread of the new farming, could well have been very rapid. It is a fundamental task for historians to identify such short periods of accelerated advance. Recently there has been a tendency to push back the timing of some of the major developments. Professor Tawney's concentration on "his" century, 1540-1640, has left the impression that the worst effects of early enclosure had already been felt under the Tudors. Professor Kerridge has identified the technical innovations that improved farming output from the later sixteenth century onwards, but has cited early instances of them quite out of the context of whole local economies. Professor C. Dyer has further listed preparations for agricultural revolution in Warwickshire in the two centuries before. Dr Thirsk has suggested that the new manufacturers of the Tudor period, which replaced the earlier importation of a variety of goods, already added up to a kind of consumer economy.[4] All these views, when taken together, have encouraged the conclusion that the transformation was largely complete by the end of the sixteenth century, or the following generation, and had little to do with the upheavals of the seventeenth-century "English Revolution".[5] This is endorsed by the choice of 1500-1640 as the period covered by the most important survey of the subject to date, the fourth volume of *The Agrarian History of England and Wales*, edited by Thirsk.[6]

On a broader front, Professor Hilton's studies have laid the foundation for an understanding of the changing nature of the English peasantry in the middle ages and of its role as a class within the "feudal mode of production".[7] On reaching the discussion of the transition to the "capitalist mode of production", however, the argument has tended to skip to industrial production, or at least to agricultural production in its classic nineteenth-century or eighteenth-century form, within a three-part social and economic framework of landlord, capitalist tenant farmer and wage-labourer.[8] More recently Dr Martin has further elaborated the final development of the "feudal mode" up to the time of the last great peasant rebellion that attempted to turn the clock back, the Midland Revolt of 1607.[9] Both Hilton and Martin, however, stop short of providing actual examples of the processes at work during the transition. What is needed then, and what this book seeks to provide, is an explanation, based on a variety of sources rather than a single class of evidence, of how the peasant farmer, engaged in his traditional husbandry, was able to retain increasing accumulations of capital within the local economy and thus break through to a new level of capitalist farming. This may help illustrate the way in which the "capitalist mode" was to become the dominant mode of production.

This study accordingly starts from the peasant economy of the sixteenth century and follows agrarian developments in detail through to the later seventeenth when, for the first time, the country was brought into such agricultural surplus that its corn was exported. The analysis seeks to restore the major changes to the mid-seventeenth century and to identify them as amounting to a definite leap forward in the progressive development of

English society: in other words an "agrarian revolution" that formed the background to the Civil War. It will be argued that it was only at this stage of the evolution of Midland rural communities that whole sections of them either deserted the ranks of the peasantry to become capitalist farmers or were severed from their peasant roots to become landless wage-labourers. This revolution did not bring the peasantry to an end: peasant producers continued as an ever-decreasing middle stratum of society; but they were now trapped in an outdated agrarian system which was no longer the predominant one.

A transformation of this nature can only be identified by studying the diverse changes a over a wide period such as the two whole centuries chosen. It is not sufficient, however, to set temporal limits to the study; its spatial scope must also be defined, so as to be able to identify unambiguously the processes of cause and effect at work. If peasant society were uniform, the scope would be immaterial; but social diversity at any one time means that its component elements must be distinguished and contrasted.

The basic unit of peasant society was certainly the farming community; but rural economy needs to be studied in a context wider than the individual village. In the middle ages the redistribution of produce and provisions was by no means a free market but was regulated by custom and manorial controls. What was involved thereafter was the transfer of far more of this activity firstly into the open market and, eventually, to private dealings. The peasant's increasing personal involvement in marketing was an essential element of the transformation.

Studies of trade in this period have so far concentrated on problems of urban development, with the emphasis on international or inter-regional commerce and on urban industries. As a result the classification of urban communities from the metropolis down to the market town tends to dismiss the latter as barely urban. The peasant's initial entry into the market was, however, as it had been for centuries, through the market place of his own local town.[10] Indeed in any peasant society the primary urban unit is the market town, forming the nucleus of a "local market system".[11] Analysis of such a system, little affected by any outside importance of its own, should shew most clearly the essential interdependence of urban and rural society. To elucidate the transformation of the peasant economy, therefore, this study is of necessity a study of the fortunes of the market town.

The town chosen is Lutterworth, which is situated in the southern corner of Leicestershire, near the county boundaries with Warwickshire and Northamptonshire. It is approximately at the centre of the triangle formed by the ancient boroughs of Leicester and Northampton and by the city of Coventry. Just outside the sides of this triangle lie the towns of Hinckley, Rugby and Market Harborough (see Map IX and Illustration 2). The subsequent development of these three smaller places has tended to obscure

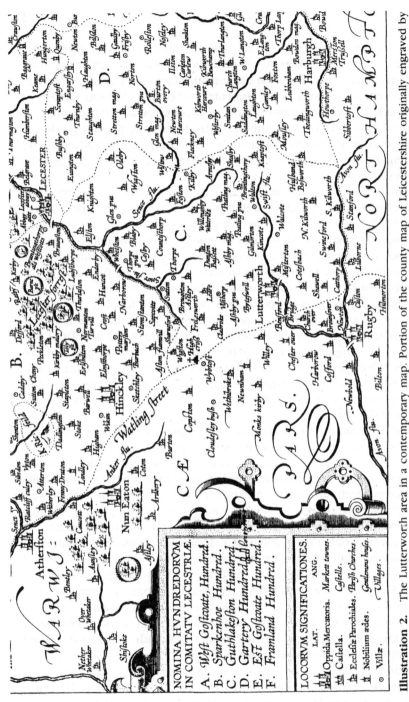

Illustration 2. The Lutterworth area in a contemporary map. Portion of the county map of Leicestershire originally engraved by Iodocus Hondius of Amsterdam in 1602. Based on Christopher Saxton's survey and improved by the addition of over 80 place names supplied by the Leicestershire historian William Burton. Market towns are clearly distinguished from other settlements.
L.R.O.

their common origin; like Lutterworth they were all formerly local market towns.[12]

Just as the individual village cannot be studied without taking into account its marketing relationships with other communities, so the market town cannot be studied without taking into account its role in a wider context. It is contended here that only in the second place should it be set in the widest context, as the lowest category in the classification of urban types: its primary role was in the local economy, as the point of exchange between villages of contrasting economic character within its immediate market area. The first chapter, therefore, sets the stage for the discussion of the role of the market town partly by using the progress of enclosure to classify in order the various types of community in the region which were involved in such exchanges, from the deserted or depopulated village upwards.

Even such a preliminary classification reveals complex interrelationships which raise many questions. These cannot be unravelled merely in terms of the town' role in the intercourse between whole villages. A further level of analysis is needed, a level which examines the fortunes of the various identifiable component groups within each community. Thus the remaining chapters will deal with the whole of the market area; and this applies even to the chapter concentrating on non-agricultural occupations and the urban influence of the town. By studying the role of the town "community" in the two contexts, firstly as the exchange point between contrasting groups and villages and secondly as a point on the regional urban network, it is intended not only to account for the rise of the market town in early modern England but also to elucidate the nature of contemporary peasant society and to demonstrate the importance to it of the seventeenth-century transition.

CHAPTER ONE

Urban and Rural Communities

To take Lutterworth as a typical market town, it is necessary first to characterize the market town in general, which will be done by drawing parallels with other towns in the region. Before that the market town will be defined by setting it in context as the lowest urban category, in contrast to the major cities, with other larger towns and cities in a middle category. Since, however, the study is primarily concerned with the town in the context of its own area of villages, the classification must be continued downwards, so to open the question of the different types of village community. This will later be elaborated by accounting for the changes brought about by agrarian development, as evidenced by the progress of enclosure. To start with, therefore, it will be most convenient to run through the whole gamut of the classification, starting at the bottom.

1. The classification of communities

In recent years much attention has been paid to the fact that a proportion of the villages that crowded the early mediaeval landscape of lowland England have since perished. Among surviving villages, moreover, there is a great diversity. It has long been recognized that, at least in the lowland regions of the country, there is a basic distinction to be made between the "close village", usually dominated by one landowner or a few farmers only, and the "open village", which was more susceptible to the subdivision of property, to immigration and, eventually, to industrialization. Such differences, it will here be argued, were closely connected with village farming economy; early desertions frequently followed soon after enclosure had brought about the abandonment of mixed husbandry on open fields, and many "open" communities were villages whose fields remained unenclosed far into the eighteenth century.

The distinction between a village and a town at the beginning of the period was not clearly drawn. The word "town", as will appear in contemporary sources quoted, carried no urban connotations and was used for villages of all kinds. There were in England well over 700 places where weekly markets were held.[1] Yet the presence of a market is not invariably a sufficient criterion for separating towns from villages and it will be helpful to make a fresh distinction. Here "town" will be reserved for a place with some urban characteristics that raised it above the level of an essentially agrarian village in which markets were held. The latter will be called a "market village".

Between the early middle ages and 1700 these places with markets exhibited great diversity in their development. On the one hand many remained mere market villages or even lost their one distinction and became ordinary villages. On the other hand the marketing importance of a few market towns, often for a particular range of produce, grew to exert an influence outside the immediate region. This occurred in the case of a town in a key position, such as at a road or river crossing on a long-range trading route. Another instance was the "cardinal" market, the point of exchange between two regions of contrasting terrain and complementary products. Within Leicestershire the early importance of Melton Mowbray as a regional market dated back to before the Norman Conquest.[2] Loughborough too occupied a key position and by the early modern period had become second only to the shire town as a market centre. It may have been a cardinal market, standing near the bridge over the Soar that linked the Charnwood Forest pastoral area with the Wolds. Ultimately of more importance, however, was its position on the main route from London through Leicester. In 1553 Loughborough bridge was said to be a much-frequented 'thoroughfare into the North parts of this Realm'[3] and this was also the export route out of the region, down the Trent to the sea.

During the later seventeenth century some market towns became populous and rapidly expanding industrial centres. Loughborough and Hinckley are obvious local examples, following the emergence of the hosiery industry, although this kind of development was, of course, more typical of the more intensively industrialized regions of the country. Meanwhile there was many a "simple" market town that merely retained or reinforced its importance within its own immediate area. Among these there is nothing to single out Lutterworth as exceptional, either in market specialization or in industrial development.

The towns of the middle category,[4] however, the shire towns and smaller cathedral cities, numbering 60 or more, did not function only as market towns. Their importance over a wide area assured them also a mixed economy as service, legal, religious and social centres. Many of them were considerably smaller than Leicester and Northampton, which started the sixteenth century with populations of about 3,000 each. The mixed economy of both these boroughs included a concentration of leather-working.[5] Shoemaking remains a speciality of Northampton and its county; but although the town was notable in the seventeenth century for its accommodation for wayfarers and as the centre of the country's horse-dealing trade, it continued into the nineteenth century without having undergone any substantial expansion as an industrial centre.[6] In contrast, the industry that took root in Leicester around the mid-seventeenth century was part of the local hosiery industry. After having grown hardly at all during the sixteenth century the town numbered around 5,000 inhabitants by the later seventeenth century.⁻

The urban centres of the top category were the half dozen-odd provincial capitals, while London must be counted as in a class of its own as the national centre. The concentration of population in these major cities and their reliance on manufactures and trade made them particularly vulnerable to changes in the economy of the nation. An extreme example was Coventry. Around 1500 it had at least twice the population of Leicester or Northampton, but well into the century it was suffering a severe decline and only found a new expanding role as an industrial centre in the eighteenth century.[8] Some of the smaller places were more or less similarly affected. In 1540, for instance, the complaint from Leicester was the usual one that competition from outsiders selling in the markets was bringing depopulation, ruin, decay and poverty to the town.[9] In general, however, these problems of decay were peculiar to the larger mediaeval city or town and lie outside the scope of the study of the market town.

2.   The characteristics of the market town

What were the characteristics that distinguished the market town?[10] The first and most obvious feature that separated it from towns in other categories was its small size. A count of the numbers of households in 1563 illustrates this.[11] Leicester was credited with 591, followed by Loughborough with 256. The five other market towns in the county each had about 100 or slightly more,[12] including Lutterworth, 'scant half so big as Loughborough',[13] with 106. This made them all about twice the size of the market villages and indeed larger than very nearly every other village in the county. The numbers of people assessed for Hearth Tax in the 1670s shew the towns in very much the same order.[14] Leicester, with 1,061, had over twice as many as Loughborough, with 413. The other five towns ranged from Melton Mowbray, with 340, down to about 200, Lutterworth having 225. None of the market villages had more than 170; but only one had fewer than 100, so that they were clearly distinguishable from all but the very largest villages. Comparing the two sets of figures suggests that while the rate of growth of the towns was higher than that of the county as a whole, the greatest growth had been among the smaller places, some of the market villages having more than trebled their numbers and most of the market towns having doubled at least. The two important exceptions were the two largest, Loughborough and the shire town.

The market town was in general more populous than most villages, and therefore presumably more extensive. What other topographical features distinguished it from the village and the market village? The layout of the simple market town, indeed the layout of all towns, altered very little after the early mediaeval period of new foundations. These foundations included the planting of completely new communities like Market Harborough and also, as at Lutterworth or Ashby-de-la-Zouch, the planned extension of existing settlements.[15] Both types of place still shew signs of the ordered laying-out of narrow burgage plots facing onto the market area. Any decay of such towns in the late middle ages and renewed growth in the early modern period can be thought of, therefore, as taking place very much within a continuously existing framework. In the case of Lutterworth this can be demonstrated by comparing closely the perambulation of the town in the complete Terrier of the town and fields made in 1509 with nineteenth-century maps or, indeed, with the present street plan (see Map I, a sketch plan displaying the details given in the perambulation).[16]

Suffice to say that the most obvious visible difference between the market settlement and the ordinary village was the area on which the market was held, a space wider than the normal village street and usually bearing some relationship to the church and the access roads.

As might be expected in a Catholic country, most mediaeval English villages probably had a simple stone cross at some focal point in the street. Certainly there was one at Walton by Kimcote, a village near Lutterworth, and one each at Clifton-upon-Dunsmore and Dunchurch, both of which lie on the other side of Rugby in Warwickshire.[17] In market villages, such as Hillmorton, also beyond Rugby, and Welford and Naseby in Northamptonshire, the cross was very likely the only permanent piece of "street furniture" in the market area.[18] The market town, in contrast, could boast much more than that. In the first place, by the sixteenth century at least, the cross was often something more elaborate, enough indeed to arouse Puritans to destructive action, as happened at Banbury and possibly also at Market Harborough. At Lutterworth in 1634 a local Puritan parson applauded a crowd of townsmen and villagers who pulled down the High Cross that stood at the centre of the town.[19] In smaller market towns the cross was sometimes combined with, or replaced by, a market shelter, a market house or a school; but in larger places the buildings for trading and for administering the market developed separately.

The buildings for trading were in effect permanent stalls, or "shamels"; hence the name by which they were often known, 'the Shambles'. In a small town like Lutterworth or Market Harborough they were just as specialized in use, for the sale of meat, as they were in a city like Coventry; the earliest references in each place call them "Fleshamels".[20] The Flesh-Shambles in the market village of Hallaton in the sixteenth century, on the other hand, appears to have been a market area rather than a permanent building.[21] Cover was also needed for the sale of cloth, the specialized building being the "Drapery". Rugby had its Drapery in the fourteenth century, and so did

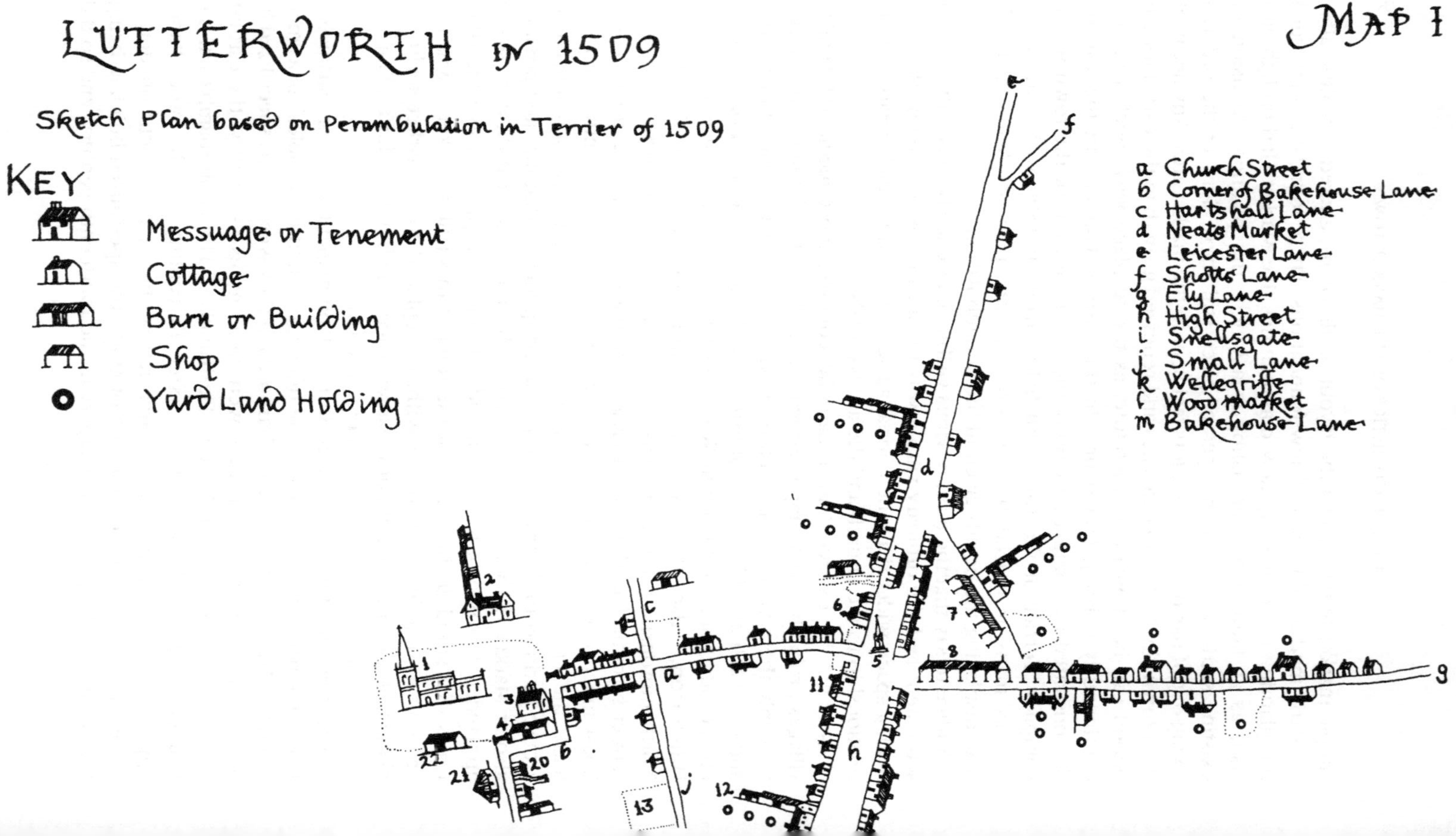

LUTTERWORTH in 1509

Sketch Plan based on Perambulation in Terrier of 1509

KEY

Messuage or Tenement

Cottage

Barn or Building

Shop

● Yard Land Holding

MAP I

a Church Street
b Corner of Bakehouse Lane
c Harts Hall Lane
d Neats Market
e Leicester Lane
f Shittes Lane
g Ely Lane
h High Street
i Shellsgate
j Small Lane
k Wellgate
l Wood Market
m Bakehouse Lane

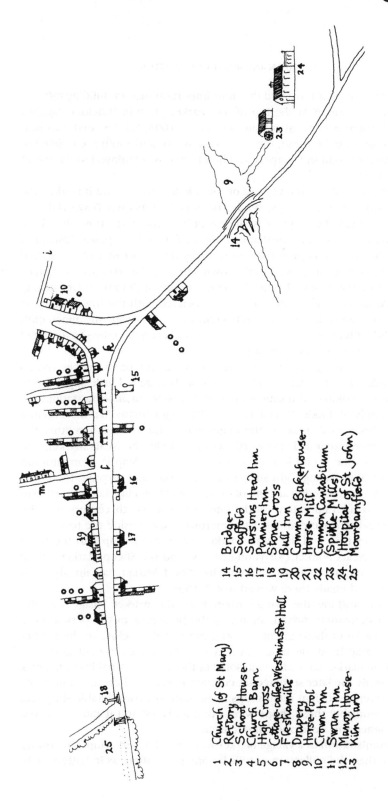

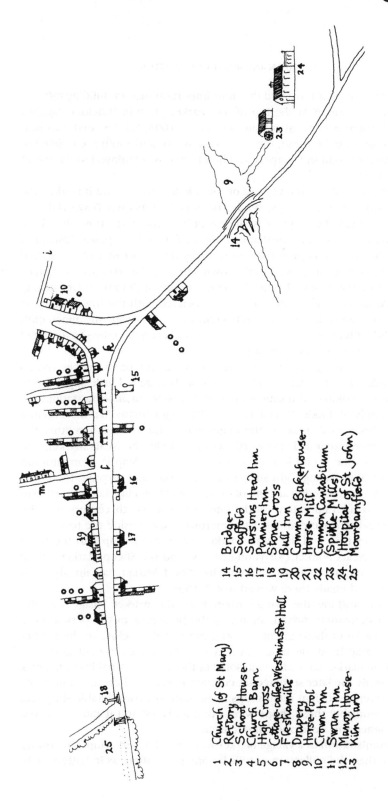

1   Church (of St Mary)
2   Rectory
3   School House
4   Church Barn
5   High Cross
6   Cottage called Westminster Hall
7   Fleshamills
8   Drapery
9   Horse-Pool
10 Crown Inn
11 Swan Inn
12 Manor House
13 Kiln Yard

14 Bridge
15 Scaffold
16 Sursons Head Inn
17 Pannier Inn
18 Stone Cross
19 Bull Inn
20 Common Bakehouse
21 Horse Mill
22 Common Cantabium
23 (Spittle Mills)
24 (Hospital of St John)
25 Moorbanyfield

Lutterworth, where it remained the most important market building into the seventeenth century.[22] At the top of the market place in Hinckley, 'against the cross', there was an island site which, by 1603, was divided into four parts. One was the Bullhead, the town's main inn, and another consisted of 'the Shoemakers Hall the Drapery and butchery now employed to the use of the Market there'.[23]

In some places the market house or town hall served for both market and town administration meetings. While Hinckley had its own Town Hall,[24] in Lutterworth it may be a sign of weakness in both these functions that there was apparently never any substantial building for such purposes. Instead of the town hall that is so prominent in so many towns because of its isolated position, there was, at the side of the town's principal market area, a cottage called 'Westminster Hall'. In the sixteenth century it did not in fact belong to the lord of the manor; but it can be associated with the town bailiffs in both the sixteenth and seventeenth centuries.[25] Not until the nineteenth century did Lutterworth possess a town hall; and even then the site for it had first to be purchased (see Illustration 3).[26]

Most of the trading would have taken place in the open market and its market buildings. In a market village it probably required little supervision. In a town the volume of business made it necessary to allocate stations for different kinds of goods. In general only the larger towns had more than a few such designated areas. At the beginning of the sixteenth century the principal market area in Lutterworth was for cattle, the Neats Market, and there was also the Wood Market, still so named (see Map I). Northampton has been cited as having eight such areas.[27] It comes as a surprise, therefore, to learn that the marketing activity of even a small town like Lutterworth had intensified to such an extent by the end of the sixteenth century that the market areas there were almost as numerous.[28] Just outside the town were the Horse Fair Leys and the cattle markets were divided up into the Beast Market, the Neats Market (for young beasts) and the Sheep Market. There was also an important Corn Market. The Wood Market has already been mentioned; and finally there was an Iron Market.

Also distinguishing the market town from the market village was the number of permanent private shops. At the beginning of the period there were at least 16 of these in Lutterworth, most of them close to the market centre (see Map I). At this time they may have been open-fronted structures used only on market days, although some of them were probably craftsmen's workshops. By the later seventeenth century, however, there are indications that there were sufficient retail shops to amount to a considerable shopping centre. Presumably these shops were open all week and it must be asked how and when this development occurred.

The administration of a village market was probably very simple, involving little more than the collection of tolls by one man, often, as in Lutterworth,

Illustration 3. High Street, Lutterworth, looking North, photograph taken by Henry Taunt of Oxford in 1878. The Denbigh Arms and the sign of the Hind shew on the western side. Beyond the nineteenth-century Town Hall at the top of the eastern side were island premises which have been demolished, as have the shops facing downhill from the top of the High Street, which formed a continuation of the frontages along the north side of Church Street.
    Oxford Central Library

the bailiff of the lord of the manor. In larger towns and cities supervision of different classes of goods required numerous officials, market lookers or searchers, usually appointed in pairs and sometimes amounting to more than a dozen in all.[29] Even in small market towns like Rugby, Melton Mowbray and Ashby-de-la-Zouch there were six in the seventeenth century.[30] In Lutterworth it seems that there were six in the mid-sixteenth century, two for tasting flesh and fish, two Bread Weighers and two Ale Tasters. By the mid-seventeenth century these had been joined by two Leather Searchers.[31]

    While the running of the markets even in such simple market towns might be a fairly elaborate process involving half a dozen officers, it nevertheless formed part of a quite elementary system of local government. The primary unit of jurisdiction, and therefore of local administration, was the manor. Throughout the mediaeval and early modern periods Lutterworth remained basically one manor with the market rights belonging to the lord, although there were some exceptions, premises and lands within the town and parish which were not subject to the manor. The most important, and one that gave rise to disputes during the period, was the Hospital of Saint John and its lands.[32] At the beginning of the period the manor was the property of the Marquis of Dorset and it was forfeit to the Crown on the execution of his son the Duke of Suffolk in 1554. It remained a Crown manor until 1628.[33]

There is no trace of any of the early lords having been in residence at Lutterworth and in the fifteenth century it was stated that there was neither manor house nor demesne there.[34] Within the manor, however, the Feilding family owned a substantial freehold estate, constituting in fact a subsidiary manor with its own bailiff.[35] There is a mid-seventeenth century reference to 'the Manor of Lutterworth called Feilding's Manor of my Lord's and his Ancestors' Inheritance above 400 years'.[36] Although they made their chief residence their Hall at Newnham Paddox, just across the Watling Street, and let off their manor house and farm in the town, they were the most obvious influential patrons of the town (see Illustration 4). When the principal manor left the hands of the Crown it was very soon snapped up by them.[37] The transaction in effect brought about the enfranchisement of all the remaining tenants by demise, as they in turn bought their freehold reversions from the Feildings, leaving the latter to add only the manor itself and the market buildings and rights to their freehold estate.[38] Thus the subsidiary estate was merged in the principal manor and the Feildings became the only important manorial influence in the town.[39] It seems, however, that while the manorial courts continued their business, they had at this stage lost effective control over the town economy.

In the early middle ages a most important feature of the town community was that the leading traders and craftsmen held their premises by burgage tenure, a free tenure carrying with it some independence from manorial domination and some opportunities for self-government.[40] Lutterworth was among the numerous seignorial "petty boroughs" that failed to survive as such into the early modern period. The only trace that remained there, as in Hinckley and Ashby-de-la-Zouch, was the odd burgage plot which, although it retained its title and identity, had long since lost any legal significance or privileges.[41] These three towns, together with Atherstone and Nuneaton in Warwickshire and Rothwell in Northamptonshire, while losing their borough organizations, at least remained market centres. Other petty boroughs, such as Belvoir, Mountsorrel and Castle Donington in Leicestershire, Brinklow and, possibly, Bretford in Warwickshire and Rockingham in Northamptonshire, seem to have been founded mainly as appendages to castle establishments. At best they only survived as market villages.

An integral part of mediaeval urban life, and one closely connected with borough administration, was the system of guilds. In Leicester, as in some

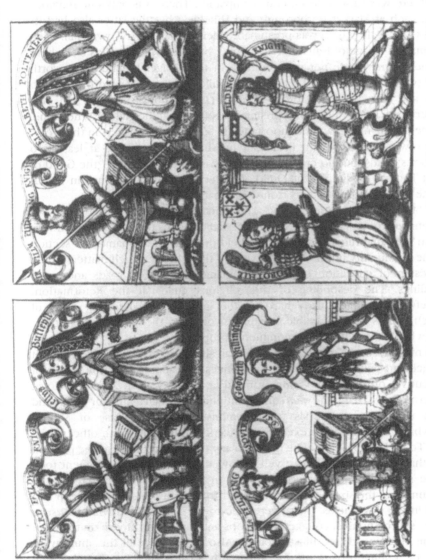

Illustration 4. Contemporary representation of the Feilding family succession. Portion of the parlour window at Newnham Paddox, from an engraving signed by Wenceslaus Hollar and published in 1656 with heraldic colours indicated. Sir Everard was followed by Sir William, who married a Pulteney.

W. Dugdale, *Warwickshire*

other towns, the Guild Merchant had at an early date effectively become the governing body of the town.[42] Market towns usually had their social and religious guilds, although in Loughborough six such guilds were matched by six craft guilds. At Stratford-upon-Avon the three religious guilds had merged and there were also a dozen craft companies. There was only one religious guild each at Market Harborough and Hinckley; but the latter also had its own Guild Hall, which was presumably identical with the Town Hall. Even the market village of Hallaton had a guild; but then village guilds elsewhere in the country were not uncommon.[43] In the villages around Lutterworth only two have been traced, Saint John's Guild in the will of a North Kilworth man and 'the gylde of Morton church' (*i.e.* Gilmorton) in the will of a Lutterworth man.[44] It is not surprising, therefore, that the guild at Whetstone, further to the north, was of importance to some of the villagers in the area.[45] The town of Lutterworth itself can be shewn to have had at least two religious guilds, but no craft guilds. 'The Guild of Saint Anne', 'the Guild of Saint Thomas' or simply 'the Guild of Lutterworth' are mentioned in 12 out of the 22 wills of inhabitants from 1500 to 1535.[46]

A borough corporation, being a continuous legal entity, could own and administer communal property. In the smaller towns the guilds fulfilled very much the same function, since they held property in the name of a section of the community but often for the use of the whole, in such matters as the provision of education or the maintenance of bridges, roads and town buildings. The despoiling of the religious guilds at the Reformation, therefore, was particularly hard on the unincorporated towns, many of which, unless they were able to suppress or divert the foundations in time, lost what was in effect their communal property.

In many cases the town could rely on an alternative device. Property might be held on behalf of the town by feoffees and administered by a pair of executive officers, who thus formed a primitive but effective local government.[47] That there was some continuity between a guild or guilds and such a "town estate" has been demonstrated in the case of Melton Mowbray.[48] Although the executive powers of the Lutterworth officers, the two Town Masters, cannot be traced in any detail, it must at least be pointed out that its Town Estate was well endowed and that this endowment took place not around the Reformation but in the period before that. At the beginning of the sixteenth century, apart from farms outside the parish and land in the town fields, there were held to the use of the town, '*ad usum ville*', several houses, cottages and shops and the School House on the edge of the churchyard (see Illustration 5). Also on the edge of the churchyard was the 'common *cantabilum*', apparently a cattle shed for the town bull kept in the adjoining Bull Close.[49]

Several sixteenth-century wills of inhabitants, in fact 10 out of the 52 dated before 1585, include bequests towards secular town works such as the

Illustration 5. Church Gate, Lutterworth, looking West, towards the parish church, photograph taken in 1878 by Henry Taunt of Oxford. On the south side the inn started as an alehouse built at the beginning of the seventeenth century as an encroachment adjoining the end of the Spittle Row. The new Reading Room beyond the top of Bakehouse Lane replaced the early School House. On the north side is the end of the row of former church cottages.

    Oxford Central Library

highways, the pavements and the two bridges. Occasionally the wording gives a clue as to the town business. Sir William Feilding mentioned contributions by 'the most honest men of the parish' . . . 'whereby every man in the town is compelled to pay his portion'.[50] Another man had little confidence in the system. He left a sum 'being in the town's hand . . . if the township be wilful to pay it without strife' and two other sums, one of them in the hand of the Master of the Hospital, 'and if the township be not diligent I will that . . . my son shall dispose the said money as he knoweth my mind in that behalf'.[51]

The device of the town estate gave market towns a certain amount of self-determination and was important in dealing with the problem of poverty. The Lutterworth Town Masters, although chosen in the manorial court, would appear to have been nonetheless accountable primarily to "the majority of the inhabitants", and in the seventeenth century the inhabitants are sometimes mentioned as taking independent action.[52] In 1610/11, for instance, a letter was addressed to the Mayor of Leicester during a visitation of the plague. It was signed by the two parish constables and various other notables, including the Lutterworth attorney, and when it says 'we have resolved' to exclude Leicester traders from the town, it probably refers to a town meeting rather than to a manorial court.[53] Similarly in 1631 one of two petitions from the town to the central government was made in the names of 36 men of all ranks and occupations, amongst whom were the curate schoolmaster, the bailiff, the constables, the church wardens and the overseers of the poor.[54] Later in the century another petition carried the signatures and marks of 70 inhabitants, a very high proportion of the town, considering that only twice that number were paying the Hearth Tax in 1670.[55] The measure of self-government that the Town Estate gave the inhabitants may have been an important factor in opposing the domination of a town by the manor and other gentry. For Lutterworth, as elsewhere, there are records of several disputes concerning the manorial monopoly over milling and baking in the parish, even after the break-up of the manor. Shortly after the Crown parted with the manor, it was a petition by the inhabitants that caused the rates and levies on the enclosed grounds of Moorbarns within the parish to be raised to match their high value.[56] Conflicts such as these were evidently part of the seventeenth-century transition in local government from the manor to the parish as the primary unit of administration.

So much for the topography and administration of the simple market town. When it comes to dealing with the town's social and economic structure, it is evident that even the most basic questions remain to be answered. At the beginning of the period these towns were small and largely agricultural. In 1524, for instance, there were 32 substantial taxpayers in Lutterworth; and yet there were about 36 holdings in the town fields.[57] At that time, just as in Coventry, Leicester, Loughborough and other places,[58] the personal wealth of the town was mostly concentrated in the hands of a few exceptional men, in this case two members of a merchant family named Paver and the bailiff. Below them there was probably little in the way of an urban concentration of traders and craftsmen; for towns like these in fact only became commercial places on market and fair days.

Over the two centuries covered by this study it is highly unlikely that the number of farm holdings attached to such towns increased in pace with the phenomenal growth of their populations. On the contrary, by the later seventeenth century their economic structures had evidently become more urban in the modern sense. In Ashby-de-la-Zouch, for instance, it has been shewn not only that agriculture played a less important part in the town economy but also that hardly any of the more prosperous inhabitants were now involved in farming.[59]

By this time the leading people in such a town were often its innholders and traders. Most of the mid-seventeenth century trade tokens from this region were issued by men of this sort.[60] After them in importance came the wealthier craftsmen among the woodworkers and shoemakers, and also those responsible for supplying provisions, the millers, bakers and butchers. Alongside these were the new professionals, such as surgeons and attorneys, and also a few gentry, who either belonged to the town or were drawn into it from the surrounding area. From these gentry and "pseudo-gentry", or rather "new gentry", evolved the narrow range of families that, by the end of the century, came to view the running of their particular town as their duty and right.[61]

Below these men were a number of smaller shopkeepers and also a large number of craftsmen. In Melton Mowbray and Ashby-de-la-Zouch shoemakers, and then tailors, shewed as the most numerous occupations, and the same was true in Lutterworth.[62] At the bottom end of the scale the small town, like the larger urban centres, also had a concentration of labourers who swelled the number of potential paupers. In 1603 it was alleged that 'Hinckley is a poor market Town and hath many poor inhabitants therein that have great need of relief'.[63] Melton Mowbray was described as 'a poor market town populous and full of poor people' and in 1610 a levy was made to build a House of Correction. In Ashby in the 1620s and 1630s it has been shewn that a considerable proportion of the population received payments from the overseers of the poor.[64] The 1670 Hearth Tax return for that town lists 167 assessed to pay the tax and only 49 exempt; yet a hitherto unnoticed exemption certificate from the same year lists 138 people as exempt.[65] Among Leicestershire towns the exemptions in the returns varied from one third to one half of the total number of households assessed. The situation appears to have been graver still in a couple of the more remote market villages in the eastern half of the county. Billesdon had 71 people paying and 63 exempt and Hallaton had 73 paying and no fewer than 92 exempt.[66]

The emergence of a prosperous middle class of traders and craftsmen and the presence of a large section of the population living in comparative poverty have here been emphasized as the most important developments in the structure of the simple market town during the period. Clearly, then, some account must be offered as to the timing of these changes and as to how such communities developed out of what, at the beginning of the sixteenth century, appear to have been very little different from villages. It must be remembered, however, that throughout the period agriculture remained the essential context in which the town functioned; not only the agriculture of the area around, but also that of the town community itself.

In the early middle ages it appears that there had commonly been a sharp division between the farming and the commercial interests within such towns.[67] Sometimes there was even a division of functions between different settlements within the parish. Hard by the then comparatively new town of Market Harborough, for instance, was the village of Little Bowden where, in 1341/2, there were 'no traders or dealers there except those who live by agriculture'. In Ashby-de-la-Zouch there was a subsidiary settlement, Blackfordby, which apparently remained entirely agricultural. But the division might equally be within one settlement. Hinckley has preserved in its street names to this day the ancient distinction between its "borough" and its "bond". A part of mediaeval Lutterworth too, through which a highway passed, was known as 'Ly Bonde-end' and evidently lay outside the central area of burgage plots.[68] Even the nearby former market village of Monks Kirby still has its Bond End. Such divisions, however, seem to have lost their significance by the early modern period and few of a town's traders and craftsmen had no farm stock at all. In Lutterworth, although there were naturally few shops far from the market centre, there were farmsteads all over the town and some of them even fronted onto the main markets (see Map I).

The agriculture of the parish was one part of the town economy; but it was the agriculture of the immediate area that was the foundation of the town's commerce. Among the distinguishing features of the simple market town the first has been taken as its small size; the last and most important must be the small scope of its market influence. In fact it may reasonably be postulated that the further down the scale of urban categories a market came, the less independent its economy was from the farming in its area.

This point can also be illustrated by the fate of the market settlements that never even graduated to an urban status, the market villages. In the later middle ages the lack of customer demand in areas experiencing population shrinkage allowed rural markets to decline into obscurity or lapse completely. The new expansion of economic activity in the sixteenth century granted a fresh lease of life to those that did survive and even led to the foundation of some new markets. The population of these places rose particularly rapidly, but on the whole their business activities failed to match the more general increase in the range and volume of internal trade, which thus left them as unimportant backwaters. This can be seen in one later seventeenth-century topographer's contempt for the five village markets in Leicestershire and for others in the region, dismissing them as 'small', 'very mean' or 'very inconsiderable, and in a manner disused'.[69] Obviously this is not a sufficient account of the effect, which must, as suggested above, be explained mainly in terms of the agricultural development of the market areas.

Where a market lapsed, however, the annual fair that had usually been granted with it often did survive. Here something should be said of the network of local fairs which, although similar to the pattern of markets, overlapped it. At the opposite end of the spectrum from purely local fairs there were fairs whose importance was wholly independent of any permanent settlement, such as the great international concourse at Sturbridge Fair near Cambridge. In between were fairs of an inter-regional significance, such as the fair for timber and wooden products at Boughton Green in Northamptonshire. Harborough Fair at Market Harborough was widely noted for cattle and horses and by the early eighteenth century Atherstone Fair was the gathering point for much of the cheese produced in north Warwickshire.[70] Although the fairs at Lutterworth were not especially renowned, they were no doubt attended by buyers and sellers from a wide circuit. In one year in the 1580s, for instance, the Isham family of Lamport in Northamptonshire stocked up with beasts from Coventry and Rothwell fairs and from Uppingham and Lutterworth.[71]

Apart from their economic significance in drawing people from well outside the market area, however, these fairs also had a local significance as social gatherings for townspeople and villagers, just as the annual wake in any parish did for the parishioners. Whatever the standing of the Lutterworth fairs in other counties, there is no doubt that their importance within the town's own area was great. On Ascension Day in 1632, for example, 'only a very few of the meanest sort of the parishioners' of the nearby village of Shawell were not at the fair in the town.[72] Beyond the immediate area, however, it may be that county boundaries were decisive in defining loyalties to local fairs. The most important date in the calendar for inhabitants of the neighbourhood of Lutterworth was Harborough Fair, starting on the 9th of October, the date on which debts were paid[73] and by which local husbandry practices were timed.[74] Across the boundary in Northamptonshire the main attraction was Rothwell Fair[75] and the inhabitants of the Northamptonshire village of Naseby resorted there, even though Harborough is in fact nearer to their village.[76]

3. The survival of markets

Following on this general examination of the characteristics of the simple market town and to set the stage for a study of Lutterworth as a particular example, there are questions which need to be settled about the reasons for the survival or failure of Leicestershire mediaeval rural markets. The answers must be sought in two fields of activity, which relate the one to a place's connexions with outside markets and trade and the other to its immediate market area.

It is obvious that a market could best serve its area as a collection and distribution point if it stood on a through-trade route. Here it is no doubt significant that the markets that were founded earliest were also the ones

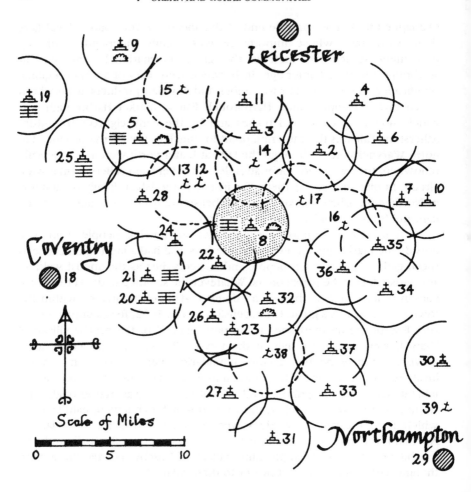

that remained important. In Leicestershire, besides the shire town, all six market towns had markets by about 1220.[77] It is not surprising that four of these, including Lutterworth, were places which the Leicester Portmanmoot designated a generation later as wool-collecting centres when restricting the wool-buying activity of foreigners in the county (of the seven places named, the four which are south of Leicester are marked on Map II).[78] There were also merchants living in these towns, and in some of the smaller centres too, during the middle ages.[79] Doubtless they were involved, along with Leicester, Melton Mowbray and Loughborough merchants, in exporting wool *via* the eastern ports, such as Boston, Lynn and Kingston-upon-Hull or *via* London.[80] Further evidence of such trade is the presence of Merchants of the Staple of Calais in these towns in the later fifteenth century, including one based on Lutterworth.[81]

MAP II
EARLY MEDIÆVAL MARKETS
KEY

≡ Petty Boroughs
〰 Wool Markets for Foreigners

LEICESTERSHIRE		WARWICKSHIRE		NORTHAMPTONSHIRE	
Leicester	1	Coventry	18	Northampton	29
Arnesby	2	Atherstone	19	Brixworth	30
Cosby	3	Bretford	20	Daventry	31
Glen magna	4	Brinklow	21	Lilbourne	32
Hinckley	5	Churchover	22	Long Buckby	33
Kibworth Beauchamp	6	Hillmorton	23	Naseby	34
Lubenham	7	Monks Kirby	24	Sibbertoft	35
Lutterworth	8	Nuneaton	25	Welford	36
Market Bosworth	9	Rugby	26	West Haddon	37
Market Harborough	10	Willoughby	27		
Narborough	11	Wolvey	28		

Markets ⊕

Possible Markets

Claybrook magna	12	Kilsby	38
High Cross	13		
Dunton Bassett	14		
Earl Shilton	15		
Husbands Bosworth	16	Boughton Green Fair	39
Walton	17		⫸

These merchants were of national or even international importance and the wealth of families like the Wigstons in Leicester, the Burtons in Loughborough or the Pavers in Lutterworth, when compared with the rest of the town community, was immense.[82] Some explanation must be offered, therefore, as to how their business fitted in with the town economy and how it disappeared in the early sixteenth century to be replaced, eventually, by a more broadly based commercial section of the community.

The export abroad of wool was not, of course, the only business of such merchants. During the early modern period wool from the Midlands was marketed in all directions according to the specialized needs of different cloth-weaving areas. Some of it would return as woollen cloth to be offered for sale in the Draperies alongside linen cloth from abroad. In fact the increase in internal trade involved the redistribution of all kinds of goods over a network of routes approaching a "national market". It is necessary therefore to identify the more important of the routes through the region.

Lutterworth stands near to the intersection of the Roman Watling Street and Fosse Way at High Cross (see Map IX). Although the directions of these two roads remained important trade routes, in the early middle ages Coventry had become the principal exchange point, drawing aside the main through-traffic from the central sections of both of them.[83] The development of a through-route from London to York by way of Leicester was already apparent in the eleventh century,[84] but the section of it between Northampton and Leicester seems to have become firmly established through Market Harborough in preference to the Welford route.[85]

Many of the places with market grants that did not have the advantages of such through-routes lost their markets in the later middle ages. Even those that retained their markets, like Market Bosworth and Hallaton, did not rise above market village status and were backwaters by the later seventeenth century.[86] On the other hand the presence of such a route was no guarantee of success, especially if the place did not stand at an intersection between routes. Among the six places with grants along the two roads from Leicester to Northampton the only survivals were Market Harborough and the fair at Brixworth (compare Map II with Map III). How was it that Lutterworth prospered when it seems to have been largely bypassed by the three major routes mentioned?

The road from Leicester to Lutterworth has some claim to be of Roman origin. Beyond Lutterworth it is assumed that it followed through to Tripontium, the station on the Watling Street at Caves Inn.[87] A mile further south, where the three counties meet, Dow Bridge carries the Watling Street over the River Avon (see Illustration 6). Immediately south of Lutterworth, however, the Leicester road has to cross the River Swift and it is no doubt significant that it was just here that the Hospital of Saint John was founded to accommodate poor travellers in the same generation that the original market grant was obtained.[88] Very likely the Spittle Bridge dates from this time too. Nearly every principal road bridge in the county had been built in stone by the early fourteenth century and the Spittle Bridge was certainly in existence by the beginning of the fifteenth century.[89] No doubt the road to Leicester was used by merchants, such as those who exported wool *via* Leicester and the Trent valley. What was the significance of this route as it left the town towards the south?

High Cross and the central sections of the two Roman roads whose intersection it marks are shewn on various early county maps. In spite of such antiquarian interest in it as a Roman road it seems fairly certain that the Fosse Way beyond Sapcote out from Leicester remained disused as a principal through-route. William Camden noted traces of its causeway 'in pastures now trackless and unfrequented' near Chesterton in Warwickshire,

Illustration 6. Dow Bridge, carrying the Watling Street across the River Avon, at the point where the three counties of Leicestershire, Warwickshire and Northamptonshire meet, drawn in 1796. A team of six horses, drawing a four-wheeled wagon for heavy road freight, and a wayfarer on foot with his bundle both travel along the main road through the area.

J. Nichols, *Leics.*

although Daniel Defoe implied that it was in use later at least from High Cross to Dunsmore Heath.[90] The main wool traffic from the region to the south-west weaving areas, even to Cirencester, would have followed the diversion *via* Coventry and Stratford-upon-Avon. This was the probable route, for instance, for the wool crop bought in 1554 by a Gloucestershire wool merchant from off the Misterton estate next to Lutterworth. The road surface in August was good enough for the one-and-a-half ton load to be carried in four carts.[91]

Even in the early sixteenth century, on the other hand, the Watling Street further down towards London was a very busy thoroughfare[92] and the fact that Bransford Bridge, which carries it over the River Swift, was then standing suggests that the central section of the Street was by no means deserted.[93] It was recognized as one of the great droving routes from the north-west.[94] To the drovers the condition of the bridges and of the road surface, so often the despair of literate travellers, was usually immaterial and one of the route's attractions was the very fact that it did not pass through any sizeable towns. Besides, anyone in need of the services of a town could easily make a short detour, as indeed the later coaching traffic did, so as to pass through Hinckley or Lutterworth.[95] This was no doubt the practice in the early seventeenth century too, when the Leicestershire historian William Burton described Lutterworth as 'very much frequented, standing not far from the street way'.[96]

The important coaching route through Lutterworth, however, was the Chester to London road, which left the Watling Street at High Cross to reach the town *via* the Claybrooks and Bitteswell and then went on to Northampton *via* Welford. This was precisely the route that nineteenth-century Welsh drovers took on their way to the markets and fairs in the region and there is no reason to doubt that it had long been used for this and other traffic.[97] Misterton estate dealings in the 1550s shew that the main outlet for beasts, especially Welsh cows, was Northampton Fair. Even fat stock for household consumption in Middlesex started out *via* Welford and Northampton, before being driven south to cross the Watling Street at Stony Stratford.[98]

Some Misterton estate oxen were sold at Harborough Fair, which has already been mentioned as important in the Lutterworth area.[99] An example of inter-regional traffic on the Harborough road out of Lutterworth was the laborious progress of north-Warwickshire cheese as described by Defoe. Gathering each autumn at Atherstone Cheese Fair it left the drove route just mentioned beyond Lutterworth on its way to Sturbridge Fair.[100] Each year in the eighteenth century, and probably in the late seventeenth too, this road must have been alive with cheese factors for several weeks. Much of the cheese never reached Sturbridge Fair, as it encountered a string of cheese fairs on the way, including one at Lutterworth. In return from Sturbridge Fair the Midland region was supplied with hops from the South East and other special goods. Purchases there for the Misterton estate, for instance, included cord and tar.[101]

The north-west was not, however, the main direction from which cattle from outside entered the area. Most of the Misterton estate Welsh beasts were bought at fairs at Coventry and Birmingham. These would have reached the town *via* Cross in Hand on the Watling Street. There is seventeenth-century evidence too that the bridge over the stream between there and the town, the Wood Bridge, was an ancient stone-built cart-bridge used not only for carts and carriages but also, in times of flood and frost, by droves of sheep and other cattle.[102]

The importance to the town of the road south from Leicester is obvious. Cattle coming to the Misterton estate from far north naturally passed this way.[103] But while the town, to judge from its present layout, might appear to have grown on a north–south axis, the chief routes over the river crossing by the Hospital turn out to have been connected with long-range traffic through from the north-west and west towards the east and south-east. This may help to explain the only substantial difference between the present town plan and the plan at the beginning of the sixteenth century. At that time the road from the west, Woodway or Coventry Way, entered the town *via* the Wood Market. Since then the Wood Market has been superseded by a more northern way in. Yet both the name and the generous width of the Wood Market suggest that it was formerly one of the main market areas in the town. At the beginning of the sixteenth century, moreover, it contained three of the town's five inns (see Map I).

The increase in the volume of traffic in the sixteenth and seventeenth centuries along roads of the kind mentioned made greater demands on the towns along, and just off, the route. Clear evidence of this is the accommodation provided not only in the towns but also in thoroughfare settlements that never became true market towns, like Weedon and Fosters Booth, both on the Watling Street.[104] Even along the open road there sprang up isolated inns and alehouses to serve the through-traffic, such as the New Inn, later called Caves Inn, and the inns at High Cross and at Smockington, all of them on the same road (see Map III).[105]

Many market towns had their own carriers journeying regularly to London, as is shewn by the first published list, John Taylor's *The Carriers Cosmographie* of 1637.[106] The increase in trade and traffic brought new life to their streets. And yet, paradoxically, it also helped to sweep away their prime importance as the "capitals" of their own areas. The townspeople who benefited were the keepers of public houses and shops; but dealings in local produce were taken on more by middlemen trading over long distances than between producer and consumer in the open market.[107] Defoe noted the adverse effect that the London market and the practice of selling corn by private agreement had on the prosperity of even quite large towns.[108] A similar effect may be discernible in the case of the smaller towns faced with the new trading in the later seventeenth century. It was at this time too, if not earlier, that those mediaeval market villages that had survived were sinking into obscurity.

Defoe also noticed that the towns that were able to maintain their positions were the ones that had some special contribution to offer.[109] If this was in the form of a specialized market, this might be reason for placing them in a separate category of towns. Many of another type too, the expanding industrial towns of the eighteenth century, originated as simple market towns. In the larger town of Leicester and nearby villages it was claimed in the 1670s that there were 2,000 men, women and children employed in stocking-making.[110] It can be shewn, moreover, that even the smaller town of Hinckley contained men of substantial wealth dependent on the hosiery industry. It is significant that this is the place where the first knitting-frame in the county is supposed to have been set up, before 1640 by one William Iliffe,[111] and that it is the one market town in the county which grew appreciably in the seventeenth century. At this time hosiery was not essentially a town-based industry, so that the substantial hosier or woolcomber living here depended on an activity spread through the villages.[112] Once again, therefore, the discussion returns to considering the way the economy of the market town was embedded in that of its market area.

The second field in which reasons for the survival of some mediaeval markets in preference to others are to be found concerns the nature of the market area. It is clear from the profusion of market grants that in the early middle ages most settlements were within easy reach of a trading point.[113] Their distribution in the region in the three counties around Lutterworth, for instance, is shewn on Map II.[114] The circles are drawn with a diameter of five miles, which is the average distance between neighbouring places with markets. This leaves spaces where there could well have been untraced markets, at Earl Shilton, where there was, a castle, at Claybrook magna, or perhaps High Cross, at Dunton Bassett and at Husbands Bosworth, or perhaps Walton (was the cross here a market cross after all?), in Leicestershire and at Kilsby in Northamptonshire. Even without these, however, there were few villages that were not within 3½ miles of at least two places with market grants.

Here again it is relevant to mention the chronology of the foundation of the markets. It has already been noted that all seven towns in Leicestershire that remained important into the early modern period had markets by about 1220. Similarly the 13 places that retained their markets had all gained them by about 1290. In the meantime there had been another 10 grants, including the ones for Great Glen and Kibworth Beauchamp, all of which later lapsed; but there were still another 16 to come, including the ones for Arnesby, Cosby and Lubenham, all of which lapsed too. There is indeed a case for maintaining that most of the earlier grants were for markets which were needed as central trading points within potential market areas and that they retained this significance throughout.[115]

This kind of market is likely to have pre-dated its first traced grant. Thus Loughborough probably had a market before 1221 and Hinckley may have had one even before the Domesday Survey. In the case of Lutterworth, it is true, there is no suggestion of any trading before the original grant of 1214, but there is evidence that before the end of that century the market was used for the sale of corn, presumably to local inhabitants, both for consumption and for sowing. Many of the later grants, on the other hand, including the ones for Great Glen, Kibworth Beauchamp and Lubenham, appear as less spontaneous foundations and probably only had a very local significance. Where the grant was obtained mainly for the disposal of produce from a demesne farm or for the provision of a manorial establishment, a change in circumstances could result in the disappearance of all trading activity. The grant to hold markets obtained by the priory of Monks Kirby in Warwickshire probably lapsed with the disappearance of the priory, which did not last into the fourteenth century.[116] Other examples may be the grants for Lilbourne and West Haddon in Northamptonshire and the two petty boroughs at Brinklow and Bretford in Warwickshire, all associated with castle establishments, except Haddon, which belonged to the convent at Daventry. Other small markets appear to have been submerged within the market areas of more important urban centres, such as Narborough, Cosby and Great Glen, all within seven miles of Leicester, Brinklow and Bretford, seven miles from Coventry, Willoughby and Long Buckby, five miles from Daventry, and Brixworth, seven from Northampton.

The distribution and relative importance of the market centres that survived into the early modern period have altered very little since then. This is shewn on Map III, where the sizes of the circles are intended to reflect the relative importance, the three large urban centres, for instance, having circles of 16 miles in diameter. With the disappearance of lesser markets, places like Hinckley, Market Harborough and Daventry emerged with substantial market areas, shewn as eight-mile circles. Lutterworth's only close rival was Rugby. The market there had been founded in the first place to dispose of the produce from a grange farm, but soon became the main exchange point in the area.[117] The town had a Drapery in the fourteenth century and was later noted for its butchery business.[118] It never, however, managed to draw away from other centres in the area all the business arising from the traffic across Dunsmore Heath.[119] Thus it was not so well coordinated a centre as Lutterworth. Moreover the county boundary which separated the two, and which also separated the even closer centres of Hinckley and Nuneaton, appears to have acted as an economic as well as a cultural barrier. No use was made, for instance, of Rugby market or fairs by the Misterton estate in the 1550s. Apart from this, from the point of view of Lutterworth the three towns of Hinckley, Market Harborough and Daventry stood outside the triangle formed by the three main urban centres, Leicester, Coventry and Northampton, leaving the middle clear as the market area for this town.

Next in order below the market towns were the market villages, shewn with four-mile circles. Although their markets continued to serve the immediate area, they were of declining importance. What places like Market Bosworth and Hallaton appear to have missed was an infusion of new life through being on main trading routes. Conversely, when it comes to studying places that had once been mediaeval market centres of some importance, it turns out that even though they lost their markets they still responded to the demands of through-traffic. Hillmorton and Welford both offered more accommodation than either of the market villages just mentioned. This activity even gave rise to new settlements, like Fosters Booth, or added new significance to existing ones that had never had markets, like Weedon.[120] Such places are all shewn with two-mile circles, while some ordinary villages with inn accommodation and some wayside

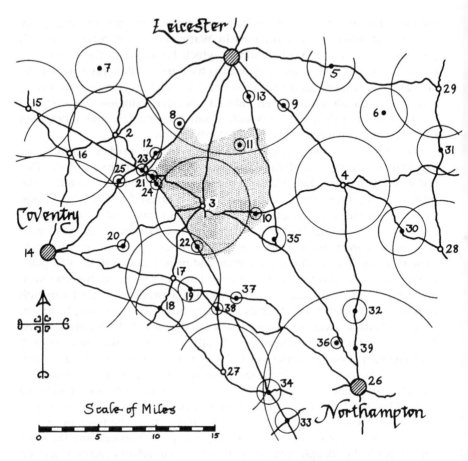

inns are marked with smaller circles.[121] This activity also affected the classification further up the scale. Billesdon and Dunchurch, for instance, both actually acquired new markets in the early seventeenth century and, although they hardly even qualified as market villages, they at least remained important for their fairs and their roadside accommodation.[122]

Comparatively little is known about village shops in this period and in this region seventeenth-century trading tokens were rarely issued from villages.[123] As there was a tendency during the century, however, for the open market to be supplanted by private trading, the existence or absence of a market may no longer have been a decisive factor. Thus a village that had lost its market might still be serving a small area, at least for some purposes, as a modest shopping centre. A place like Welford very probably did so; but that a place like Arnesby, which neither retained its market nor offered significant wayside accommodation, was in this respect different from its neighbouring villages is more doubtful.

EARLY MODERN TRADING AND ACCOMMODATION

————— Main Roads
Lutterworth Area

MAP III KEY

LEICESTERSHIRE | WARWICKSHIRE | NORTHAMPTONSHIRE

8 mile radius	Leicester	1	Coventry	14	Northampton 26
4 mile radius Market Towns	Hinckley	2	Atherstone	15	Daventry 27
	Lutterworth	3	Nuneaton	16	Kettering 28
	Market Harborough	4	Rugby	17	Uppingham (Rutland) 29
2 mile radius Market Villages	Billesdon	5	Dunchurch	18	Rockingham 30
	Hallaton	6			Rothwell 31
	Market Bosworth	7			
1 mile radius Thoroughfare Villages			Hillmorton	19	Brixworth 32
					Fosters Booth 33
					Weedon 34
					Welford 35
½ mile radius Wayside Accommodation in late 17th century	Croft	8	Brinklow	20	Brampton 36
	Glen magna	9	High Cross	21	Crick 37
	North Kilworth	10	New Inn	22	Kilsby 38
	Peatling magna	11	Smockington	23	
	Shamford	12	Wibtoft	24	Boughton Green Fair 39
	Wigston magna	13	Wolvey	25	G

These varying degrees of survival and the effect of the demands of through-traffic to some extent cut across the concept of the market area. Attendance at markets overlapped for different purposes, especially in the Midlands, where much of the business was the buying and selling of livestock.[124] At one extreme certain fairs attracted custom from several counties away. At the other, however, it may be supposed that each place had an immediate area of villages over which its hold for essentials was fairly exclusive. As the choice of an area for study must be made at the outset, the obvious method is to imagine a "watershed" half-way between similar markets and to allow for physical and other barriers.

Between Lutterworth and the three next market towns, Market Harborough, Hinckley and Rugby, the obvious half-way frontiers are the Welford Road, the Fosse Way and the Watling Street. This last has, throughout the ages, represented an astonishingly consistent cultural frontier across the Midlands.[125] It is also here the county boundary, as is the

THE PROGRESS OF ENCLOSURE

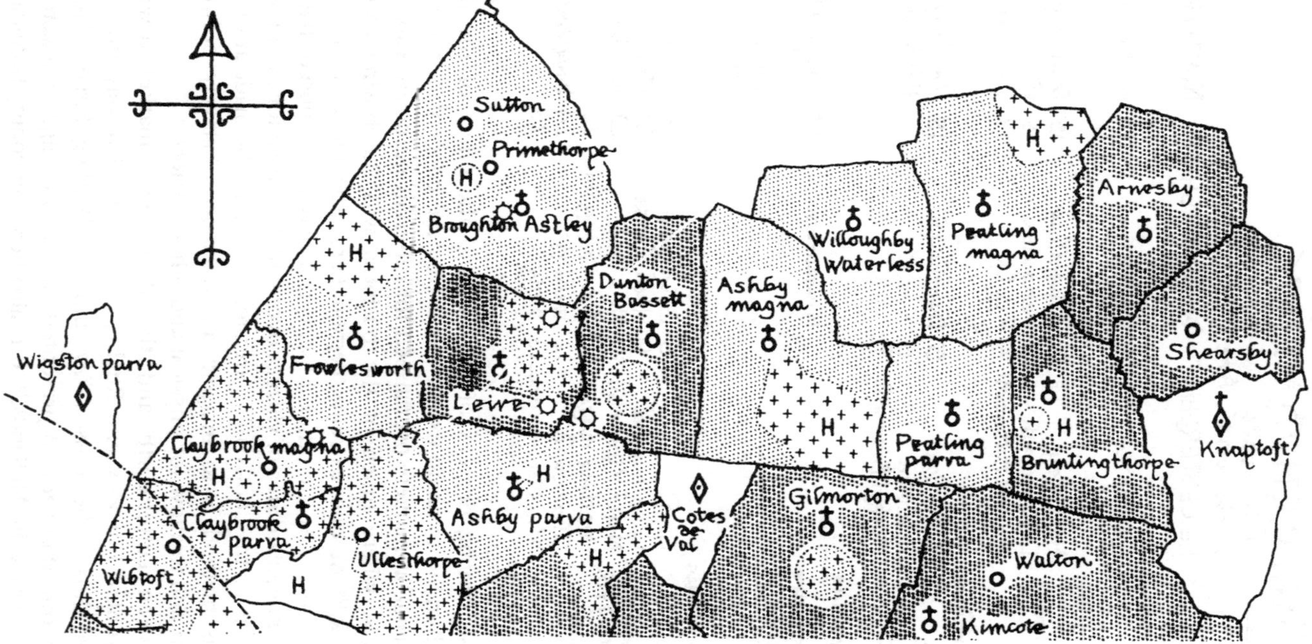

MAP IV

Sutton
Primethorpe
Broughton Astley
Frolesworth
Claybrook magna
Claybrook parva
Wibtoft
Wigston parva

Dunton Bassett
Leire
Ashby parva
Ulleshorpe

Willoughby Waterless
Peatling magna
Ashby magna
Peatling parva
Gilmorton
Cotes de Val

Arnesby
Shearsby
Bruntingthorpe
Walton
Kimcote
Knaptoft

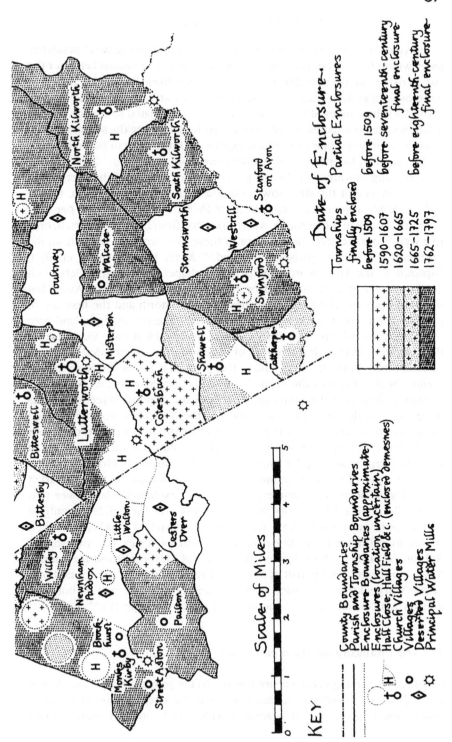

KEY

County Boundaries
Parish and Township Boundaries
Enclosure Boundaries (approximate)
Enclosures (location uncertain)
Half Close, Half Field &c. (enclosed demesnes)
† Church Villages
H · Villages
◇ ○ Deserted Villages
⚙ Principal Water Mills

Scale of Miles

0 1 2 3 4 5

Date of Enclosure

	Townships finally enclosed	Partial Enclosures
	before 1509	before 1509
	1590–1607	before seventeenth-century final enclosure
	1620–1665	
	1665–1725	before eighteenth-century final enclosure
	1762–1797	

Morris Kirby
Street Ashton
Brock-hurst
Pailton
Newnham Paddox
Little Walton
Cesters Over
Willey
Bittesby
Bitteswell
Lutterworth
Misterton
Cotesbach
Shawell
Poultney
Walcote
North Kilworth
South Kilworth
Stormsworth
Westrill
Swinford
Cotthorpe
Stanford on Avon

5

River Avon, which forms another obvious frontier; and these two boundaries meet where the road crosses the river at Dow Bridge. Towards Leicester the last parishes included to the north form a line from Broughton Astley to Arnesby. Altogether, therefore, the Lutterworth area as chosen comprises about 75 square miles of land divided among 36 nucleated townships. In fact it follows the boundaries of Guthlaxton hundred, forming the southern three quarters of it, and coincides almost exactly with the Leicestershire parishes in the nineteenth-century Lutterworth Poor Law Union.[126]

If anything this area may be too generous and, in view of the greater size and importance of the shire town, especially so towards the north. Out of 245 Leicester apprentices engaged in 1646–50 and 1678–82, 45 *per cent* were from outside the borough. Apart from two from Lutterworth itself, only five were from the area chosen. Four of these five, however, came from the northernmost line of parishes included.[127] Again the origins of children baptized at the Lutterworth Independent chapel in the early eighteenth century cover an area confined by the Watling Street and the Avon, but omitting both another line of parishes along the north and the first line of parishes on the nearer side of the Fosse Way.[128] The remaining upland core of the Lutterworth area is a fairly discrete geographical unit. Viewed from the Leicester direction it is that part of the county that is excluded by reason of its altitude from the Soar Valley, the plain that forms the heart of the county. Within the area the Swift Valley, with Lutterworth at its centre, is a miniature version of this, although it faces in the opposite direction and its waters end in the Bristol Channel and not the North Sea. For the detailed examination of records, however, in particular the probate records, it was decided to concentrate on a substantial area of villages within the county of Leicester, on the assumption that they should sufficiently characterize the different types of village community to be found within the town's market area. One adjacent area, however, cannot be excluded. The power that eventually replaced the priory in Monks Kirby was the Feilding family of Lutterworth, who made their residence at Newnham Paddox and then retired from the town. For this reason the parish of Willey, the township of Wibtoft (actually in the Leicestershire parish of Claybrook) and the various townships in the large parish of Monks Kirby, all of which later formed part of the Warwickshire extension of the Lutterworth Union, will be borne in mind when considering the economy of the area (see Map IV).[129]

4.   The changing agrarian economy

Contrasts in farming economy are the key to the primary role of the market town. Just as a "cardinal" market town was the exchange point between contrasting regions, so, on a smaller scale, every ordinary market town depended on exchange between communities within its area with complementary economies and between individuals with contrasting livelihoods. For this reason it is necessary firstly to build up a picture of the farming economy of the area, not only in general terms alone but also in detail, and secondly to identify the interests of the different elements in local society so as to be able to assess how far they remained self-sufficient or became dependent on trading of one sort or another.

Between 1500 and 1700 there were fundamental changes in the economy of England. In the first place there was a great increase in the population. Part of the increased agricultural production needed to feed the growing numbers was achieved by a continuing process of specialization. Of course it should not be supposed that even at the beginning of the period any settlement was entirely self-sufficient. Nevertheless, any concentration on the produce particularly suited to the soil of the locality would have involved farmers in considering markets progressively further afield than their local market centre.

The Midland counties of Leicester, Warwick and Northampton, situated on the central watershed, were hampered by lack of waterways in the transport of heavier produce such as grain. Typical of this region is the rolling landscape of more or less heavy clays, of which the Lutterworth area is an average example. In his descriptions of it Burton several times commented on the 'exceeding good soil' and these soils were then, as they are now, for the most part equally suitable for arable crops and for pasture.[130] The first steps towards increasing production for the outside market, therefore, tended to be away from grain production and in the direction of grazing, especially of sheep for wool and mutton, both easily moved out of the region. The dilemma was that these claylands were almost completely occupied by the common fields which already supported considerable village populations. The transition here from the peasant husbandry of the common fields to a more commercial farming, concentrated in the hands of fewer farmers and relying on wage-labour, involved a radical transformation of rural society.[131]

The uneven progress of this transition further emphasized contrasts between regions and stimulated internal trade. At the same time, on the smaller scale, it saw the emergence of contrasts within rural society between the economies of adjacent villages and also between the livelihoods of individuals, both of which contrasts depended on local trading. The most easily traced indication of the progress of these changes is the spread of enclosure. This invariably brought to an end the mixed husbandry of the common fields and so transformed the economy and the society of a whole village at a time. In order to characterize the different types of village within the area, therefore, it is necessary to make a detailed study of the progress of enclosure there. The study of enclosure in the Midlands has already been advanced by examining various classes of evidence; commission returns, deserted villages, glebe terriers, Chancery decrees, parliamentary acts and surviving ridge-and-furrow landscapes. More detailed work has been done on Leicestershire and in the case of the Lutterworth area it has been possible to supplement the information in these studies from other sources (see Map IV).[132]

The complete enclosure of the region took several centuries and falls into five definable periods. At each stage the movement appears to have spread into the region from further south and to have affected Leicestershire later than Warwickshire and Northamptonshire. The first period covers the desertion of settlements, for various reasons, up to the later middle ages. In the Lutterworth area this accounted for Westrill, possibly identical with the untraced Domesday vill of Lilinge, and Cotes de Val, two small villages whose fields became pasture grounds.[133] But the greatest source of what was later termed 'ancient enclosure' was the movement in the late fifteenth century. This appears to have been the time when the home closes and crofts that formed a ring around the village farmsteads became established as "several" pasture, instead of common, freeholders having the advantage in this development. The greatest advantage, however, was for the lord of the manor who could lay down his own manor farm, his "demesne", to pasture. This regularly involved the winding-up of common-field husbandry so that the village was absorbed into the manorial establishment or disappeared completely.

Reluctance to accept the possibility of a positive enclosure movement in the context of fifteenth-century economy has led to distrust of the significance of the returns of the first enclosure commissions, held in 1517 and 1518.[134] Detailed study of the returns and the cases that followed the hearings, however, has shewn that, on the contrary, the returns only accounted for a fraction of the area enclosed at this period.[135] Time and again the contention was over the last few farms in what was, to judge from the small number of taxpayers in the 1520s or from the deserted site, doomed as a village. Moreover much, if not most, of this enclosure had taken place before 1488 and was therefore outside the scope of the commissions.[136]

Of the 36 townships in the Lutterworth area only two failed to survive as villages into the fifteenth century. By 1507, however, a further six, Bittesby, Knaptoft, Misterton, Poultney, Stormsworth and Wigston parva, had been enclosed and almost completely depopulated. The evidence points to this having happened during not more than the previous generation. In addition there were the large enclosures of Moorbarns in the parish of Lutterworth and the Hall Field, representing the demesne farm, in the adjacent parish of Cotesbach, both formed in the first years of the sixteenth century. The Spittle grounds at Lutterworth were in effect another demesne enclosure. There were many other enclosures in the area and just beyond, including at least nine Hall Closes. Some cannot be proved to date from this stage; but the total so far was certainly as much as 7,000 acres, approximately 15 *per cent* of the whole area.

The fact of this spectacular phase of enclosure cannot be denied. How is it to be explained in the context of the fifteenth century? In the absence of detailed information about the farming economy and the actual process of enclosure at the time, some account can at least be given of the character of the ancient enclosures in the sixteenth century and the uses made of their resources. This should also help to explain why this phase of enclosure came to an end. The effect on the enclosed townships is obvious; they became estate pasture-farms. Apart from the success of these farms, however, it remains to be seen what was the effect on the economy of the area as a whole. Evidently some balance was reached which held off further enclosure, a balance that was maintained for two generations or more.

The third phase started with increased enclosing activity in the county from 1570 onwards. This time the initiative was not so much with manorial lords creating pasture estates as with landowners and farmers of all kinds converting their individual farms.[137] Nevertheless, when the spate of enclosure that followed the relaxation of the anti-enclosure legislation in 1593 led up to 'the rising of the commons' in 1607, the anger of the rioters, of their popular leader John Reynoldes, 'whom they surnamed Captain Pouch' and of 'the Diggers of Warwickshire' was directed against some recent examples of deliberate and ruthless estate-improvement in Northamptonshire and Warwickshire (see Illustration 7).[138] And the Leicestershire rallying point for this Midland Revolt was Cotesbach, just outside Lutterworth, where the lord of the manor was attempting finally to enclose the common fields.[139]

Some of the 'men, women and children to the number of full five thousand' who assembled at Cotesbach had followed the spread of the disturbance from Northamptonshire and Hillmorton, just beyond Rugby:[140] but no doubt most were from the villages in the area and from the town; and over 70 were recorded as coming out from the town of Leicester.[141] The riot was, moreover, condoned by John Moore, the rector of Knaptoft, in his preaching against enclosure in the years following.[142] Yet the final enclosure at Cotesbach, involving 1,000 acres, was exceptional in being apparently the only final enclosure in the county at this stage. In fact this third period of enclosure made very little impression on the Lutterworth area as a whole. It seems, therefore, that, to upset the balance which was unusually stable in the area, there must have been special forces at work in the case of Cotesbach.

The next 50 years saw an irrevocable swing in government opinion in favour of a more commercial use of the land.[143] The key word was "improvement" and the encloser's improvement was assumed to contribute

ANNO QVINTO
IACOBI REGIS.

ᴠ¶ A Proclamation for fuppreſsing of
perſons riotouſly aſſembled for the
laying open of Incloſures.

Illustration 7.   Royal Proclamation of May 30th 1607, made by James I at the
outbreak of the anti-enclosure Midland Revolt; heading and first paragraph.
    P.R.O.

as much to the common good as it did to his own profit. Emphasis on this
change and on the fact that the Midland Revolt was the last great peasant
uprising against enclosure has tended to obscure the facts of continued
public opinion against enclosure, the adverse social effects of enclosure and
indeed of the full extent of the enclosure movement in the seventeenth
century.[144] It should be emphasized that the century and a quarter after 1607
saw the enclosure of at least 40 *per cent* of the area of the county of
Leicester. In the Lutterworth area 19½ *per cent* was enclosed by 1607. In
1725 47 *per cent* remained to be enclosed in the fifth and final phase, which
was almost entirely confined to the last four decades of the eighteenth
century. The main phase of seventeenth-century enclosure, therefore, had

accounted for one third of the area. The majority of this fourth phase, involving 11 villages and 26½ *per cent* of the area, took place in the 45 years starting in 1620 (see Appendix Table 1 and Map IV).

The intellectual device by which seventeenth-century enclosure was justified was to distinguish between improving enclosure and depopulating enclosure and to deny the necessary connexion. In the broader context the enclosed regions cited as not having suffered depopulation were counties like Kent, Essex, Somerset and Devon, where the agrarian economy was patently different from common-field husbandry on the Midland claylands.[145] The witness most frequently quoted as proving the case for this dissociation within the context of the Midlands is Joseph Lee, the rector of Cotesbach, where he farmed the enclosed glebe land.[146] His family farm too was in the Lutterworth area, in the fields of Catthorpe, the final enclosure of which he was at pains to justify in the 1650s in an exchange of pamphlets with the second John Moore. The latter, like his father, was rector of Knaptoft. In 1647 he was also appointed to the Rectory of Lutterworth in the place of an ejected Royalist.[147] It was here in May 1653 that he started the controversy by making an impassioned attack on enclosures in 'two SERMONS, Preached at the Lecture at *Lutterworth*'. These formed the basis of the first pamphlet, *The Crying Sin of England, Of not Caring for the Poor*, and by the end of 1656 they had published three pamphlets each (see Illustration 8).[148] Moore exclaimed:

> Yes, but they say there may be an inclosure without decay of Tillage or Depopulation. Surely they may make men as soon believe there is no sun in the firmament as that usually depopulation & decay of Tillage will not follow inclosure in our Inland Counties. We see it with our eyes: It is so.[149]

The core of Lee's closely reasoned vindication of enclosure has been taken to be that 'from his own personal experience (he) could compile an impressive list of Leicestershire villages which had been enclosed in the previous fifty years without depopulation and without decay of tillage.'[150]

Leaving to subsequent chapters the question whether the villages Lee named were free from depopulation and decay of tillage, it is important to note that he made not one list but a separate list for each of the two points and that there is only one name which appears in both.[151] As to the list produced to counter the charge of depopulation, it is suspicious that the main part of it names villages which are outside the Lutterworth area, a point taken up by Moore. The significant thing about the latter list is precisely that here Lee named not recent but ancient enclosures, calmly implying that they were living villages. This enraged Moore; for only a local reader would know that most of these places had been depopulated a century and a half before and that some of them were enclosed grounds which never had supported separate townships (see Map VII).[152] The final condemnation of Lee as a

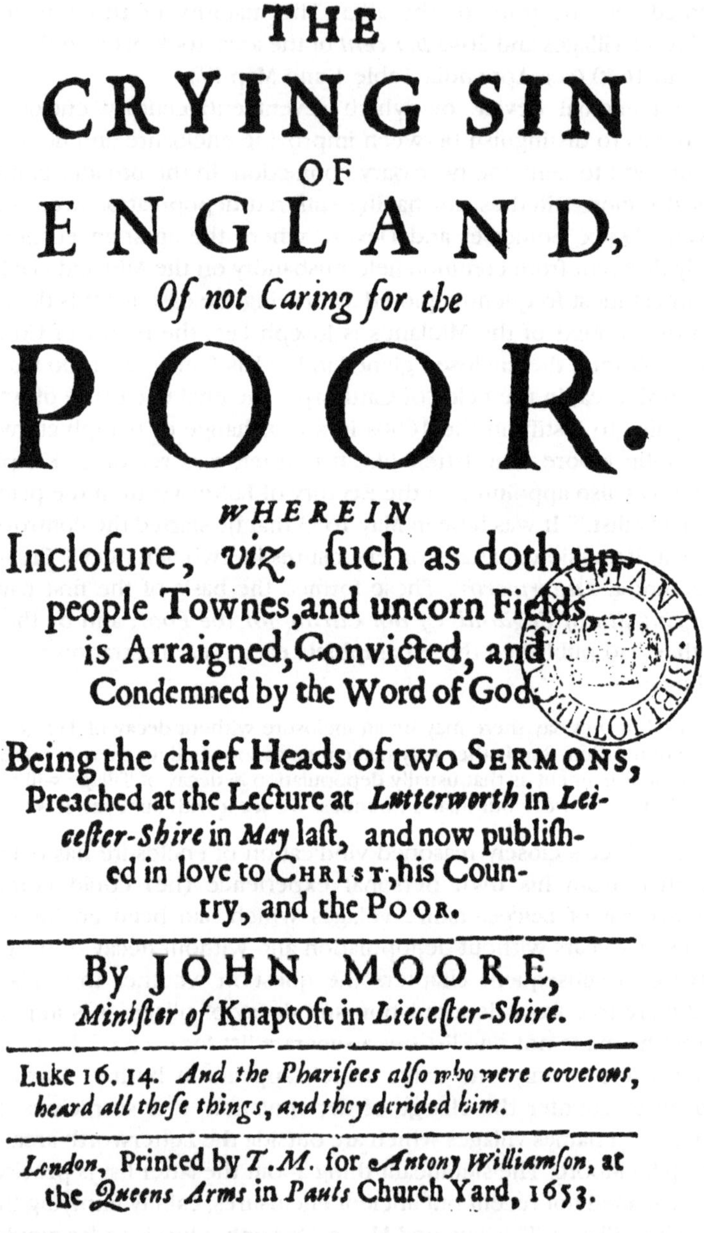

THE
CRYING SIN
OF
ENGLAND,
Of not Caring for the
POOR.

WHEREIN
Inclofure, *viz.* fuch as doth un-
people Townes,and uncorn Fields,
is Arraigned, Convicted, and
Condemned by the Word of God.

Being the chief Heads of two SERMONS,
Preached at the Lecture at *Lutterworth* in *Lei-*
cefter-Shire in *May* laft, and now publifh-
ed in love to CHRIST, his Coun-
try, and the POOR.

By JOHN MOORE,
Minifter of Knaptoft in *Liecefter-Shire.*

Luke 16. 14. *And the Pharifees alfo who were covetous,*
heard all thefe things, and they derided him.

London, Printed by *T.M.* for *Antony Williamfon,* at
the *Queens Arms* in *Pauls* Church Yard, 1653.

Illustration 8.   Title page of the first of the six local pamphlets from the 1650s,
which were written by John Moore of Knaptoft and Joseph Lee of Cotesbach.
   B.M. and Bodleian Library

witness to the innocence of enclosure from depopulation is the fact that he himself admitted that the one was usually followed by the other; although of course he argued that the fault lay in the men who enclosed and not in the enclosures themselves.[153]

Was Moore a 'ghost from the past' launching an 'ineffective and outmoded diatribe against greed'?[154] There is copious evidence of the contemporary belief that enclosures were connected with depopulation and with local scarcity of corn in years of dearth.[155] Following the Civil War the phenomenon of law-defying "Diggers" cultivating commons spread up into the Midlands and in 1650 one group was apparently based near Husbands Bosworth on the edge of the Lutterworth area, where there had been anti-enclosure reaction over a century before.[156] Public feeling against the activities of 'those cruel inclosers and caterpillars of the Common-wealth'[157] in the region were channelled into three petitions to London, in 1651, 1653 and 1656.[158] Moore was closely involved in their preparation, apparently going to London himself all three times before he died in 1657.[159] Support came from all over the county and the protagonists were the Mayor and aldermen of Leicester.[160] The culmination of this work was when Edward Whalley, the Major-General for the Midland Counties, introduced into the House of Commons his 'Bill for Improvement of Waste-Grounds, and Regulating of Commons and Commonable Lands, and preventing Depopulations.'[161] This has been called the last anti-enclosure bill; and the fact that it got no further than its first reading, the turning point of parliamentary opinion in favour of enclosure for good.[162] The cause, however, was far from being rejected on the grounds that no case was proven. It wanted but a couple of votes in the House to refer the second petition to a committee. The very next business was the referral 'to the Committee for the Poor, to consider of the Business where Inclosures have been or shall be made, how there may be a prevention of Depopulations, and decay of Tillage'.[163] In the end the argument that prevailed against the Bill was rather the inviolability of the property of the landowner. The Master of the Rolls 'was for rejecting it, for he never liked any Bill that touched on property'.[164]

In the seventeenth century the characteristic means of achieving enclosure became the enclosure agreement, often enrolled in Chancery. It must be asked how far such agreements were truly voluntary or arrived at under manorial or economic pressures. Moore was explicit that many cottager and husbandman families were driven from their villages on enclosure and took refuge in the towns and villages that retained their common fields.[165] An important part of the study of the population changes in the area will therefore consist of comparing the two types of village for signs of depopulation in the former and of otherwise unaccountable growth in both the latter and in the town of Lutterworth itself.

The second half of the dispute concerned the laying-down of arable land to pasture. An examination of farming practice in the newly enclosed parishes, and indeed in the ancient enclosures, in the later seventeenth century will shew in what way Lee was justified in maintaining that enclosure did not decrease the output of corn. But what was the fate of the villages that retained their common fields? It might seem that they were trapped in a more primitive agrarian organization, unable to adapt to the demands of the new economy. Certainly it was claimed that they had to bear an unfair burden of paupers as a result of immigration from the enclosing villages.[166] But it does not necessarily follow that their more important farmers were dragged down and kept less prosperous than their counterparts in the successfully enclosed villages. These and other possibilities will have to be explored in order to explain why this phase of enclosure came to an end in the balance which was not upset until a century later, when the final, "Parliamentary" stage of enclosure put an end to common-field farming and, indeed, to the Midland peasantry.

To return to the mid-seventeenth century controversy, even where the facts of depopulation and of the laying-down of the old husbandry have been admitted, the changes have still been defended by asserting that the new style of enclosure by agreement made provision for both cottager and poor and that the depopulation was but 'abridgement of labour', 'one of the mainsprings of industrialization'.[167] These are arguments which were used by Lee too. Obviously the question of how far the "Cottage Pasture" and the "Poor's Plot" laid out at enclosure compensated for loss of common rights can only be answered in the context of the farming economy of the time.[168] It is worth asking here, however, what opportunities there were for alternative employment in the area. Moore maintained that, in comparison with other regions, there were none; for tillage was the only industry.[169] What of the emerging hosiery industry? Lee did, it is true, observe that 'combing of wool for jersey is likely, by the new manufactures, to prove a far greater benefit to the Commonwealth, than clothing alone, either is or can be'; but this hardly advocates it as a fully established alternative, especially in the immediate Lutterworth area, where it never became deeply rooted in the way it did in the Hinckley neighbourhood.[170] Were there, on the other hand, less industrial crafts which could absorb the area's redundant labour? Lee held that 'our people may be employed in the working of wool, flax, hemp, woad, and other commodities, which are very beneficial to the Common-wealth'.[171] It will be necessary to establish what scope there was for such non-agricultural employment in the different types of village and in the town, and also how far the town was involved in dealing with the materials for and the products of the various crafts. An understanding of all such matters, however, depends heavily on how the movements of population in the area as a whole may be interpreted and so it is this subject that must be dealt with first.

CHAPTER TWO

Population and Poverty

It is well established that the two centuries after 1500 included a period of outstanding population growth in England. In the case of the Lutterworth area this involved a doubling in numbers. This increase, however, was distributed evenly neither in time nor in space. The town of Lutterworth, for instance, grew much more than the villages in the area; indeed it may have trebled its population. This chapter is concerned with the extent and timing of these changes and with identifying where the increased population was accommodated, both as between the different types of village, those that enclosed and those that retained their open fields, and within the town itself.[1]

1. Lutterworth area villagers

The later middle ages were apparently a period of comparative population stagnation, which may well have lasted into the sixteenth century. Subsequently the main period of growth was the latter part of the sixteenth and the first part of the seventeenth centuries, the rest of the seventeenth being another period of slow growth or even of decline in some areas. This is well illustrated in the study by Professor C. T. Smith of the population of Leicestershire.[2] He based his conclusions for this period mainly on a comparison of the four records that, for all their defects, must be accepted as coming the closest to providing general estimates of the county population. These are the Diocesan Return of households in 1563, the *Liber Cleri* of communicants and recusants in 1603, the Hearth Tax assessments for 1670, which include exemptions, and the 1676 Ecclesiastical Census of Anglican communicants, Papists and Protestant Nonconformists. Comparing the number of households counted in 1563 with the number of Hearth Tax assessments in 1670 shewed a 69 *per cent* increase during the intervening century. On the other hand the number of communicants hardly altered between 1603 and 1676, so that the greater part of the increase must have taken place before the turn of the century. This was confirmed by his estimate of the population change between 1563 and 1603. He divided the ratio of 2.8 communicants *per* taxpayer, found to apply in the 1670s, into the figures for 1603 and compared the result with the figures for 1563. This shewed an increase of 58½ *per cent.*

Smith's examination of a sample of parish registers suggested that from 1630 to 1660 village populations were hardly replacing themselves. This makes it likely that the phenomenal increase of the later sixteenth century had not come to an end at the turn of the century, but that when it did it was followed by an actual decline. A major factor in the fall of the growth rate was undoubtedly the rapid rise in the numbers of deaths. This is confirmed by counting the numbers of probates granted in the Leicester Archdeaconry Court. Comparing the average totals for the four decades before 1610 with those for the three following decades shews an abrupt rise by 68 *per cent* (see Figure I).[3]

If the seventeenth century was not on the whole a period of great population increase, it was nonetheless a period of great population redistribution. The most obvious instance was the growth of the metropolis; but many other industrial centres were growing too. Moreover the trend was not confined to cities and towns but affected entire rural regions as well. In the sixteenth century the population increase in Leicestershire had been fairly equally distributed throughout the county. It was during the seventeenth century that the western half of the county for the first time reached a population density equal to that of the eastern half. But there was redistribution not only between different areas, as in this case, but also between different types of settlement within the same area.

Exploring the relevance of enclosure to these changes, Smith found that population trends were unaffected by the late sixteenth-century enclosure, but that the seventeenth-century figures supported the contemporary view that enclosure involved depopulation. This effect was most marked on the heavy clays of the eastern uplands. In the south-west, on the other hand, enclosing villages even exhibited a slight growth. Here the changes in the economy seem to have been more favourable to the smaller farmer and there was still evidently room for immigration. While the population of the county as a whole remained the same, the south-western hundred of Sparkenhoe, which included the market centres of Hinckley and Market Bosworth, increased its numbers by a quarter. It evidently had a considerable population of smallholders and labourers, not to mention cottagers settled on heath land; for towards the north it merged into the Leicester Forest area. These people together no doubt formed the foundation on which the local hosiery industry was established during the century.

If the two extremes were exhibited by the eastern uplands and the west of the county, the fate of the Lutterworth area lay somewhere in between. To return to the pamphlet controversy, did Lee succeed in demonstrating that enclosure in the area did not necessarily lead to depopulation? It is suspicious that the 13 places he named as recently enclosed without depopulation are nowhere near his village of Catthorpe, but form a group in Sparkenhoe Hundred. In fact they were growing less than that hundred as a whole and some even declined between 1603 and 1676. In his tentative additional list of five names, even more damning to his argument, Lee

FIGURE I

NUMBERS of PROBATE ACTS by DECADES
(see Appendix Table 2)

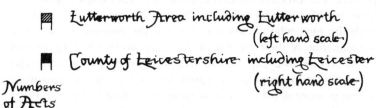

Lutterworth Area including Lutterworth
(left hand scale)

County of Leicestershire including Leicester
(right hand scale)

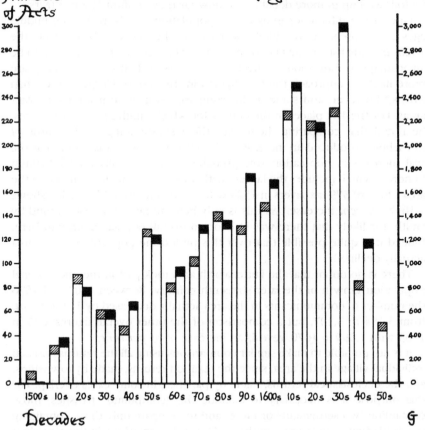

Decades

G

actually dared to include one Lutterworth area village, Ashby magna.[4] Moore
retorted that although the lord of this manor may have postponed the effects
of his enclosure at the beginning of the century by granting long leases, 'the
time of depopulation of that Town is not yet come'. Sure enough it lost 42
of its 110 communicants between 1603 and 1676. In conclusion, therefore,
as Moore expostulated, Lee's writings 'scrabble up a few towns that are
innocent (as they say) which are just none at all in comparison of those many
hundreds are guilty . . .'[5]

In the end Lee was forced to admit that enclosure was usually followed by
depopulation; but of course he argued to the last, as already noted, that the
fault lay with the men who enclosed and not in the process of enclosure
itself. An examination of the economy of the Lutterworth area will put this
problem in its context and explain the disagreement between Moore and
Lee. In the meantime the population figures for the Lutterworth area must
be followed up in more detail to see how far they confirm Moore's fears.

One of the difficulties in assessing population trends in the late middle
ages is the absence of reliable local statistics. The Lay Subsidy rolls from the
1520s provide lists of the taxpayers in individual settlements but prove to be
an inadequate indication of the total numbers of householders. They are
more likely to approach the true figures in the case of villages rather than
towns,[6] however, and some useful comparisons may be made over larger
areas. For the 184 places in the county for which Smith found assessments,
he noted that comparing them with the corresponding 1563 returns of
households produced an increase of 31 *per cent*; but he suggested that the
real increase in population was probably less.[7] The rolls for Guthlaxton
hundred, which includes the Lutterworth area, are complete. Comparing the
area's total of 579 taxpayers in 1524 with the 675 households in 1563 shews
a 16½ *per cent* increase.[8] As this is only half the rate of increase found by
Smith it is likely that there was little or no overall population growth here.
Indeed it is quite possible that over this period the population of the area
actually declined.

There is no doubt that the Lutterworth area took part in the phenomenal
population growth of the later sixteenth century. Between 1603 and 1676
the number of communicants in the area actually decreased by 1½ *per cent*,
from 3,154 to 3,107; but a comparison of the other overall figures, 675 in
1563 with 1,099 in 1670, reveals an increase of 63 *per cent*.

It is not possible to make similar comparisons using all the returns for each
individual village in the area, since the taxation returns, made by townships,
and the ecclesiastical returns, made by parishes, in some cases overlap. For
this purpose it is necessary to exclude the "compound" parishes, those
containing two settlements or more, and to compare only those containing
one settlement, the "single" parishes. Of the 36 townships in the area eight
had already been enclosed by the early sixteenth century and retained only

an insignificant population. Of the remaining villages those that were to be enclosed in the next century comprised nine single parishes and those that were to retain their open fields comprised 19 townships, including, conveniently, nine single parishes. The population of the compound parish of Broughton Astley, enclosed in the early seventeenth century, appears to have been more typical of the "open village" economy, or rather of the Hinckley area, and it has here been classified as an open-field parish. Such detailed comparisons as are possible between the various sixteenth-century returns for the two types of village reveal no very convincing contrasts either in their size or in their composition. In 1524 there were on average 24 taxpayers to each village, practically the same as the county average of 22. The fact that in 1603 the nine single parishes of both types averaged almost exactly 100 communicants each shews that they had so far shared equally in the growth.

It was only in the seventeenth century that the marked divergence in the figures started. The two sets of single parishes, enclosing and open-field, averaged 30 and 52 Hearth Tax assessments in 1670 and 74½ and 160 communicants in 1676 each respectively. In other words whereas they had been of even size at the beginning of the century, the enclosing villages were by then only half the size of the others.

Comparing again the two sets of figures, 1563 with 1670 and 1603 with 1676, the enclosing villages shew an increase of 43 *per cent* over the longer period and a 25½ *per cent* fall between 1603 and 1676. Both the increase and the fall varied from village to village; but they were unanimous in their decline in numbers of communicants in the seventeenth century. This is the clearest refutation of Lee's contention that enclosure would not involve depopulation.

What Smith did not investigate was the corollary to the dwindling numbers in the enclosing villages. As the county population did not fall, it would follow that the open-field villages were actually growing. Sure enough, in the Lutterworth area the longer period saw an 80 *per cent* growth in the nine single parishes of this type, twice as much as in the others. Taking into account five more villages, moreover, settlements within compound parishes for which the figures can be compared, makes the growth very nearly 90 *per cent*. Over the shorter period, however, far from decreasing like the others, the nine increased by 57 *per cent*. Estimates of the numbers of families in the parishes were made by the clergy in the early eighteenth century. It is clear from these that the spectacular divergence in the size of the two types of village had not ceased by the 1670s but continued beyond the end of the century. The nine single open-field villages contained on average 64 families each, a 24 *per cent* increase on the number of Hearth Tax assessments, and the nine single enclosed parishes 27½, a decrease of 10 *per cent*.[9]

To sum up the principal changes in the size and distribution of the population of the area which an examination of these six records can shew, the most important fact is the doubling of the population between the mid-sixteenth and mid-seventeenth centuries. This can be illustrated by the overall figures; 579 taxpayers in 1524 and 675 households in 1563, swelling to 1,227 Hearth Tax assessments (including original exemptions) in the 1670s and 1,101 families in the early eighteenth century. The period of growth appears to have been confined largely to the last three or four decades of the sixteenth century. As, however, there are no records to shew the size of the population between 1603 and 1670, the possibility must not be ruled out that the apparent lack of growth between these two dates conceals a continuation of the sixteenth-century increase, followed by an actual decline in the. mid-century. What has been shewn, however, is that this period of 70 years, far from being one of population stability, saw a striking redistribution of population in the area, a trend which continued into the eighteenth century. Now that the overall changes have been outlined, the parish register figures can be used for filling in the details to explain how this phenomenal growth and spectacular redistribution were achieved.

The most obvious feature of the parish register figures is that while the population doubled during the later sixteenth and early seventeenth centuries, the figures by no means did.[10] This is apparent from the annual averages calculated by decades for 21 parishes in the area (see Figure II). Taking the baptisms first, the average number each year remained about 150 or over for all but one of the decades from 1570 to 1650, after which it fell to around 135. There were what appear to have been temporary checks in the 1590s and 1690s; but the 1650s evidently marked the start of a more serious and lasting demographic set-back. Whether this is to be ascribed to the upheavals connected with the Civil War or, more likely, to the plagues and other epidemics in the mid-century, it is probable that the 1660s opened with the population of the area seriously depleted.

If there was a fall in the population in the mid-seventeenth century it follows, as pointed out above, that the overall growth before then must have been even greater than the records so far used have been able to shew. Looking at the annual average burial and probate figures suggests that there was a period of great natural increase up to 1610, which could have been sufficient to provide for the doubling of the population in a short period; for the numbers of burials did not increase until then so as to cancel out the increased number of baptisms. In fact, with the exception of the 1590s, the four or five decades before 1610 each saw about half of the baptisms unmatched by burials (see Illustration 9).

Like the county as a whole the area shews an abrupt rise in the probate numbers from 1610 onwards, in this case by 70 *per cent*. The parish register

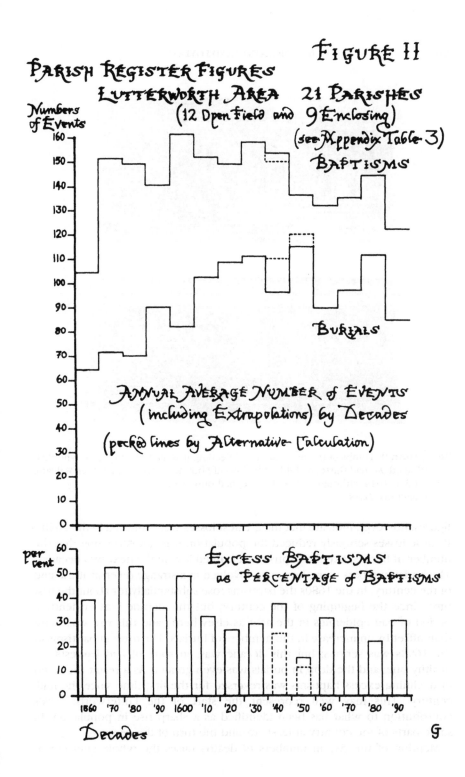

FIGURE II

PARISH REGISTER FIGURES
LUTTERWORTH AREA   21 PARISHES
(12 Open Field and 9 Enclosing)
(see Appendix Table 3)

Numbers of Events

BAPTISMS

BURIALS

ANNUAL AVERAGE NUMBER of EVENTS
(including Extrapolations) by Decades
(pecked lines by Alternative Calculation)

per cent

EXCESS BAPTISMS
as PERCENTAGE of BAPTISMS

Decades

G

Illustration 9. Tombs of the Jervis family of Peatling magna. William Jervis, who died in 1597 aged 94, had thirteen children by his wife but his successor, another William, who died in 1614, although married twice, had only five.

　　J. Nichols, *Leics.*

figures, however, indicate that the greatest losses were suffered in the 1650s. If these losses seriously reduced the population it is not surprising that the number of burials, like the baptisms, remained low in the next two decades. The burial numbers were, however, involved in a strange reversal at the end of the century. In the 1680s the baptisms rose substantially for about the first time since the beginning of the century; but this decade was evidently a period of bad epidemics in the area as elsewhere[11] and this rise was more than offset by an increase in the numbers of burials. The drop in baptisms in the 1690s was serious; but this decade was, in spite of bad harvests,[12] a healthy one, and the drop in burials was even greater. As a result the trend of declining excess baptisms was reversed for the first time since the mid-century. This may well represent the start of the Lutterworth area's contribution to what has been identified as a sharp rise in population, in some parts of the country at least, around the turn of the century.[13]

Mention of the rise in numbers of deaths raises the whole question of epidemics and harvest failures throughout the period. There are numerous examples of unusually high burial figures in single years, often concentrated into a couple of months, from nearly every parish in the area at one time or another. Unfortunately few of the parish registers start before the late 1550s; but the burial figures can be supplemented by the annual numbers of probate acts.

The numbers of probate acts for the county and the area point to no years of any exceptional mortality before the mid-sixteenth century. The late 1550s, on the other hand, which included the dearths of 1555 and 1556 and widespread disease, raised the figures to a high level from 1556 to 1560. The peak was 1558, the year in which, according to local tradition, 'Corn was so dear that people made bread of Acorns which were sold for 8d. a strike'.[14] It is very likely that these years saw a considerable depletion of the population. The Lutterworth area, being more densely populated than other areas, was evidently particularly vulnerable, which might explain why there was apparently no increase in numbers between the 1520s and 1563, while the county as a whole shewed some increase. In other words such increase as there may have been in the population of the area was probably cut back by the ravages of the late 1550s.[15]

The combined evidence of the parish registers and probate figures indicates that the following two decades were comparatively free from epidemics. The first serious set-back was not until 1587, following the bad harvest in 1586. Prices of all types of grain reached their highest so far across the country and the Lutterworth area fared rather worse than the county as a whole. The disastrous 1590s, bringing dearth throughout Europe and plague as well, saw unusually high numbers of probate acts both early and late in the decade. The parish registers confirm the high mortality at both these times, but do not in fact point to any epidemics in the area.[16]

The first decade of the seventeenth century provided a brief respite. There is no trace of the plagues of 1604 and 1609, or any other epidemic, having affected seriously either the county or the villages in the Lutterworth area. With a good run of harvests too[17] the numbers of deaths stayed comparatively low. The one exception was in 1609, when the plague in Lutterworth evidently spread to the neighbouring village of Cotesbach as if it were a suburb of the town. This village normally had only a couple of burials a year and appears to have been growing in the years 1593 to 1608. In 1609 there were 12 burials, all but two of them at the time when the plague was raging in the town. The plague was here working in concert with the enclosing lord of the manor who, in the proceedings following the anti-enclosure riot here in 1607, was accused of decaying 16 houses supporting 80 people.[18] All this is reflected in the numbers of baptisms, which dropped from an annual average of 3.8 in the years mentioned to 1.4 in the years following up to 1620.

Throughout the three decades after 1610, by contrast, the probate figures ran at a new high level in both the county and the area. Among the bad years in the 1620s, 1629 was a bad year in the Lutterworth area, and the burial figures confirm this. They also confirm, however, that nearly every year in the decade saw a high number of deaths in one parish or another in the area. The worst years in the 1630s were 1638 and 1639, the former producing very nearly as many probate acts as 1558 had done; but the burial figures shew that in the area other years too, especially 1635, saw unusual numbers of deaths.

By the 1640s the probate records are no longer complete, although they do suggest that 1647 and 1648 may both have been bad years. There was a series of bad harvests.[19] In 1647 'wheat was at 9s. a strike' locally[20] and there was a visitation of the plague in Loughborough;[21] but there is no proof that the Lutterworth area suffered unduly during these 'heavy times'.[22] Although the parish registers are deficient for the 1640s and even more so for the 1650s, there are enough complete figures to indicate what the probate records cannot shew, that there was a terrible loss of life in the late 1650s, the worst year being 1658.

In the following two decades the burial figures do not suggest any serious epidemics in the area, which even appears to have been unaffected by the plague of 1665. The 1680s, however, as mentioned above, were a decade of epidemics, the worst year being 1686.

To return to the contrast between the two types of village, the figures available do not suggest any great divergence in their development in the sixteenth century. Both of them shared in the period of natural growth between 1570 and 1610. Subsequently the numbers of baptisms for the villages that retained their open fields, instead of rising, appear to have fallen slightly towards the end of the seventeenth century. Meanwhile those for the enclosing villages held up right through to the 1660s, after which they declined steadily. This can clearly be seen in comparing the excesses of baptisms over burials (see Figure III). The great rise in mortality after 1610 affected the open-field villages far more than the enclosing villages, with the result that, save for the 1650s which were in any case exceptional, each decade between 1610 and 1680 saw the enclosing villages maintaining a high proportion of baptisms unmatched by burials. Yet these were the very villages that were shrinking while the others at least doubled in size. Moore insisted that the effects of enclosure were to depopulate the enclosing villages and to overcrowd the remaining open-field villages. Short of checking the movements of large numbers of individuals, this is the clearest confirmation of such migration that can be expected.

Finally in the 1680s and 1690s it was only the open-field villages that were involved in the sudden reversal mentioned above; for by then the numbers of burials in the enclosing villages had nearly caught up with the dwindling

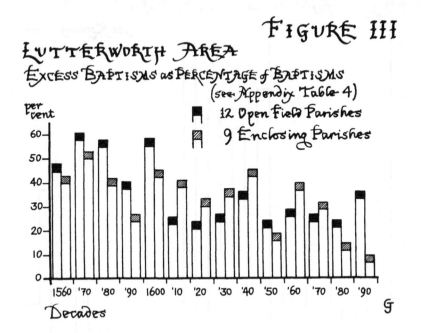

FIGURE III

LUTTERWORTH AREA
Excess Baptisms as Percentage of Baptisms
(see. Appendix Table 4)

per cent

■ 12 Open Field Parishes
▨ 9 Enclosing Parishes

baptisms.[23]

An examination of the year by year and month by month burial figures for the individual villages reveals no contrast in the susceptibility of the two types to epidemics in the sixteenth century. In the three decades after 1610, however, there are practically no cases of an unusually large number of burials in a year among the enclosing villages. Such cases are, on the other hand, a striking and frequent feature of the new high level of mortality in the other villages. This is probably connected not only with the incidence of epidemics but also with the standard of living and of accommodation there.

After the 1630s the burial figures for the enclosing villages become even steadier, except during the 1650s, when they suffered rather more than the other villages. For the last three decades of the century the records are complete and provide telling examples of the different responses to epidemics in the two types of village (see Figure IV). The 1680s evidently saw the outbreak of two epidemics in the area, each of them affecting the open-field villages for longer, so that the high mortality of 1686, the last bad year of the decade, was entirely confined to them. In the mid-1690s a similar pattern on a lower level may be noted, one bad year in both types of village being followed by a year of normal burials in the enclosed villages but even higher figures in the others. Finally, two pairs of bad years in the 1670s affected the open-field villages only, and the last two years of the century

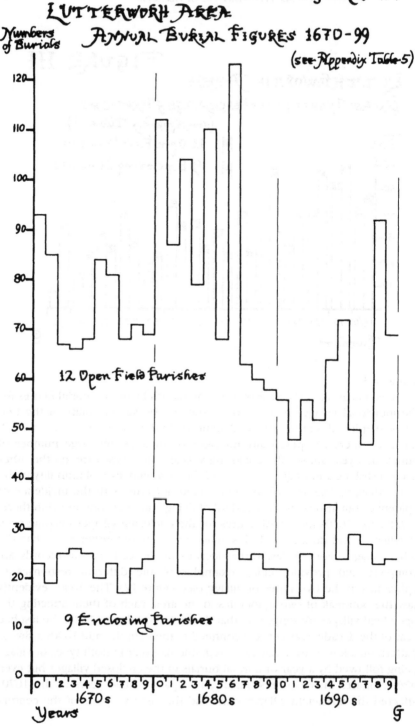

FIGURE IV

LUTTERWORTH AREA
ANNUAL BURIAL FIGURES 1670-99

Numbers of Burials

(see Appendix Table 5)

12 Open Field Parishes

9 Enclosing Parishes

0 1 2 3 4 5 6 7 8 9 | 0 1 2 3 4 5 6 7 8 9 | 0 1 2 3 4 5 6 7 8 9

1670s   1680s   1690s

Years   G

brought a peak in the numbers of burials in the open-field villages which had no effect at all on the enclosed villages.

All this suggests that the seventeenth-century redistribution of population within the area had an effect on the two types of village beyond the difference in their average sizes. A petition against enclosure signed by the townsmen of Leicester in the 1650s expressed the fear that:

> [The] labourer and cottager wanting work and means in such inclosed Towns to maintain hims[elf at] Home [?] turn thief, vagrant, or remove to some open Town or Corporation [and increase the] burden of the poor there. These said Borough and open towns in this county [?] [find their] poor by such Inclosures so great of late years that they are not [able to relieve them][24]

Moore was quite explicit about the effect:

> But woeful experience tells us, a short time forced all the Tenants and Cottagers out of most of those places into the open fielded Towns to seek for a livelihood where they can find it, to the great oppressions of those Towns.[25]

And again:

> And hence it comes to pass, that the open fielden Towns have above double the Number of Cottiers they had wont to have, so that they cannot live one by another, and so put the fielden Towns to vast expenses in caring for those poor, that these *Inclosures* have made . . .[26]

It has already been demonstrated that these fears were justified as far as the movement of population was concerned. Do the records shew that the villages that received additional numbers were also overloaded with poor?

It might be expected that the 1670 Hearth Tax returns should illustrate this effect. Even enlisting the further evidence of the original exemption certificates, however, they do not provide strong grounds for contrasting the composition of the two types of village.[27] Such a contrast does, on the other hand, shew in a comparison of the ratios of communicants in 1676 to Hearth Tax assessments in 1670. The nine enclosed parishes had on average a ratio of 2.45, well below the county figure of 2.8; but eleven open-field parishes had an average of 3.1, only three being below the county figure. It could be argued that this merely reflects the fact that the open-field farmers maintained larger households, including servants in husbandry.[28] It seems more likely, however, that these villages also contained a proportion of families that were not accounted for in the Hearth Tax returns. The exemptions listed were for people who were assessed; recognized paupers were not even assessed in the first place.[29] The higher ratio of communicants to taxpayers in the open-field villages, therefore, probably reflects the presence of larger numbers of poor families there.

Although there are insufficient records to demonstrate the extent of poverty, an examination of charitable bequests in the sixteenth-century wills of inhabitants serves as a reminder of the kind of regular provision made for the poor of each parish. On the other hand the bequests were sometimes distributed 'to every poor cottage' or even 'to every poor household' and there is no indication that the occupants were denied the minimum rights of a cottage cow pasture. Indeed no clear dividing line appears between gifts to such people and gifts to all the husbandmen or all the householders in the parish. On the contrary there seems to have been an assumption that it needed little to put them in the way of being able to produce for themselves their chief need, a supply of bread-corn. Bequests were sometimes in the form of a distribution of bread or corn. One Broughton Astley man left corn 'to every poor man within the parish . . . having no parcel of a plough going' and the vicar of Ashby magna left 'to every one of my po[or neigh]bours that be occupiers so much plough timber as shall make every one of them a plough'.[30] In any case the numbers were not large and probably the majority of the poor were old or infirm husbandmen and labourers unable to work and their widows.

By the early seventeenth century the references in the parish registers to poor may suggest that the term was changing from a description to a recognized status. In the late 1630s there occur a dozen odd entries of this kind, only two of which are from enclosing villages.

To return, therefore, to the difference between the two types of village, the records from the 1670s pointed to the burden falling more heavily on the open-field villages, but were insufficient to illustrate this village by village. While the Hearth Tax returns for a start did not list the recognized paupers, there was also some confusion in the preparation of the Ecclesiastical Census of 1676 so that, even where it appears to have been made conscientiously, it may underestimate the problem.[31] A proportion of the immigrants into the open-field parishes would have formed a fringe of squatters and more settled vagrants whom the parish clergy felt entitled to ignore as outside their cure until death and burial in the churchyard brought them within the fold.

As for civil responsibility for the poor, it was no doubt in these villages that the parish overseers of the poor were especially active in carrying out their statutory duties. Half of the paupers mentioned above as recorded in the registers of these parishes were specified as living "on the collection". In the enclosing villages, on the other hand, the landowners were better organized not only in preventing settlement of new paupers, but also in maintaining those that they had by means of bequests and endowments rather than by rates. When the rector of Ashby parva left three pounds to the poor there in 1604, he was clearly making more than a token offering. Yet the problem was never very extensive. His predecessor had made a bequest 'to five poor cottiers' there in 1573. In 1633 a husbandman making a bequest to the poor was able to name them – all eight of them. At the enclosure in 1655 the Poor's Plot of 14 acres cannot have been intended to accommodate the cows of more than seven paupers.[32]

Both the paupers from enclosing villages mentioned above were termed 'almsman'. One came from Shawell, where he no doubt lived in the Almshouse for six poor men that had been endowed there in 1604.[33] Eleven more almsmen were buried there in the period 1661 to 1695, accounting for just under 10 *per cent* of the burials recorded for these years. Even if the Almshouse was the same as 'the Townhouses' referred to at the enclosure in 1665 as accommodating five poor, this might have been considered ample provision in a village of under 30 households.[34] The other almsman belonged to Catthorpe. The enclosure of the open fields of this village, including the farm that Lee had inherited, was the central arguing point of the pamphlet controversy. Lee was able to report, with satisfaction, that 'there are not above twelve persons, men, women and children, that do, or at least can, pretend to poverty'. Apart from five or six 'ancient Cottages . . . there are only four erected Cottages in the Town' and 'two or three old men, who are unable to work', could be maintained by their sons who, like the rest of the cottiers, were in work. Otherwise 'there are only three day-labourers in the Town'.[35] With so few paupers and their place in the community so well defined, the problem in such villages was less acute and more contained. If the Shawell almsmen are typical, it is well to remember that their conduct was as closely regulated as that of the scholars at the village school there. They were also identified by their blue gowns, which bore the letters J and E, the initials of their benefactor John Elkington, the gentleman who had endowed the Almshouse for six men at the beginning of the seventeenth century. Some almsmen may even have lived in comparative comfort; one Shawell almsman died worth £23.13.4d.[36]

A certain hostility is evident in the way the poor were provided for in these villages. Such provisions have been quoted as evidence of the humanity of this phase of enclosure;[37] yet smallholdings and cottage cow pastures were easily swallowed up in the transition.[38] Moreover even rights of grazing in the plots allotted for the poor had to be paid for, and the administration of them was somewhat precarious when entrusted to the freeholders together with either the lord of the manor or the minister.[39] Following the enclosure of Peatling magna one freeholder was able to advertise his farm for sale in 1659 as 'free from the poor by Articles from the Freeholders at the inclosure to maintain every man his own poor'.[40] Here the average number of baptisms *per annum* sank steadily from 5.5 in the 1660s to 1.9 in the 1690s. In 1670 23 paid Hearth Tax and 16 were exempted; but by 1716 there were only two dozen households, the overseers of the poor being concerned with but four of them.[41] This would have been gratifying to another inhabitant of an enclosing village who, according to Moore, complained that '*The poor increase like fleas, and lice, and these vermin will eat us up unless we inclose*'.[42]

Thus landowners in the enclosing villages were not only more vociferous in complaining about poverty, but also more effective in dealing with it. At the same time, and partly as a result, the problem was far more acute in those villages that retained their open fields. Here the contribution of the ancient enclosures, at least, to the present difficulties was recognized. In open-field villages the practice was 'that all public payments, as taxes and the like, are laid according to the number of yard lands as they are usually accounted'.[43] It was also possible, however, for the inhabitants of a township to secure payments from the occupiers of enclosed grounds within their parish. In the 1670s the Quarter Sessions dealt with claims of this sort from Claybrook magna, Ullesthorpe and Mowsley over the depopulated townships of, respectively, Wigston parva, Bittesby and Knaptoft.[44] The mid-century enclosures, however, were each of the fields of a single parish with its own village and its own paupers to relieve and under the Elizabethan Poor Law, moreover, there was technically no possibility of enforcing contributions to any place outside the parish. Some indication of the extent of the problem in the villages that did not enclose is provided by the entries in the parish register of Bruntingthorpe in the period leading up to this time of change. In the years 1606 to 1638, 20 of the people recorded as buried, making 13 *per cent* of the total, were poor men and women, all but four noted as old. Thirteen more of them were noted as old, lame or blind. The entries include a 'stranger and a poor travelling man' and 'an old widow that was living upon alms'.[45]

*   *   *

It is now possible to sum up how the major changes in the size and distribution of the population of the villages were achieved. The remarkable growth of the later sixteenth century was based on natural increase and continued throughout the area into the seventeenth century. From 1610 onwards it was severely cut back, especially in the villages that were to retain their open fields, by a rise in mortality. Possibly some slight increase in the population lasted until the end of the 1630s; the middle of the century, on the other hand, saw an actual loss of population. Up to this time, however, the villages retaining their open fields had continued to grow, although the major source of their new population was no longer natural growth so much as immigration from the enclosing villages. This redistribution, indeed, carried on after the crisis of the 1650s; but by the 1680s the enclosed villages were very much reduced and as a source of population for the area they were a spent force. The strange reversal of the last two decades was, not surprisingly therefore, a phenomenon which concerned only the remaining open-field villages. And these villages have continued to flourish in this way: they all, for instance, now embrace council houses and other housing estates.

One way of illustrating the overall change is to compare the figures for the two sets of nine "single" parishes. Between these the open-field ones accounted for half the taxpayers in 1524 and half the communicants in 1603, but 63 *per cent* of the 1670 Hearth Tax assessments, 68 *per cent* of the communicants in 1676 and 70 *per cent* of the families in the early eighteenth century. This shews them nearly doubling in size in comparison with the enclosing villages; yet the omission of the "compound" parishes excludes from this comparison just the "open" villages that were most susceptible to immigration.

But the difference in size between the enclosed and open-field villages was not the only result of these changes. Closely connected with this population shift was the greater proportion of poor living in the latter. No doubt their lower standard of living and poorer housing conditions contributed to the higher mortality there and the greater susceptibility of these villages to epidemics. These effects were all, as will be explored in the following chapters, concerned with the changing availability of employment. In this sense, therefore, the contrast between the two types of village foreshadows the contrasts in the following century, when the pattern of employment changed again during the final phase of enclosure.[46]

2.   Lutterworth townspeople

Among the places that retained their open fields was, of course, the town of Lutterworth itself. The growth of the town population on the whole followed the pattern that has been identified in the area. The problems of the town, however, cannot be treated as if it were merely an example of a large open-field village; for demographic characteristics were emerging which came to distinguish its development as truly urban.

To begin with, it is necessary to trace the overall growth of the town during the sixteenth and seventeenth centuries. The six records used for the comparative study of the villages prove of little value in estimating the town population and will be mentioned only briefly here. Fortunately it is possible to supplement them with information from other sources.

At the outset the detailed Terrier of 1509 shews that there were at least 116 dwelling houses in the town, presumably all occupied.[47] Much use has been made of the Lay Subsidy rolls for estimating the populations of towns.[48] The case of Lutterworth is an illustration of the fact that on their own they cannot provide an approximation of the number of households in a town. The 42 taxpayers in 1524 represent little more than the principal householders,[49] since the Terrier lists 37 messuages and tenements and at least 79 cottages. It also records some empty plots along the town streets and it is possible that the town was still losing population over the following 15 years, which might account for some of the difference in the figures. Nevertheless, the main reason of the roll covering only 36 *per cent* of the households is likely to have been the shortcomings of the tax assessment. In Coventry the same assessment covered only 45 *per cent* of the households.[50]

How far the 1563 Diocesan Return under-counted the number of households must remain a matter of conjecture;[51] but the figure of 106 at least encourages the assumption that there had been no great increase in numbers in Lutterworth during the first half of the century. The numbers of communicants given for 1603 and 1676, on the other hand, 564 and 644 respectively, confirm what might have been expected, that the town grew considerably in the second half of the sixteenth and continued to grow in the seventeenth. Finally the estimates of the number of families made in the early eighteenth century vary from 300 to 315.

The Hearth Tax assessment of 1670 goes some way towards listing the households in the town: 225 people were assessed, 142 paying and 83 exempt. The original exemption certificate of 1672 lists 111 people, adding 39 new names for exemption, but omitting 16 previously exempted.[52] Combining the two returns, therefore, shews that the total number of households liable to assessment was at least 248. Supposing there to have been under 150 households in the 1560s and over 300 by the early eighteenth century, it is already clear that the majority of the growth had taken place before the 1670s.

For the six market towns in Leicestershire taken together, the ratio of 1676 communicants to 1670 tax assessments is on average 2.7 to one. For Lutterworth it is 2.85. Both these figures are very near the county-wide average of 2.8. Substituting in each case the largest number of exemptions found in the series of original certificates from the 1670s for the number given in the 1670 return reduces the ratio for the towns to 2.3. As this calculation does not start to deal with the recognized pauper households, it casts doubt on the worth of the 1676 figures. What can be said is that Lutterworth, with 2.55, had the highest ratio, making it even more likely that there were numerous pauper households not assessed for 'Hearth Money' by the 'chimney men'.[53] All this emphasizes the difficulty of dealing with a taxation return that excluded pauper households and with an Ecclesiastical Census which may seriously have under-counted the poorer potential members of the congregation. In any case, as already mentioned, there was some confusion among the clergy responsible as to who exactly was to be counted.[54]

Perhaps for once the attempt to reconcile the unsatisfactory statistics gleaned from the various official records should be abandoned and more attention paid to the impressions of contemporaries. In giving evidence in a legal case in 1630 five aged inhabitants were in agreement that the number of houses and families was about 300 and that it had doubled within the previous 40 years, or since they first knew the town.[55] As they were aged from 70 to 87, this cannot have been earlier than the 1560s. The figure of 300 was obviously an approximation, but not necessarily an exaggeration. More precise estimates were given by another aged inhabitant in a case in 1658.[56] This was Edward Overing, shoemaker, who came from a Lutterworth family and was 75 years old. He referred to a count of communicants about 20 years before. As he had been church warden in 1642, it is possible that he himself had conducted the count. On one day in that year the rector, Nathaniel Tovey, wrote to a relation 'I am very weary having had a communion of above four hundred communicants'.[57] Overing recalled the total number of communicants counted, however, to have been 700 or 800 and also estimated that there were not less than 240 families in the town in 1658. When it is recalled that a dozen years later the number of people liable to assessment for Hearth Tax was at least 248, quite apart from any recognized paupers, it seems that this man too, like the tax assessors or the minister counting communicants for the Census, was ignoring the poorest families in the parish; unless, of course, the numbers in the town were still rising rapidly. It all depends on how many poor families there are assumed to have been; but at the most the total of 300 families may not have been so far from the truth.

If it is to be believed that the town doubled in numbers of families and houses in the half-century before 1630, the numbers of baptisms and burials ought to reflect this. Unfortunately the surviving parish register does not start until late in 1653 and the registration appears to have been defective in the mid-1660s. Looking at the few figures for those years before the 1650s that can be retrieved from the Bishop's Transcripts, the baptisms shew a spectacular rise from about 25 a year at the beginning of the seventeenth century to over 40 by the 1630s (see Appendix Table 6).[58] From then onwards, however, the number of baptisms in a year remained fairly constant, except for the familiar drop in the 1690s. The baptism figures, therefore, are compatible with a doubling in the population between the late sixteenth and mid-seventeenth centuries; but they suggest that the growth may have ceased by then.

Even supplementing the burial figures with the probate figures, little can be said about the occurrence of epidemics in Lutterworth in the sixteenth century. The probate figures were surprisingly low; presumably the section of the population most susceptible to famine and epidemics was below the probate level. For the early seventeenth century, however, the two series of figures combined help to identify the worst years as 1604, 1609, 1634 and 1638. The figure of 44 probates for the 1630s represents a rise by 20 *per cent* over the average for the three preceding decades and identifies this as the decade with easily the highest mortality so far. Ignoring the burial figures for the exceptional years named and following those for the other years, as if they were in some way "normal", shews that the normal number of burials rose sharply from an average of 16 early in the century to 26 by the 1630s (see Figure V). Moreover it looks as if all the five years from 1657 to 1661 inclusive, when the average was 44, should be counted as years of exceptional mortality. As in the case of the villages the loss of lives in these years is presumably the reason for the dip in the numbers of baptisms and the lower level of burials that followed; for the remaining four decades of the century the average annual burials were never far from 35. The burial figures too, therefore, are consistent with a phenomenal growth leading up to the middle of the seventeenth century; but they also raise the possibility that the late 1650s actually saw a fall in the overall population of the town.

If, however, the town doubled in numbers between about 1590 and 1630, it is likely that a slightly wider period, from the 1560s to the mid-1650s, accounted for just about all the growth of the whole of the two centuries. This has been assumed to have been in the order of 150 to 200 *per cent* and, if there was an actual drop in numbers in the mid-seventeenth century, it may have been even greater. There can be no doubt that the town was far outstripping the area in population growth. How did it achieve this?

The first possibility that must be raised is that the growth represented natural increase from within the town; this, after all, was the case in all the villages up to the beginning of the seventeenth century. There is no reason to suppose that the rate of natural growth was higher in the town or would have continued so longer into the seventeenth century. On the contrary, among the few parish register figures available from before 1660 the proportion of baptisms unmatched by burials was generally between 12 and 15 *per cent*, which compares very unfavourably with the figures from the area. Moreover, taking the numbers of children mentioned in the wills of inhabitants as an indication, the prevailing size of family rose to a peak in the 20 years from 1590 and then fell again. This suggests that the contribution of natural increase to the town's growth was already dwindling in the early seventeenth century, exactly at the time when the town was growing at its fastest (see Table 2.1).

Whatever contribution natural increase made to the overall growth, there is no reason to doubt that immigration was the main source of new population and was responsible for the spectacular rate of increase. Indeed it became still more important during the seventeenth century. The parish register figures are all but complete from after the 1650s and shew that the unmatched baptisms declined from 24 *per cent* to a miserable 3½ *per cent* (see Table 2.2).[59] By the end of the century, then, it is clear that the town was relying on immigration to retain its numbers, let alone increase them.

If the rise in numbers in the town depended largely on immigration, what were the origins of the immigrants? Urban immigration was a nationwide problem in the late sixteenth and early seventeenth centuries. Lutterworth

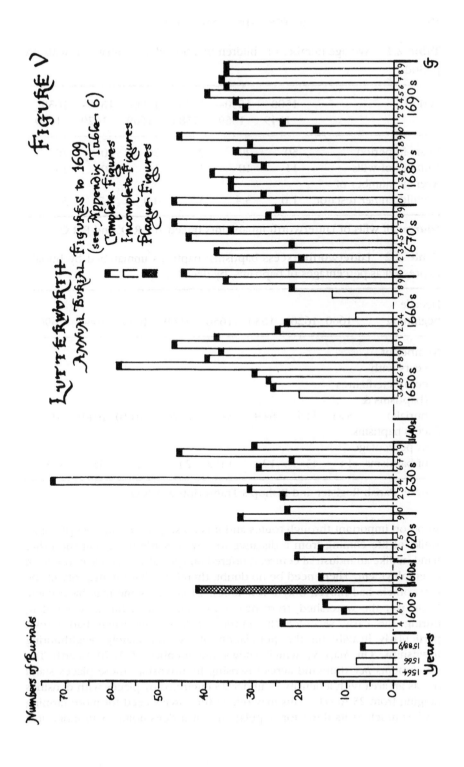

FIGURE V

LUTTERWORTH
Annual Burial Figures to 1699
(see Appendix Table 6)

Complete Figures
Incomplete Figures
Plague Figures

Numbers of Burials

Table 2.1   Average number of children mentioned in Lutterworth wills, by periods

Period	1500–1549	1550–1569	1570–1589	1590–1609	1610–1629	1630–1649
Years in period	50	20	20	20	20	20
Number of wills	11	10	20	13	20	25
Average number of children *per* testator	1.6	3.4	3.7	4.0	3.7	3.2

Source: all wills of Lutterworth inhabitants traced at L.R.O. and P.R.O.

Table 2.2   Lutterworth excess baptisms: baptisms unmatched by burials, expressed as percentages of baptisms, by decades

Decade beginning	1600	1620	1630	1650	1660	1670	1680	1690
Number of years with complete figures (baptisms & burials)	5+4	3+4	8+8	5+6	8+6	10+10	10+10	10+10
Excess baptisms as percentage of baptisms	14	45	12	14½	24	24	18½	3½

Source: Parish Register and Bishop's Transcripts at L.R.O.

stood on important through-routes and it is no surprise to find people of all walks of life coming from a distance to stay or settle there. On the other hand, unlike an industrial centre, it offered no special attractions in the form of employment. There need be no doubt, therefore, that the majority of the newcomers had moved only a few miles. Of course some may have come from over the watershed, from nearer to other towns; but it seems that, during the early seventeenth century at least, the town had drawn particularly heavily on the population of its immediately neighbouring townships. On Map V, which shews the number of 1670 Hearth Tax assessments *per* thousand acres township by township, these places stand out as an area with a density of under 25 encircled by places with densities ranging from 25 to 60.[60] This may reflect the town's need for more farming land as much as its thirst for population, but it does point to an inner area

MAP V

POPULATION DENSITY IN 1670

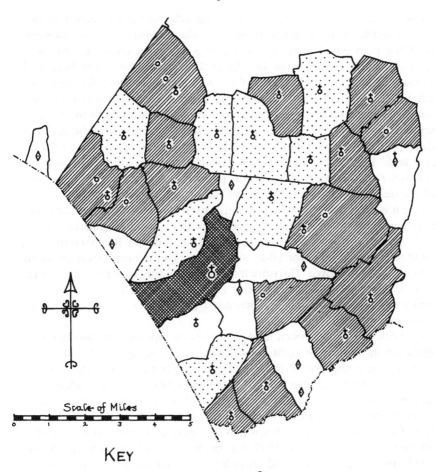

Scale of Miles

0 1 2 3 4 5

KEY

```
— — — —   County Boundaries
————————   Parish and Township Boundaries
   ♀       Lutterworth
   ♀       Church Villages ⎫ of the
   ○       Villages        ⎬ Lutterworth
   ◊       Deserted Villages⎭ Area
```

Density: Number of Hearth Tax Assessments
          for every thousand acres
          by Townships or Parishes

under 15

under 25

under 60

Lutterworth 119

G

over which the town exerted a very strong influence and which does not shew on similar maps prepared from any earlier record. Of course to some extent the map merely reflects the changes following enclosure; but it is worth noting that only three of the villages that retained their open fields had a density of under 25. They were Bitteswell and Gilmorton, the only two such villages left whose fields matched with those of Lutterworth, and Dunton Bassett, which was only separated from the town's fields by the early enclosed township of Cotes de Val. Indeed the proximity of these three villages to the town very likely strengthened the farming economy of their open fields. In 1754 Sir Thomas Cave wrote of Bitteswell that 'The number of land-owners (or freeholders) in this parish has probably been the reason that the destructive genius of inclosure has not yet prevailed here'.[61]

Since it is clear from the various records used above that the population of Lutterworth did not constitute a large proportion of the population of the whole area, probably never as much as one fifth, it can be imagined that any overall tendency to leave the villages could have had a considerable effect on the numbers in the town. The principal instance of this appears to have been during the period of agrarian change from near the end of the sixteenth century until around the mid-seventeenth; but the effects also continued, to a lesser extent, until after 1700.

Reference has already been made to the contemporary opinion that this population movement brought great problems for the open-field villages. It was also clearly understood that the towns suffered as well.[62] This was no doubt the reason for the anti-enclosure feeling in Leicester, the evidence for which weighs against Thirsk's assertion that 'the citizens of Leicester . . must have been among the least affected by the inclosure'. The sustained intensity of this feeling in the county town may be measured by the rejection of a parliamentary candidate in 1597 for being 'an incloser, and therefore unlikely he would condescend to redress that wrong in others wherein himself was faulty'; by the numbers of townsmen who joined the riot at Cotesbach in 1607; by the complaint from the Mayor and others in 1614 'of the present misery and future danger both of ours and other Corporations by means of depopulation and decay of Tillage'; and by the widespread support there for the petitions in the 1650s.[63] The draft of one petition stated that:

> . . . many of the Inhabitants are constrained either for want of work, or through the cruelty of Landlords to fly to other places and especially to market towns, whereby they are not only oppressed with multitude of poor, but disable to maintain them through the decay of the market, and traffic.[64]

Moore too emphasized the plight of the market towns:

> for when these Inclosures have made Farmers, Cottagers; and Cottagers, Beggars; no way of *livelihood* being left them: These poor with their families are forced into *Market-towns*, and *open-fielded Towns*, hoping

they may find some employment there to preserve them and theirs from perishing. Whereupon, these open fielded places are so loaden with poor, that the Inhabitants are not able to relieve them.[65]

It may not be fanciful to suppose that he had in mind his own market town of Lutterworth, where he was also rector, when writing these lines. Certainly in the minds of his contemporaries the question of immigration into market towns was inseparable from the problem of poverty there. An illustration of this is the provision made in 1638 by the Justices of the Peace for Leicestershire in the case of Melton Mowbray, requiring the church wardens and overseers of the poor to take security from and tax for poor relief anyone entertaining strangers or taking in inmates. This was in view of the 'great increase of poor people within the Towns and villages of the said County'.[66] What evidence is there that Lutterworth was overloaded with poor at this time?

There is no way of determining precisely the extent of poverty in the town of Lutterworth during the sixteenth century. For a start it is evident from what has been said above that the Lay Subsidy rolls of the 1520s are of no help here. For instance Lutterworth, with 42 taxpayers in 1524, and Rugby, with 56, may have had very similar populations. They both had 32 inhabitants assessed at over one pound; but this says nothing about the poorest sections of their communities.[67] In the sixteenth century there was some charitable provision for the poor (see Illustration 10). Five bedeswomen were accommodated in cottages belonging to the Hospital of Saint John, were paid a few pence weekly and were given a gown each winter. As the property changed hands during the course of the century these charitable uses were conveniently "forgotten", although the distribution of distinctive black gowns and some money at Christmas continued into the next century on an *ex gratia* basis.[68] Among the 71 wills of inhabitants from the sixteenth century also there were 10 bequests, all of them made after 1540, to small numbers of the poorest people in the town. In some cases the bequest was to a few of the parishes in the area, which might suggest that the problem in the town was not felt to be particularly grave; on the other hand a bequest by a town baker in 1564 was 'to forty of the poorest people inhabiting in Lutterworth'.[69]

More positive evidence of the problem, however, dates from the seventeenth century. Encouraged, no doubt, by the Elizabethan legislation dealing with poor relief and charitable uses, bequests to the poor, usually of a pound or two, suddenly became more common. There were none in the 21 wills from the 1580s and 1590s, but in the 37 wills from the first three decades of the new century there were 18. In 1631 the town complained in a petition of the difficulty of maintaining a supply of barley in the market as bread-corn for the poor.[70] A little later the church wardens' accounts shew

Illustration 10. Giving drink to the poor. Painted glass panel from the end of the fifteenth century, depicting a merchant engaged in one of the Seven Corporal Works of Mercy. From the house in Leicester associated with Roger Wigston, Merchant of the Staple and Mayor. The cans held by the servant were a product of the cooper's craft; the companion panel, giving bread to the poor, shews a baker's pannier made of wicker-work.

Leicestershire Museums

how money collected at communion was being distributed by order of the overseers of the poor and the rector. On the whole these payments, about 92 in all and amounting to £13.0.9½d. in the seven years from 1639 to 1645, seem to have been *ad hoc* payments to people in difficulties or in need of sums to place their children. Although other payments recurred, no doubt the regular maintenance of the poor was attended to by the overseers raising a rate. Yet over the seven years the number of recipients covered by these payments alone added up to 62 people in all.[71]

The account books of the town overseers survive from 1673 onwards. The amount of money they handled each year apparently responded to changing conditions. For the first decade recorded it averaged about £60 a year; it then rose and fell in the 1680s, the highest total being just over £90 in 1686. In the 1690s, however, it rose steadily, reaching in the last two years of the century over twice the average mentioned. The principal expenditure was in the form of fortnightly 'standing collections' paid throughout the year to a list of people who usually numbered around 30. These were doubtless the town's recognized paupers, the old, disabled and widowed. The rates of payment did increase; but the main increase was in the *ad hoc* amounts paid 'by collection', which included attending to cases of destitution as well as expenses such as setting pauper children to apprentice.[72] However all these figures are taken, it cannot be said that the overseers were dealing with the full range of poverty that has been suggested overtook the town in the seventeenth century. The majority of the landless labourers and poor craftsmen that came in hopes of employment there would not be classified as paupers. Indeed in so far as they were immigrants from villages, provided they did not threaten to become a charge on the parish, they were probably never even counted as officially settled in the town but as more or less permanent inmates or sojourners.

The greater part of the burden of dealing with vagrants in the area under the various vagrancy laws would have fallen on the market town. The Lutterworth constables made the usual payments, such as to lame soldiers, and both they and the church wardens made frequent payments to outsiders with passes. The constables' account book, which starts in 1651, also records the sad periodic lists of vagrants whipped in the town. The nineteenth-century workhouse, the centre of the Lutterworth Poor Law Union, superseded an eighteenth-century workhouse in the town. Already in the seventeenth the four town overseers too were evidently tackling a poverty problem beyond that of the town parish. On the other hand each parish had its own paupers to relieve; even the overseers in the enclosed parish of Shawell were handling around ten pounds a year in the 1690s.[73]

The clearest indication of the wider significance of the town's poor relief is the extended range of sources from which the income to the town overseers was drawn (see Table 2.3). As has been mentioned, levies might

Table 2.3   Lutterworth overseers of the poor, sources of income, 1673

	£	s	d
Levies on:			
monthly men (68 entries)	32	16	0
quarterly men (35 entries)	5	0	8½
out-town quarterly men (21 entries)	4	2	7
out-dwellers (see below)	24	14	8
Other income	3	4	6
Total	£69	18	5½
Levies on out-dwellers (paid on each property by one landowner):			
Moorbarns	12	10	6½
Spittle	2	10	1½
Misterton and Poultney (13 properties)	2	14	0
Cotesbach	2	10	0
Westrill and Starmore	2	0	0
Bittesby	1	10	0
Cotes de Val	1	0	0
Total	£24	14	8

Source: Overseers of the Poor Account Book, L.R.O., DE 2559/35

be raised on ancient enclosures within a parish. Sure enough, a provision very important to the town was the order of 1628, following a petition to the king, which ensured that the Temple family, or their tenants at Moorbarns, should contribute one quarter of what the rest of the town paid. A similar arrangement applied to the Spittle, so that together these two properties supplied over a fifth of the total poor rates in the 1670s. Another important order, obtained at the Quarter Sessions in 1693 to settle 'several differences between the husbandmen and Tradesmen of Lutterworth', provided 'That all lands and tenements there be taxed according to the Intrinsique value'. Whether farm holdings were still assessed by the yard land or not, presumably premises in the town centre now had to pay rates related to their full commercial value.[74] What was, however, in comparison with normal practices, quite extraordinary was that the town had managed to secure payments from the owners of all the neighbouring depopulated townships, despite the fact that these lay outside the town parish and, in the case of Bittesby, apparently in defiance of the more legitimate claim of Ullesthorpe. Added to this there was even a payment from the squire of Cotesbach, which parish still contained a living village, albeit a much depleted one. These sources of income confirm the inner area of the influence of the town shewn on Map V.

It is very likely, therefore, that poverty first became a serious problem in the town in the early seventeenth century and that the way it had to be dealt with during the century further reinforced the town's role as the centre of its area. Even though it is not possible to quantify the general extent of poverty, beyond the provision made for recognized paupers, it is worth investigating the timing further in relation to two constant companion problems of urban poverty, high mortality and unhealthy housing.

The evidence that survives from the sixteenth century does not shew the town as having suffered from any of the epidemics of the period. On the contrary the probate figures remained low in both the late 1550s and the 1590s, although there is a hint that the town may have suffered in the late 1580s, a time of famine rather than epidemics. Of the five bad years identified in the first three decades of the seventeenth century, however, 1604 almost certainly saw the bubonic plague in the town and in 1609 32 of the 42 burial entries were marked in the parish register as plague deaths. 1629 and 1638 were peak years of mortality in the town and in the area as well and the 73 burials in 1634, the highest number in a year recorded for the town, testify to an epidemic which appears to have spread to the area in the following year.

It will be recalled that the burial figures for the five years from 1657 to 1661 all appear exceptional; in the area, on the other hand, the worst year was 1658, after which the burials fell off. After these five bad years in the town the number of burials in a "normal" year was down, but then rose again steadily until 1690. In the villages the 1650s were followed by decades of low mortality, the only exception being the 1680s. The town evidently succumbed to the epidemics in the 1680s; but whereas the last bad year was 1684 in the enclosed villages and 1686 in the open-field villages, the town suffered again badly in 1689. In the area the ravages of the 1680s were followed in the 1690s by a reduction in the numbers of baptisms and, in the open-field villages, an even greater reduction in the numbers of burials. The town figures might be expected to follow the same pattern. Sure enough the baptisms dropped. The burials dropped too, from an average of 35½ a year in the 1680s to 17 in 1690 and 24 in 1691. After this respite of two years, however, the next ten years returned to exactly the same average as the 1680s.

Thus although, as elsewhere, the last four decades of the century were not punctuated by the odd years of terrible fatality like earlier periods - and no doubt the final disappearance of the bubonic plague was largely responsible for this change – the exceptional years in the town became more frequent and the number of burials in the "normal" year rose, so that after 1691 the distinction can no longer be maintained. As the average numbers of baptisms were not increasing at the same time, this was not a case of the population rising, but of the "normal" mortality rate rising to meet the exceptional. In several instances, moreover, it appears that when there was high mortality in the area, the town was affected at the same time and for a year or two afterwards as well. This happened in the late 1650s, in the mid-1670s, in the 1690s and twice in the 1680s (compare Figure IV with Figure V). If these were epidemics, the infection evidently lingered longer in the town.

Although there is nothing to suggest an urban pattern in the mortality in Lutterworth in the sixteenth century, the town suffered seriously from epidemics, some of them plagues, in the early seventeenth century. The greatest rise in mortality came in the 1630s and there was also a great loss in numbers in the 1650s. These developments no doubt reflect the population increase of the late sixteenth century and first half of the seventeenth. From that time on, however, the pattern of mortality took on a new form, strongly suggesting a more urban problem. This effect was no doubt connected with the lower standard of living among the poorer section of the town community and it is appropriate at this stage to raise the question as to how all the additional population was housed in the town.

It has been mentioned that the 1509 Terrier lists at least 116 dwelling houses in the town. A detailed comparison between the Terrier, the 1607 Survey and the 1790 Inclosure Award and Map shews that the 'ring of the town' formed by home closes and crofts remained unaltered.[75] There is no possibility that the growth in the size of the town involved anything in the way of an extension of the built-up area. There was plenty of room, as there is no indication that frontages were originally continuous except in the very centre of the town facing onto the markets. Some new accommodation was built by squatters on waste ground, but since the only waste in the town was the busy market areas and the streets themselves, there was not much scope for encroachment of this type. The 1607 Survey accounted for four cottages on the waste. Two were newly erected and one of these was on a site 20 feet by 10½ feet and included a shop. The main source of new accommodation must have been more intensive use of existing sites. For instance a barn could be converted to a dwelling house, as in two cases recorded in the Survey, or one plot could be divided to provide the site for a second house. Shortly before 1638 one inhabitant had allowed a weaver to build a 'little house' to live in on part of a half croft that he held of the manor.[76] The most important development of this nature was the dividing of existing tenements so as to accommodate more than one family. This is clearly attested for the early seventeenth century by Edward Overing, the inhabitant who gave evidence in 1658 about the growth of the town. He went on to say that some former single tenements now contained three or four families.[77] An example of both conversion and division was a barn in Bakehouse Lane which by 1629 had become accommodation for three households.[78]

Most of the actual examples that can be produced to illustrate these developments come from the detailed records of the principal manor, which date from before 1610. They cannot therefore be used to estimate the date, the nature and the location of the new housing that accommodated the increased population in the seventeenth century. An important proportion of the houses in the town, however, between a fifth and a quarter, belonged to the Feilding family freehold estate. In both 1509 and 1607 this included 34 houses. An exhaustive analysis of the estate records shews that by the mid-seventeenth century this number had increased to 50 or 60. This is confirmed by Edward Overing's statement that the estate included about 60 messuages, farms and cottages in the town. By 1682, however, the number had further increased to 70.[79]

The cadet branch of the Feilding family also owned an estate in the town. In 1629 this was listed as consisting almost entirely of five messuages with yard land holdings, one of them also with two cottages.[80] In 1695, however, apart from four houses with farm holdings, four more houses had no such land. Meanwhile the cottages, or 'little houses', had proliferated; seven of them had gardens, but 11 had no ground with them at all and together they now numbered 24.[81]

As to the nature of the housing, some of the rebuilding involved the transformation of agricultural cottages into town houses, several of them with shops. Apart from messuages and cottages, a deed of 1726 credits the principal Feilding estate with 17 'messuages or cottages' and many of the tenants of a 'messuage or cottage' were craftsmen or traders.[82] Actual new houses, however, judging from the rents paid, were often very humble accommodation. It seems that farms were set at several pounds half-yearly, town houses at 30 shillings and upwards and anything at less than five shillings was a simple cottage. Sixteen of the houses on the estate were simple cottages in the 1650s and 29 of them in the 1680s. Some of the tenants paid as little as one shilling. In the 1660s, however, a new class of tenant appears, eight of them paying only twopence or a penny. It is clear that these were people who could not afford to pay rent, but were nonetheless required to make a token acknowledgement to the lord of the manor. Many of them were widows.

It is notable that although the number of houses in the town probably trebled, on the main Feilding estate it only doubled. It is possible that by virtue of their subsidiary manor or, after 1629, as lords of the principal manor they were able to exercise some restraint on settlement. What town premises were there outside the manor where manorial control could successfully be flouted? In the first place the properties belonging to the Hospital were outside the manor. The Spittle Row, where the five bedeswomen had been accommodated, occupied the southern side of Church Street, from Bakehouse Lane to Dead Lane. It has evidently been a continuous frontage since the seventeenth century at least but has not suffered from subdivision. By 1607, however, it seems to have been extended to the west by an encroaching one-and-a-half bay cottage 'lying upon the Corner of the Spittle Row' and occupied by Alice Peppercorne, presumably a widow (see Illustration 5).[83] The subsequent development of the other town properties belonging to the Hospital cannot be traced in sufficient detail; after they passed into private hands, this no doubt depended on the interests of the owners.

The mention of charity accommodation raises the question of the role played by the town administration, with or without the blessing of the manorial court, in providing additional housing. The Lutterworth Town Estate included various properties in the town. One site in Hartshall Lane (now George Street) was occupied in the early eighteenth century by almshouses and the workhouse, which was built around 1721.[84] Throughout the sixteenth century only one cottage stood there, but there is a possibility that already in the seventeenth century the site was being used for housing of one sort or another for the poor. Whether by design or not, however, the Town Masters turn out to have been administering some of the most crowded housing in the town. In the sixteenth century the Town Estate property included only half a dozen houses; but by 1761 the Town Masters were collecting money, not in fact rent but 'annual acknowledgement', usually one shilling, for 28.[85] This was a seventeenth-century development; the eighteenth century, especially the first half of it, saw little or no increase in the number of houses in the town. This is confirmed by a study of the Feilding estate properties and by comparing the early eighteenth-century estimates of 300 to 315 families with a rating valuation of about 1794, which accounts for 333 houses at the most.[86] Another Town Estate site was an area 30 feet by 126 feet 10 inches behind Spittle Row, occupied throughout the sixteenth century by only one house with its garden, but by 1761 being covered by no fewer than 12 houses. Map VI, based on a plan of these premises datable to 1811, shews that a couple each end faced onto streets, but the rest only fronted onto the Cutchell, a narrow passage running along the southern boundary of the site.[87] This too was an early development. Most of the houses along the Cutchell had disappeared by the mid-nineteenth century.[88] Indeed the plan shews only 10 out of the 12, one of which was already described as uninhabitable by 1761; and another had apparently blown down in 1728.[89]

Other similar housing may be attributable to the seventeenth century. There was a continuous row of cottages perched precariously along the edge

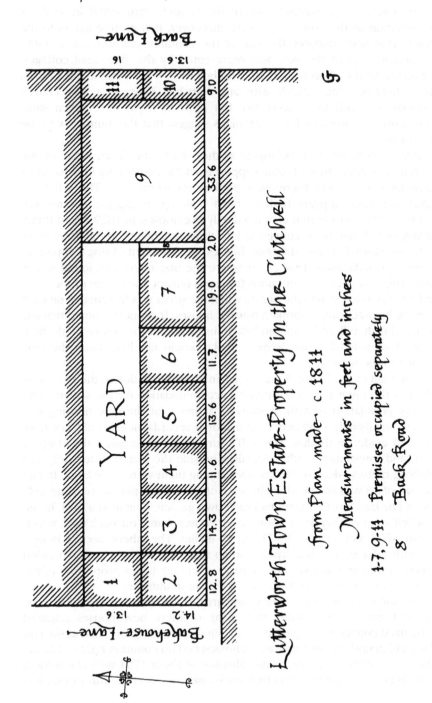

MAP VI

THE CUTCHELL

Lutterworth Town Estate Property in the Cutchell

from Plan made c. 1811

Measurements in feet and inches

1-7, 9-11 Premises occupied separately

8 Back Road

of the churchyard, precisely where the Church Barn stood in 1509. A continuation of this row to the west, moreover, had no frontage onto the street. This was probably the site of the common *cantabilum* in 1509. Presumably part of this row was represented by the 'five small cottages' belonging to the church in 1679. Another row of cottages, along Church Street between the church gate and Hartshall Lane, was also church property. In 1606 there were five but in 1679 there were seven small tenements and nineteenth-century maps suggest that the number went on increasing.[90]

Settlers on these sites, belonging as they did to the Town Estate or the church, may have enjoyed some support from the community in defiance of manorial control. But there were settlers elsewhere too. The whole of Bakehouse Lane appears to have been built up during the seventeenth century. In the sixteenth it contained only five houses. In 1629 a barn there, already noted, had been converted into three tenements and in 1662 there were mentioned 'Three thatched houses, or tenements Lying contiguous together in Bakehouse Lane'.[91] These are the first references found which prove the existence of continuous frontages outside the centre of the town and it looks as if this was the period when the street was hemmed in on both sides by its practically unbroken rows of houses. It should be noted that the manorial malt-mill and common bakehouse stood at the centre of all these areas of crowded housing, where smoke would not have been the only offence to the senses.

If the plan of the Cutchell may be taken as an illustration of the type of in-filling of the town plan that provided accommodation for the seventeenth-century population growth, it shews that much of the new housing was indeed surprisingly crowded. The manorial records alone could not have supplied evidence of this. The 1607 Survey, which omitted the Hospital itself, and, presumably, other premises outside the manor, listed only 112 dwelling houses. Many of the cottages among them were quite large. In fact the size of 18 was specified; eight were of three bays, nine of two and only one of one bay. Most cottages had their own garden, or at least a yard. In the Cutchell, on the other hand, about seven houses shared the back yard, which measured 13 feet 6 inches by 71 feet 10 inches. The others, like the houses along the edge of the churchyard, had no space of their own at all. This kind of concentration may have been typical of a much larger proportion of the housing in the town than it has been possible to indicate.

With the increase in population and greater demands being made on the common fields it is unlikely that many of these new houses acquired recognized cottage grazing rights.[92] It is significant, therefore, that at the end of the eighteenth century at least 90 houses had no common rights.[93] On the other hand, comparing the rating valuation of about 1794 with the records of the Feilding property shews that any house rated at under three pounds is

Table 2.4 Representation of population in probate records, Lutterworth, Lutterworth area and Leicestershire: numbers of surviving probate inventories related to numbers of communicants and to numbers of burials

	Town of Lutterworth	Lutterworth area	County of Leicester
1590s			
Number of inventories in 1590s	22	114	1,672
Number of communicants in 1603	564	3,004	39,160
Inventories as percentage of communicants	3.9	3.8	4.3
1680s			
Number of inventories in 1680s	28	202	2,483
Number of communicants in 1676	644	3,234	41,084
Inventories as percentage of communicants	4.35	6.25	6.0
Number of burials in 1680s	370	1,189	–
Inventories as percentage of burials	7.6	17.0	–

Sources: *V.C.H. Leics.*, III, 168-9 and 173-4; probate inventories at L.R.O.

likely to have been a simple cottage. In this case 215, or 65 *per cent*, of the 333 houses were simple cottages.

All this evidence adds up to confirmation of the increase in the number of poor households in the town during the seventeenth century. Further confirmation is provided both by a comparison of the town with the villages with respect to the numbers of probate records surviving and by the estimates of the numbers of communicants in 1603 and 1676 (see Table 2.4). At the former date the town and village populations were equally well represented in the records, but at the latter the townspeople were less well represented, presumably because a greater proportion of them were too poor to be concerned with probate. A comparison of the later figures with the numbers of burials, moreover, shews that the villagers were over twice as well represented in the probate evidence, while the discrepancy between these two comparisons further suggests that the figure for the number of communicants in the town in 1676 was indeed an underestimation. In these circumstances, therefore, an attempt should be made to estimate the extent of the poverty problem. It will be recalled that a total of 300 families in the town has been proposed as a maximum; yet in the early 1670s under 150 inhabitants were actually paying Hearth Tax. Possibly, therefore, the number of potential paupers in the town was approaching half of the total population.

Whatever the proportion of poor households, however, the housing that accommodated them presents two striking features. In the first place all the new accommodation was contained within the existing framework of the town and in the second place, although there was plenty of room, it was very unevenly distributed. Within the green and open texture of this country market town, with its home closes, crofts, orchards, gardens and yards, the seventeenth century saw the development of small areas of housing of truly urban concentration. Research by the Cambridge Group for the History of Population and Social Structure has confirmed that all over the country market towns behaved like marshland and city parishes in suffering a high rate of mortality during the century after 1650.[94] It has been shewn that Lutterworth was no exception. No doubt the health hazard presented by these slum areas was an important contributory factor.

*   *   *

On returning to the comparison between the town and the other places in the area that retained their open fields, it seems that although they were subject to the same pressures, the responses were, in degree at least, very different. Both grew between the later sixteenth and mid-seventeenth centuries; but whereas the villages doubled in population, the town trebled. To achieve this it no doubt relied on immigration from the area more than on natural increase within the town population. Similarly both suffered a loss in numbers in the mid-seventeenth century. After this, however, immigration into the open-field villages continued and the low mortality there meant that by the 1690s there was considerable natural increase again. In the town, on the other hand, mortality remained high. But for immigration, it is doubtful whether it would have maintained its population. In the 1690s, especially, the numbers of burials and baptisms were so close that the town may be seen as a drain on a proportion of the natural increase in the villages. There were no doubt pockets of poor people living in miserable housing in the villages; but only in the town were there sufficient numbers in sufficient concentration to suggest that this inability to replace its own population differentiates the problems of Lutterworth as truly urban ones.

If the pressures were the same but the responses were different, the cause must be sought in the unique nature and role of Lutterworth as the market town of the area. This is the subject of the rest of this study. Throughout, however, the economy of the town will be treated in the context of the economy of the area. And since in this period the economy of the area was almost entirely agricultural, the next chapter will concentrate on the agriculture of the whole of the area, including the town.

CHAPTER THREE

The Farming Economy

The first stage of the study of the context in which the market town of Lutterworth operated has revealed three periods of contrasting population trends. In the first half of the sixteenth century numbers apparently did not increase in the area. In the later sixteenth century and the early decades of the seventeenth the population grew at a great rate. In the remainder of the seventeenth century, although there was no overall rise in numbers, there was a remarkable redistribution between the two types of village: those that enclosed were depopulated and those that retained their open fields still increased and had to support a larger proportion of paupers. The period of growth saw the town grow faster than the villages and the period of redistribution saw it rely heavily on immigration at first to continue its growth but later even to maintain its numbers so that, on a small scale, it was behaving like an urban centre.

Enclosure, population changes and the emergence of a poverty problem are three aspects of the fundamental changes in the economy. The purpose of this next stage is to characterize the economic context within which the town operated by tracing the development of the agrarian economy of the Lutterworth area as a whole. The basis of that economy was, of course, open-field husbandry, the subject with which anyone studying Midland peasant economy must inevitably begin, as Hoskins did in his pioneering essay 'The Leicestershire Farmer in the Sixteenth Century'.[1]

1. Village economies

Although at the beginning of the sixteenth century open fields still predominated in the Lutterworth area, at least 15 *per cent* of it was already enclosed (see Appendix Table 1 and Map IV). Eight of the 36 townships either no longer existed or had been reduced to little more than a single household, the manorial establishment. In 1524 and 1525 only 5 *per cent* and 6 *per cent* respectively of the area's Lay Subsidy assessments were on people living in enclosed townships. Some of their minimum assessments, moreover, represent personal attendants taxed on wages rather than separate householders. Thus the enclosed grounds supported no true village communities and probably well under 5 *per cent* of the total population.

Each of the other 28 villages survived by means of mixed husbandry on, to adopt the precise definition used repeatedly in the local pamphlets from the

1650s, 'the fields lying open . . . used in common'. There was a move towards enclosure at the turn of the sixteenth century, and the pressures behind this will be identified. On the whole, however, the situation remained unchanged and the majority of the enclosures in the second phase did not take place until over a generation later than this. An explanation must be given, therefore, as to how the increased population was both fed and employed without overthrowing the existing farming system. This development constituted progress away from peasant subsistence husbandry, with no more than its traditional market involvement, towards truly commercial farming. The men who were able to seize the advantage at this stage must therefore be identified, in relation both to their own villages and the area and also to the market town as the exchange point.

When it comes to considering the seventeenth century, the central topic is the transformation of the peasant economy, of which the enclosures are the most striking evidence. The fact that enclosure at this stage involved, in the long run, the conversion of regularly tilled lands to pasture ground is, as Hoskins noted in his essay 'The Leicestershire Farmer in the Seventeenth Century', proof that the transformation constituted a great stride towards the grazing farming of the eighteenth century for which the region was famous.[2] In the context of the area, however, it must again be asked whence the pressures for change came and who were the greater beneficiaries of the changes. It might be assumed that those who profited most were the pure graziers who remained to occupy the fields of the enclosed villages. What has not been appreciated hitherto, however, is that once these fields had been released from the constraints of traditional husbandry they became available as additional resources to be taken in hand by the area's more commercial mixed farmers, whose farms were still, in fact, based on *common-field* holdings in neighbouring *unenclosed* villages. Turning to the other end of the economic scale, the expulsions from the enclosing villages might be taken to have represented a victory for the landlords, since this process left them free to draw into their own hands all the resources of the fields and to farm them more efficiently. The corollary of this, however, the immigration into the remaining unenclosed villages and the town, turns out to have been of equal or even greater significance. One way of looking at this movement is that people were driven to take refuge in places where there was less strict manorial control; the opposite way of looking at it is that labourers were being attracted to the only places that offered prospects of large-scale employment, the enclosing villages in this respect being backwaters.

At each stage of the analysis, therefore, it will be necessary to consider not only the economy of the common fields and of the enclosed grounds, but also the interaction between the two. Since, moreover, any interaction between them is likely to have involved the town as the point of exchange, study of this will help to identify the role of Lutterworth in its area at each stage and so reveal how the development of the town community itself was affected. As the economy of the town will be the subject of the next chapter, where the distribution of non-agricultural activity in the area as a whole will be examined, the present chapter can concentrate entirely on what was, of course, the principal activity throughout the area, farming.

The main source of information for this study is the series of probate inventories (detailed valuations of personal property) at the Leicestershire Record Office. Sample decades have been chosen (1530s and 1540s together, 1550s, 1590s, 1630s and 1680s) and the inventories tabulated to calculate the average figures and values. For this purpose the inventories of the townspeople have been omitted. Among the inventories that include the farming stock of more than a mere cottager there are well over ten times as many from the area as from the town. There are also sufficient differences to make it worth taking the farming of the townspeople separately at the beginning of the next chapter. Here, however, their farming will be mentioned where it helps to illustrate, sometimes by way of contrast, the general practice. The structure of the town fields, moreover, is especially well documented and so will be frequently used as an illustration of the common-field background to peasant husbandry.

2.   Peasant husbandry in the sixteenth century

Hoskins, with his essay on the sixteenth century, was the first to explore the analysis of probate inventories. In it he attempted to divide Leicestershire inventories between yeomen and husbandmen, although the farming activity of both was basically of the same nature. It is more helpful to separate the social from the economic questions and to start by classifying the different layers of the village community according to scope of farming activity rather than social or tenurial status.[3] Contemporary classification depended on the rights a householder had in the common fields and on the vital question whether or not he possessed his own independent means of cultivation, a team of draught animals. In this way the fully equipped farmer, who will here be called the "mixed farmer" and who usually had a holding of one yard land or more, was distinguished from what will be called the "smallholder" and from the third category, the cottager, whose rights in the fields were usually limited to common grazing alone. This triple classification was spelt out for rating purposes in Claybrook parva in the early seventeenth century:

1.   The 'husbandman that keepeth a team'
2.   The 'one that hath land and keepeth no team' or
     the 'man that hath half a yard land' or

the 'man that hath half a yard land or a quartern'
3. The 'cottenger'.[4]

The majority of the sixteenth-century inventories of villagers analysed here concern mixed farmers: to be precise, four fifths of the 186 such records from the 1530s to 1550s and half of the 114 from the 1590s, which together make two thirds of the total of 300 (see Appendix Table 7). While a group of 11 exceptional inventories have been isolated to be dealt with later,[5] initial analysis of the average totals of the remainder shews no contrast between the two types of village and suggests that, even allowing for inflation, mixed farmers greatly improved their position in the second half of the century, not only in agricultural wealth but also in household furnishings and money resources (see Table 3.1.a). Splitting the values of the farming stock between livestock, including animal products, on the one hand and all the crops together with implements and gear on the other, further suggests that their success was in the main attributable to the arable side of their farming (see Table 3.1.b). Comparing the 1550s with the 1590s, the national average prices of horses, cattle and sheep, taken together, rose by 77½ *per cent* while the average livestock total in these inventories increased by over 120

Table 3.1 Lutterworth area: sixteenth-century mixed farm inventories. (a) Average value sub-totals (b) average farm stock value sub-totals

(a)

Period	Number	Farming	Houshold	Money	Total
1530s and 40s	38	£16½	£3½	Under £½	£20
1550s	101	£26	£5½	£½	£32
1590s	55	£67	£17	£5	£89

Values to the nearest £½; values of leases excluded

(b)

Period	Livestock	Crops	Implements	Total
1530s and 40s	£11	£4½	£1	£16½
1550s	£17½	£6½	£2	£26
1590s	£39	£22	£6	£67

Values to the nearest £½; 'Livestock' includes animal products (wool and cheese); 'Crops' include hay

Source: probate inventories at L.R.O. for inhabitants of the Lutterworth area, from decades as defined in Appendix Table 7

Table 3.2   Lutterworth area: crop acreages in five early inventories

(White corn field)	Wheat	8	acres
	Rye	10	acres
	Barley	35	acres
(Pease field)	Peas	41½	acres
	Oats	10	acres

Source: probate inventories at L.R.O. for:
  Elizabeth Arnold, Walton, widow, Wills and Invv. 1544
  John Dawkyn, Peatling parva, Inv. file 6c, no. 2
  John Hunt, Dunton Bassett, husbandman, Wills and Invv. 1558
  Thomas Lord, Cotesbach, husbandman, Wills and Invv. 1557(K-Y)
  Thomas Marson, Frowlesworth, Wills and Invv. 1560/1

per cent; but while the national average corn crop prices rose by 70 *per cent* (including the important barley crop by only 34 *per cent*, the probable figure for peas too), the average crop total in these inventories increased by nearly 240 *per cent*.[6]

A variety of arable crops was raised on the common fields in fairly constant proportions. It is clear, however, that the word "corn" could be used to embrace the crops of both arable fields. On the other hand the inventories often describe the crops as 'corn, pease and hay'. To make it clear when it is intended to exclude the pulse crop the term "grain" will be used here. Five early inventories list all the corn crops and acreages precisely so that it is possible to set out the proportions in which they covered the 105¼ acres concerned (see Table 3.2). This shews almost exactly the proportions found by Hoskins for the late 1550s, and in many other inventories where full details are not given the acreages or values of the crops listed conform to the same proportions.[7] The grain crop covering the largest area was barley. Any increase in corn production in the first place would have required more labour and in the second place would have made more grain available, in particular more barley, which was needed for malting for ale and was also the bread-corn for the poorer sections of the population. Thus it would have helped to employ and to feed the increasing numbers of people.

Apart from the question of labour, however, in the context of sixteenth-century husbandry any increase in yield from the arable side of farming can only have been achieved by means of more intensive use of livestock. Animals were not only the source of power for cultivating but also the only local source of manure for improving the soil. Just as the crops on the mixed farm were diversified, so the full range of animals was kept there too. Here the contemporary terminology will be adopted. The general term for livestock was "cattle", divided into "great cattle" and "lesser cattle", the former comprising horses and beasts and the latter being sheep.[8] "Beasts" comprised oxen, bullocks, steers (all castrated males), bulls, cows, heifers (young cows), calves etc., for which the restricted use of the term "cattle" is now generally reserved.

No farmer owned a plough without horses to draw it and oxen were used for draught hardly at all. Presumably ordinary farmers found horses more versatile and in any case lacked sufficient rich pasture to keep oxen in working condition.[9] Indeed there is evidence that ox-draught was rare in the county as a whole by the sixteenth century, in spite of Hoskins's assertion that he found a yoke of oxen 'frequently mentioned'.[10] Within the Lutterworth area there were two exceptional contexts in which ox-draught survived, the one on a few farms in the line of parishes along the Fosse Way and the other on estate pasture-farms.

The standard team was four horses and the average number of horses of all kinds kept on the farm actually increased towards the mid-century, from 5¼ in the 1530s and 1540s to six in the 1550s. Connected with this may have been the increasing area under oats. Of ten inventories from the 1530s naming crops only two include oats, from the 1540s five out of ten and from the 1550s 21 out of 34. Oats was also sometimes classified with hay, suggesting that it was used as a fodder crop. There are three indications that by the 1550s horses were in fact being kept quite extravagantly, many an inventory including eight or nine, even when the total value was not more than £50. Firstly they were readily available, being bred on the farms. Out of 409 horses clearly classified in inventories from that decade one quarter were young and the ratio of horses and geldings to mares was five to four. Secondly they were not particularly valuable. They averaged 17/7d. each, little more than one third again as much as the beasts in the same inventories. In particular a type of horse confined to the parish of Claybrook, the "capel", was only worth 13/9d., the same as the average beast. Thirdly they were not being used to the full for farming. Sixteen of the 101 mixed farming inventories list no plough. Presumably these farmers relied on communal husbandry like smallholders;[11] yet they kept on average 4½ horses each.

By the 1590s, although the average number of horses remained six, they were evidently much more useful farm animals. There were no capels and no mixed farmers without a plough. The average value of a horse had risen by 145 *per cent*, far beyond the national average rise of 78 *per cent*.[12] The opportunities for breeding, however, had diminished, at least in the villages that were to retain their common fields. In the enclosing parishes the proportion of young horses and the ratio of horses and geldings to mares remained the same as they had been throughout the area in the 1550s; but in the others the young horses were down to one fifth and there were nine horses and geldings to every four mares. Evidently the practice was more a question of buying horses in as working animals so as to make the best use of the grazing rights allotted to them.

The number of beasts kept, on the other hand, remained fairly constant at an average of ten throughout the century. They were not used for draught; what balance was struck, therefore, between dairy, breeding, rearing and fattening for beef? Analysis of the beasts classified in the inventories is less conclusive, as a dairy herd is of necessity also a breeding herd. The proportions altered little during the century. In the 1550s the animals listed as calves accounted for nearly one fifth of the beasts. In the villages that retained their common fields they were down to only one tenth in the 1590s, suggesting that the opportunities for breeding may have decreased here. Similarly the practice of keeping older beasts specifically for beef dwindled to insignificance, presumably for lack of rich pasture. The number of steers and bullocks listed fell from 5½ *per cent* to 3 *per cent* of the total, the latter figure representing only 16 beasts out of 562. The way that calves were classified suggests that they were not usually kept beyond yearlings before being sold. It is significant that although flitches of bacon were common, only one inventory lists a flitch of beef. There is also no trace of grain crops having been used for fattening.[13]

What remained appears to have been a mixed breeding and rearing herd, part of the general drift of beasts from the highland regions, such as Wales, towards areas more suited to fattening. One man owed ten shillings to 'a m(an) of Walys', possibly for a beast, and another bequeathed 'a heifer that was bought at Coventry'.[14] As for the dairy side of the herd, there is no indication that, so long as the farmer could obtain what was needed for his own household, any further demands were made on the cows beyond their role in breeding and rearing calves. Equipment such as cheese boards began to be listed in the 1590s, but even then actual cheeses in store were never valued at more than a few shillings. Similarly the swine that were kept and the varied poultry - mainly "pullen" (hens, cocks and chickens) and geese but also ducks and, once, turkeys - appear only to have served the needs of the household.

The stock that varied most in numbers on the mixed farm was the flock of sheep. This was possible because it formed a fairly discrete part of the farm stock. The horses and cows returned each night to the farmstead, but the sheep spent most of the year out on the fields as part of the common flock. The evidence points to a considerable increase in the numbers kept towards the mid-century. The proportion of inventories which included no flocks of sheep fell from nearly one third in the 1530s and 1540s to one tenth in the 1550s. The result is that while the average flock size remained about 46, the average number shared amongst all the farmers increased from 27 to 41½. In this the farmers would have been encouraged by the rising wool prices, especially during the boom years of the 1540s. Judging from the wool in the inventories from the 1550s, the wool yield was on average one tod from each score of sheep, or a 1½ pound fleece, and the year's clip was worth between one fifth and one third of the flock.[15] The reversal of the market in the early 1550s would have brought a change in emphasis in production away from wool towards mutton, for which there would be a rising demand as the population increased towards the end of the century. This change is reflected in the outstanding rise in the average value of the sheep kept. Comparing the 1550s with the 1590s, national wool prices rose by 53 *per cent* and sheep prices by 79 *per cent*; but the average price of sheep in the inventories rose by 130 *per cent*, from 2/2d. to 5/-.[16]

Buying, breeding and selling sheep for mutton involved a greater turnover, more detailed flock-management and a closer controlled use of the feeding resources of the fields than simply maintaining the common flock. There was little chance of increasing the hay crops from off the meadows; the chief fodder crop to draw on, therefore, was the peas crop. In parallel with the increasing yields of grain from the fields, there would also be a larger peas crop available for this purpose. The smaller farmer, however, would need all his to maintain his team of horses. Evidently some farmers avoided the problem simply by keeping no sheep to feed at all. By the 1590s the proportion of inventories listing no flock had risen again to well over a quarter. They shew no seasonal bias, except perhaps for the fact that out of 11 inventories from June, July and August only one was without. This might suggest that such farmers were nevertheless buying in sheep to stock the commons for the summer months only, when of course they would have been needed for the folding. The average farm stock total in those inventories which include no sheep was three fifths only of the value common to the whole group. The fact that the smaller farmers were keeping sheep less regularly and that flock-management was changing would have gone some way towards removing the communal aspects of the common flock and probably interfered with the common folding programme, especially where it was possible to set sheep commons to other men.

Considering, therefore, the increased cropping in terms of livestock use, in the first place the teams of horses on the mixed farms at the end of the century were undoubtedly capable of carrying out a more intensive programme of tillage over a larger area of crops to be raised each year. It is also worth emphasizing the rise in the value of the implements they drew. In the 1550s it was common for a farm to include a couple of carts (each with a pair of wheels, which were usually iron-bound), ploughs, harrows and gears together worth 30 shillings. In the 1590s similar equipment was regularly worth at least £4 and the average value of all the equipment on the farm was £6. The beasts, secondly, did not contribute directly, unless more care was taken to carry their manure out from the homesteads to spread on the arable lands. In the inventories from the 1550s there is no mention of manure, apart from the muck forks listed; but by the 1590s a couple of inventories list manure worth valuing. The third and greatest contribution to the fertility of the soil, however, was made by the increased numbers of sheep kept. Probably the effect was the greater early on, when there was ample room for them to graze. Through the common folding this would have boosted the yields of every farmer's arable lands.

A few pairs of inventories, one each from the 1550s and 1590s and each of farmers with the same surname, offer an opportunity for comparison which bears out the conclusions drawn from the average figures. One pair in particular is worth setting out in detail as typical, not only because both were taken in October when 'the whole crop' was valued as gathered in, but also because the two men concerned, both named Thomas Heyere (or Eare), the latter probably grandson of the former, evidently farmed the same 2¼ yard land holding in Catthorpe (see Table 3.3).[17] While the value of their household goods more than quadrupled, the farm stock valuation did not even double. The numbers of cattle, especially the sheep and beasts, decreased. Yet although there were two fewer horses, the value of their equipment and the crop valuation itself trebled.

Having established the main successes of common-field farming in the sixteenth century, it must be asked how they were achieved within the existing system without necessitating its overthrow at this stage. A clear definition of the common-field holding, giving all the elements to be examined here, was published by Fitzherbert in 1523:

> It is undoubted, that to every township that standeth in tillage in the plain country, there be
> (1)   errable lands to plough, and sow,
> (2)   and layse to tie or tedder their horses and mares upon,
> (3)   and common pasture to keep and pasture their cattle, beasts and sheep upon.
> (4)   And also they have meadow ground to get their hay upon.[18]

Any such "yard land" holding was in effect a "bundle of rights" over the different areas in the fields, which were used more or less "in common". The rights approaching closest to exclusive occupation, to ownership "in severalty", were those over the "lands", the narrow strips of arable grouped in "furlongs", which are often still visible in the ridge-and-furrow landscape. A study of the fields of Lutterworth, based on the Terrier of 1509, the Survey of 1607, the Inclosure Award of 1790 and the Tithe Award of 1849, shews that even at the beginning of the sixteenth century the furlongs of lands occupied very nearly all of the open fields.[19] In this respect Lutterworth was probably typical of the villages in the area too. It might be argued that this merely reflects the land-hunger of the early middle ages and that many of the furlongs had reverted to permanent pasture. What seems more likely, however, is that they all remained "arable", that is, suitable for or capable of cultivation, but that lack of pressure on the land resources allowed farmers

Table 3.3 Summary of a pair of typical inventories

	7th October 1558 Thomas Heyere of Catthorpe, husbandman	£	s	d	18th October 1586 Thomas Eare of Thorpe Thomas, husbandman	£	s	d
Farming stock:								
Livestock:								
	6 horses, 2 yearling foals	5	0	0	4 horses, 2 colts	11	0	0
	4 kine, 4 heifers, 2 yearling				4 kine, 2 yearlings	8	6	8
	calves	5	13	4				
	50 sheep	5	0	0	10 sheep		16	8
	the wool	1	0	0				
	3 hogs		10	0	4 swine	1	0	0
	the pullen in the yard		5	4				
		17	8	8		21	3	4
Crop:								
	the crop in the barn and yard	6	0	0	the whole crop of corn, peas, hay etc.	18	0	0
Gear:								
	1 cart, 1 plough, with the harness	1	13	4	2 carts	2	13	4
	1 hatchet, 1 spade, 1 muck fork,				1 plough, 2 harrows		6	8
	1 pitch fork etc.		1	6	1 pair of horse gears		5	0
	hovel timber		1	0	plough timber and boards		15	0
					hovel timber and other wood	1	0	0
		1	15	10		5	0	0
Farming stock total:		25	4	6		44	3	4
Household total:		1	15	6		8	6	8.
Inventory total:		£27	0	0		£52	10	0

Source: L.R.O., Wills and Invv. 1558(G–O) and Inv. file 8, no. 125(128)

to crop them more or less frequently according to their convenience of access or suitability for different crops and for different periods of cropping. In Lutterworth one furlong, on light, sandy soil just to the east of the town was called Ryehill and another was located in 1509 'in the pease field'. Thus the unit of cropping would have been the furlong,[20] although there is no reason to doubt that the cropping was organized on a rotating three-course system confined to three areas within the fields. All the cropping details given in the inventories conform to this and the two fields under crops, the white corn field and the peas field, are sometimes named. In so far, however, as the three-course system had not expanded fully so as to coincide with the three-field system, the actual line of division between the fields may have remained imprecise. Although the three field names occur in the 1509 Terrier, the furlongs are not clearly listed under them. The lack of constraint on the farming community as to which lands should be cropped may account for the regularity of the proportions occupied by the different crops each year. Many furlongs would remain fallow for longer than one year in three, regaining in heart and providing more or less permanent leys of pasture. The existence of these leys has long been recognized but has been misinterpreted; it does not of itself prove any new form of improving farming.[21] There was no need for lands and leys of pasture to be clearly distinguished. A couple of furlong names in the 1509 Terrier include the word 'ley', but all strips of land are listed indifferently as 'lands'. The result was that, without changing the system, farmers were able to achieve the great increase in their crops partly by cropping under-used lands more frequently and thus in effect extending the area of crops sown in any one year.

The limits of this kind of expansion, however, had been reached by the end of the century. This seems to be indicated by the rise in the crop values in the inventories and is highlighted by the few local prices that can be calculated from them. In the 1550s local corn prices appear to have corresponded with national averages. This is also confirmed by the Misterton estate accounts. From different harvest years in the 1590s, however, local prices contrast markedly with the national averages (see Table 3.4). The smaller discrepancies for winter corn, especially wheat, are not so significant; being more valuable its market price tended towards a national standard. The markets for inferior crops were more confined, so that their prices fluctuated more widely from year to year and from area to area and make a better indicator of local hardships. The two most important crops in this area, barley and peas, both shew the widest discrepancies.[22] This suggests that by the end of the century, even in such an area of mainly arable farming, crop shortages in years of dearth like 1596 were very serious and there could still be local shortages in otherwise normal years.[23]

Maintaining the condition of a larger area of arable lands made further

Table 3.4   Corn crop prices *per* quarter

Harvest year	Crop	National average price	Local price
1594	Barley	14/8d.	32/-
1596	Winter corn (wheat and rye)		50/-
	Wheat	51/4d.	
	Rye	48/8d.	53/4d.
	Barley	27/5d.	40/-
	Peas	29/4d.	40/-
	Oats	22/1d.	16/-
1600	Wheat	26/4d.	
	Barley	16/6d.	
	Wheat and barley (equally)		93/4d.

Sources: probate inventories at L.R.O. for:.
  John Currall, Frowlesworth, Inv. file 15, no. 78
  Peter Dawes, Sutton, Broughton Astley, Inv. file 16, no. 110
  William Smart, Claybrook, husbandman, Inv. file 16, no. 66
  Thomas Thornton, Claybrook, husbandman, Inv. file 18, no. 77
P. Bowden, Statistical Appendix to *A.H.E.W.*, ed. J. Thirsk, IV, 818 *et seqq.*

demands on the manuring available, that is, principally, the sheep fold, and required a more intensive programme of cultivations. But the sheep and horses needed were both competing for the common grazing which at the same time was diminishing; for the reduction of the fallows to a uniform one year in three reduced the area of the natural sward in the fields, and more regular and thorough cultivation reduced its density. Thus intensification of the arable side of the mixed farm was meeting all round the limits of the feeding resources of the fields.

The small home closes and crofts were ignored by Fitzherbert in his definition of the resources of the farm. At Lutterworth the total area of the 'ring of the town' never amounted to more than about 100 acres. In 1607 every farmer had a close or a croft there, in very few cases amounting to more than an acre or two. The areas were not specified in 1509, but a detailed comparison suggests that there was no difference. Some of the crofts near the homesteads, however, were not yet enjoyed by individuals in severalty. All the closes beyond were, which might suggest that they represent a more recent development, perhaps coinciding with the first phase of enclosure. At all events these grounds contributed little grass, although they were no doubt vital for the private management of flocks and herds. What, therefore, were the grazing resources of the remainder of the parish?

The meadows were a separately organized part of the common-field system. This is reflected in the way Fitzherbert added them to his definition in a separate sentence. Although they were thrown open for grazing for part of the year, their main function was seen as providing a hay crop. Shares in this crop, however, were limited to the mixed farmers. In Lutterworth in 1607 no tenant of a holding of less than one yard land had any share in the meadows. Both cottagers and smallholders would thus have been expected to maintain their beasts on the commons alone.

In the fallow field the furlongs of arable land, together with all the odd pieces of grass among them, became part of the common grazing. The fallow field was, however, especially the preserve of the sheep flock. But sheep-keeping was becoming less general among the less prosperous farmers and out of the 19 inventories of smallholders from the 1590s only seven include more than a couple of sheep. So the benefit of the fallows tended to be concentrated into the hands of the larger farmers.

Who benefited from the grass growing on the leys? In the fallow field these too contributed to the common grazing. This shews in a case dated 1397 from Littlethorpe, 7½ miles north of Lutterworth, where the rights held in severalty by the tenants over 'a separate pasture' were confined to the years when the field was under corn.[24] Where a farmer kept individual lands as 'leys within the corns', the phrase used in regulations for Wymeswold in north Leicestershire written down in about 1425, common grazing was impractical.[25] It was natural for him to retain his several rights over them so as to take a crop of hay and tether his horses there, although at this early date he did not yet enjoy them completely in severalty. Where a whole furlong of leys was involved, on the other hand, both these early examples shew farmers retaining such several rights. In Littlethorpe tenants were dispasturing 'fallow wongs' in the 'separate pasture' and in Wymeswold individuals were using their 'several grass' for tethering draught animals. By the late sixteenth century the distinction between lands and leys had hardened. They were regularly listed separately, as in the 1607 Survey of Lutterworth. That there was some room for individual variation is shewn by the most unorthodox holding, the Kirby family freehold. Here the high proportion of leys suited them as the town's chief butchers.[26] It is clear that the farmers used their leys as permanent pasture grounds during the cropping seasons to the exclusion of other people with grazing rights. Thus the first of August, Lammas day, when all the leys reverted to common pasture, was of great significance to all users of the common fields. This applied to the Littlethorpe 'separate pasture' and the Wymeswold 'several grass', which were thus in effect both 'Lammas lands'.

If the grass on the furlongs of lands and leys and in the fallow field was becoming less generally available to the community as a whole, what other areas remained free for common grazing? Within the three fields there were common roadways, balks and other pieces of ground which were left uncultivated. The Lutterworth 1509 Terrier mentions ways, slades, gores and a common balk and that 'one place called Redmore is common pasture'. Such pieces were carefully designated for supervised grazing by beasts or horses. Herds of beasts were tended by common herdsmen, like 'the herdman of Lutterworth' rewarded for 'his diligence about his herd of cattle' in 1551.[27] Horses could be tethered; in Wymeswold they were tied 'on . . . havedes (hades, headlands) or by syk sydes (beside sikes)'.

The remaining commons outside the fields, the wastes and heaths, came to be associated with the beasts of those who had no rights other than grazing rights, the cottagers with a couple of house-cows. These "Cow Pastures" were thus confined to the poorest land in the parish, which doubtless represented the last areas of woodland to be cleared in this former "wolds" landscape.[28] The one in Lutterworth, listed in 1607, occupied an area that in 1509 had been furze ground, in the northernmost corner of the parish and adjoining 'Bitteswell and (Gil)Morton Furze'. In Wymeswold in the previous century there had been no shortage of grazing ground, such as 'for neats pasture', so that their Wold could even be 'leyd in several' early in the year, allowing individuals to take hay crops off their leys there. The situation in the Lutterworth area in the later sixteenth century was very different. As the numbers of "illegal" cottagers increased, moreover, these barren Cow Pastures were also in danger of becoming overcrowded.

In spite of the developments noted it is clear that even at the end of the sixteenth century the common-field mixed farm remained essentially a peasant family farming unit. Perhaps it already employed more labour; but the numbers of livestock shew that the average farm was not a larger holding. It is now possible, however, to outline the stages by which such farms were able to adapt to support the growing population. In the first half of the century the most important development was the increase in the numbers of sheep in the common wool flocks, especially in the 1540s. By raising the yield off the arable lands through the common folding this may well have formed the foundation on which the expanding economy of the rest of the century was based. Indeed, since it would have benefited the farming of everyone with lands, still a large proportion of the householders in a mainly subsistence economy, it may well have been an important factor contributing to the population growth in the first place.

In the mid-century there was still scope to expand the area of tillage and to intensify the arable side of the mixed farm by concentrating on horses for cultivation and keeping up sheep numbers; although to do the latter meant thinking of sheep more in terms of mutton than as the source of an annual wool crop. By the end of the century, however, although they had drawn into their hands the control over and benefit from so many of the resources of the fields, the mixed farmers were up against the limits.

At the lower end of the scale this left the ordinary subsistence farmers at a disadvantage in competing with the more commercial farmers for the same resources. By the end of the century, it is true, a few smallholders, and even a few cottagers, appear among the probate records, although this may not indicate increasing prosperity so much as greater involvement in the market. Apart from their small amounts of crops, the most constant farming stock of the smallholders, as illustrated by the 19 inventories from the 1590s, was the herd of beasts, on average three cows each. Similarly the most constant feature of the 16 cottager inventories from the same period was the house-cow, on average four for every three cottagers. It is certain, however, that there were many more smallholders and cottagers who do not appear in the records and it may be imagined that the difficulties they faced already foreshadowed their elimination in the next century. It may be significant that all but one of the 16 cottager inventories are of inhabitants of villages that retained their common fields. One reason for such people not generally being recorded may be that even their house-cows were not private property. There is evidence from the earlier sixteenth century of villagers hiring cows from a common herd, one man, for instance, owing four shillings 'to the town for a cow's hire'.[29] The best documented case, however, concerned the market town. Before he died in 1547 Sir William Feilding had provided a stock of 120 cows at Lutterworth, to be hired out half-yearly at tenpence a head and to be managed by a paid Deputy.[30]

So far the common-field farmer has been discussed as if his activities were confined to the fields of his own village. While this was no doubt true in most cases, especially among the smaller farmers, common-field farming in the sixteenth century cannot be understood fully without reference to the use made of neighbouring enclosed grounds. It has been shewn that the advances in the mixed husbandry of the common fields were achieved by extending and intensifying the existing system rather than by innovation. Before going on to examine the fundamental changes of the seventeenth century, therefore, it remains to be seen whether any innovations may be associated with the farming of the enclosed grounds in the area.

3. Enclosed ground farming in the sixteenth century

As the enclosure of the common fields took several centuries to complete, allowance must be made for enclosure having had different causes and different effects at different periods. This may help to solve some of the puzzles about Tudor enclosures. For example, contemporary voices were raised against the evil effects of enclosure throughout the sixteenth century: yet there was little enclosure in Leicestershire in the middle decades of the century, and in the Lutterworth area the two phases were even more clearly separated. On the other hand the majority of the early enclosures took place before the later fifteenth century; in other words Tudor enclosures were only the tail end of a fifteenth-century movement. Reluctance to accept the possibility of an active enclosure movement in the context of fifteenth-century economy has even led to distrust of the evidence for this. The solution to this disagreement may be found in the changing nature of enclosure. At this stage enclosure was not necessarily a positive act of policy on the part of a landlord leading to a higher level of farming directed at the market. Even if these enclosures are rightly blamed for depopulation, they should not for that reason alone be equated with later depopulating enclosure that made way for improved farming. The early enclosures, on the contrary, appear to have been cases of lords of manors finishing off already moribund farms and communities and making the best use they could of the resources of the fields which, as a result, fell into their hands.

If the key to these questions is to be found in the changing nature of enclosure, a comparative study of the two phases of enclosure should be made. In the Lutterworth area the majority of the early enclosure can be ascribed to the second half of the fifteenth century. By 1507, when it ended, at least 17 *per cent* of the area as a whole, including Lutterworth, was enclosed ground. For want of direct evidence about the motivation and mechanics of enclosure at this stage, a study of the uses made of enclosed grounds during the sixteenth century will serve two purposes. Firstly it will help to establish the reasons for enclosure and secondly it will provide a basis for a comparison with the later phase. It emerges that these early enclosures did not merely foreshadow the familiar seventeenth-century improving enclosures but were in fact a very different process.

The most conspicuous type of enclosure, a type confined to the first phase, was that of the whole township converted to an estate pasture-farm. There were eight such deserted villages in the Lutterworth area (see Map IV). Apart from the Misterton estate, the main ones were: the deserted township of Knaptoft, run by the Turpins of Knaptoft Hall (see Illustration 11); the deserted townships of Westrill and Stormsworth, forming a part of the mainly Northamptonshire estates of the Caves of Stanford on Avon, just across that river from the Lutterworth area; the deserted township of Bittesby, farmed by the Salisburys; finally, just across the Watling Street, the Feilding family had replaced the deserted township of Cold Newnham in Monks Kirby, which was the centre of their mainly Warwickshire estates, with their Hall at Newnham Paddox. Other enclosures, usually called 'Hall Close' or 'Hall Field', represented former demesne farms or demesne grounds, like the Hall Land which went with the Manor House at Ullesthorpe and to which the Salisburys moved from Bittesby, or the Hall Field which went with the Manor House at North Kilworth, run by the Belgrave family as the centre of their expanding estates. There were a score of such enclosures

Illustration 11. Knaptoft Hall, the home of the Turpin family, in ruins, viewed from the North in 1791 shortly before it was demolished. A manor house from the early sixteenth century, built of brick with stone details. The church of this early depopulated village fell into disuse during the seventeenth century and the Hall was occupied as a farm house. Note the two-wheeled farm cart and the crop stored on a staddle frame.

J. Nichols, *Leics.*

in the area, of varying origins and sizes (see Map IV).

The largest estate of enclosed ground in the area is also the best documented. It belonged to the Pulteneys of Misterton Hall, one of the very wealthiest squire families in the county, and comprised Misterton itself and Poultney, two of the three townships in the parish, together with the small township of Cotes de Val which, although within the adjacent parish of Kimcote, actually lay on the western side of Gilmorton. Michael Pulteney was under-age when he succeeded to the estate in 1550. A detailed analysis of the very full accounts kept during the years of his wardship offers an insight into the economy of enclosed ground farming at an important point of transition. What is remarkable is that comparison with the scattered records of other such estates in the area does nothing to dispel the impression gained that it constituted extensive farming on a very low level.[31]

The principal crop grown was, of course, grass and hay, all of which was consumed on the estate. Cultivation played only an insignificant role and so no working horses were kept, any draught work, such as bringing in the hay, being done by oxen drawing wains. The hay harvest and the shrunken cropping programme were in fact a survival of the common-field farming, being undertaken by men (and women as haymakers) of husbandman families from the neighbouring villages of Walcote, the third township in the home parish, and Cotesbach, all of whom were part of the same manorial organization. The Belgrave family of North Kilworth provides another example of this kind of farming. When Robert Belgrave, gentleman, died in 1550 his well-stocked manor farm included very little corn and no plough of his own.[32]

The numerous markets and fairs attended from the Misterton estate in purchasing and selling various beasts, or "rother cattle", provide an excellent example of the cross-country drift of livestock. The principal sources, especially for Welsh cows, were Coventry and Birmingham, although apparently Burton on Trent and Ashby-de-la-Zouch too were sometimes used. The principal outlet, again especially for Welsh cows, was Northampton, other outlets being Coventry and Market Harborough. No calves were bred on the estate and beasts were sold off within a year of purchase, presumably to pass on to areas better suited to fattening.

The fattening of oxen and steers for beef and of wethers (castrated rams) and ewes for mutton, which might appear to have been a more commercial activity, turns out on closer analysis to have been mainly to supply the manorial establishment. Beasts were bought at Leicester, Coventry, Tamworth, Burton on Trent, Derby, Mansfield, Newcastle-under-Lyme and even Pontefract and Adlington in Yorkshire. Some sheep were bought at Lutterworth and Leicester and there was one long-range purchase of 79 fat wethers at Pontefract Fair in 1553. They were soon suspected of rot and had to be resold 'with all speed'.[33] The majority of sheep were purchased from local farmers, apparently privately. The list of men owed money by Sir William Turpin of Knaptoft at his death in 1523 may be another illustration of this kind of transaction.[34] All the beasts and half the sheep fattened at Misterton had to be bought in for this purpose and, since the supply of grass and hay varied from year to year, there were times when maintaining a constant supply for the household involved buying in stock already fattened at great expense. Thus the Royal Proclamation in September 1551 limiting the price for the best sheep to 5/- actually benefited the estate. Previously they were being bought in at up to 9/8d. each. Afterwards, where the vendor's shepherd could be bribed to part with any, they cost only 'the king's highest price'.[35] As for dairying, the estate farm administration did not bother with it. Special arrangements even had to be made to supply the warrener's ferrets, 'we having no melche cow'.[36]

In terms of cash income from rents on the estate, the accounts shew that year by year, after deducting similar outgoings such as chief rents and tithes, very little remained. The principal revenue came from the sale of the wool crop each year. The whole aim of the wool flock, some fifteen hundred

(1,800) strong, was to provide the finest quality and so the fleece, here and on Robert Belgrave's manor farm, averaged no more than two pounds in weight, only half a pound more than the common-field fleece. Heavier fleeces, averaging 2½ pounds, were clipped from one hundred (120) wethers that had to be bought in fat one year; but it was 'rough wool . . . too gross for sorting with our store wool'.[37] The high quality of the main crop is reflected in its destination, being sold to clothiers and merchants from Coventry, Gloucestershire and London. The estate farm of the Turpins of Knaptoft was even more extensive at the beginning of the seventeenth century. In 1617, on the death of the then head of the family, another Sir William, there were over 150 score sheep (3,100 in all) valued at nearly £1,800 and divided into five flocks, the principal of which were grazing at Knaptoft and Misterton. The wool in the wool house was worth £445.8.0.

Special trouble was taken to maintain the stock of fish (carp) in the pools at Misterton, which meant regular visits from a local otter-hunter with his hounds. Even the swans that nested by the pools were protected. Of all the game and fish resources exploited, however, the most spectacular was the coney warren (rabbit warren). There was probably a warren worth exploiting at Knaptoft too;[38] like Misterton it still has a Warren Farm. The large warren at Misterton was run by the Warrener at his lodge, aided by his sub-warrener, and so required fewer regular staff even than the sheep farming (although in the winter armed patrols had to be enlisted 'much part for more defence and company to the Warrener being manessed (menaced) with knaves hunting in the night'[39]). The returns from the sales of thousands of conies, probably direct to London, were therefore almost pure profit.

During the years covered by the accounts, however, the important returns from both wool and conies were halved. The gross return from wool was £141.2.0 in 1550 and £171.0.0 in 1551. It dropped to £84.13.4d. in 1552 and remained slightly below that figure in the following two years. The gross cash return from conies was £89.7.10d. in 1550, dropped to £74.4.4d. in 1551 and sank further to £50.10.7½d. by 1554. In both cases, even if this was only a temporary set-back, it was warning of an ultimate decline. Certainly in 1622 Burton mentioned Misterton's fame in London for its conies, 'sending thither great abundance, and those which (for the goodness and sweetness) were preferred before any other that were brought thither', but only as a thing of the past.[40]

Even within the parish of Lutterworth itself there were two large areas of enclosed ground, Moorbarns, measuring 565 acres, and the Spittle grounds, measuring around 100 acres. The former had been part of one of the common fields and in 1636 ancestors were still recalled who 'could go into Moorbarne grounds . . and set their foot upon land and ley sometimes belonging to their farms'. In particular Martin Woolman was quoted, 'a very old man', grandfather of John Woolman, husbandman, whose family had

Illustration 12. View towards Lutterworth from the Watling Street, with the town's now spireless church tower on the far skyline. This part of the parish, Moorbarns, was enclosed for sheep pasture at the beginning of the sixteenth century but there was no farm house here until a century later. Sheep still graze permanent pasture over ridge and furrow which bears witness to the former common-field husbandry of the townspeople.

Photograph: Wordscan, Lutterworth

been 'of very long continuance in Lutterworth'. He lived at least until 1587 and yet claimed to have seen rye growing there on two ridges or leys of theirs (see Illustration 12).[41] During the sixteenth century, however, Moorbarns grounds became a very profitable sheep walk for wool flocks. The Temple family of Warwickshire acquired a reversionary lease of them in 1557 at an annual rent of £37 and four years later gained possession. In 1607 they were stocked with ten hundred (1,200) sheep and 40 rams and were valued at £300 or £400 a year; yet the rent paid remained at the original figure.[42] Similarly the Spencers of Althorp in Northamptonshire took occupation in 1573 of the two fields in Poultney that had formerly been used by the Caves of Stanford on Avon.[43] The Spittle grounds at Lutterworth, together with the house of the former Hospital there, were occupied at the end of the century by Thomas Farren, who also owned the Spittle Mills, the common bakehouse in the town and the Bailiwick. He was engaged in large-scale pasture farming ranging into Northamptonshire and involving very valuable stock, especially sheep. In 1598 he informed the Northamptonshire Justices that he was willing to undertake the provision of cattle: 'The ox at the Queen's price is 7l.10s., the fat sheep 17s., the lean sheep 13s.4d., and the lamb 7s.6d.'. At this time his partnership flock of twenty hundred (2,400) sheep and 60 rams grazing on the Hatton family's Holdenby Grounds in Northamptonshire were 'of the best stock of sheep of Lady Hatton' and worth 29 shillings a sheep and £3 a ram. Farren also played a part in the enclosure of Cotesbach at the turn of the century. Thus, although he should be classified as an estate-pasture farmer, the more commercial basis of his farming was actually enabling him to build up a new estate. His will shews that at his death in 1613 he was increasing his holdings in Clay Coton, a village just inside Northamptonshire where he was lord of the manor.[44]

These families, however, were exceptional. The Temples specialized in sheep farming and had the advantages of scale and diversity across their estates. The Spencers not only dealt direct with London butchers but also specialized in sheep-breeding.[45] On his death in 1523 the largest debt of Sir William Turpin of Knaptoft was £20 owed 'unto Spenser of hallthorpe', presumably for livestock purchased.[46] Farren's prosperity depended partly on his involvement with the affairs of the town. In general it can be concluded that in the sixteenth century the Lutterworth area pasture farms represented farming at a very low level, little more, in fact, than the exploitation of more or less natural resources employing very few staff. There need be no doubt of their success and prosperity early on, but as the century passed their inflexibility in a changing economy left them as backwaters.

In view of the importance of grass and hay in the second half of the century, it may seem strange that there was no further enclosure at that time. Judging by what has been said here, on the other hand, it might be advanced that pasture farming was still no serious rival to the mixed farming of the common fields. If that was the case, why was there no reconversion of pasture to arable lands? The answer must be sought in the role of the pasture grounds in the economy of the area as a whole. The success of pasture farming cannot be judged merely by the performance of the estate farms. It is necessary, therefore, to pursue in detail the uses made of these grounds to identify the men who benefited from them both directly and indirectly.

The nature of the labour employed on pasture farms raises the question of the fate of the populations of the deserted villages. It is not possible to ascertain the proportions that were absorbed into the local economy or were forced to seek a living in the town or further afield. It should not, however, be assumed that all the householders were transformed overnight into wage-labourers on their lords' estates. Where a township was replaced by an estate farm, or a demesne by a Hall Field, it usually appears that mixed husbandry was already dying out, so that although the tenants still worked on the manor, their rights over the land itself were also already evaporating. A stage would then be reached when a change in the running of the manorial establishment, such as rationalizing a series of residences or giving up the demesne arable farming, would confront them with the fact that they had no more security than household dependants. Thus the enclosure of the Hall Field at Cotesbach in 1501, alleged to have been responsible for the expulsion of 30 people, was probably connected with the abandonment of the early Manor House there.[47] In the parishes of Misterton and Knaptoft, that is, including their satellite common-field townships, the majority of the taxpayers in the 1520s were assessed on only one pound each and were probably wage-earners. The fate of such men, who depended on the manorial establishment that replaced a township, may be personified by the solitary almsman at Misterton, father John, who ended his days in poverty and squalor in 1554. He was at least housed, fed and clothed at the expense of the estate, payment even being made to a woman 'for Washing the Alms man's clothes and Seething them in hot water to destroy lice in clothes Sundry Times'.[48] Tenants in a small township supporting no substantial Hall or Manor House, however, would obviously have been even worse off when its grounds were occupied by a local man more interested in his farming. The only other place in the area where early enclosure was associated with expulsions was Bittesby. By enclosing this township in 1494 the Earl of Shrewsbury was alleged to have evicted the last 60 inhabitants and his family was continually held responsible under various anti-enclosure measures. The real beneficiaries, however, were the Salisburys, who exploited these grounds for their own profit as tenant farmers. After a generation they too deserted the former village.[49]

In so far as it was a successor to the common-field farming it is no surprise to find that the labour organization on the estate pasture-farm was neither close-knit nor flexible. Where it consisted of labour service, the husbandry was no more than a survival of the customary common-field husbandry and was in no way specially adapted to enclosed ground farming. In any case it was confined to time-honoured practices and, more surprisingly, could actually be more expensive than wage-labour. On one day in 1554 three regular Misterton estate workers were paid 8d. each for reaping six loads of barley. On another day in the same harvest 32 "neighbours" were paid 6d. each for reaping 11 loads of rye. The former cost 4d. a load and the latter, taking into account the payment 'of custom for a drinking on the field in reaping', 1/7d. a load, nearly five times as much. Even where there was no cash payment to the 'neighbours' or 'tenants' for their labour service, the dinner and refreshment in the field cost over 3d. a head.[50]

Much of the additional estate work was undertaken by neighbouring husbandmen paid by the day like wage-labourers. Of the permanent employees, on the other hand, some were in effect household servants or attendants. Others, the keepers and shepherds, held positions of responsibility dealing in valuable livestock. Of more importance to these men than their wages, however, were the perquisites of the posts they held. Some could run their own wool flocks on the pastures and most of them grazed a small herd of cows there to supply a dairy based on the home. In effect, therefore, although they were employees, they were able to engage in the kind of farm production more typical of the peasantry in the pastoral regions of the country. This was in sharp contrast to the estate farm, where commonly no dairying was undertaken at all.

Of the various shepherding families employed at Misterton, Cotes de Val, Knaptoft, Bittesby, Cotesbach and Moorbarns in the sixteenth century, those who were 'keepers of the pasture' at Moorbarns are particularly well documented. Here it must suffice to cite only the wealthiest of them all. When he died in 1614, Robert Car of Moorbarns had goods worth £111.4.8d., including household goods worth no less than £51.4.8d., the highest total recorded so far for an ordinary household in the town. Yet his daughter referred to him as 'servant unto Sir Thomas Temple'.[51]

The employees who fared best were those who were also based on their own common-field holdings, which they were able to enrich out of the benefits they derived from their posts. The contrast is neatly illustrated by the two shepherds employed on the grounds round Misterton in the 1550s. One relied entirely on his post, so that although he received wages and board, in his last years, when he was too old or weak to take on extra work, he had to be supported practically as an almsman.[52] The other lived in the dependent common-field township of Walcote, where he rented a two yard land holding. He died worth £36.12.10d.[53] Robert Car of Moorbarns not only took a lease of half a two yard land holding in the fields of Lutterworth but he also replaced the barn on it with a farm house (see Illustration 12). The lease was still worth £50 when he died.[54]

If interaction of this sort between the two types of farming land was particularly profitable for the keepers and shepherds towards the end of the century, further enquiry is needed into the precise nature of the relationship by studying the use made of the enclosed grounds by completely independent farmers.

Even from the early sixteenth century there are a few clear examples of yeomen in the area supplementing their common-field farming with grazing in pasture grounds. Best known are the Bradgates of Peatling parva, identified by Hoskins as the wealthiest yeoman family in the county, who occupied pasture grounds, notably in Knaptoft and Elmesthorpe, which is across the Fosse Way from the Lutterworth area.[55] Other local yeoman families with access to Knaptoft fields were Cattell of Ashby magna and Dawkyns of Peatling parva.[56] Needless to say, marriage connexions can be found between such yeoman families in the area and they tend to shew them as a class fairly discrete from the foremost gentry.

Extending their grazing in this way enabled these men to fatten oxen and steers for beef and wethers for mutton. The main advantage, however, was the opportunity for keeping larger flocks of sheep. The importance to them of their wool crops may be seen in the connexions between a couple of them and the Wigston family of Leicester Staplers. The principal creditor of Richard Cattell of Ashby magna on his death in 1521/2 was 'Mr. William Wygeston of Leicester', while Thomas Dawkyns was William Wigston's attorney in Calais and all the Dawkyns property in the parish of Kimcote passed to Wigston.[57]

The practice evidently became more common and of more significance as the century progressed. In the mid-century it was this type of farmer that was supplying the pasture estates with wethers for fattening and, in bad years for grass, already fattened. It is no coincidence, then, that the first instance of the term "grazier" so far traced in the area was applied to such a man in 1588. This was 'Thomas Button Grasyer', a member of a Kimcote family of yeomen who occupied the Cotesbach Hall Close.[58]

In the supply of sheep and, more particularly, in buying sheep for mutton, the Misterton accounts shew that the principal men were farmers based on holdings in Lutterworth, some of them, of course, being the town's butchers. The Kirby and Lussell families of butchers naturally appear chiefly as purchasers, but they also sold fat animals to the estate when it was short. The only sale of a large number of fat animals off the estate, five score fat wethers in 1553, was to a partnership consisting of Thomas (Kirby) butcher, Hugh Lussell and Richard Pratt. Lussell had access to 'Misterton fields' for his sheep. Pratt too, apart from his various farms in Lutterworth and in nearby villages, had access to pasture grounds and, to judge from the accounts, he was active mainly as a sheep-dealer.[59]

At the end of the century there were, apart from Farren, two arms-bearing families of gentry in the town, Insley and Gore, both with large holdings in the fields and making use of pasture grounds.[60] At Bittesby in 1599 Thomas Gore had 247 sheep worth 17/- each and four bullocks or steers worth £3 each.[61] These families were connected not so much with the foremost gentry as with the leading yeomanry in the area; they were thus the forerunners of the new local gentry of the next century.

What were the special advantages that a farmer of this type enjoyed? The size of his enterprise gave him the advantage of scale over the ordinary common-field farmer, so that he could, for instance, sell or withhold his corn crop as the market suited him. Similarly, since his peas crop was not all needed for his horses, he would have had surplus fodder available for fattening. Of greater significance, however, the occurrence of complete folds of hurdles in a few inventories suggests that pasture-fed sheep may have been folded privately on individual farmers' arable lands in the fields to supplement the folding by the common flock.

Over the estate farm, by contrast, these farmers had the advantage of greater flexibility and closer control over labour, so that they were better equipped for detailed stock-management. Moreover for feeding they were not limited to grass and hay. Of especial importance was the opportunity of fattening mutton on peas in the early spring before the first grass-fattened sheep were ready. The pasture farm could only achieve this by buying in peas for the purpose or perhaps, as in the case of the Misterton estate, by securing the tithe peas from a neighbouring common-field township. The peas rick at Knaptoft belonging to Sir William Turpin in 1617 was probably grown not on his estate farm but in one of the other townships in the parish and perhaps represented tithes.[62] Although this device made sure of a supply which might not have been otherwise offered on the market at all, it was not necessarily cheaper. In Misterton, over four years in the 1550s, payment for both the tithe itself and the labour involved brought the price of the tithe peas to an average of 9/- a load. Yet in one winter when the estate was short, 4½ loads were bought in at only 6/8d. a load.[63]

With his labour force based on the family farming unit, this type of farmer was also well able to undertake dairying for the market based on a small herd of cows grazed on the pastures. Richard Bradgate, when he died in 1572, had 12 cows at home in Peatling parva with more in Knaptoft pasture. Their produce was represented by 60 cheeses in store valued at 30/-.[64]

The way the benefit of the pasture ground was being drawn off into the hands of the larger farmers in the area may best be illustrated by the reconstructed life history of a sheep, as assembled from numerous regular entries in the Misterton accounts. Born in the first place among the estate flocks, if it was more suitable for fattening it would be culled as a lamb too coarse for the quality of the store flock. Bought by a local farmer it would be brought on by him on the common fields and then, perhaps, sold back to the estate for finishing off on grass. In a year when the estate was constrained to buy in mutton sheep already fattened it might be fed on the farmer's peas crop in the early spring and then sold to the estate. Later in the year, however, the estate might be buying back a sheep that had actually been fattened on estate grass. Thus it emerges that although the pasture breed of sheep was being evolved on the pasture grounds, this was being done actually in conflict with estate farming policy. For, all the while, probably right through to the 1620s, the estate farms maintained the fine quality of their wool by keeping down the size of their sheep and, in consequence, the quantity of wool and mutton that they yielded. Burton, whose own enclosed estate at Lindley was 12 miles up the Watling Street from Lutterworth, gives that impression in praising the sheep pastures of the Lutterworth area and the fineness of the wool in south-east Leicestershire. The 'fair and thick woolled sheep' he noted at Misterton were presumably not part of the store flocks but belonged to outsiders.[65]

The diverging interests of the grazier and the estate pasture-farm are the clue as to the unique position of the enclosure at Cotesbach at the beginning of the century. The new lord of the manor, John Quarles, a London draper, has usually been blamed alone. Was Quarles, on the contrary, merely late in the day in attempting to form an old-style pasture-estate farm? John Moore, the rector of Knaptoft, dedicated his contemporary anti-enclosure pamphlet to his patron Sir William Turpin, lord of one of the largest pasture estates in the region and an active encloser himself, who was also related by marriage to Quarles. Sir William was even one of the commissioners who decided in favour of Quarles concerning a petition to the Crown from the tenants at Cotesbach.[66] Possibly he was at the time sitting beneath the biblical inscription in his Hall at Knaptoft that read 'Witness against me before the Lord. Whom have I done wrong to? Whom have I oppressed? . . .' (in the room marked B in Illustration 11).[67] To Moore, however, the villains were the 'many graceless Graziers' with 'Their innumerable tods of wool, their herds and droves of fatlings'.[68] Also interested in this enclosure, however, and the ultimate beneficiary of it after Quarles went bankrupt, was Thomas Farren, the Lutterworth gentleman whose grazing activities, based on his residence at the Spittle, have already been mentioned.[69] So far as the ordinary farmer was concerned the common fields of Cotesbach were already hemmed in by the pasture grounds of Misterton to the east and of the Hall Close and Moorbarns to the north. It seems that grazing interests from outside the parish, and in particular from the town of Lutterworth, were the main moving force behind the enclosure.

Early in the sixteenth century the common-field farmer was not in competition with the lord of the manor to enclose, since there was no possibility of his surviving other than in the context of the mixed husbandry of the common fields. It is even possible that the enclosure of demesne lands and other areas such as Moorbarns aroused little resentment at the time. Later in the century the farmers were reaching the limits of the grazing capacity of the common fields and were therefore in competition for the use of the enclosed grounds, but still only as a source of grazing, or occasionally for hay.

That outsiders used the enclosed grounds only as sources of grass is clear from the nature of the rights they took in them; not leases of the grounds themselves, but grazing rights for so many beasts or sheep. Some yeomen, it is true, secured leases of whole grounds and prospered; but even then it is not certain that they always enjoyed exclusive possession. Normally the management of "agistment" was in the hands of the estate shepherd or keeper on the spot. In 1607 there were 30 cows in Moorbarns. Yet it is certain that the Temple family ran no dairy there and the keeper had only seven of his own. The rest no doubt belonged to inhabitants of the town, who could pay sixpence a week for agistment there. One townsman also took hay crops off one of the Moorbarns meadows. At Clifton-upon-Dunsmore, just across the Watling Street in Warwickshire, the Hall Field was held in customary units of stint and some of it was still 'unknown ground' in the mid-seventeenth century. The arrangement was probably similar at Primethorpe in Broughton Astley, where one man mentioned in his will in 1558 his lease 'of a quartern of the alle land (Hall Land)'. In Monks Kirby, Walton Fields, near, and possibly constituting part of the former common fields of, the deserted township of Little Walton, were leased to the inhabitants of Pailton 'because this hamlet was destitute of pasture'. They became the Bullocks Field, later known as 'Pailton Pasture'.[70]

What prevented outsiders gaining more than limited rights over pasture grounds was the continuing presence of the estate store flocks. In fact there was probably very little difference in appearance between the enclosed fields and the common fields, apart of course from the absence of tillage and the presence of the indispensable ring-fence. Elmesthorpe was enclosed under Henry VII and, 'from traditional accounts, is supposed to be one of the earliest inclosures in the kingdom by ring-fence, the usual mode of inclosing at that time; excepting it being afterwards divided into two or three divisions, for the convenience of farming.'[71] Flock-management in such large grounds, which were simply the three open fields hedged round, was indeed not necessarily any easier. To form smaller closes by hedging and ditching, moreover, was a considerable expense in the first year alone. To fence off the corner of one of the Misterton fields, forming a new close of possibly 20 acres, cost £7.16.1d. in 1551. Even when it was established the maintenance of a hedge was an expense and damage was caused not only by animals but also by poor hedge-robbers desperate for fuel.[72]

In conclusion it can now be said not only that were there ways in which the ancient enclosures remained to be improved as much as did the common fields, but also that the chief obstacle in each case was the store flock, whether it belonged to a community of farmers or to one man only. This throws new light on Burton's remark that the adjacent part of Leicestershire, the south-east, was 'almost all champain'; for this description may not have struck him as inconsistent with the fact that much of it was also ancient enclosure.[73] Indeed although the words 'field' and 'ground' usually distinguished common from enclosed land, the early enclosed townships were still sometimes referred to as 'fields'. In the terms employed by the pamphleteers in the 1650s, all the fields were 'lying open', but not all of them were 'used in common' (see Illustration 13).

Illustration 13. The two Kilworths, North and South. This tiny engraving of 1792 comes nearest to portraying the last of the unenclosed open-field landscape in the area.

J. Nichols, *Leics.*

4.   Enclosed ground farming in the seventeenth century

It has been seen that the first phase of enclosure involved the lord of a manor drawing into his hands all the resources of his demesne or township. In this way he improved his position for production for the market, or rather for reaping the more or less natural crops of his enclosed grounds. There was some hardship for the displaced population in adjusting and, although initially there may have been employment for them on the pasture estate, in the long run the activities there were on a low economic level without prospect of improvement. The productivity of the common fields, on the other hand, was raised until it reached the limits of their resources, some time before the end of the sixteenth century. By this time the larger common-field farmers were improving their situation considerably by taking grazing rights over neighbouring enclosed grounds and this move was especially significant as the emphasis in sheep farming shifted from wool to mutton.

In the introduction the rate of enclosure was taken as an indication of the rate of change in the farming economy and it shewed that the critical period was the years from 1620 to 1665. This was confirmed by the study of the population trends. It is not surprising to find a period of transition starting with the 1620s, a key decade in the development of the economy of the nation. Apart from plagues and dearths, there was also a serious slump in industry and trade. One important result was that while the price of corn remained high, especially in the years of poor crops, the demand for wool in general, and for the fine short-staple wool in particular, fell right back, never again to recover its prime position in the farming economy. Thus there were strong reasons for abandoning wool flocks, for taking pasture ground in hand and for stepping up corn-production.[74]

The effects of the next phase of enclosure, that is the success of the conversion of arable to pasture, the displacement of sections of some village communities and the changes to the landscape, are well known. What of the other villages? The question of how far the villages that retained their common fields after 1665 were unaffected at this time will be dealt with later. Before examining the new enclosures, however, the discussion of the deserted townships and ancient enclosures will be resumed to see how they were affected at this stage.

As elsewhere in the Midlands, the years following 1620 saw the winding-up of the great estate pasture-farms in the Lutterworth area.[75] By the time he was writing, Lee was only just able to couple the Pulteneys with the Caves as surviving landowning families. The Pulteneys, the Turpins and the Staresmores were all Royalist families and their estates were being sold off during or just after the Civil War.[76] The Misterton estate was effectively broken up on the death of John Pulteney in 1637. Of the sale price of the Knaptoft estate in 1648, £13,460, only £4,220 remained to Richard Turpin, out of which he had to find £939 for a delinquency fine. The Staresmores parted with their Frowlesworth estate by stages.[77] The Feildings and Caves were both of divided loyalties, apparently concluding with the Parliamentarians. Their respective estates survived to support Newnham Paddox and Stanford Hall, the only two "stately homes" in the district; yet both these establishments were more typical of Warwickshire and Northamptonshire, in which counties respectively they stood and the majority of their lands lay. The Feilding family accounts shew that they were certainly not farming in the 1650s and indeed there is no trace of estate farming by any of these families after the 1620s. The end of the Temple family's enterprise at Moorbarns can be dated precisely; they sold off their flocks and herds in 1623 and 1624.[78]

This change in farming practices amongst the gentry of the first rank was mirrored by the lesser gentry of the town of Lutterworth. Whereas they had once been common-field farmers involved in grazing on pasture grounds, they now tended to invest in tenanted property in the district and to become in effect local landed gentry. The Insleys and Gores were soon joined by the Pratts, who were enriched by a marriage with the Gores and made their residence at Cotesbach. Similarly the senior line of the Gores took up residence in Ullesthorpe as lords of the manor there.[79]

The new occupants of the ancient enclosures were no doubt the same as the men who had previously held grazing rights over them. Once the estate store flocks had gone, however, they could divide the grounds up into more manageable closes for controlled grazing, taking leases so as to secure exclusive possession. In 1629 half of the township of Bittesby consisted of 'the two great fields'. By 1679 these had been 'divided for better conveniency into several parcels', comprising six closes averaging 45 acres each and six meadows averaging nine acres each. Moorbarns had formerly been divided into two great grounds. Now the Further Grounds were let to a grazier and the Hither Grounds were split up among various townsmen.[80]

So long as the ancient enclosures were used only as sheep walks, they were being under-used, or rather robbed for the benefit of the common-field arable. An even stronger reason, therefore, for subdividing them was to enable them to be taken in hand and cropped again. This is what was happening on the Hither Grounds in the 1630s. The clearest evidence for this new practice is the eyewitness list published by Lee in 1656 referring to the ploughing-up of enclosures going on at the time and in the previous 30 years (the places named are shewn on Map VII).[81] Corn prices may have been decisive in these changes. In general they remained high until the mid-century, after which they declined, at least in the years of better weather. In 1654, for instance, wheat was cheaper than it had been since the early 1590s. The following year it fetched no more than two shillings a strike in Leicester. Lee acknowledged the influence of the weather, but he was nevertheless satisfied that the main reason was that 'the late plenty and double quantity of corn is got in new broken up inclosed grounds, whereof there are now very many in all places'.[82]

This subdivision of ancient enclosures, by following earlier field and furlong divisions and natural features, tended to produce an irregular landscape of hedges. The resulting closes varied in shape and size as areas were taken in hand for cropping piecemeal. The 100 acres in tillage in Moorbarns in the 1630s was probably exceptional and each smaller area, such as the 16 acres of wheat at Misterton in 1682, would have needed protection from grazing cattle.[83] It emerges, therefore, that these fields, which enclosure had already released from common-field farming over a century ago, were now undergoing practically the same process of subdivision as the common fields of the villages that were being enclosed at this stage. Where an estate was split between several tenants they may have found it convenient to establish yards and buildings out on their grounds. Eventually isolated "lodge" farm houses were built, even in townships like Bittesby and Poultney where, throughout the sixteenth century, the villages had been 'utterly decayed, not one house remaining'.[84] In 1681 it was

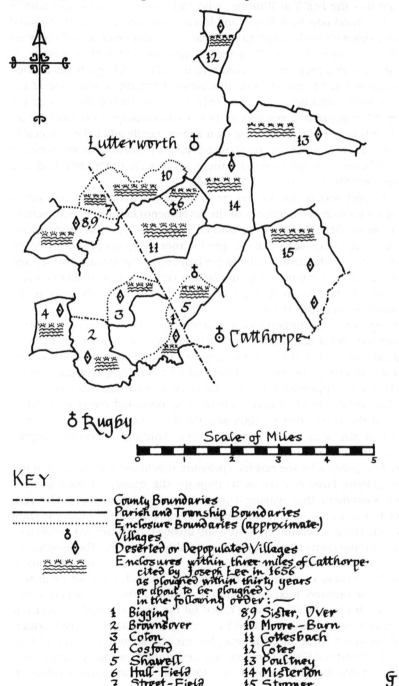

MAP VII

CROPPING OF ENCLOSURES 1620s-1650s

Lutterworth

12

13

10

7

14

8,9

11

15

4

3

5

2

1

Catthorpe

Rugby

Scale of Miles

0   1   2   3   4   5

KEY

—·—·—·— County Boundaries
———————— Parish and Township Boundaries
················ Enclosure Boundaries (approximate)
Villages
Deserted or Depopulated Villages
Enclosures within three miles of Catthorpe
    cited by Joseph Lee in 1656
    as ploughed within thirty years
    or about to be ploughed
    in the following order:—

1 Bigging   8,9 Sister, Over
2 Brownsover   10 Moore-Barn
3 Coton   11 Cottesbach
4 Cosford   12 Cotes
5 Shawell   13 Poultney
6 Hall-Field   14 Misterton
7 Street-Field   15 Stormer

G

reported that the bailiff at Bittesby, who had taken on land worth £200 a year, had a good new-built house and it was suggested that another should be built to go with lands worth £150 a year.[85] The severance in 1654 of what in a fine was described as 70 acres of meadow and 630 of pasture in Misterton and Poultney, at an annual rent of £371.16.8d., probably created one of the isolated farms in those townships. Certainly at least one of the Poultney lodge farm houses was in existence well before the end of the century.[86] The separate properties in these two townships were assessed for Lutterworth poor rates under their own names, nearly all of them traceable as the names of grounds on the sixteenth-century estate farm and some of them still borne by lodge farmsteads there, such as Thornborough, Holbeck, Wakeleys and Sharrag (shear-hog) Grounds.

In a parallel way it was the common flock which was the chief factor holding up those new enclosures of the seventeenth century which were to bring common-field farming to an end in so many villages. In these places, however, it has been seen that the profits from sheep-keeping were being concentrated into the hands of the larger farmers, so that eventually they and the lord of the manor would together be in a very strong position to control the fate of the common flock, especially after the decline in the price of the short-staple wool in the 1620s.

In recent years the importance of enclosure in the seventeenth century has been somewhat underrated. In the Lutterworth area, however, by 1665 very nearly one half of the land was enclosed ground and two thirds of this enclosure, involving the final enclosure of 12 townships, had taken place since 1600 (see Appendix Table 1). The Leicestershire-based anti-enclosure campaign and the local pamphlet controversy occupied the years 1650 to 1656, and the years 1655 to 1665 saw the final enclosure of at least five parishes in the area, namely Ashby parva, Catthorpe, Peatling magna, Peatling parva and Shawell.

Here too, judging by the results, enclosure would seem to have been the tool of grazing farmers anxious to improve the quality of their pasture ground, something that remained impossible so long as the fields were subject to the round of common-field husbandry and to common grazing rights. One thing is certain: enclosure still involved both the laying-down of ploughs and the conversion of permanent arable to pasture. The inventories from the enclosed villages in the 1680s shew conclusively that the mixed husbandry of these communities had come to an end. None of them was typical of the ordinary mixed farm and in several of the cases where crops are listed it is clear that they were raised on the common fields of adjacent unenclosed townships. One indeed has been classified as of a mixed farmer, that of Elkington Kirke of Catthorpe; but his will shews that his £45.10.0 worth of 'all sorts of Grain Thrashed and unthreshed' probably represented his tithes stored in his tithe barn and hovels in the unenclosed village of

Newton on Dunsmore, just across the Watling Street in Warwickshire.[87]

Lamenting this decay of traditional husbandry, Moore cried, 'where are those every years crops, and all those Tenants, Cottiers, and servants that were wont to be kept there?' But, as Lee pointed out, it did not mean that no corn was being raised in these parishes. There is ample evidence for cropping, not 'every years crops', but the occasional cropping of pasture ground for a few years, 'five, or six crops, once in thirty, or forty years', exactly in the same way as on the ancient enclosures.[88]

As in the ancient enclosures, the subdivision of the fields of the newly enclosed villages produced separate farms made up of manageable closes, as can be seen in a survey of Willoughby Waterless made in 1675.[89] The only major difference was that the new enclosures were based on existing villages. Here the farmsteads remained sited together along a village street and the isolated farm house was probably a later development. A reconstruction of the enclosure map of Ashby parva, which was enclosed in 1665 – albeit not at the will of any lord of a manor but by agreement among the farming inhabitants[90] – shews the kind of layout more usually ascribed to eighteenth-century enclosure, with a farmer's allotted plot 'at his yard's end' and 'shooting' out towards the parish boundary. The two isolated farmsteads in the parish were evidently not built until some time in the eighteenth century (see Map VIII).[91] The enclosure of Bitteswell later in that century was typical in making way for 'several neat houses interspersed throughout the field, and annexed to their respective farms'.[92]

Apart from these obvious differences, it emerges that both the ancient enclosures and the newly enclosed fields were undergoing a very similar transformation. In the former the common-field husbandry had died out over a century before; but although common grazing rights had been extinguished, the store flocks remained as much an obstacle to subdividing enclosure as the common flocks in the latter. The villages enclosing in the seventeenth century, on the other hand, had to go through both stages at the one time. Despite the fact that, to the mixed farmers, or at least to the larger ones among them, from the 1620s onwards everything must have seemed in favour of enclosure, there still remained two important obstacles. One was the common husbandry of the smaller farmers and the other was the grazing rights of the smallholders and cottagers. It might be expected, therefore, that there would be a difference in date and pace between the carving-up of the ancient enclosures and the final enclosing of whole villages. For this reason it is worth studying the chronology of the various stages in these changes.

The late sixteenth century had seen rival demands made on the land threatening to come into conflict. Both the grazing farmer who raised livestock for the market and the arable farmer who grew corn for the local population now began to break down the established distinctions between permanent pasture and permanent arable. How, then, was the innovation of

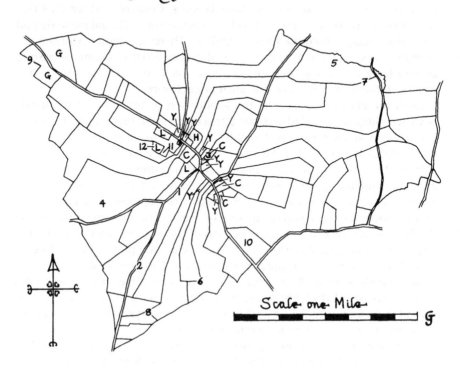

MAP VIII

ASHBY PARVA ENCLOSURE AWARD MAP
Plots laid out by Agreement in 1665

Scale one Mile

KEY

C	Close	
H	Hall Close	pre-existing
L	Lammas Close	
G	Glebe allotted	in Award
Y	Yard mentioned	

Furlong names, close names &c. mentioned in text

Cole Lane	1	Hemp Brooks	7
Colepit Way	2	Lincroft (Furze)	8
Coventry Close	3	Redham	9
Cow Pasture	4	Poor's Plot (Meach Close)	10
Flaxen Knolls	5	Three Leys	11
Fullpits (Furze)	6	Leicester Close (Top of Town Close)	12

cropping pasture grounds related to the demand for corn? In times of dearth it was of course the poor that had the greatest difficulty in securing barley or even peas for their bread-corn. In Leicestershire it is clear that the problem concerned not only the great quantities of barley bought up for malting but also the peas used by graziers for fattening mutton. The situation was acute in 1622/3 and it is to this year, at the beginning of the 30-year period referred to by Lee, that the first instance in the area – a 'close of corn of Oliver Cave gent . . . lying near Morton's orchard' in Swinford – may be traced. No indication of its size was given, but it was probably a small home close and part of his demesne farm.[93] In 1630/1 the situation was even worse and there is evidence of difficulty in maintaining a supply of barley for the poor in the market at Lutterworth. It can hardly have been a coincidence that it was in 1631 that 100 acres of Moorbarns, formerly part of one of the town's three fields and untilled for over a century, was suddenly turned over to tillage again. Ever since the Temples had abandoned their sheep farming in this pasture ground there had been disputes as to its future both within the family and between the family and the town.[94] Only now was pasture converted to arable on such a scale and it is significant that part at least of the task was undertaken by Francis Billington, a leading yeoman baker in the town who also ran its most important inn.[95] This was a very different operation from the former occasional tillage of furlongs of lands here by Lutterworth common-field farmers.

Such cropping at this stage thus seems to have been more in the nature of a response to emergency than a consistent policy; certainly there was none at Moorbarns after the first round until the late 1650s.[96] Moore and Lee both give the impression that it had only just become general in the mid-century, by which time it was a major factor in the arguments in favour of enclosure.[97] Seventeenth-century enclosure, however, was not confined to the 1650s and 1660s. What form did the earlier enclosures take?

It is surprising to find that at first enclosure was not in fact incompatible with the survival of wide-ranging grazing rights. At Ashby magna, enclosed at the beginning of the century, holdings appear to have been consolidated but to have remained open.[98] Similarly at Cotesbach it was not the ring-fence round the parish that the rioters pulled down in 1607 but the internal divisions between the grounds of the larger farmers. As late as 1625, indeed, one such holding there was still apparently lying open.[99] According to the arrangement which Quarles attempted to impose in 1603, the smaller farmers, the remaining eight husbandmen, were to share jointly enclosed grounds amounting to 169 acres. The three remaining cottagers were to receive no land but to have grazing rights in the lord's closes. Two of them had expressly refused plots of land offered in lieu and had demanded their 'kyes grass' in Quarles's pastures.[100] Improving farming, therefore, cannot have been the main motive for enclosing at this stage. Contemporary outbursts against enclosure continued to be directed at 'Pasture-men' like 'You gentlemen that rack your rents, and throw down Land for corn'. The elder John Moore addressed himself to 'the tyrannous dealing of unjust inclosers and needless overthrowers of tillage' and throughout his pamphlet equated enclosing with 'turning commons into pastures, and tilled fields into closing for . . cattle'.[101]

Later on both husbandmen and cottagers were confined to smaller areas for grazing, like the 'Husbandman's Pasture' and the 'Cottyers' Pasture' at Frowlesworth. Eventually cottagers were reduced to accepting a share in a Cottage Cow Pasture or just an allotment of an acre or two. An early instance of separate allotments was the enclosure of Leicester Forest in 1627/8, when numerous ancient cottages received two acres and new erected ones only one acre. At Willoughby Waterless in 1675 there were a dozen two-acre plots, half of them called 'Dale (Pasture)' and half 'Cow Pasture'. At least five of them were occupied by men known to have been cottiers. These plots may represent Cow Pastures awarded at the enclosure and later subdivided.[102] The dozen acres set aside as the Poor's Plot in each of the enclosure agreements of the mid-century appears as the direct successor to the former Cow Pasture in the open fields; although by that time few of the needy could afford to keep a cow and the plot came to be treated more as a source of income for the overseers of the poor.[103] One device by which the enclosing villagers freed themselves from the poor was to covenant to maintain 'every man his own poor'. Accordingly in respect of cottages on men's farms the two-acre plots were allotted to the owners and not to the occupiers. Lee 'would have them left to the owners discretion, when they grow void, either by the decease, or voluntary departure of the present inhabitants . . .'. This practice was no more convincing in the seventeenth century than it was to be in the nineteenth.[104]

This suggests that after the 1620s cottage grazing rights presented less of an obstacle to enclosure and that the main factor was the survival of the communal husbandry among the smallholders. It is worth noting that the last dissenter to the enclosure at Catthorpe, on whom Lee poured all the scorn of a fourfold argument, including a discourse on Naboth's vineyard, was a smallholder. Like the cottagers at Cotesbach he was refusing an allotment and asserting, against all odds, his rights of common, in his case for seven sheep.[105]

It is also surprising to find that these earlier enclosures were not always incompatible with the survival of common husbandry, or at least of some form of mixed farming. The method of obtaining the agreement of tenants to enclosure, still the time-honoured granting to them of leases for the duration of three lives, may have had a bearing on this. The terms in the leases could have helped preserve former husbandry practices for a while.[106] Moore, indeed, saw this as only having deferred, but not prevented, the depopulation of Ashby magna[107] and certainly there are no mixed farming inventories from Cotesbach after the enclosure there. The survival of older practices, however, is particularly noticeable in the row of parishes along the north-western edge of the area, against the Fosse Way. Their farming economy shews them to have been exceptional or, even, hardly part of the Lutterworth area. Here mixed farming, even on smallholdings, did not die out completely and it remained possible, moreover, for a cottager to engage in some dairy production.

Elsewhere the smaller farmer was not so well off. Only so long as he could still maintain a plough team could he raise enough corn to support his own household and to that extent remain protected against the vagaries of the market. But as Lee's account confirms, he was in fact losing ground; the yields from his lands, so laboriously tilled, were dwindling. When the cropping of enclosed grounds became general, Lee pointed out, such a man was faced with the impossible situation of corn being cheaper in the market than the crops he could raise on his own land; yet the corn crops may have been the only produce that he could spare for sale.[108] This then appears to have been the critical set of circumstances that induced the final capitulation on the part of so many small farmers, which in turn opened the way for the spate of enclosures between 1655 and 1665. It may even have been responsible for the apparent population crisis in these villages in the 1650s.[109] The character of enclosure at this stage was very different from what it had been in 1607. Moore, writing in 1656, might well distinguish between the activities of the 'former Inclosurists' and 'these inclosures of the *last Edition* which they are now about'.[110]

It is thus certain that the immediate cause of the abandonment of common-field farming in so many villages in the mid-seventeenth century was the success of cropping on the ancient enclosures. In a broader context what this meant was that the common-field husbandry was facing direct competition from improved farming; for there is no suggestion that there was ultimately any difference between the farming methods used, whether the enclosures were ancient or new. What was it that constituted improved farming in the Lutterworth area?

The most conspicuous change was the abandonment of the inflexible distinction between land permanently tilled and ground under permanent grass.[111] When pastures were broken up for a period of cropping they commanded an enhanced rent. In instances of such arrangements which have been traced, the period ranged from three to six years and the 'improved rent' could be double the 'grazing rent'.[112] Apart from the practical advantages of large-scale cultivation, the crop yields benefited enormously from the soil having rested under turf.[113] This system also dispensed with fallowing and with that vital feature of the fallow year, the folding of the sheep flocks on the arable.[114]

All this can be found broadly described in the local pamphlets. The inventories reveal the details of the change. They shew that the main corn crop used for feeding was now oats; indeed on some farms it had become the only corn crop. This may reflect a change in the feeding of the working horses; no longer dependent on the peas crop, they could be fed on pastures in summer and on hay, supplemented by oats, in winter. Peas were no longer an important crop here and a grazing farmer wishing to fatten spring mutton could continue to rely on peas grown on neighbouring common fields, still commonly secured in the form of tithes. There is no trace of turnips having been grown in the area as fodder until the end of the century.[115]

The chief crops for the market, by contrast, were, inevitably, wheat and barley. But if the attractions of the town market and the needs of the area's population appear to have stimulated the initial cropping of enclosed grounds, there are also signs that local corn-dealing was beginning to respond to yet wider market demands and that by the mid-seventeenth century this had become the deciding factor.

The breaking-up of substantial areas of old pasture ground necessitated the growing of "pioneer crops" to protect the corn from the pests which thrive in turf and to prevent it from growing too rank and lodging.[116] The increasingly specialist demands of the wider market may have encouraged experiments in exploiting these crops. Lee's claim that flax, hemp and woad were already local crops is borne out by the evidence. Woad was almost certainly used for the first round of tillage at Moorbarns. Woad-working also made way for the first years of cropping in Misterton and Poultney. The growing of flax at Catthorpe apparently continued for a time after enclosure. A 15-acre ground within the precinct of the Feildings' Newnham Park called 'the Hopyard' suggests that hops too may have been grown on more than a domestic scale.[117] These industrial crops provided employment in the area for numbers of labourers, but only on a seasonal and temporary basis; and they all appear to have declined in importance as the century progressed. In spite of Lee's complaint of the scarcity of labourers and the high wages they demanded, labour would have been available around the time of the expulsions connected with the mid-century enclosures.[118] Later it was presumably found better to leave these labour-intensive crops to districts more suited to specializing in them.

Such crops required reserves of capital and a labour force; another use of enclosed ground which needed neither but which could be founded on a family unit was market gardening.[119] The names of half a dozen village gardeners have been found, all from villages with enclosed grounds and including one named Reynolds. A family of the same name was running the only considerable market garden traced in the area, a plot of 3½ acres in Moorbarns. This family of gardeners lived in Lutterworth and doubtless their business was based on the demand for fruit and vegetables in the town. The importance of their enterprise is shewn by the high rent they were paying in the 1660s, ten pounds a year, well above the rate for meadow ground and nearly three times the rate for ordinary pasture ground there.[120]

Farmers with enclosed grounds could in general respond more flexibly to changes in the market. In periods when corn prices ran low, common-field farmers were in difficulties. According to Defoe, during the 'uninterrupted series of plenty' in the eight years beginning with 1680 'it was impossible that those who depended on nothing but their labour and the crops could pay the rent'.[121] Enclosed grounds, however, could always be laid down again to grass. In 1682 it was reported that the tithe in the Wheat Field and other grounds at Bittesby 'ceases for the present because they have laid it down from ploughing'. In the long run, of more significance than the improved arable farming, therefore, was the opportunity it offered for enriching the quality of the pasture. The tenant of the Further Grounds at Moorbarns in the 1660s 'designed as well to advance his grazing condition as to better himself by ploughing'. In 1659 part of an estate in newly enclosed Peatling magna 'would be better for ploughing which will be a great improvement to the owner'.[122] Lee mentioned 'improved grounds' and ground bearing better grass after being corned. The success of this treatment was reflected in the improved rents paid; Moorbarns, valued at £300 a year in 1608, was bringing in £582.0.2d. by 1663, so that the capital value of the property was considered to be well over £11,000.[123] It also finally reduced the great contrast in value between meadow ground and pasture ground in both new and ancient enclosures. The ratio sank from 3:1 at the beginning of the century to 2:1 or 1½:1 in the 1650s and 1660s.[124] Much larger areas could be mown for hay according to the condition of the grass and in fact hay became by far the most important fodder crop; £10 worth of hay was not uncommon in the inventories of grazing farmers. The 16 inventories of pure grazing farmers from the enclosing villages in the 1680s averaged £34 in livestock and £2 in crops, all of which was hay. There is a strong possibility that whereas grass ground had hitherto been formed by natural swarding only, it was now sown down with selected seeds. There is one instance traced of a close sown down with clover. This is the lease of a close in Lutterworth in 1682/3 specifying that the tenant 'do sow the same into good clover seed at least twelve pounds upon an Acre, and after one mowing keep the same in grazing and lay at least twenty load of good Dung upon the same'.[125]

If the main result of the changes was so much improved pasture, what was the effect on livestock-farming? The most important overall change was that it meant that fewer "cattle" of any kind were kept, whether great cattle or lesser cattle. This is one complaint of Moore's that Lee did not refute, as he maintained that each animal kept on enclosed ground could be three times as profitable.[126]

Lee was contemptuous of the common-field horses and held that only pasture horses were worth anything or were capable of military service. Moore retorted that there were so few of the latter that the war could not have been fought without relying on the former.[127] There had always been a few horses kept on the pasture estates; yet these were not working horses, just personal mounts and the occasional team of coach or carriage horses.[128] Thus there were horses of superior stock within sight of, but out of reach of, the ordinary farmer. The improved farming, however, no longer limited by the peas crop for fodder, was able to support teams of larger horses. It can have been no coincidence that the farmers who owned these valuable horses were also the ones who owned wagons by the 1680s. This makes it very likely that the horses they were using were descended from coach and carriage horses that had previously been limited to road work.

Comparing the herds of beasts, on the other hand, reveals no great contrast in values or in the herd structure such as to suggest that there were now different breeds in the area. The main difference seems to have been in the end-products. Lee mentioned that the graziers had a monopoly of all the fat beef to themselves and certainly the inventories of the largest pure grazing farmers confirm that some of their beasts were fat bullocks, steers and cows.[129] Dairying for the market, on the other hand, was not confined to the larger grazing farmers nor was it practised on a large scale. For the most part it remained a household occupation based on a herd of half a dozen cows. Some of the farmers built up stocks of several pounds worth of cheese and butter. Also it was more usual than it had been in the sixteenth century for an inventory to list, among the household swine, one or two fat hogs, which may have been fed on dairy by-products.

As enclosure has been seen to have brought an end to the mixed husbandry, the decline in the numbers of horses and beasts kept in the enclosing parishes is not unexpected. But the pamphleteers were also quite explicit in including sheep among the cattle that declined in numbers on enclosure. This no doubt partly reflected the abandonment of the old wool flocks of the smaller and less demanding fallow sheep. On the 'extensive sheep-walks' at Misterton, according to the second edition of Burton's book, 'the breed of sheep are noted for their size, and the extraordinary quantity of wool they yield', possibly already a five or six pound fleece.[130] Indeed the distinction maintained in the inventories between 'follow sheep' – sheep kept on the 'follows' (fallows)[131] – and 'pasture sheep' makes it clear that they were considered separate breeds, the latter being worth up to twice as much. In seven inventories making the distinction in the 1680s, follow sheep averaged 5/8d. each and pasture sheep 10/3d.; in four of them some of the pasture sheep were worth well over twice the average follow sheep. This tends to confirm Lee's assertion that the graziers also had a monopoly of all the fat mutton. He mentioned too the advantages for 'the new manufactures' of hosiery, in that, doubtless because it was of an appropriately long staple, 'the fleece in grounds inclosed is usually fit to be combed for jersey, which in common Fields it is not'.[132] Where such wool is listed in the inventories, it appears to have been valuable, in a couple of cases amounting to one quarter of the value of the flock of sheep.

To sum up the changes in livestock that accompanied the improved farming, therefore, the numbers decreased but the quality, or rather the profits to be made, increased. Only in the case of beasts is there no suggestion of a change of breed. It is thus not surprising that the selective breeders of the eighteenth century found little that needed to be done to improve the Leicestershire draught horse.[133] The pasture sheep that had been developed in spite of the old estate farms became general throughout the area on pasture grounds and was no doubt the foundation of the Old Leicester breed.

It is now possible to identify one of the most significant changes in the farming economy of the area. Whereas during the sixteenth century there had developed a sharp contrast between the ancient enclosures and the common fields, these two types of field both still shared one important feature, the old-style wool flock, which in each case stood as a barrier to progress. In the 1620s this barrier was swept away, and the next generation saw changes in the use of the ancient enclosures, and also changes in the use of the fields of many of the villages in the area, which involved the end of the mixed husbandry of the common fields. These changes constituted a new type of farming, improving farming. Previously the two types of farm, the estate pasture-farm and the common-field holding, had been poles apart and the only progress that had been possible had depended on the interaction between the two. The new changes broke down the old distinction and saw the rise of two new kinds of improving farmer, both producing for the market, namely the large-scale arable farmer and the grazing farmer taking advantage of improved pastures.

The innovation of cropping pasture grounds provided an opportunity of improving the quality of the pasture when it was laid down again. There is no doubt that the great achievement of this period was the new high level of grazing farming that this made possible, and landlords were able, by means of short leases at rack rents, to have their land improved for them and to let it again at enhanced grazing rents to grazing farmers. This would open the way for a new kind of gentry, rentiers rather than manorial lords. If this was the achievement, what was the means of achieving it?

It will be shewn below that large-scale corn-production, involving the ploughing and cropping of areas of pasture ground, was at first undertaken by townsmen in response to local needs which were centred on the town's corn market. But the developments which this triggered off spread throughout the area, and before long the initiative had passed to a new breed of farmer in the area, the large-scale arable farmer. At first sight there is a paradox here, as it has been emphasized that there was no mixed farming based on holdings in enclosed townships, and this applies whether they were of ancient or of new enclosure. The solution will be seen in the fact that the principal agents in the transformation, whether townsmen or villagers, were the large mixed farmers based on common-field holdings and taking pasture grounds in hand. These were the men who owned the large horses and heavy equipment, including wagons, whose dairies, unlike those of other farmers in the same villages, built up stocks of produce and whose sheep were of both types, follow and pasture sheep.

Such farmers no doubt took advantage of the availability of large numbers of labourers, not only in the town but also in those villages where they had managed to settle precariously. The enclosures themselves released a whole new wave of labourers. At first the activity in the area, not only the ditching and hedging within enclosed grounds of both types, but also the large-scale arable farming itself and the cultivation of labour-intensive pioneer crops, provided additional employment. By the later century, however, it must have been apparent that the overall effect was an increase in the profits to be made by commercial farmers, whether they concentrated on grazing alone or on grazing and arable farming, and a decline in the amount of labour needed as a result of improved efficiency. In other words the seventeenth century saw a great stride being taken from the inflexible economy of the open fields of both types – both common fields and ancient pasture grounds – towards the almost exclusively grazing economy of the later eighteenth century. But if in the long run the end of the changes that went with enclosure at this stage was the improved pasture farming, the means was improved arable farming; and as nearly all arable farmers in the area, including large-scale improving farmers, were based on villages that retained their common fields, it is necessary to explore this matter further with a study of common-field farming in the seventeenth century.

5.   Common-field farming in the seventeenth century

Sixteen villages in the Lutterworth area retained their common fields after 1665 and all but three of these for another century as well (see Map IV). It might be assumed that this was a case of the old peasant husbandry surviving while external influences brought the mid-seventeenth century phase of enclosure to an end. It appears, however, that the internal structure of these villages was so altered at this stage that further enclosure was unnecessary. The inventories continue to list all the component parts typical of the mixed husbandry; but a closer examination, with the benefit of the local pamphlets, will help to shew the influence of the changing economy and to reveal the conflicts within the villages.

How did the communal husbandry survive? At the top of the economic scale it has already been seen that there were commercial farmers who had a new opportunity of adapting their production to suit the markets. At the other end how did the small farmer, the husbandman, fare, and the cottager too, at a time when their counterparts were being squeezed out of the enclosing villages?

Mixed farmers, smallholders and cottagers

When it comes to examining the fortunes of each layer of the common-field farming community in the seventeenth century it is at once apparent that the top layer has already been described. It consisted of the large-scale mixed farmers, heavily equipped for improved arable farming and for improved grazing, achieving these ends by taking on enclosed grounds outside the common fields. It might be expected that these cuckoos ill-fitted their common-field nests. What effect did their presence have on the husbandry of the rest of the village working alongside them? Were the ordinary farmers also able to benefit from the use of heavy horses, wagons, improved stock and even convertible husbandry?

The overlap between the two types of farming land appears to have been so general among the larger mixed farmers, even where it cannot be proven, that it is not possible to separate out the inventories of those whose farming activity was confined to the fields of their own village. The different crops were not so often named as in the sixteenth century and acreages were never specified, except where a crop was growing on enclosed ground. This makes it unlikely that a table like the one provided by Hoskins in his essay 'The Leicestershire Farmer in the Seventeenth Century', which shews the acreages of crops in inventories from 1669 to 1672, will be informative about common-field farming practice. In any case some of the places listed in that table were already enclosed.[134] While the fortunes of ordinary common-field farming cannot, therefore, be demonstrated by comparing inventory average totals, the development of its main features can at least be traced by taking all the inventories of mixed farmers as one class.

By the 1680s it was rare for the fully equipped mixed farmer in the Lutterworth area to have crops worth under £20. Wheat and barley remained the chief grain crops. Rye was grown less frequently; perhaps its former use had been to diversify the winter bread-corn when husbandry had been more in the nature of subsistence farming. Oats still featured, but mainly on the larger farms, which may confirm its connexion with the larger draught horses kept there. The most important fodder crop, and the one universally grown, remained the peas crop. It seems, therefore, that the common fields, once the only source of corn for the market, remained the main regular source.

As the proportion of the average inventory total attributable to crops held up in the 1680s, in spite of low grain prices, it might be argued that the common-field farmer was concentrating more than ever on producing crops for the market. On the other hand the crop valuations included not only the peas crop but also the hay, and there are indications that the quantity of hay taken off the common fields increased during the century. It remains possible, therefore, that the common-field farmer was also very much in competition with the pasture farmer in the market for selling animals and their products. What sort of livestock was being kept on the common-field mixed farm?

Lee's contempt for the quality of common-field horses could not conceal the advantage they had in numbers. By the 1680s, however, common-field farms supported a great range in value of horses.[135] Those forming the heavy plough and wagon teams were worth up to £10 each, while on the mixed farms in the crowded village of Ullesthorpe the average value was £3.3.9d., and in Lutterworth no more than £2.4.6d. At the same time the chances of the ordinary common-field farmer being able to breed his own working horses had still further declined; the proportion of young horses was down to 7 *per cent*, and there were three horses or geldings for every one mare. This highlights his need to make the best use of his grazing rights in the fields.

If these changes give the impression that the ordinary common-field farmer was relying more on the arable side of his farm, this is confirmed again by the beasts he kept. The common fields were still further from being able to fatten any beasts for beef. The chief activity remained the buying and selling centred round the small dairy herd. Indeed the average value of a beast here actually fell from £1.19.0 in the 1630s to £1.13.0 in the 1680s. If there was any intensification it was more in the direction of dairy production for the market. It was still, however, very unusual for anyone to keep more than half a dozen milk cows. Here again it is hard to avoid the suspicion that the farmers with considerable stocks of dairy produce all had access to pasture grounds. One such farmer, who died in Claybrook magna owning 100 cheeses and 40 pounds of butter, together worth £7, had taken a lease of 35 acres of enclosed ground in Wibtoft.[136] Meanwhile among the nine mixed farming inventories from the adjoining township of Ullesthorpe the only trace of dairying is that one yeoman owned a cheese rack.

The fall in the size of the sheep flocks kept on the mixed farms, which is shewn by a comparison between the inventories from the 1590s and those from the 1630s, no doubt reflects the further change in emphasis away from the store flock towards feeding for mutton production, especially after the fall in the profits to be made from the short-staple wool of follow sheep in the 1620s. The figures in Table 3.5 are based on all the mixed farming inventories specifying sheep numbers, including those from the enclosing

Table 3.5 Lutterworth area: sizes of sheep flocks in mixed farming inventories (flocks of more than five sheep)

	1590s	1630s	1680s
Number of flocks	37	35	32
Average number in flock	59	48	58½
Number in median flock	48	33	46/50

Source: probate inventories at L.R.O. of inhabitants of surviving open-field villages in the Lutterworth area

villages before enclosure. It will be seen that the flock size recovered by the 1680s, perhaps suggesting that the larger farmers had succeeded in engrossing to themselves the sheep commons of those who could no longer keep sheep. The will of one mixed farmer records his purchase of 'one land and six sheep commons' but it may have been normal practice to let grazing rights too.[137] The figures for the 1680s, however, are considerably affected by the larger flocks, including pasture sheep, of those who had resources outside the common fields; so the density of sheep-stocking on the fields may in fact have remained at the lower level.

The contrast between follow and pasture sheep has already been emphasized. Between the 1590s and the 1680s the average value of all the sheep kept by common-field mixed farmers, including their pasture sheep, increased only slightly. In the villages that retained their common fields it was 4/11d. in the 1590s, 5/1d. in the 1630s and 5/4d. in the 1680s. So it is quite possible that the value of a follow sheep was actually declining during the seventeenth century.

In the 1630s the proportion of mixed farms with no flocks of sheep shewed a marked seasonal variation. Of the 63 mixed farming inventories from the villages with common fields, including those about to be enclosed, 18 list no flock. Among the 13 from the months of January and February there are seven without, but among the 24 from the following four months there are only two without. This too points to the abandonment of the common wool flock. Whereas previously every farmer had in effect owned a share in the common flock of "store" sheep, he was now either more involved each year in buying and selling "feeding" sheep which were ultimately intended for mutton[138] (in which case he may have been unwilling or, in some years, unable to keep any at all through the winter), or else he gave up sheep-keeping completely.

When it came to fattening for mutton on grass the common-field farmer could not compete with the pasture farmer. Perhaps he had settled down to breeding and bringing on sheep suitable for finishing off on pasture grounds.

In other words the activity which in the sixteenth century had been limited to those common-field farmers who had access to pastures had spread further down the scale. Using the static information in the inventories it is not possible to be sure on this point; but it seems likely that the situation was a complex one. The fact that a distinction was made between fallow and pasture sheep makes it certain that different breeds were involved. Probably the core of the common flock remained unchanged in breed; for although the return from its wool never revived after the 1620s, its role in the husbandry cycle was still vital. Moreover it was by no means useless as a mutton animal and was very probably prized as being 'particularly agreeable to the taste'.[139] In the meantime, those farmers who were involved in buying and selling sheep to be finished off as fat mutton, either by themselves or by others, no doubt made sure that as many as possible were of the pasture breed.

While Lee maintained that graziers had the monopoly of fat mutton, Moore claimed that common-field farming produced great numbers of fat muttons for the market. The pure grazier was limited to the grass yield of his grounds; but the muttons Moore referred to were fed on the peas crop.[140] In this the common-field farmer still had the start on the grazier in the spring. Consequently, as Moore pointed out, the two methods of fattening worked to some extent as complementary supplies: 'The Common fields breed Cattell, and in fruitful years feed them too.'[141] In a year when grass was short, a year which might well favour the peas crop, the common-field farmers would be able to take a larger share of the market for fat mutton.

> But also we have fed them with fat mutton, and swines flesh, yea also with victualling our ships by our pease and beans that come by the plough. As our open fields breed abundance of sheep, so the plough provides abundance of the aforesaid provisions to feed them fat; yea, at such times when no fat flesh is to be had elsewhere in the Nation.[142]

Fattening mutton on peas, however, for sale, rather than for home consumption, was an activity beyond the smaller farmer. All of his peas crop would be required to maintain his horses; '. . . the pease for the most part being all spent in seed and keeping of horses, and seldom any profit made of them', as Lee put it.[143] In conclusion he was no doubt correct in holding that sheep fed from the common fields were, 'neither in their bodies, nor in their fleeces', as profitable as they might be in enclosed grounds.[144]

What other meat did the mixed farmer produce? Moore claimed swine's flesh as an export from the region. The fact, however, that he mentioned beans in this context, a crop hardly grown at all in the Lutterworth area, suggests that he may have been thinking of elsewhere, such as the Hinckley area. Hinckley market was noted for swine.[145] Swine were certainly kept on every mixed farm in the Lutterworth area, but not in such numbers as to suggest that they were bred for sale; and they were only fattened one or two at a time, no more than might be expected to go with the domestic dairy. It is also worth noting that poultry was listed neither so regularly nor in such variety as in the sixteenth century. Presumably the more commercially minded farmer found it easier to purchase trifles like eggs and chickens as and when needed.

To sum up, therefore, it can be said that for the larger common-field farmer agriculture had become a much more commercial activity. His arable side was heavily equipped for raising large crops and for transporting them. But he was also concentrating on his livestock, not only the new breed of horses, but also cows for dairying and sheep for mutton, involving the pasture breed of sheep. The poorer common-field farmer, on the other hand, was not only confined to the common fields of his own village, but was also being held back in the economy of the old husbandry. His horses were limited both by the commons and by the peas crop, his beasts were limited so far as beef production and dairying were concerned and he had little or no chance of taking advantage of the pasture breed of sheep.

One of the most striking features of the series of inventories is the sudden increase in their numbers in the early seventeenth century, there being well over half again as many from the 1630s as from the 1590s (see Appendix Table 7.b). This increase was largely confined to the villages that retained their common fields. Comparing their inventory figures and population figures with those of the enclosing villages shews that they were under-represented in the records in the 1590s, while by the 1680s, and possibly the 1630s, the representation was more even. This suggests that the change was due not so much to their population growth as to a larger proportion of their inhabitants being concerned with probate. Breaking the figures down between the different types of farmer, the most remarkable increase was in the number of inventories ascribed to smallholders. There were four times as many from the 1630s as from the 1590s. There is no need to suppose that this represents any great subdivision of holdings to accommodate more husbandmen. It was evidently a case of a new layer of the farming community, people previously concerned with supplying the household, being launched into market production. It is possible to identify how this came about and what were the products that they were able to sell.

The factor that distinguished the smallholder from the cottager was that he occupied a small common-field farm, usually a fractional yard land holding. The factor that distinguished him from the mixed farmer was that he owned no team of horses. So few horses were kept by smallholders that it is unlikely that they regularly contributed to shared teams; presumably they relied on communal husbandry or had their lands tilled along with those of the farmers for whom they worked. If a man could survive without a team, what was to be gained by keeping the odd horse? It might consume more peas than he could raise on his holding and make demands on the grass and hay needed for his cows. There was usually a prohibition on the letting of horse commons, as at Ullesthorpe and Gilmorton; so if he did not stock them he would lose all the benefit.[146] The few horses that smallholders did keep might well have invited Lee's contempt. Eleven of the 40 smallholders' inventories from the 1680s include a horse. They were worth only £1.14.0 on average, under half the average on the mixed farms, and several were actually described as 'poor' or 'old'.

Beasts were, of course, the smallholder's most indispensable livestock, the average number being three, often specified as two cows and a heifer. Any extra calves would have had to be sold off owing to restrictions as to common pasture.[147] The average value of the beasts kept on the mixed farms rose from £1.7.0 in the 1590s to £1.19.0 in the 1630s. On the smallholdings it rose distinctly more, from £1.6.4d. to £2.1.6d., suggesting that the smallholder was concentrating as far as possible on dairying. Half of the inventories from each of these decades do in fact contain clues confirming this activity. Conversely, by the 1680s the smallholders' beasts had fallen more in value than the others, down to £1.11.0 as opposed to £1.13.0, and only a quarter of the inventories suggest dairying. In other words the beasts kept by the smallholders were reduced again to no more than a couple of house-cows and a follower.

Of the smallholders who left inventories a number had small flocks of sheep, but half of them kept no sheep at all, so that the larger flocks among them appear not so much as an integral part of their regular farming as an extra undertaking. The number of sheep commons that went with a fractional yard land holding probably offered no possibilities for a wool flock of any significance and the holding itself none for fattening mutton. The smallholder that Lee termed 'the weak and unstocked husbandman' was thus a very pervasive figure. It is quite clear that what caused Lee anxiety was that such a man kept no sheep; he was 'An husbandman unstocked and unfurnished with sheep'.[148] If he was not using such sheep commons as he was entitled to, he would be reduced to buying his mutton from the local butchers. He probably had to buy any wool he needed as well; only two of the 40 smallholders' inventories from the 1680s list any wool worth valuing. About half of them include a swine or two and sufficient poultry to suggest that some was generally kept. Otherwise in each decade a few of these people kept hives of bees valuable enough to be included.

At best, therefore, the smallholder had calves, poultry, eggs and pigs (young swine) for sale; but his main source of regular income of this sort, his dairy production, died out during the mid-century, presumably because of competition from more commercial farmers. At worst his holding offered him little entry into the market, especially so far as sheep-keeping was concerned. In this respect, therefore, he was no better off than the cottager. To return to what did distinguish him from the cottager, his lands in the fields, it must be asked what use he could make of them.

In the first place it is obvious that the smallholder would have been anxious to keep as many of his lands as possible under crops, unlike the larger farmer who was interested in keeping lands as leys of pasture. In Lutterworth in 1607 nearly 15 *per cent* of the area of lands held in the fields by tenants by demise was in leys. Of the nine smallholdings only two included leys, amounting to half that proportion of their area. The smallholder had no meadow ground; but so long as he could gather enough hay to winter his couple of cows from off his odd ley and any of his headlands kept as headleys, he could concentrate on raising corn on the rest of his lands. Whether or not he was constrained to raise peas in the peas field, his corn crop must have been his most important insurance against the vagaries of the market, providing at least for his own household in all save the very worst years. Indeed it seems that his corn crop was also the one regular product of his holding which he might take to market. Several of the smallholders' inventories from the 1680s mention wheat, in particular seven out of the eight from Arnesby and Shearsby. Perhaps here this was intended for the Leicester market. But the smallholder could only continue in this so long as the yield from his lands and the price in the market both held up. By the mid-century uninterrupted cropping was exhausting the former and the latter was depressed by the improved arable farming. At such times the smallholder found himself, for all his labours, hardly any better off than the cottager. In Lee's words:

> . . the arable Land turns the husbandman to little profit, his great pains and cost considered, which I conceive is the reason of that maxim of the husbandman, That he that gives more Rent for his Land than the Hay and Commons are worth, hath but a hard bargain: his labour and charge in dressing seeds and inning, amounting to near as much as his Crop of grain is worth.[149]

The cottager too was being pinched, not only by the over-stocking of the commons, but also by regulations designed to restrict the use made of the commons by new inmates and new cottagers. Complaints among common-field farmers concentrated against these new arrivals, so that a distinction was made between the "ancient cottage" and the "(new-)erected cottage" or "illegal cottage". Generally the enclosing villages were more successful in excluding immigrants or in preventing them acquiring grazing rights. As already noted, Lee boasted of his own village of Catthorpe that in addition to the 'five or six ancient Cottages', 'there are only four erected Cottages in the Town'.[150] On the other hand:

> In all, or most towns where the Fields lie open and are used in common, besides houses of husbandry, and ancient cottages, that have right of common, there is a new brood of upstart intruders, as inmates, and the inhabitants of unlawful cottages erected contrary unto law; who live upon the spoil of other men . . .[151]

In such villages, however, the owner of a cottage who had a use for the labour of its occupant was quite prepared to contravene the law requiring four acres for each cottage. In Gilmorton notice was taken in 1607 of four newly erected cottages and by 1629 11 men were paying a fine of £2 each 'for continuing of one Cottage one month without land contrary to the statute'.[152] Lee pointed out the impossibility of preventing the new cottagers from taking a share in communal property, such as by putting a house-cow on the commons.[153] The inventories cannot, of course, be used to prove the seriousness of the problem, but the few that can be ascribed to a cottager confirm that his most important farming asset was a couple of cows and that he kept neither a horse nor any sheep. The beasts were worth almost exactly the same as those of the smallholders in the 1590s and 1630s; but by the 1680s they had declined dramatically, from an average of £2.2.0 a head to £1.7.0, back in fact to the average value of a beast in the inventories from the 1590s. This at least is evidence of the over-stocking of the fields or rather of the restrictions on the cottagers' grazing there; for, as they had no lands in the fields and no share in the meadows, their cows were entirely dependent on the commons.

The common-field villages, therefore, contained the widest range of types of farmer in the area, only the small dairy farmer and the large pure grazier being generally absent. At the top end of the scale was the commercial mixed farmer, able to undertake the improving cropping of pasture grounds and also to fatten stock on both pasture and fodder crops. At the other end were the smallholders struggling to maintain their few arable lands as some sort of subsistence farm, exhausting the soil in the process and being reduced to little better than cottagers. Together with the cottagers they tended to join the landless labourers who crowded these villages seeking work on the large farms and, for want of work, swelling the numbers of poor to be supported there.

Some idea of the proportions in which these elements made up the village communities may be gained from an analysis of the occupations given in the parish registers in the 1630s. Evidently the main changes were yet to come, as there was no great contrast between the two types of village, those that were to retain their common fields and those that enclosed at this stage. Taking together, therefore, all the people whose occupations were given, just under half of them were yeomen and husbandmen and other farmers, including gentry and clergy, and just under 30 *per cent* were labourers, cottiers, servants, etc. The inventories do point to one contrast, in that there was a greater proportion of them with no farming stock from the common-field villages in the 1630s and 1680s. The commonest feature of these 53 inventories is a sum of money or debts owed; but around half of them are of women, mainly widows. The six of labourers and two of servants, however, serve to shew that not all the landless here were poor.

Having identified the interests of the different classes dependent on the common fields, an examination of the uses made of the different resources there will help establish what effect the changes in the farming economy had on the common-field farming system.

The common fields

The most characteristic feature of the common-field holding was the dispersal of the lands over the fields. This obviously was best suited to the communal husbandry that had given rise to the system. So long as the fields remained truly open and were farmed in common the compulsion to consolidate lands was probably never strong, but as farmers became independent of each other they would have found disadvantages. The fully equipped farmer would have agreed with Lee's criticism:

> . . in common fields, where divers mens lands lie intermixt, and every mans lands dispersed so, that many parcels in many places, and sometimes far asunder, go to make up one Acre, there is occasion of great inconvenience, and charge to the owners divers ways. Many days works are cast away, and much labour is lost in the ploughing of the land, in the carriage of Manure, and inning of the crop, which might be spared, if the land lay all together, as it doth in Inclosures.[154]

To these disadvantages of the scattered lands Lee added the troubles of trespass and trampling resulting from over-stocking and from increased livestock movements and droving.[155]

There was probably nothing new in the substance of these complaints. More important, however, was Lee's assertion that the arable lands were being exhausted:

> . . there is a great deal of land in common fields, which formerly hath been good, and might be so again, utterly spoiled for want of good husbandry.[156]

Who was responsible for this? When Lee wrote:

> Tillage lands in Common-fields have no rest at all, wherewith to be rich and fertile; and so the husbandmen are necessitated to plough the same land each year, though it be barren, to the utter undoing of the weak or unstocked husbandman.[157]

his sympathy appears to have been with the poor husbandman; in truth, however, it is clear that he believed that it was the perversity of such men that was the cause.[158] Who was this husbandman but the smallholder that has already been described as desperate to keep up the area of his crops?

Wherever it was decided to leave a proportion of the arable lands down as leys, this would have been of least advantage to the smallholder. Eighteenth-century examples of such agreements included leaving narrow balks of grass between each of the lands in a furlong. There was at least one such provision in force in the Lutterworth area in the later seventeenth century. This was in Ullesthorpe, where the balks were to be three feet wide.[159] Similarly fines for ploughing up more ground than was allowed were heavy. In Ullesthorpe every man was 'stinted as to ploughing' and to prevent such cheating the village jury had the responsibility of marking out the lands before ploughing started.[160]

What prevented the complete exhaustion of the soil was the preparation that was possible every third year in the fallow field. Apart from the folding, this involved repeated tillage. Moore mentioned 'the *following tilth*, . . the *stirring tilth*, . . the *airing up tilth*, (and) the *sowing tilth*' and according to Lee 'The white corn, as Wheat and Barley, hath 4 or 5 tilths yearly where it is sown'.[161] This endless labour may well have been tolerable in a largely subsistence economy, but could hardly continue, especially on a small scale, when competing in the market with the improved arable farming.

It has been suggested that the common fields remained the principal regular source of corn for the market. Here too, however, the larger farmers, with their heavy horses and implements, were at an advantage in comparison with the ordinary mixed farmer. Moreover there is every likelihood that they were also able to increase their advantage by folding their pasture-fed sheep privately on their own arable lands. The inventories shew that on larger mixed farms fleaks, hurdles and pales worth valuing were not unusual. They would be required for contributing to the common fold. A large number of fleaks or a complete fold, which could have been used for private folding, was normally only to be found on the farm of a squire with enclosed demesne grounds in addition to his common-field holding. Private folding by men in this position is implied by Lee.[162] The heavy yields achieved on these well-manured lands would have thrown into relief the poverty of the ordinary farmer's lands alongside them. It was clear to Lee that the husbandman, with his 'hard bargain', was fighting a losing battle: for his complaints that bad husbandry was exhausting the lands cannot have referred to the arable of the largest and most successful farmers.

As for the grass resources of the fields, the old low-lying meadows remained the primary source of hay. The only chance of increasing the yield here was to enclose them and so restrict their use as common pasture. As Lee noted, this was in fact done in some places where the rest of the fields remained open.[163] Since only the mixed farmers had a share of the hay crop there, however, this was yet another case of excluding the smallholders and cottagers from one of the common resources of the fields.

The largest area of common grazing was the fallow field. This was, however, for the summer months at least, reserved for the fallow flock.[164] Any increase in the area of ground left under grass in the fields, therefore, especially the balks between the lands which were too small for use except as grazing in common, tended to benefit mainly the sheep-owners. And these, as has been pointed out, were by the seventeenth century a more or less restricted class. This may partly explain the orders limiting ploughing.

After the harvest the two stubble fields also were thrown open for common grazing. This continued into the winter, even over the young winter wheat. Careful grazing of wheat can be beneficial; but where there was over-stocking or where many of the sheep belonged to men who had no interest in the arable crops, it did more harm than good. The regulations at Ullesthorpe shew that the great cattle were taken off the two corn fields before Christmas,[165] but not before they too would have contributed to the damage done in a wet year. In Lee's words:

> . . for the most part in the winter time cattle of all sorts, both small and great, are suffered at their pleasures to go over the fields, where Corn is sown, and do more hurt with their feet than with their mouths, especially when the weather is wet . .[166]

The problem that haunted the common-field farmers was how to accommodate the great cattle when the sheep were in the fallow and the other two fields were under corn. So far as horses were concerned, the mixed farmers, who were of course the principal horse-owners, could solve the problem largely by tethering them on their leys in the two corn fields. But, in addition to the horses and beasts of the farmers and smallholders, there was the problem of the house-cows belonging to the occupants of cottages, both ancient and illegal. The worry was mainly, therefore, how to provide cow pasture for a herd several hundred strong. Lee mentioned that '. . . Cows, 200, 300, or 400 are kept on a ruck, or herd, driven to and fro by day . . .'[167] In Lutterworth in 1607 the formal stints allowed for 204 beasts among the farmers. There were 51 cow pastures listed for smallholders and cottagers; so any unofficial cottagers' cows would have swelled the number here at least towards Lee's middle figure.

All the small areas of grass ground within the three fields, such as roadways, slades and meres, were carefully pressed into service for grazing the great cattle. Of course only two parts of them would be available in any one year, the other part being in the fallow field. This could be one reason for fines levied in Gilmorton 'for tying a Cow upon broken grass'. Ploughing up these areas was either impossible or else actually forbidden. In the same village the fine was 3/4d. 'for ploughing out into the Common high way contrary to a pain'.[168] The smaller pieces were used for grazing tethered horses and the larger for grazing beasts under supervision. In Lutterworth the 40 such pieces provided 46¼ acres of common pasture for draught animals, just under half designated as for horses and the rest for *averia* (draught beasts). The only men to keep such great cattle, however, were the mixed farmers. Evidently the men with holdings of lands in the fields were reserving the benefit of this grass for themselves to the exclusion of others with common grazing rights.

Another source of common grazing was the last of the waste or heath ground left outside the fields, brought under control and forming the area known as the 'Cow Pasture'. Such pastures have been hailed as a seventeenth-century innovation, formed by laying down common-field arable to grass and possibly connected with "convertible husbandry".[169] This may have been the case in other regions better endowed with grazing ground, where the farmers could use such pastures for beasts, oxen, neats or bullocks.[170] In this region, however, its name proclaims it to have been primarily intended for the beasts of the poorer members of the community so that it was, in effect, no more than what in some places was called the 'Cottage Pasture'. As to quality, it was the worst ground in the parish. In Ashby parva it was on a poorly watered plateau near the western edge of the parish, recently known as 'Poverty Knob'. In Kettering in Northamptonshire 'The Cottagers Common called Kettering Links' had formerly been the manorial coney warren.[171] Apart from this the cottagers, even those with legal rights of common, were not allowed undisturbed and exclusive occupation of their pasture. In 1670 four Monks Kirby husbandmen agreed to resign their rights in the Cottage Pasture and to take instead part of the New Inclosure, presumably the New Cottage Pasture. At Stoneleigh, also in Warwickshire, in 1597 ' 'the cottingers . . now hold in regard of their common new tilled' a field of 37 acres called Stony Dales' to share between all 27 of them.[172] It is very likely that the cottagers received the worst of the bargain at each such exchange. But there were also simultaneous rival claims made on their pasture. In Monks Kirby farm holdings included 'leys in common saving to cut the furze thereon growing' and in Lutterworth the interest that the mixed farmers had in 27 acres of heath called 'the Cow Pasture' consisted of leys of furze or gorse. Such leys, rather than being evidence of recent pasture-improvement by ploughing, should perhaps be thought of as the last vestiges of an occasionally cropped outfield. Whatever their origin, however, the farmers no doubt prevented any improvement in the quality of the grazing there which would have endangered their source of fuel.

By the late sixteenth century the leys of pasture in the three fields, the 'Lammas Lands', had become a more or less regular and permanent feature of the farming system. When in one of the two fields under corn they provided the farmers with an important additional source of hay; indeed they were probably charged with the same rates as meadows. They also allowed the farmers greater flexibility in grazing their own stock, especially the great cattle. A suggestion has also been made that some furlongs of leys were at this stage cropped occasionally and that this gave the farmers an opportunity of improving the quality of their pasture when laying it down to grass again.[173] So long, however, as the leys remained part of the open fields and subject to common grazing, there was little to be gained in this way. The local evidence that has been produced to support this theory is in fact negative. This was an order made around 1624 in Leicester to restore to grass leys ploughed there during the preceding eight years. Similarly in Gilmorton in 1622 one man was fined 3/4d. for ploughing up two headleys and the offender already quoted as fined the same sum for ploughing out into the common highway was also fined 10/- for ploughing a ley.[174] Like the early cropping of closes, these appear to have been *ad hoc* responses to corn shortages in years like 1608, 1615 and 1622 rather than a deliberate farming policy.

To save the constant supervision of the cows and tethered horses grazing on the leys in the corn and to avoid spoiling their neighbours' crops, farmers in some villages were apparently allowed to form temporary fences or even ditches and hedges around their permanent leys. This is recorded in the case of Wigston magna, ten miles north of Lutterworth. Perhaps farmers with adjacent leys cooperated in this; and consolidation may have been an important issue at this stage.[175] As, however, the benefit of the grazing of all the grass growing in the fallow field went chiefly to the sheep-owners, it may eventually have been easy to agree that such hedges might be used to withhold the Lammas Lands from the common pasture during the cropping season in the fallow year as well. In other words barriers erected originally to keep farmers' cattle in were later used to keep the commoners' cattle out.

This would have been a crucial step in the transformation of leys into Lammas Closes; for, after this, by careful mowing and grazing, a farmer could retain for himself practically all the benefit of any improvement he might make to the quality of the grass on them. As, moreover, their only contribution to the common grazing in any of the three years would be the aftermath, it would not be difficult to withdraw them for longer periods so as to carry out a programme of private cropping and pasture-improvement. Thus it seems that the changing uses made of the leys in the seventeenth century opened up by degrees the way for some improving farming within the common fields. In this case the possibility of pioneer crops being grown there too should not be ruled out. At Ashby parva furze called 'Lincroft' and furlongs named 'Flaxen Knolls' and 'Hemp Brooks' in the early seventeenth century possibly reflect no more than domestic crops grown there before final enclosure. Similarly at Leire there was 'a little close of two leys called Flax lands'. At Shawell, on the other hand, there were actually leys called 'Flax Leys' and both there and at Catthorpe there was a roper or linen-dresser at work a generation before the final enclosures in the mid-century.[176]

The first Lammas Close traced in the area was in existence in 1618. This was in Ashby parva, which had two next to the village and an isolated close, later known as 'Top of Town Close' or 'Lammas Close', not far from the churchyard. Possibly the nearby closes called 'Three Leys' and 'Six Leys' and the 'three leyes close' in Wigston magna also functioned as Lammas Closes. In Claybrook parva there was 'hard-by the town side a close called the Lammas Close, hedged round about, containing ten leyes'.[177] All the Lammas Closes traced in the area were of only a few acres each, but the fact that they all appear to have been extensions to 'the ring of the town' round the home closes suggests that they were important not only for the crops that they yielded. Home closes were vital for private livestock-management and in particular the feeding of fodder crops in the winter. Other benefits may have followed, such as the opportunity for a farmer with no pasture grounds to engage in some private folding and perhaps eventually this development made way for the raising of new fodder crops. Moreover it is by no means certain that piecemeal enclosure at this stage was limited to Lammas Closes near the village. Land just inside the township of Ullesthorpe and belonging to the Beales, the chief yeoman family in the adjacent parish of Ashby parva, was described in 1613 as 'land in the fields of Olesthorpe called Reddwong or Reddong' but by 1639 as 'one Close in Ullesthorpe called Redham Close'.[178]

Thus it can be seen that, beyond the home closes round the farmsteads, the common-field parishes contained different types of grass ground ranging from common pasture to what came to be virtually closes held in severalty. While the most spectacular changes were taking place in the enclosing parishes in the mid-century, it may be that the developments outlined here as taking place in the common fields, which gave the larger farmer some measure of freedom to improve his holding, were part of the same transformation and happened at exactly the same time. Even if the majority of the leys were concerned, however, the area involved was not sufficient to revolutionize, let alone to overthrow, the common-field farming system. In any case the greater part of the demand for improved pasture ground was no doubt met by the new enclosures outside these parishes. It is also conspicuous that the use made of leys does not feature as a matter of contention in the pamphlets of Moore and Lee.

The more settled state of affairs that followed these changes after 1665 was not without its internal conflicts of interest. At the top end of the economic scale both arable farmers and grazing farmers were pulling in the same direction, towards commercial agriculture, alternately raising increased crops, possibly on a reduced area of tillage, and raising grass on which to rear and feed improved livestock. At the lower end of the scale the interests were in opposition; on the one hand the smaller farmers were reduced to keeping more of their lands under corn than their farming could stand, thereby endangering the condition of the soil, while on the other hand the most harmful feature of common grazing, the menace of the cottagers of all kinds over-stocking the commons with house-cows, had to be contained and kept under control.

The problem of over-stocking was a notorious source of conflict by the mid-seventeenth century: 'neither is the way of intercommoning without its great disorders . . . so that the commons being overstinted . . . occasions many to think of Inclosure as the only Remedy'.[179] How was stocking of the fields regulated and who were the offenders?

In despair of actually preventing those cottagers who could afford cows from grazing them in the fields, the solution was to circumscribe as far as possible the commons available to them. As for mixed farmers and smallholders, their stock was stinted according to the size of their holdings. The yard land stint at Cotesbach was recorded in 1612 as three horses, four beasts and 30 sheep. At Monks Kirby, where the holding was more generous in size, it was eight beasts and 60 sheep in 1611. The 1607 Survey of Lutterworth gives it as three horses, three beasts and 35 sheep, making a total of 230 horses, 256½ beasts and 2,381½ sheep. Over the common fields of the town the density of stints going with the yard land holdings was one horse and one beast to every seven acres and five sheep to every three acres. These stints had become formalized and attached to their holdings as part of the property, like the 15 beast pastures mentioned as going with a lease of three yard land in Bitteswell in 1582.[180] The Lutterworth stint was already antiquated in 1607 in that 141 of the beasts were specified as draught animals (*averia*). By the mid-seventeenth century it was evidently acknowledged that the old stints were impractical, as the effective stints were being reduced in the manorial courts. At Shawell the sheep stint was reduced by six in 1639. At Wigston magna only about half of the total allowances of cows and sheep under the 'old stint' was being kept by the later seventeenth century. At Ullesthorpe the stint was set at three horses and 28 or 32 sheep in the 1680s.[181] Over the common fields there this made the density of stints going with yard land holdings one horse to every ten acres and one sheep to every acre. Being a crowded township, it may here be comparable with the town of Lutterworth, suggesting a reduction in stock density during the century. Lee cited one place he knew where 'the inhabitants agreed to abate of their ancient usual stint, one sheep in six, and one cow in three'.[182] A similar reduction in the enclosing village of Shawell made in 1656, three years after Lee was writing and ten years before the final enclosure there, increased the area from one acre for each sheep to four acres for every three and, very likely, the area for each cow from 12 acres to 18.[183] In so far as the problem was a numerical one, it may be seen as a parallel to the development in the enclosing parishes. The larger farmers in the common-field villages too were not interested so much in numbers as in quality. So long as stocking was by numbers, their larger horses and sheep took a greater share of the common grazing than the mean stock of the poorer farmers: in Lee's words, '. . . he that is rich, and full stocked, eateth with his cattle, not his own part only, but likewise his neighbours, who is poor, and out of stock'.[184] A reduction in the stint might satisfy the former as being in the best interests of good husbandry. Yet the smallholder stood to lose, perhaps, one of the three cows that were so vital to him, as did any farmer with a single yard land in Shawell in 1656. This was, therefore, another of the ways in which the smallholder was being reduced to little better than a cottager. At Wigston magna in 1707 under the 'new stint' a man with a quartern of a yard land could only tether either one horse or one cow. At Ashby parva in 1622, a generation before the final enclosure there, the owner of a quartern was already reduced to one cow common.[185]

The inhabitants of the place Lee cited 'yet did confess, that formerly their cattle had fared better at the long stint, than afterward they did at the short' and again 'they thought it necessary to make a greater abatement in the numbers of cattle . . .' Evidently the problem was not entirely one of numbers. It might be thought that the smallholder could well afford to forgo some of his sheep commons. Lee's preoccupation with the 'poor unstocked husbandman', however, gives warning that the position was not so simple. The dilemma that faced this man was that he could no longer afford to keep sheep of his own. At Hallaton, 17 miles north-east of Lutterworth, a case in 1665 dealt with this problem, starting with 'divers commoners, not being able to stock their commons' with sheep.[186] So as not to lose all the benefit of his commons, the obvious course for the husbandman was to set them to another man. In some places this was not allowed; perhaps these were the places where the smaller farmers capitulated at this stage and enclosure followed. Lee denounced the practice of setting commons as a case of the poor commoner being exploited by a rich man. But his specific proof is uncharacteristically vague; 'A sheeps grass in the Common-fields is not worth more than 2d. 4d. 6d. or at most 12d. per annum'.[187] This may be compared with valuations of 5d. at Lutterworth in 1607 and 4d. at Monks Kirby in 1611. Clearly what alarmed Lee was that this perverse bad husbandry was admitting onto the commons in rivalry to the farmers a man whose stock might be a match for theirs in feeding demands. If such a "common-field grazier" was an outsider, as at Hallaton in 1665, where the lettings were to 'all inhabitants of other towns', he might be beyond the scope of the common-field farming organization.

Owing to the overlap in their activities between the different kinds of land and between townships, it is not easy to separate out examples of common-field graziers from among the inventories. The inventories of eight men from the 1630s suggest this line of business. One was of a smallholder with half a yard land but 70 sheep worth, with their wool, £19. Another was William Coltman of Claybrook magna, shepherd, a pure grazing farmer with 15 barren sheep and 26 ewes and lambs 'in the fields of Claybrook'. The fact that there is none from the 1680s may indicate that by then the larger farmers had succeeded in bringing the practice under control. Among the

Lutterworth inventories there are several which suggest common-field graziers, but only from the 1630s onwards. They include the first Lutterworth man recorded as 'grazier', James Coltman, who died in 1658 owning 40 sheep.[188] The important difference is that in Lutterworth the practice continued. Out of seven such inventories from the last quarter of the century four expressly record the sheep as being in the (follow) field. In general, however, the introduction of outsiders as common-field graziers brought into the open the conflict between grazing and arable interests and was a crucial step towards the dissolution of the communal husbandry. A closer examination of the function of the sheep flock is needed to explain this.

The overnight folding of the sheep flock on the arable lands was an essential part of the common-field farming cycle, even on the heavy clays of the Midlands and where the villages had no extensive sheep walks outside the arable fields. Apart from the laborious carting out to the lands what little farmyard manure there was, it was the only means of fertilizing the soil. Lee noted the shortage of dung and straw for manuring the arable lands in the common fields.[189] A detailed analysis of the occurrence of manure among the inventories suggests that horses were only kept in until spring, while the manure from cows went on building up through the summer. The latter provided some smallholders with a useful amount of manure in the 1630s; but, in parallel with the decline in their stock, none by the 1680s. Meanwhile the increased quantities of manure on the larger farms, usually valued at three pounds in the 1680s, almost certainly came from the larger horses more than from the beasts. No lime has been traced in the area during the period, apart from that used in building. Nevertheless Moore claimed that 'Land folded with Sheep . . . affords as good Crops of Corn as any the earth brings forth'.[190] How was the folding organized?

Folding took place on the fallow field, that is in preparation for the winter corn crops in the white corn field. Presumably it started at some time when the ground was dry enough to stand the treatment. During the summer months the sheep would graze the fallow field. They would find grass only on those parts of the field that were not being tilled. This area, however, was probably being reduced by the withdrawal of leys or Lammas Lands as Lammas Closes; hence the importance of the pieces of grass ground and the balks between the lands, even though they were too narrow to graze by tethering when in one of the corn fields. Of much the greatest importance, however, was the period after Lammas, when Lammas Grounds were thrown open, and after harvest, when the sheep were allowed onto the stubble and grass in the other two fields. At Hallaton it was noted that 'The fields are always fresh and good at Lammas' and it was at Lammas that a regulation at Ullesthorpe compelling the overnight folding of sheep came into force. Depending on the weather, this might mean that the only really effective part of the common folding programme was very short. In 1685 the Ullesthorpe regulation lasted until the 10th or 11th of November but in the following year only until the 9th of October; but the sheep were not admitted to the peas field until the 25th of September, leaving only a fortnight of folding with the benefit of the grass from that field.[191] The operation could not be prolonged many weeks into the autumn for fear of the sheep-rot setting in, especially in a wet year. Lee pointed out several times that common-field flocks were far more susceptible to rots than pasture flocks precisely because of the folding. It is likely that the change in the breed of sheep aggravated the problem too; and a loss of potential mutton animals rather than part of a store flock would have been financially more serious.

The system could work well so long as farmers owned sheep to contribute to the flock in proportion to the size of their holdings. What happened when so many owned no sheep at all? In theory the men to whom they let their commons should have put their sheep into the common fold. The regulation at Ullesthorpe was that no man should set his sheep commons during folding time 'except their sheep be folded every night'. What the common-field grazier was interested in, however, was the grass that had been saved until Lammas. At Hallaton 'the commoner and stranger . . . make their bargain at or before that time', so that the strangers 'when the fields are fresh and full of grass, bring great flocks of sheep into the fields, and eat out the commoners of the town'. Such outsiders, with no interest in the arable lands, might have no scruples in drawing off the benefit of the fold of their sheep onto their own arable or pasture elsewhere. At Hallaton these common-field graziers, instead of folding the arable, were apparently folding their own closes of grass or pasture ground. Such sharp practice would doubtless have enraged Moore, who had disapproved of those who 'delight to sow the land with Sheep-trickles alone without Corn'.[192]

Of greater significance is the implication in Lee's writings that by this time private folding was not confined to pasture sheep and that it was possible for the farmers to discriminate against one who contributed no sheep to the commons by withholding the common fold from his lands. He exclaimed that 'The fallow field, to the weak or unstocked husbandman is a great charge, and of no profit'.[193] But, if the common fold still progressed over everyone's lands regardless, far from being of no profit, it should have been an unfair advantage to him. The sheep that stocked his commons, whether his own or another's, however, were of no use on their own; the folding operation depended on large numbers being penned into a small area. Accordingly he was forced to sell the folding of his sheep, no doubt to swell another farmer's private fold.[194] This throws new light on Lee's complaint about the bad husbandry of men who persisted in cropping more land than they could manure, thus wearing the land quite out of heart.[195] This may after all have resulted not so much from any wilful negligence on their part as from the strangle-hold the larger farmers had on a vital limb of the common husbandry.

Lee summed up the fate of the smaller farmer: 'The unstocked husbandman is consuming every year, like one in a consumption, and cannot help himself'.[196] He touched on the problems of such men in no fewer than 15 separate passages in his three pamphlets. Yet his anxiety on their behalf barely disguised his hostility towards them. They were, after all, the very class of farmer that he was advocating should be freed by enclosure from their agricultural labours for other employment. No doubt along with other landlords and farmers in the area, he was convinced that they were responsible for undermining the common-field system, to the disadvantage not only of themselves but also of the larger farmers engaged in serious farming. By hanging onto more arable than they could keep properly folded, they landed themselves in the impossible situation of raising corn at greater cost than the corn they could usually buy in the market while at the same time dragging down the condition of the arable lands. By hanging onto their sheep commons as a disposable asset when they could no longer use them as part of their own husbandry, they opened the door to the grazier whose activities could not be controlled by the farming community.

It is not surprising, therefore, that the problems of intercommoning were central to the enclosure controversy in the mid-century. It is well to remember that Moore's campaign was not aimed blindly at prohibiting enclosure but at avoiding it by bringing intercommoning under control.[197] Among Lee and other men advocating enclosure, however, the cow commons of the cottagers and the sheep commons of the poor husbandmen were singled out as targets to prove that the only solution was enclosure. But, as has been seen, the problem originated in the fundamental transformation of the local farming economy.

Before leaving the subject of the uses made of the common fields, one other aspect should be discussed. It was a commonplace among topographers throughout the period that the champion region of south Leicestershire was deficient in timber, wood and fuel.[198] Furze has already been mentioned and the "kids" of furze listed in the inventories confirm its importance. Farmers were able to keep some of their leys in the fields for this fuel; but the inventories also suggest that they at least were not short of wood, probably grown in the hedgerows around the home closes. There were also the common heaths and areas of furze near the boundaries between townships. Nevertheless, especially where the furze here too was claimed by the farmers, the poorer inhabitants were reduced to burning straw or cow dung, further contributions to the impoverishment of the arable lands. This was presumably the reason for the prohibition in Ullesthorpe against gathering muck 'off any known ground' without the owner's consent.[199]

It was asserted that enclosure would help solve the fuel shortage;[200] and of course the ancient pasture grounds were ringed by hedges and grew hedgerow timber and wood, like the 45 ashes and elms in the hedges round the Cotesbach Hall Close in 1589. The contrasting landscapes are well illustrated by the appearance of Lutterworth in 1607. Not one of the 1,223 trees within the manor (all but 15 of them ash trees) stood on the open fields; 916 were in Moorbarns and all the rest were in the closes forming the ring of the town.[201] It has now been seen that in the seventeenth century even the common-field landscape included a growing network of hedges, though not such an extensive one as came to cover the ancient and new enclosures. In dealing with the shortage of fuel Lee was uncharacteristically hesitant in advancing the argument that the new hedges would help in an area 'where wood is scarce, and coal not to be had, or only at excessive rates'.[202] There had been trouble in the sixteenth century from poor hedge-breakers from Lutterworth and elsewhere desperately taking fuel from the Misterton estate hedgerows.[203] The situation would become even more desperate as all the land of different kinds was subjected to intensive farming. Farmers in the area could doubtless grow more timber, wood and fuel in the later seventeenth century than had been growing there in the sixteenth; but it was far from being freely available. A report on Bittesby in 1681 stated 'that some of the fences are bad and there is but little wood upon the Estate' and 'That Pit coals are generally burnt in those parts'. In Ullesthorpe it was even ruled that 'No man woman or child shall cut or fetch any thorn boughs or furzes or break any hedges except (on) their own ground'.[204]

In conclusion it can be stated that at the upper end of the economic scale the strength of the surviving common-field villages was in the heavily equipped mixed farming that spread out to make use of the pasture grounds. Any industry, however, which expands to use more resources and improves in efficiency brings with it problems of redundancy and poverty. So the people at the lower end of these village communities were suffering in the changes. As control over the resources of the fields was drawn more tightly into the hands of those engaged in the serious business of commercial farming, so the smallholders were squeezed out of their subsistence farming. Similarly just as cottagers were reduced to squatting on what scraps of waste there were left, so their cows were confined to the worst pieces of pasture on land the least worth taking in hand and improving. Even the rights to take fuel from the commons were circumscribed.

Much of the land resources taken over by this farming, however, consisted of grounds outside the village where it was based. This included not only the ancient enclosures but also the new enclosures of the seventeenth century. Many of the labourers swelling the population of these villages, moreover, would have been from families driven out of the other villages by these very enclosures. It is necessary, therefore, to consider the changes that have been noted in the common-field villages in the context of the economy of the area as a whole.

6. Improving farmers and dispossessed peasants

Returning to a consideration of all three types of land in the area, the ancient enclosures, the new enclosures and the surviving common fields, it appears there are close parallels between the two phases of enclosure. In the period of early enclosure whole townships disappeared. There was no question of the small producer, the husbandman, surviving outside the context of the mixed husbandry of the common fields. So long as the main market output of sheep farming was wool there was, for instance, no place for the small grazier. The tracts of land enclosed at this stage, therefore, were for the most part taken over by the large-scale but low-level farming of the pasture estates. During the sixteenth century, and especially after the set-back in the woollen cloth industry in the mid-century, the benefit of the occupation of these grounds was increasingly drawn off by the more progressive members of the remaining farming communities. Until the 1620s, however, the grounds were still not free from their manorial ties in the form of the open-field wool flocks, albeit not common flocks but belonging to individuals.

By the early seventeenth century the remaining village communities were beginning to split into two types. In fact the occupation structure in the 1630s suggests very little in the way of a contrast that could not be ascribed to the changing concentration in population. The difference may have been more in the control of the husbandry and of the resources of the fields. One vital factor that has been pointed to was the control of the common flock. Where private folding of arable lands was allowed or where the letting of sheep commons was forbidden, the position of the subsistence farmers was very much weakened, especially after the 1620s when the returns from the wool of the follow sheep fell. It seems that, apart from any squire and leading yeoman families in these villages, the remainder of the community formed a more or less uniform peasant class, still embedded within the manorial organization. Whatever the reasons, however, this type of community was more vulnerable in the face of economic change and when its common fields were enclosed the old mixed husbandry died out completely. Thus whereas the early enclosures had started with the dying-out of mixed husbandry, and were not followed until over a century later by subdivision and improving farming, the seventeenth-century enclosures involved all these steps being taken in one generation.

Even if a smaller farmer survived enclosure so as to take occupation of his allotment, he could not continue his mixed husbandry. After the initial expense of ditching and hedging, without a team and implements he could not take advantage of the enclosure by improving his pasture quality. No doubt, therefore, many such people, even if their land was freehold, either sold out or let their holdings. The larger farmer stood to gain from the conversion if he continued as a grazier. He too, however, was being overtaken by the tide of change. He owned the land resources, but not the means to improve them. Whether or not he continued to farm, he had to leave the serious business of improving farming to the large mixed farmer based on a common-field farm, while he tended to isolate himself from the farming community as a member of the new local landowning class.

The places that retained their common fields were able to respond more vigorously to the changes and to accommodate a fuller range of activity. This explains not only the extraordinary rise in the number of smallholders appearing in the probate records between the 1590s and the 1630s but also the emergence of cottagers into the probate records in the 1590s from these villages only. Less rigorous control over immigration here led to poverty problems, but it also meant a freer supply of labourers to work for the larger farmers. The latter already occupied ancient enclosures and, when the wool store flocks were once out of the way, they were the men who took the initiative towards improving farming by breaking up these grounds for corn crops. This was no doubt prompted in the first place by the needs of the local population and the town's corn market, but the effect that the practice had on the local corn supply was probably the principal factor in the enclosures of the mid-century that represented the capitulation of the old mixed husbandry in the other villages. Even in the villages that retained, in theory, their common-field farming system, the effects of the transition were not so very much less serious for the lower sections of the community.

A simple way of ascertaining how the new commercial farming was based within the area in the period after the mid-century enclosures is to examine the farms of the wealthiest of the villagers who left inventories in the 1680s. Omitting the smallholders, the cottagers and all those with no farming stock, there were 85. Twenty eight had farming stock worth over £120. Out of the eight of these who were based on enclosed townships, only two were pure grazing farmers, namely John Haines, a shepherd from the anciently enclosed Misterton, and John Wigfall, the rector of the newly enclosed Peatling parva. The former may be taken to personify the triumph of professional stock-management over the old pasture-estate farm. He was probably the son of Thomas Haines, who had been the Misterton estate bailiff, and he owned £7 worth of cheese in the cheese chamber and £15 worth of wool.[205] The latter may be taken to personify the clerical interest in improvement at this period.

While Moore and Lee were disputing over the changing ideals, it is well to remember that as rectors they were also involved practically in farming, as occupants of glebe farms. Tithes were important in releasing fodder crops locally and also had an influence on local markets. Improved farming enormously enhanced the value of tithes. The rector of Lutterworth was beside himself with joy on being told by Anne Newcombe, widow, of the intended first cropping in Moorbarns. He promised 'that upon condition of that news to be true . . he . . would give her . . . a new gown, the best that ever she did wear, if she would wear one of silk for that good news'. On the enclosure of Peatling parva Wigfall was allotted 104½ acres, only about 35 of which would have been for his glebe farm and the rest in lieu of his tithes.[206] Walter Blith, the enthusiastic writer about improving farming, was living in Cotesbach in 1649, the year his book *The English Improver, or a New Survey of Husbandry* was first published. Perhaps he was staying at Cotesbach Rectory as a guest of Lee in order to exchange ideas with him. His expanded revision, *The English Improver Improved or the Survey of Husbandry Surveyed*, appeared in 1652, just before the local exchange between Moore and Lee started.[207] Another author, John Worlidge, in compiling his comprehensive treatise *Systema Agriculturae, The Mystery of Husbandry Discovered*, published in 1669, consulted the writings of both Blith and Lee as authorities.[208] Unlike Moore, who died in 1657, Lee lived to witness the full range of consequences of the seventeenth-century phase of enclosure, from the depopulation and deprivation, which he had predicted would not follow, to the new prosperity, which he doubtless had a share in as owner of the family farm in Catthorpe. Presumably he found a way of adapting to the changes in his subsequent Nonconformist career, firstly as an active "ejected minister" in his native village and finally in Leicester where, at the time of his death in 1694, he valued his house at over £200.[209]

The other half-dozen wealthy farmers from enclosed townships were all more or less involved with arable farming. In nearly every case, however, it is possible to shew that the cropping was not in fact divorced from common-field farming. At a later period the kind of village a farmer was based on may not have mattered; in the seventeenth century it did. Not only did the ordinary mixed husbandry fail to survive in the villages that enclosed, as in the first phase of enclosure, but even large-scale arable farming could not be undertaken unless it was based on common-field farm holdings.

The only man apparently breaking this rule was William Seale of Peatling magna, whose inventory total, £2,286.1.8d., is easily the highest from the 1680s. He had taken short leases in his own parish for improving farming, but his cropping activities spread widely over the area. His crop valuation was £235.5.0, including £20 for a rick of oats at Ashby parva and £20 for 16 acres of wheat at Misterton. He also owned a wagon. Even Seale's crops were not entirely independent of common-field farming; he owned tithes from the common-field village of Newton on Dunsmore and possibly his peas stack in

Mowsley Field, worth £23.5.0, represented tithes of the crop grown in the common fields of that village too. His major asset, however, was his livestock, valued at no less than £1,250.16.8d., and he was also owed £650 for more sold in London and for wool. Obviously Seale was a grazier, but on his death he was in fact styled 'butcher and grazier'. About £107 of his crop valuation consisted of hay.[210]

The member of this group with the next highest livestock total, £366.10.0, was Thomas Simons of Shawell. He had the stock of a pure grazing farmer, including cheese and wool valued at £50. He was almost certainly a butcher too; a later Thomas Simons was apprenticed to Anthony Prowitt, butcher, of the neighbouring Northamptonshire village of Lilbourne and was one of the country butchers made free of Leicester for market days only in 1719. Similarly one of the 20 wealthy farmers from the open-field villages was a butcher with grazing stock only. Some of his sheep were grazing the common fields of his own village and he had wool worth £21.10.0. This was an earlier Anthony Prowit, of Swinford, a parish which adjoins Shawell and Lilbourne. These inventories are the clearest indication that commercial grazing farming at a new high level and directed at the meat market was by this time a major force in the area.[211]

In spite of all this, and although his inventory total of £1,762.6.6d. was not so high as Seale's, John Hall, based on the unenclosed village of Arnesby, must be taken to represent the greatest successes of the new improving farming. His corn crop valuation was the highest of all, £134, and he had two wagons. He also had wool in his wool chamber worth £40 and his additional resources included mortgages from the squire families in the villages where he took grounds.[212] Not so very far behind Hall in farming stock, however, the other 18 common-field farmers formed a pretty uniform group. The highest farm stock valuation amongst them was just under £350, but for 13 of them it ranged from £120 to £177. Their livestock valuations varied according to the amount of pasture ground they had in hand; the lowest figure was just over £50, but the average was £104. But they were all equally committed to large-scale arable farming. Only three of their crop valuations were outside the range from £40 to £90, and they were higher. Where valued separately, hay shews in some cases to have been an important part of the crop total. The average figure for crop valuation among them was over £70 and for implements £10. Half of them were wagon-owners.

In contrast to these, out of the 36 Lutterworth townspeople who left inventories which included farming stock in the last 35 years of the century, only two qualify to be added to this group. They were in no way remarkable, save that one represents the last involvement in farming of the Insley family of town gentry that had been influential in the late sixteenth and early seventeenth centuries. Both were wagon-owners.

It is worth emphasizing the significance of the introduction of the wagon into the area at this stage. The group of wealthy farmers mentioned included all but two of the 14 wagon-owners among the village inventories from the 1680s. There is no reason to doubt that the usual distinction was being made between the two-wheeled cart and the four-wheeled wagon (see Illustrations 11 and 6). What was reputed to be the first wagon in Northamptonshire belonged in the early seventeenth century to a Naseby squire family who also owned the tithes of the village. In Wiltshire the first was introduced in 1632, but they only became common after about 1655. In Oxfordshire the wagon was little used in 1677, except by carriers, but was soon to become common. The wagon had hitherto been used on the roads as a heavy freight vehicle. It has been assumed that all that was involved was simply its adoption as a farm vehicle. The owners of the first Wiltshire wagon mentioned 'saw the use of them by the professed wagon drivers to London'.[213] In view of the importance of arable farming to these wealthy farmers, however, it seems more likely that they brought these juggernauts of the open road along the village lanes mainly as road vehicles for transporting their crops in bulk to market when and where it suited them best. Every one of the 14 wagon-owners had at least one cart as well for farm work. Five of them had two, as did all but one of the town-based wagon-owners from the last 30 years of the century. Francis Billington, the area's pioneer improving farmer, whose wagon is easily the earliest farm wagon traced in the area, had three carts. His four vehicles were together valued at £13.[214]

Such men were undoubtedly the largest employers in the area. They were also presumably responsible for the building of most of the fine brick houses in the area that date from the later seventeenth century. While they may have had larger houses, however, they did not usually have extensive households, frequently being assessed for Hearth Tax on only two hearths, or even one. Their employees would not be servants in husbandry but wage-labourers. In the words of Moore, 'the great *Manufacture and Trade of Leicester-Shire*, and many (if not most) of the Inland Counties, is *tillage*'.[215] His fear was that enclosure was endangering its survival. As it turned out, however, the changes constituted not a defeat but a victory for common-field farming. It survived in a new and flourishing form; but, as this was achieved by what was in effect a territorial expansion, it only served to aggravate the problems that distressed him. In other words, this was the Lutterworth area's experience of an agrarian revolution, a revolution in agricultural production of the kind that helped lay the foundations on which the Industrial Revolution was to build. The timing suggests that the Civil War was crucial in encouraging or releasing the commercial forces involved. During the following century there may have been further agricultural progress; but the final agricultural revolution needed to underpin industrial expansion was to be the replacement of common-field farming by commercial farming based entirely on enclosed farms, which was achieved by the enclosure of all the surviving common fields.

By the mid-seventeenth century it is no longer possible to treat effectively the economy of each village in isolation. The study of the sixteenth-century farming economy has shewn that real progress was made not so much on the common fields or in the ancient enclosures as in the interaction between the two, the one supporting farming communities and the other all but empty. In the seventeenth century there was a similar relationship between the two types of village, but a much more complex relationship in that the enclosing villages, albeit more passive in the transition, were nonetheless living communities.

The contemporary pamphleteers were well aware of the cross-influence between the two types of village. Moore noted that the end of mixed husbandry in the enclosing villages was driving tenants there, 'inclosed wretches', to compete for holdings in neighbouring common-field villages, thus increasing the difficulties for inhabitants farming there.[216] To this Lee retorted by citing the farmer who has become so familiar in this study, the common-field farmer renting enclosed grounds:

> Those that live where the fields lying open are used in common become tenants themselves, and rent inclosed grounds round about them, or near unto them, that they may be better able to maintain their own families, and manage their tillage in the common fields with more advantage; for which inclosed grounds, in that respect, they can afford to give greater rents, than they that live only upon inclosure can do.[217]

Lee even pointed his finger at one of Moore's supporters in the campaign who 'living himself where fields lying open are used in common, doth take to rent of other men, in other places, grounds inclosed to the value of 2000 *l. per annum*'.[218] From what has been said there can be no doubt that this latter was the more important of the two types of farmer, and in fact the most important figure in the economy of the area.

Such men were able to achieve the enormous increase in production from their farms by taking advantage of the new kind of landless wage-labourers now made available. Indeed Moore characterized the campaigners for enclosure and those who profited from it as 'make-beggars' and was quite specific in dramatizing the displacement of different levels of the village communities:

> First, they make Beggars of *Tenants* upon such *Inclosure*, for the *Tenant* forthwith is discharged of *tillage*, and farm, to seek a living he knows not where. Truly it would make a charitable heart bleed to come now into our Markets, where we are now so busy upon such *Inclosures*, in *Leicester-Shire*; where the Market is full of enquiry, and complaint of such *Tenants* to all they meet, 'Can you help me to a farm, or a little land to employ my team? I am discharged, and if I sell my Horses, and Cattle,

I shall never get a team again, or so many Milk-cows to maintain my families. Alas, all my money will be spent, that I shall sell them for, ere I shall hear of any land to be set.' And in some Towns there is *fourteen*, *sixteen*, or *twenty Tenants discharged* of ploughing, all in this sad condition, besides many other teams, and farms of free-holders laid down in the same Towns.

And now in the second place, we shall truly shew you how they make Cottiers Beggars. In these inclosed Towns in laying down the plough, and taking away the crop of corn, how many crops do they rob the poor Cottier of? This poor man had a crop and income in every tilth of the plough . . . 'And now alas', saith the poor *Cottier*, 'there is no work for me; I need not be thrust out of the Town, I must be gone where I may get my living, and if I can get no house else where, I, and mine must starve.' . . . and what enquiring every where is there of these poor Cottiers (after the Town is inclosed) to get an house in any place, where they may have work.

Thirdly, such inclosure make Beggars of the children both of Tenants, and Cottiers; the children of both usually become servants to the husbandman, and brought up at the plough, &c. But now in such inclosed Towns, where there were kept 30, 40, 50 servants, there is not above three, or four. Hence the droves of poor children, when they are reproved for begging, are complaining, 'We would willingly work, if any would set us on work.'[219]

Thus in the questions of depopulation, immigration and poverty Moore was painfully alive to the effects of the interaction, and Lee was in the end forced to agree with him. It can now be seen that the depopulation of the enclosing villages and the immigration into the common-field villages were both aspects of the changes in the economy of the area. These changes affected the availability of employment not just in the enclosing villages, but throughout the area, where the new improving farming not only took over ancient enclosures but also altered the farming organization of the common fields where it was based.

Finally Moore recognized the direction in which events were heading. Of enclosure he observed that 'it takes away the *general Trade* that all the Inhabitants of these Counties live on, except some great ones and Trades-men in Market-Towns, etc.'[220] While such men prospered, Moore and his supporters in his campaign, many of them townsmen of Leicester, went out of their way to emphasize that it was the towns in particular that suffered in the population redistribution. It has already been seen that Lutterworth grazing interests were of first importance in the second half of the sixteenth century and were involved in enclosure around the start of the seventeenth, and that the town's corn market was in turn of first importance in the agricultural changes in the period after the 1620s. It remains, therefore, to study in more detail the role of the town as the exchange point between the different types of economy within the area and beyond, in order to shew how the town community itself fared at each stage.

CHAPTER FOUR

The Town Economy

The divergence in population trends used in the second chapter to characterize the different types of village has now been shewn to have been one aspect of their contrasting farming economies. Within this area of villages, however, the population of the town was exceptional; not only did Lutterworth grow faster, no doubt because of immigration from the villages, but towards the later seventeenth century it was only such immigration that enabled it to maintain its numbers. The reason for this was the unique role of the town as the market centre of the area.

Since this study is offered as the first detailed analysis of the economy of an English market town in this crucial period of transition, no apology should be needed for the fineness of detail to be pursued in this chapter. Here the sample decades of probate inventories have been filled in by examining all the probate records for Lutterworth inhabitants and also the inventories of any villagers with traceable non-agricultural occupations. Hitherto one of the principal means of distinguishing the different types of early modern urban community has been to make comparisons between their occupation structures. To describe the actual functioning of an urban community like Lutterworth, however, it will be appreciated that occupational labels on their own are not sufficient and occupations within the town must be judged in the context of the wider economy of the area of its influence. The present chapter will, therefore, define the town's role by examining all the non-agricultural occupations in the area as a whole.[1] Indeed for a study in urban history this chapter may seem perversely preoccupied with village and rural matters; but the contention is that the best way to identify the points at which the various non-agricultural activities converged on the town to form an emergent urban economy is to keep in focus at the same time their background, the economy of the area in its entirety. In this way their concentration in the town at each stage of development can be used to indicate how far Lutterworth had grown into an urban centre. Before leaving agriculture as a subject on its own, however, the role of farming in the economy of the town community must be assessed against the important changes revealed in the last chapter.

1. Town farmers and non-agricultural occupations

A detailed study of the series of manorial records and deeds that survive makes it clear that throughout the sixteenth and seventeenth centuries the town fields supported what was in many ways a typical common-field farming community.[2] The years either side of 1630 saw considerable changes, it is true, in the split-up of the manor, which may well have released husbandry from effective manorial control, and in the dividing-up of the nearer half of Moorbarns among townsmen. Nevertheless there was no fundamental change in the structure or the landholding pattern of the common fields. There are, however, several peculiarities about farming based on the town that call for attention.

In the first place, in comparison with village-based farming, ordinary common-field farming based on the town shews up very poorly throughout the period. This was not apparently because the fields were overcrowded with too many holdings. The total of 69 yard lands was certainly the highest traced for any township in the area. Because the town parish was unusually large, however, the equivalent acreage of each yard land was quite normal; it varied from 20 to 30 acres in the villages and in Lutterworth it was 25 acres. The town fields would have suffered more than others by being overrun with cottagers' cows and certainly 'the oppression of the Commons' was a matter of contention;[3] but in the 1607 Survey only 43 cottages were listed as officially having grazing rights in the fields, while the total number of beasts allowed to the yard land holders added up to nearly 200. It seems rather that the town was ahead of the rest of the area in the separation of interests between grazing and mixed farming, so that the livestock of the stock-dealers and butchers, even if they were restricted within the formal stint numbers, kept the productivity of the ordinary mixed farm in check.

This poor performance was no doubt the reason for the relatively small number of early probate records of townspeople. From before 1600 there is only one ordinary common-field farming inventory from the town listing farm stock worth more than £50, while from the 1590s the inventories of 55 fully stocked common-field farmers from the villages in the area survive, the average of their farming stock value being £67. Town farmers suffered more than others in the 1630s. From that decade nine inventories of fully equipped mixed farms in the town survive; but only two of them include any sheep, a flock of 12 and a flock of 26 where, to judge from the sizes of the farms and the stint allowed in 1607, 600 sheep in all might have been expected. Even at the end of the century the contrast persisted among the wagon-owning improving farmers. From the 1680s there are four inventories of town farmers which include wagons, the average total value being £110. In the same decade the 54 inventories of mixed farmers of all types from the common-field villages had an average total value of £134, and the 14 of them that included wagons far more.

In view of all this, the second and third points which relate to the agricultural role of the town appear paradoxical. The second is that in both the changes of direction which affected the farming economy of the area

Lutterworth farmers took the lead. The most important men engaged in stock-dealing and stock-raising for meat in the late sixteenth century were townsmen; and Thomas Farren in particular had a hand in the final enclosure of Cotesbach. Similarly in the next generation it was the raising of crops by townsmen on the enclosed grounds of Moorbarns that pioneered the new improving farming. There was overall a sense too in which the farming activity of the town no longer operated in isolation from that of the immediate circle of townships already referred to, which encompassed the whole range of farming, from estate pasture-farms to the thriving common-field village of Bitteswell, only a mile away to the north.

The third point is that most of the wealth in the town was in the hands of the people who formed the farming community. This shews particularly clearly in the later sixteenth and early seventeenth centuries, when the increase in wealth in the town, parallel with that in the area, was very much an increase in agricultural wealth, even among those engaged in more commercial activities as well.[4] The position at the beginning of the sixteenth century might appear an exception to this generalization. In 1524 the three highest tax assessments were on two members of the Paver family and on the town bailiff, who together owned over half the taxable wealth in the town. Shorn of these assessments, however, the Lutterworth tax rolls for the 1520s are very similar to those of any village in the area. It is true that comparison with the 1509 Terrier makes it possible to say that there were many cottage dwellers who were not assessed; but whether they were mainly occupied in agriculture or otherwise can for the moment only be guessed at.

Lastly this balance of wealth was shifting throughout the two centuries in favour of townspeople who were not farming. The final reversal came quite swiftly in the last few decades. The overall shift was largely a result of the increasing proportion of non-farmers; but the final reversal was due to the increase in their wealth (see Table 4.1). By this time too there was a clearer separation between farming and commercial activities. Few of the important commercial men were farming at all, let alone as ordinary common-field farmers; and nearly all of the important farms were run by plain farmers with no commercial interests.

These last facts point to the emergence of a commercial community independent of its farming background. The first question to be asked, therefore, is what was the nature of the commercial activity in the town at each stage of its development? To a certain extent this can be answered by shewing the occupation structure of the population. From the early sixteenth century there are insufficient records, but the occupations given in one mid-century Lay Subsidy tax roll suggest that the one outstanding family of merchants was giving place to a broader commercial section of the community (see Table 4.2). On the other hand the assessments were headed

Table 4.1 Numbers of inventories of non-farmers in Lutterworth and their share of total inventory wealth, by periods

| | 1580-1699 40-year periods | | | | 1660-1699 20-year periods | | | |
| | 1580-1619 | | 1660-1699 | | 1660-1679 | | 1680-1699 | |
	No.	Inv. wealth	No.	Inv. wealth	No.	Inv. wealth	No.	Inv. wealth
Non-farming inventories	18	20%	71	47%	37	38%	34	56%
All inventories	44	£3,050	115	£9,300	61	£4,850	54	£4,450

Source: all probate inventories of Lutterworth inhabitants traced at L.R.O.

by the tenant of Moorbarns and, as just mentioned, the town was growing in agricultural rather than commercial wealth. The appearance of a man among the taxpayers will be used as an indication that he was one of the chief men in the town, as there were on average only 15 of them from Lutterworth on these rolls from this date until the early seventeenth century. By then the

Table 4.2 Lutterworth Lay Subsidy assessment, 1552

Taxpayers	Occupation given	Assessment	
Edward Feyres of Warwickshire	Gentleman	£33	(tenant of Moorbarns)
Richard Wynfellde	Gentleman	£10	(tenant of the Spittle)
Margaret Pavear		£30	(widow of mercer)
William Peyke		£28	
Richard Johnson	Yeoman	£10	(bailiff of the manor)
Hugh Lussell	Yeoman	£26	
Thomas Kyrbye	Butcher	£14	
Hugh Haddon	Mercer	£16	
Thomas Peyke	Draper	£10	
John Wheteley	Baker	£12	
John Kyrbye	Wool-buyer	£22	
John Johnson	Innholder	£10	
William Chamberlyn	Mercer	£10	

Table 4.3 Lutterworth and Lutterworth area: occupations in probate records and parish registers from the 1630s, expressed as percentages of total numbers of entries giving occupations

	Villages		Town of Lutterworth	
	Probate inventories	Parish registers	Probate records	Parish register
Food	3½	4	15	8½
Clothing	5½	8	3	11
Leather	1	1½	11	15
Crafts	3½	6¾	11	15½
Trading etc.	½	1¾	10	8
Total non-agricultural	14	22	50	58
Agricultural	86	78	50	42
	100	100	100	100
Total number	429	714	225	154

Sources: Appendix Tables 8 and 9, which shew the classification of occupations into the headings used here

assessments were headed by Thomas Farren and Thomas Gore, both wealthy gentlemen engaged in large-scale farming and livestock-dealing. The other dozen taxpayers at that time included butchers, bakers, innholders and shoemakers, but only one retail trader. The occupations shared among the 54 people taxed on three hearths or more in 1664, however, shew that by that time the farmers in the town had lost their prominence and were being replaced by various retail traders and innholders.

These short lists of the occupations of the chief inhabitants are of limited use in characterizing the economy of the whole town. A wider-based sample obtained from the probate records suggests that non-agricultural occupations were over three times as common in the town as in the area. Overall half the townsmen represented had such occupations; and the proportion was increasing throughout the seventeenth century.

All these records are biased towards property-owners. The occupations given in the parish registers in the 1630s, however, offer an opportunity of checking, if only for one decade, how representative they are of the whole population of the area (see Table 4.3). The only difference that emerges is that men with non-agricultural occupations, especially in the villages, are under-represented in the probate records. Presumably they were on the whole by no means wealthy; and indeed the inventories shew that they were usually only concerned with probate when they also possessed some farming stock. It is worth emphasizing this finding here, if only to help dispel the assumption hitherto made, presumably relying on the probate records alone, that at this period the typical Midland village craftsman was also a farmer.[5]

Analysed in greater detail (see Appendix Tables 8 and 9) these sources reveal that the more important traders were all but absent from the villages; but also that, however important they were in the town, there were even there only a few of them, except towards the end of the seventeenth century. Those concerned with provisions, again mainly confined to the town, were even better represented among the probate records, shewing that they were generally prosperous. The various wood, metal and building crafts were conspicuous in the town partly because it supported several of the more specialized skills. Clothing occupied a proportion, but there is no suggestion of weaving on an industrial rather than a domestic scale; on the contrary, people occupied in clothing were just as common in the villages and the presence of mercers and drapers in the town emphasizes the importance of cloth brought into the area from outside, some of it no doubt made up by local tailors. Only leather-working was carried on to any extent and that almost exclusively in the town. The under-representation among the probate records of the town weavers, tailors and shoemakers suggests that they were some of the men that helped to swell the body of potential paupers there.

This preliminary account of the town economy leaves untouched some of the most important questions. What, for instance, was the extent of trading in the town, not only by townspeople but also by outsiders, not only at the fairs and in the open market and its buildings but also among the wayfaring community at public houses? What was the mechanism of the primary distribution of agricultural produce within the area? Such questions cannot be answered by studying the occupation structure alone.

Another limitation of occupation tables is that they cannot take into account secondary occupations which in some cases, of course, developed into primary ones. To give one Lutterworth example, John Tarlton was named 'husbandman' in 1589, 'innholder' in 1617 and 1624, 'innkeeper' in 1626 and 'victualler' at his death in 1638. Yet it appears that he started out as a shoemaker, the occupation he himself gave in a court case in 1636.[6] Of special importance to this study is the overlap between farming and other activities. Many of those who by their occupations would appear to have been farming, not only, for example, the "new gentry" but also another group that may be termed "new yeomen", were involved in commercial activities as well; while many of the most important commercial men were at the same time heavily involved in farming of one sort or another. At the other end of the economic scale, moreover, the independence of labourers and poor craftsmen from subsistence farming and from cottage grazing rights is a vital factor in assessing the urban character of the town.

2.   Distributors of agricultural produce and provisions

The economy of the area underwent three stages of development which in turn threw into prominence as market commodities three basic agricultural products, wool, meat and corn. This account will start with the redistribution of agricultural produce in that order, taking in turn wool-dealing, then cattle-dealing and the butcher's trade and then corn-dealing and the associated trades, and so leading on to provisioning in general. In a second section the various crafts will be examined, taking, so as to preserve the same order, clothing and then leather-working before all the other crafts. A third section will then deal with retail trade of all kinds.

Dealers in wool

At the beginning of the sixteenth century the principal export from the area was, as it had been for centuries, wool. With the first phase of enclosure, however, wool-exporting had received a boost, especially as a result of the scale of production on the pasture estates. The importance of the local wool merchants in the Midlands is no doubt connected with this development. In Leicester there were several families of Merchants of the Staple, with the Wigstons towering above the rest. Merchants were not confined to the large towns; there were Staplers in several of the market towns, including one who died in Lutterworth in 1473. His name, John Reynolds, suggests that he was a member of the Reynold family of Leicester merchants, five successive generations of which produced a Mayor, two of them named John. The influential Reynolds family of Coventry too included a Sheriff of that city. There were even Staplers based on villages, like William Saxby, who died in 1517 at Stanford on Avon, the centre of the Cave family estates. Indeed, to judge from family connexions, the business did not involve anything like a clear dividing line between producers and dealers. At the beginning of the century the wife of Richard Cave, esquire, of Stanford on Avon, was daughter to John Saxby, a Northampton Stapler, and William Wigston the elder of Leicester appears to have married a daughter of Sir Thomas Pulteney of Misterton. In the mid-century Peter Temple, the Warwickshire gentleman grazier who used Moorbarns as a sheep farm, apprenticed his eldest son and heir to an Oxfordshire Merchant of the Staple.[7] If the main wool crops were following such family and trading connexions out of the area, what business was there left for a merchant based on Lutterworth?

In fact Lutterworth too was at the centre of a large estate which included several enclosures. The owners were the Feildings, the town's only family of gentry. It is very likely that the export of their wool crops was the main business of the Lutterworth Stapler. Moreover Sir Everard Feilding, the head of the family who died in 1515, was himself a Merchant of the Staple and his bequest of £100 to his daughter 'to be levied and paid out of my stock in Caleis' shews that he was personally involved in the trade.[8] The Lutterworth wool-dealing should, therefore, be thought of not so much as an integral part of the town economy but, like livestock-dealing, as another example of trading based on a large manorial farming unit.

Some time before Sir Everard's death the family had retired from the town to their nearby seat of Newnham Paddox, apparently leaving the trade in the hands of the professional merchants. Ralph and Robert Paver were two of the only three men from the area recorded as being admitted to the Leicester Chapmen's Guild during the sixteenth and seventeenth centuries. They were both mercers and, even though they were not Staplers, there is no doubt that they dealt in wool. At her death in 1550 Margaret, who was presumably Robert's widow, owned £10 worth 'in the Wool chamber'. The taxation rolls shew that the family was important not only on a local but also on a county scale. The only man in Guthlaxton hundred to pay more tax in the 1520s than Robert was Thomas Pulteney, whose £160 assessment at Misterton was one of the very highest in Leicestershire. Robert was assessed on £143.6.8d. in 1524; but if Ralph's assessment is included the family paid on £170 in 1524 and £184 in 1525. There is a close parallel between the Pavers in Lutterworth and the Wigstons in Leicester, where the roll for 1524 was headed by that family's two assessments, William the elder at £100 and his cousin William the younger at £600. Their wealth was not only pre-eminent in their respective towns in the 1520s but it also declined rapidly thereafter. In cases where direct comparison is possible the inventory totals are nearly always several times the tax assessments. Margaret Paver's inventory total, however, was £73.10.0, merely half of Robert's assessment in the 1520s, and Ralph's too was half his own assessment.[9] In both towns the reason was presumably that the export of the clips of wool from the large estates had passed out of the hands of the local men. By the 1550s the Misterton wool crops were being bought up direct by clothiers and merchants from Coventry, Gloucestershire and London.

Apart from the pasture-estate owners, only a very few of the most important farmers in the area had a wool house for sorting and packing wool crops or a wool chamber for their storage. In the town the Pavers had their wool chamber; but even such wool stores as there were in the town were going out of use in the early seventeenth century, if not before. In three pairs of inventories, describing respectively the Feilding family manor farm, the Gore freehold farm and the Billington family's Swan Inn, the earlier one mentions wool in the wool house while the later one mentions neither. In 1594 William Newcombe described in his will his two-bay building in the High Street as 'the whool shop which is now two shops'. If it had been a wool shop, and not simply undivided, wool-dealing in this case had been replaced by shoemaking.[10] The only wool stores in the inventories from the 1680s belonged to villagers, John Hall of Arnesby and William Harrison of Bitteswell, who was another of the more important improving farmers in the area.[11]

So much for the wool crops from the pasture estates. On the ordinary farm where wool was used for the household, of course, no dealing was involved; but as sheep numbers increased towards the mid-sixteenth century there would have been wool available for sale. Much of this no doubt was packed and exported from the area in the way already described. What evidence is there for the redistribution of wool for spinning and weaving locally?

The only clips of wool sold locally from the Misterton estate in the 1550s came from wethers and other sheep bought in for mutton, wool too coarse for sorting with the store wool. It was usually bought up by yeomen from the villages. In one year it went to Richard Pratt, the Lutterworth yeoman who was heir and successor to the Pavers.[12] This was small business compared to the store wool; but it was probably the only type of dealing in wool crops that was left to local men.

Whenever a sheep died or was eaten on the Misterton estate the fell was sold to one of the estate shepherds. This serves as a reminder that the changing emphasis in sheep farming from wool production to mutton production would have greatly affected the local availability of wool. While the annual shearing continued to produce clips suitable for selling to a merchant from outside, the constant turnover of sheep and their regular slaughter for mutton released small quantities of fells of varying types of wool throughout the year suited to local sorting and dealing.

The wool-dealing that grew up on this business was undertaken on a small scale and as a secondary interest.[13] In the first place there were men whose employment gave them access to wool, such as the shepherd and the wool-winder or any other labourer employed in sorting or packing wool. In the second place there were men whose trade released wool as a by-product, such as the butcher, the glover and the fellmonger, all of whom would have handled skins. All the evidence for this business in the hands of the former group in the area comes from the 1590s onwards and, as might be expected, concerned villagers only. The business in the hands of the latter group appears to have started in the mid-sixteenth century as a speciality of the town. John Kirby, a member of the leading family of Lutterworth butchers, was listed in the 1552 tax assessment as 'Wool-buyer'. Two of the debts owed in 1568/9 to John Ratclyfe, the first Lutterworth glover traced, were for 1½ stone of best wool and 2/6d. for four pounds of black wool. At the beginning of the seventeenth century four Lutterworth glovers were members of the Wood family, one of them owning one stone of lamb's wool on his death in 1614.[14]

By this time no such concentration in the town can be demonstrated. A member of the Sleath family, the principal butchers in Gilmorton, was trading as a wool-dealer (*lanister*) and apparently selling wool within their village.[15] By the 1680s the only men in the area holding large stocks of wool were villagers directly involved with improved pasture farming, such as John Hall and William Harrison and John Haines, the shepherd at Misterton. They also included important village butcher graziers like Thomas Simons of Shawell, Anthony Prowitt of Swinford and, of course, William Seale of Peatling magnà. Apart from the producers, a dozen villagers have been traced from the end of the sixteenth century onwards as dealing in wool, including three wool-winders and five fellmongers. One of the latter, from North Kilworth, died in 1684 owning two packs of wool valued at £12 and leather and skins worth £1.2.6d.[16] In the early seventeenth century the Leicester families of glovers, such as the Langtons and Dowells, were changing into fellmongers. This transition is apparent in the Lutterworth area too. Yet the group of Lutterworth glovers was not replaced by an equivalent group of town-based fellmongers. Only one Lutterworth wool-winder has been traced, a widow, and a couple of fellmongers, one of them a member of the Wood family.

There is a possibility that even before 1600 a yeoman dealing in wool from mutton animals was selling it direct to weavers in the Hinckley area. It was this coarser wool that was developed into the long-staple wool needed during the seventeenth century for the local hosiery industry.[17] Clement Stretton, an important Leire yeoman who died in 1597, had wool worth £10, but sheep worth only £15. Debts owed to him included £22 and a share of £13 by 'Nicholas Decon of Hinckley and Thomas Weaver [of?] Thornton' (or 'Thomas weaver'). Other debtors included two men from Broughton Astley and one from Sibson, a village which, like Thornton, lies beyond Hinckley.[18] One case of wool-dealing in the 1640s involved wool that could also have been used for this purpose, but further away. William Dowell of Lutterworth, woolman, was employed by a Leicester vintner as his factor or agent in buying wool in the area. The business ran into several hundreds of pounds and involved dealings with a London vintner too. Things went badly for Dowell, who was £40 in debt to his principal by 1650. This example is particularly significant, as wool-dealers of this type were just the men who were developing into the county's jersey-combers and hosiers. In Leicester Peter Dowell, fellmonger, a stranger, was made free in 1620-1. Three years later Thomas Dowell, glover and apprentice to Brian Langton, glover, was made free. Later one of Peter's apprentices was Abstinence Pougher and James Hyndman was apprentice to Thomas, now a fellmonger too. The Pougher and Hin(d)man families produced two of the county town's very first jersey-combers and hosiers. On closer examination even the one Lutterworth woolman turns out not to have been a townsman but a fellmonger based on the enclosed village of Frowlesworth, which is just across the Fosse Way from the Hinckley area. Peter Dowell had two brothers in the village. One was named William and the other's son John was a fellmonger there in the 1650s and 1660s. Nobody of this surname has been traced in the town.[19]

Thus whereas at the beginning of the sixteenth century the area and the town supported wool-dealing business of county, national or even international importance, the trade dealing with the main wool crops soon passed out of the hands of local men. As for the redistribution carried on by various yeomen and other men with different occupations, the volume of this trade probably added up to something much larger than the few references found can shew. Lutterworth may have started out as its local centre; but by the mid-seventeenth century, if not earlier, the town was being bypassed by this trade too.

Dealers in livestock

The most valuable items sold in the open market were animals. In the Midlands, where droving routes from the North and West converged and crossed on their way towards London and the South East, the various kinds of livestock were the most frequent speciality of individual markets and fairs.[20] Lutterworth had a piece of ground just outside the town used for fairs, the Horse Fair Leys, while the Neats Market, or Beast Market, and the Sheep Market were two of the largest special market areas in the town. What was the role of the deals that took place here in the economy of the area and how did they affect the economy of the town itself?

Farming in the Lutterworth area was more or less self-sufficient as far as horse stocks were concerned until the mid-sixteenth century; but by the end of the century it was more usual for a farmer, especially if based on a village that was to retain its common fields, to buy in his horses as working animals. The toll books of the Market Bosworth Fair from 1603 to 1616 include details of 53 sales and 49 purchases by men from Lutterworth and the villages in the area. This involvement in the local market was evidently no more than normal dealing among yeomen and husbandmen and hardly any of them concluded more than one sale or purchase. No doubt the Lutterworth horse fairs too grew up mainly as the local exchange point, especially between the two types of village. They have not been traced any earlier than the Survey of 1607, which describes them as 'Fairs or other markets for selling horses' held on the three Thursdays after Epiphany. This suggests that they were little more than ordinary Thursday markets and were of recent origin. Even fairs at the county town may have drawn in few outsiders, at least in winter.

Of the vendors and purchasers involved in the sale of 13 horses at Leicester on one day in January 1598/9 only three came any way from beyond the county boundary. At Lutterworth all three fairs also took place in the dead month of January, inconvenient for any other than local farmers to attend.[21]

With the advance of improving farming it became even more important for common-field farmers to buy in their working horses, as only the largest among them, those also making use of pasture grounds, could afford to raise their own. The Market Bosworth records shew that the involvement in this trade of ordinary farmers based on enclosing villages was declining. At the same time the area was also developing into an important source of the heavier horses for sale to outsiders. The local involvement in two fairs in September 1646 at Stratford-upon-Avon, admittedly a more renowned centre and twice as far away as Market Bosworth, was of a very different nature. A group of 15 men, all from three villages that were to retain their common fields, made only one purchase, but sold a total of 28 horses at an average price not far short of five pounds each. Lutterworth itself was only one of several places in the region with horse fairs which such local farmers might attend; and even within the Lutterworth area the Lutterworth fairs were never such important dates in the farmer's calendar as the 9th of October, the start of Harborough Fair. Nevertheless, whereas the Lutterworth horse fairs had been primarily of local importance, in the seventeenth century they no doubt became one of the knots on the national network of horse-dealing. One function of these fairs was to introduce superior stock to supply local needs, like the bay mare bought for £13 at the second of the January fairs in 1655/6 for the Feilding family establishment, and probably intended for their coach. The Lutterworth horse fair that survived into the eighteenth century was not in the middle of winter but in the more open month of April.[22]

On the estate pasture-farm, as illustrated by the Misterton estate accounts, all the beasts formed part of the nationwide drift of cattle towards the South East. No breeding was done and beasts were commonly bought in to be kept for less than a year. Purchases were frequently made at distant fairs, even as far away as North Yorkshire. The sheep flocks, on the other hand, were more stable units. A few purchases were made at a distance, but the majority of the deals, all of which involved sheep ultimately destined for mutton, were with local yeoman farmers. Fifty-eight wethers were purchased at the Lutterworth Ascension Day fair in 1554, 40 of them from one Thomas lloyde, evidently a Welsh drover.[23] Otherwise all such exchanges were contracted privately, thus bypassing completely the Lutterworth markets and fairs. In spite of this the unique position of Thomas Farren in the town economy at the turn of the century suggests that his prosperity was built up not so much on his own pasture farming as on the local livestock trade in the town's markets and fairs over which, as tenant of the Bailiwick, he had control.

The yeoman farmers were increasingly drawing off the benefit from the pasture grounds. Among the advantages they derived from the interaction between the two types of land was the opportunity of fattening sheep for mutton on either grass or fodder crops and also beasts for beef. As employers they too were probably able to buy at distant fairs, apart from dealing locally with the estate-farm shepherds and keepers. The fact that there was an unusual concentration of farmers of this type based on the town, however, suggests that they were also very much involved in the local markets.

The ordinary farmer was constrained by the constant stock requirements of his common-field holding and by the lack of pasture. With no chance of buying and selling beasts for beef he had to be content with concentrating on the breeding and dairying potential of his herd of cows. In so far as his sheep formed part of the common flock he would have no occasion to buy in fresh stock and for the odd cow to re-stock his herd he could rely on the nearest fairs.

When it came to selling cattle for meat, the larger producer always had the opportunity of choosing his market, by selling, for instance, direct to a London butcher. In 1553 the Misterton estate sold to such a man four beasts for beef and the disastrous purchase of wethers from Pontefract that have already been mentioned. In 1555 a South Leicestershire man was owed £21 by a butcher from London and £17.10.0 by another from Islington. In the 1680s it was reported that Richard Webster, 'the greatest tenant' of grounds at Bittesby 'now deals in grazing and drives fat cattle to London' and the £650 owed to William Seale of Peatling magna was partly, if not mainly, for cattle sold in London.[24] At the other end of the scale the ordinary husbandman selling his lambs or his few calves, which were usually sold off as yearlings, would be more dependent on the local markets, and the cottager with only the odd calf perhaps entirely so. Conversely, within the area an increasing proportion of the householders was not in a position to eat home-grown mutton, let alone beef, and would have depended on local butchers for meat supplies. How far was the local butchery trade centred on the town?

One of the two conspicuous market buildings in the centre of the town was the butchers' Shambles. In 1607 it measured 110 feet by 12 feet and contained seven shops; but the court rolls from the 1560s shew that even at that date over 20 men at a time might be selling meat in the town.[25] Two thirds of them were outsiders, from villages within the area and beyond. Although these villagers were termed 'butcher' in the court rolls, however, no villager of that occupation has been traced before the last years of the century and it is almost certain that they were primarily husbandmen who visited local markets as butchers only on one or two days a week. Several of the butchers named, on the other hand, were townsmen. The town supported three or four well-established families of butchers, such as the Kirbys and Lussells. These men were in fact some of the Lutterworth yeoman farmers and played a leading part in the livestock-dealing with the pasture estates, alongside Richard Pratt. Unlike him, of course, they were usually purchasers.

The importance of the yeoman farmers was not only that their farming drew on both kinds of land resources but also that their livestock movements and dealing bridged the widening gulf between common-field farming and pasture farming. With this activity being centred on the town as the exchange point, it is not surprising to find there the earliest divergence of interest between mixed husbandry and livestock farming and the emergence of stock-dealing more or less independent of ordinary farming. Much of the dealing at the fairs would have been in the hands of outsiders, notably Welsh drovers supplying the area with cows. Three of the suppliers of beasts to the Misterton estate in 1552 were Davye lloyde, a drover with the appropriate name of Grenwaye and 'a Walshe drover'. Only one local man described as a drover has been traced, Thomas Lussell of Dunton Bassett, who died in 1564. His goods consisted of 80 sheep, half of them fat, worth £16 in all, wool worth £3, peas and hay worth £1 and nothing else. He was evidently unmarried and based on the village because of his 'sister dwelling in Dunton Bassett', whom he made his residuary legatee. Nevertheless he was almost certainly a member of the Lussell family of Lutterworth butchers.[26]

By the early seventeenth century the town was supporting several commercial men who were farming as pure graziers and were evidently closely involved in local livestock-dealing. Nicholas Ratcliffe, shoemaker, who died in 1583, had a common-field holding; but in 1564 he had been fined for keeping four hundred (480) sheep over his stint and he was also the first craftsman to appear in the later Lay Subsidy rolls. The 1597 inventory of Edward Overing, saddler and chandler, is the first to shew a pure grazing farm. His livestock, valued at £57.6.8d., over half his inventory total, was grazing a close, probably in Moorbarns, and included ewes, with their lambs worth as much as 13/4d. each. He was a taxpayer too. Francis Pope, mercer, was also a pure grazing farmer. At his death in 1626 his livestock included steers and wethers and was valued at £188, nearly half his inventory total. Most striking is the inventory of John Hackkytt, made in 1615/16. His possessions consisted of little other than £135.7.6d. in debts due to him and £100 worth of valuable sheep, and rams, of various types and at different prices. He was a bachelor and, as he had no household goods, evidently a dealer who lodged at one of the inns in the town, although not temporarily, as he paid tax from there.[27]

Several factors, therefore, combined to reinforce the town as the centre of the area while the livestock trade increased into the seventeenth century. In the first place its position on through droving-routes supported its fairs as the exchange point between the area and further afield; secondly the markets were the most convenient outlet for farmers in the area with only a few animals to sell at a time; thirdly the town remained the natural centre for stock movements and dealing, even if the open markets and fairs were being bypassed; and fourthly, whether in the hands of townsmen or villagers, the local butchery trade was confined to the town and its markets.

During the first half of the seventeenth century, however, there emerged some village-based butchery businesses of importance. In a manorial court at Gilmorton in 1607 no mention was made of the sale of meat, but at others in the 1620s six men were cited in connexion with selling meat there, all but one being members of the Sleath family.[28] Any study of the butchers in the area would have to start with the tree of this family, with its distinctive christian name Gabriel. It produced at least a dozen butchers based on six of the villages during the century and one in the town too. Just as the Misterton accounts referred to Thomas Kirby of Lutterworth as 'Thomas butcher', the Leire yeoman Clement Stretton referred to a debt owing by 'Gabriel the butcher', evidently meaning Gabriel Sleath. Such village butchers were the successors to the husbandmen trading as butchers on market days only. With the spread of improving farming through the area, however, they were nearer to the new sources of livestock reared for meat. Needless to say, the majority of them were based on villages with the mixed economy associated with the retention of common-field farming. Here they would be selling meat to the other villagers from their shops; but they no doubt continued to sell in local markets. In Leicester in 1635/6 a new type of freedom of the borough was introduced, making foreign butchers free on market days only. Among the 84 men who took this up during the remainder of the century were a dozen from the villages along the northern edge of the Lutterworth area, and one of the very first was a member of the Sleath family.[29] In Lutterworth itself such men may have taken a greater share of the business at the expense of the town butchers. For, while the village butcher was in the ascendancy by the later seventeenth century, at the same time the town butchers lost their leading position in the economy of the area. In the last three decades of the sixteenth century half a dozen Lutterworth butchers were concerned with probate; but in the whole of the seventeenth century only John Taylor and William Winterton were, and they probably owed their wealth to the important public houses they were running.[30]

Such butchers as remained in the town were in general full-time tradesmen with no farming interests. Some of the village butchers, on the other hand, were the chief grazing farmers to take advantage of the improved pasture grounds, men like William Seale, Thomas Simons, Anthony Prowitt and Richard Webster. Thus in an important sense they were the successors to the Lutterworth yeoman farmers who had dominated the livestock-dealing in the area at the beginning of the century. In other words with the spread of improved farming the greatest share of the local livestock market, which had been a town monopoly, passed into the hands of the new class of commercial farmers, who could see to their own marketing, whether in the town, at other markets and fairs or in private dealing.

Lutterworth market day would also have been the main time for local men and women to sell all kinds of lesser produce. Only half a dozen fishers selling in the market there have left any record, in the court rolls of the 1560s. They mostly came from down the River Swift towards the Avon at Rugby.[31] No doubt such wares as butter, cheese, poultry, eggs and honey, and also fruit, vegetables, herbs and flowers, were all set out for sale and this would have been especially important to those smaller producers who have been mentioned as being thrust into the market from the late sixteenth century onwards, the smallholders and cottagers.

Dealers in corn

There is evidence for the sale of bread-corn and seed-corn in Lutterworth market in the early middle ages. The volume of this business must have increased greatly in the later sixteenth century and Burton noted the 'exceeding good Corn in great abundance', no doubt sold in the Corn Market, as the most conspicuous feature of the town's Thursday market.[32] The mid-seventeenth century changes in the economy involved a far greater proportion of the population of the area being dependent on corn grown commercially. How did this affect corn-dealing in the town? At first sight there is practically no trace of corn-dealers trading in the town, so that it would seem that all dealing must have been direct between producer and consumer in the open market. In order to trace the patterns of redistribution for consumption, therefore, it is necessary to make a closer study of the successive stages of processing, namely milling, baking, malting and brewing.

Over the two centuries mills or millers have been traced in 20 of the 23 village parishes in the area. In fact nearly every village had its own mill, at least a windmill if not a water-mill; but only a few supported a miller who could raise himself out of the context of the manorial economy to attain any independent wealth. When, with the increase in population, the business built up in volume the miller could sell the surplus of the tolls he took in kind to satisfy demand within the village communities or in a nearby town. Town customers were likely to be keepers of public houses but village customers were primarily those who grew no corn of their own, the poorer inhabitants. The will of the Claybrook miller who died in 1557 prolonged this aspect of his role in the parish; for he not only gave fourpence a house 'to every poor household' there but also specified 'I will there to be dealt the day of my burial to the poor people twenty dozen of bread and the thirty day ten dozen and the year's mind twenty dozen of bread'. It is presumably corn-dealing business of this kind that is reflected in those inventories of millers that consist mainly of a list of debtors, some of them owing very small sums. The assets of another Claybrook miller, who died in 1591, consisted almost entirely of £7 in ready money and 27 debts amounting to £22.10.3d. Three quarters of this was owed by 17 people within the parish, one seventh by five people from the parish of Monks Kirby, just across the Watling Street, and in addition 6/- by a Hinckley woman and 18/- by a woman from Coventry. Similarly among the assets of a Leire miller who died in 1598/9 were four debts amounting to £7.10.0. His debtors included one man from Broughton Astley, one from Sapcote, just across the Fosse Way, and Robert Shakespeare of Lutterworth. In such cases, or in the event of the local demand for grinding outstripping the capacity of the mills, the "custom of suit and grist" or monopoly of the manorial mill over its "soke" became a matter of contention.[33] Of the village mills which rose in this way to more than local importance by the late sixteenth century onwards some of the chief were the two water-mills (Bag Mill and Stemborough Mill) at Leire and the ones at Dunton Bassett, Claybrook, Swinford and North Kilworth (see Map IV). All of them, needless to say, belonged to villages that continued to support the mixed economy of common-field farming, while there was also at least one important water-mill in the exceptional parish of Broughton Astley. Of the millers for whom probate records have been traced 13 were from such villages, two from Broughton Astley and only one from an enclosing village, from Catthorpe before in fact it was enclosed. The only wind and water-mills in the area shewn on the county map prepared by John Prior in the 1770s were seven in such villages and the two in Broughton Astley.

The greatest demand, of course, came from the town community and the capacity of the Lutterworth manorial mills, the Lodge Mills whose soke was the principal manor, was outstripped by the 1580s if not earlier. These were separated from the common fields by being in the middle of the enclosed grounds of Moorbarns and from Lutterworth by being 'a long mile' or 'a good mile from the town'. The Spittle Mills, on the other hand, which were outside the manor, were only 'about a bow shoot', 'about a flight shoot' or 'a land's length or two' outside the town.[34] At first it was the more independent millers at these rival mills that took advantage of the situation. One miller there, appropriately named William Snow, was taxed on one pound in wages in 1524, but also was the first Lutterworth miller to feature in the probate records, his personal goods being valued at £7.8.8d. in 1571. In the late 1580s, to increase the capacity of the mills, the first windmill was built there, 'in the middle of a close anciently called the Park' but thereafter 'the Milne Close'. By the end of the century, however, it was the proprietor and not the miller who was investing in improvements; and the proprietor at this time was, of course, Thomas Farren. Shortly after purchasing the Spittle estate in 1596 he rebuilt the water-mills. Meanwhile the millers were reduced to employee status. In about 1610 he had to rebuild the windmill which had been burnt down 'by the negligence of . . . a miller at that time belonging to . . . Thomas Farren'.[35]

Paradoxically it was now the town's manorial mills that offered prospects for an ambitious miller. It is remarkable that during the 40 years after 1570 three millers in turn, John Vicars, Thomas Swancote and Thomas Chamberlaine, each graduated from the Spittle Mills to the Lodge Mills. The lease of the latter continued to be held on a nominal or fixed rent of £5 a year, despite the fact that by 1607 it was valued at £25.6.8d. The millers there found it profitable enough to invest their own money in improvements. In the late 1580s Swancote rebuilt the water-mills at a cost of £20. In 1609 Chamberlaine built at his own expense the first windmill at the Lodge Mills, evidently a substantial mill, as it was still valued at £50 in his inventory six years later. They even tried hedging-in their monopoly by engrossing into their hands other mills in the neighbourhood. These men were important figures in the town in the early seventeenth century. Their debtors included villagers, but were mainly townspeople. Chamberlaine's inventory total was £181.17.11d., of which £83.8.8d. was owed by four men from neighbouring parishes, including John Pulteney of Misterton, and 23 others, nearly all of whom can be identified as townsmen. Swancote paid tax in 1610, but was probably retired as yeoman when he died in 1625. His inventory total was £143.1.0, of which £93.6.0 was due from his debtors, who included a glover and a husbandman in the town, both kinsmen of his, and four village yeomen. Already in the 1590s the complaint had been that 'there are many bakers and victuallers now in the town that heretofore have not been which do grind at the mills, by reason whereof the tenants' corn cannot be ground'. Other evidence confirms that the chief customers of the mills were the bakers and innholders in the town, including Robert Smith and Robert Billington. The latter owed as much as £15 to Chamberlaine in 1615 and was himself in occupation of the Spittle Mills in 1622. These millers, therefore, were able to rely on their monopoly over all the milling by tenants of the manor to obtain some hold over the expanding corn market in the town. In other words they were principal corn-dealers in the town and area.[36]

Upon the sale of the manor at the end of the 1620s the Lodge Mills finally went the same way as the Spittle Mills. A lease was taken by a member of the town gentry, Thomas Insley, who invested his own money in it. At a cost of £100 he rebuilt the water-mills from the foundations up. The two wheels were changed from over-shot to breast-shot and their capacity greatly increased, to five quarters a day.[37] From then onwards no town miller of any independent wealth is recorded. There followed renewed litigation between the proprietors of the two mills over the monopoly. This time, however, the aim seems to have been not so much to settle the rivalry as to attempt to establish control over the business of all the inhabitants, whether tenants of the manor or not.[38] The cases may well have been collusive, as Farren's heir had already mortgaged the Spittle Mills to the Temple family, the head lessees of the Lodge Mills.[39] Later in the century the latter still claimed the monopoly for their mills; but when the windmill at the Lodge Mills burnt down in 1667 they had to make their tenant, the then Thomas Insley, a £20 allowance off his rent in return for his rebuilding it.[40]

There is a long history of substantial townspeople setting up domestic querns or mills in defiance of the monopoly and being compelled to take them down.[41] The chief offenders were the bakers and innholders, including, again, Robert Smith and Robert Billington. Enforcement was becoming less effective and the final judgement asserting the monopoly of the two mills over the whole town turned out to be a hollow victory, as the manorial court was evidently no longer able or concerned to enforce it rigorously. In the mid-sixteenth century a manorial court had sufficed to compel several townsmen, including a member of the Paver family of mercers, to pull down their private mills. An Exchequer case in 1587 had succeeded against the three offenders, who included the tenant of the Swan and, ironically, Thomas Insley's grandfather. Out of the dozen offenders at the turn of the century, however, half of them innholders and a couple of them bakers, only two appear to have complied, in spite of another Exchequer case in 1597. In the final cases in 1630–1 another seven offenders were cited. The result was a more or less free market in which outsiders, "foreign millers", could compete with townsmen on a commercial basis. Thomas Chamberlaine's son and heir left Lutterworth and removed to Biggin Mill, just across the Watling Street; but this did not sever his connexion with the town. Together with a Lutterworth baker, Richard Hallam, he owned a windmill in Bitteswell, so that his business in fact straddled the town.[42]

Thus milling within the area during this period exhibits all the stages of progress from a service embedded in the manorial economy to a commercial business run for the profit of its proprietors. In the years of transition the town millers were able to exploit their monopoly position so as to grasp an important share of the local corn trade; but with the dissolution of the manorial structure in favour of a more commercial economy the town millers soon lost their commanding position.

Baking was like milling in the sixteenth century in that it was undertaken for the most part in manorial common ovens. A common bakehouse had been in operation in Lutterworth since the middle ages;[43] but if there were any full-time bakers in the villages they were not prosperous enough to leave any record. Apart from the use made of the bakehouse at manorial establishments, the only evidence for village baking is one bakehouse and some baking vessels, both in the inventories of ordinary farmers.

In the mid-century as many as 20 townsmen and women at a time, or more, were presented at the manorial court in connexion with baking. Most of this baking was still done in the common bakehouse. Two of the offenders, however, John Saunders and the wife of John Wheteley, were common bakers paying substantial fines. They, together with a few other important householders, had their own ovens. One presentment in 1562 was 'for baking at Home weekly 2 days' and in the 1590s two bakers, William Jones and William Hallam, were presented for not baking at the manorial bakehouse.[44] Various records confirm the wealth and influence of the two common bakers, Saunders and Wheteley, and their successors. Saunders was worth £84.11.6d. at his death in 1569. Wheteley paid tax from 1546 to 1552 and was worth £148.10.4d. at his death in 1564.[45] William Jones also paid tax in the 1570s. By the turn of the century the two yeoman bakers Robert Smith and Robert Billington were the main bakers, supplying the town and also selling in the villages. Smith first paid tax in 1599 and Billington in 1611. They were the principal, or the only, common bakers cited in the North Kilworth and Gilmorton manorial courts in 1597, 1602 and 1607.[46]

Seventeenth-century bakers have been traced in 12 of the villages in the area, eight of which were villages that retained their common fields. Of the four others the Willoughby Waterless references date from before the enclosure there and the final enclosure at Cotesbach actually seems to have compelled the baker to leave his village to set up business in the town. He was selling bread from Cotesbach in 1597, but later from Lutterworth, where he already owned a cottage in 1607. There was at least one thriving bakery in the exceptional parish of Broughton Astley, where the first of three successive bakers with identical names in Sutton was worth £107.6.2d. on his death in 1675. The adjoining parish of Frowlesworth had some similarities and its modest bakery also features more than once in the probate records. Part of the baker's business there, on the other hand, depended on the town. In 1657 he, together with seven other outsiders, was selling bread in the Lutterworth Thursday markets. He was not the only village baker recorded as owning a horse and panniers with which he could transport his products. Conversely the town remained very much the centre of the bread supply for the villages. In the mid-century it was stated that 'besides other inhabitants in the town of Lutterworth there are seven common bakers to sell at home and abroad into the country'. Two town bakers, Thomas Alsop and John Newcom, were still the main sellers of bread cited in North Kilworth in the 1670s and town bakers also had panniers in which to deliver it. In the mid-century it was also estimated that 40 quarters of grain were baked in the town each week, an amount which might have fed about twice the town population. The town population itself relied very heavily on its bakers; for only 'the better sort of housekeepers', estimated to number 16, or at the most 20 or 30, had private ovens. In fact the number of town bakers had already increased to seven by the early 1630s.[47]

The common bakers were men of some importance in the town. Four families produced bakers who served as church wardens during the second half of the seventeenth century, including Mr Thomas Alsopp. He was presumably related to Mr William Alsopp, baker, twice Mayor of Leicester in the same period. These families frequently retained the same business for two generations or more. William Hallam, who came to Lutterworth some time before 1600, almost certainly from Leicester, was the first of a line of bakers lasting into the eighteenth century.[48] These businesses were, with few exceptions, entirely independent of farming. This throws into relief the farming undertakings of the Smith and Billington families early in the century. They were setting about solving the corn supply problems by direct action; in other words they were the first commercial arable farmers in the area.

At the other end of the scale, the baker at the manorial common bakehouse used to have a holding in the common fields; but this, 'the bakehouse yard land', became a separately occupied farm well before the end of the sixteenth century.[49] This left the family running the bakehouse hampered by the customary basis of the business and their efforts in the mid-seventeenth century to establish a monopoly of baking over all the tenants of the manor were ineffective. One of the two ovens in the bakehouse was disused and the capacity of the other was only 18 to 20 strikes a day, that is, no more than 15 quarters a week, under half the baking needed in the town. Besides, the manorial court was no longer able or concerned to enforce such a monopoly. In the 1590s it had taken steps to suppress the use of private ovens; but in 1658 the baker tried resorting to an Exchequer action.[50] The chief role of the bakehouse appears to have been to bake for the poorer inhabitants, many of whom thronged in that part of the town immediately round the bakehouse and the baker's home. This might be the reason for the short working life of the Clarke family. In the period 1607 to 1681 no fewer than eight of them in turn were baking there. Nevertheless they managed to increase the charges and go a long way towards commuting them from voluntary contributions in kind to money payments. At the beginning of the century people baking there gave one penny and a piece of dough for every strike baked. By the 1640s the charge had been raised progressively to twopence and a piece of dough, or twopence-halfpenny without. By the later seventeenth century bakers there were even building up some independent wealth.[51]

Commercial baking became well established in the town during the seventeenth century; and yet the inventories shew the bakers to be less prosperous than either the Smiths and Billingtons or even their sixteenth-century predecessors. As with livestock-dealing, this points to the dissolution of a practical monopoly within the local economy. Whereas, like the millers, the town bakers had apparently been principal corn-dealers in the area, the greater part of the trade now passed out of their hands. Unlike the town butchers, however, they faced little serious competition from village bakers. Their role as the chief suppliers of bread in both the town and villages was therefore able to support them as full-time commercial bakers.

Unlike milling and baking, malting lent itself to small-scale production in the home, as initially only modest equipment was required. The simple domestic kiln was little more than a wooden box set over a low fire and the only part of it worth valuing separately was the cloth of horse hair stretched across the top, on which the malt was carefully dried. So long as malt was for consumption within the household or within the community, little account needed to be taken of the time and labour of the women-folk in its preparation. The ordinary farmers in the area, however, were able to respond to the increased demand and to supplement their income by selling off part of their grain crop already processed in this way. Only one village inventory has been traced listing a kiln house before the 1590s. From that decade, however, 15 mention 5 kiln houses, 11 pairs of querns and a mill and from the 1630s 25 mention 20 pairs of querns and 14 malt-mills.

At the same time malting was being undertaken in Lutterworth on a scale far larger than the domestic. By the beginning of the seventeenth century the kiln houses and malt houses were some of the very largest buildings in the town. Of the six kiln houses listed in the 1607 Survey, there were two of two bays of building, two of three and one of four; of the four malt houses there were one each of three, six and seven bays. Pairs of querns, however, were not so common as might have been expected. This was no doubt because the town was served by powered malt-mills. Here again the most important householders were trying to break free of the custom of grist to the manorial mills; for with the Lodge Mills went the manorial horse malt-mill in Bakehouse Lane. Such men patronized foreign millers, like the millers at the Spittle Mills where there was also a malt-mill, or else set up their own pairs of querns or domestic malt-mills. Malt was the main source of contention in the litigation over the milling monopoly. This monopoly was still being considered a practical proposition in 1630. Unlike the Lodge Mills with respect to bread-corn, the Horse Mill was said to be capable of grinding all the malt needed by the inhabitants.[52]

Apart from the gentry, the principal offenders against the monopoly were innholders. Substantial stocks of malt were kept by such men, especially from the 1630s onwards. In 1634 Francis Billington had £17.10.0 worth in the malt chamber at the Swan. From this decade too date the first mentions of maltsters in the area, like John Flude of Lutterworth. From the second half of the century there are records of half a dozen maltsters. In addition ten more townspeople, half of them men and half women, were, to judge from their activities and possessions, equally involved in malting. Thomas Goodacre, for example, occupied 'three bays of building being a Kilne and Maulting room' in the 1690s. With few exceptions all these people were independent of farming and often their stock of malt made up half the value of their goods. Even one who was also a "common-field grazier" had 40 quarters which were valued at £40, a large proportion of his inventory total of £100.5.0. Malting in the villages, meanwhile, was dying out, save in the largest households. Fourteen of the inventories from the 1680s mention only eight pairs of querns and six malt-mills. The sole kiln house listed belonged to a Swinford yeoman with 'Debts due for malt of several persons'. As his name was James Flude this may have been part of the family's town-based business.[53] All this points to malting having become established as a separate and commercially based occupation, even more prosperous than baking and very much centred on the town.

The malt prepared in the area in the sixteenth century was doubtless consumed locally and in the form of ale. The wives of some of the larger farmers may have brewed on a small scale at home, but other villagers would rely on the various communal ales that punctuated the calendar and on the manorial brew-houses, like the ones at Misterton Hall, Knaptoft Hall and Monks Kirby manor house.[54] There is no trace of brewing in ordinary households on a scale that required a special room. Moreover so long as brewing was for immediate consumption in the home or in the community the introduction of hops made little headway and beer was only drunk at the establishments of the gentry who were in a position to raise their own hops. Out of 95 gallons of drink bought in by the Misterton estate for two annual audit feasts in the 1550s only seven were specified as beer.[55] The first local mention of hops traced is in the inventory of a Lutterworth parson in 1588. The Spittle and Monks Kirby manor house both had domestic hop-yards at the beginning of the seventeenth century and a larger one was recorded at Newnham Paddox later on.[56]

In Lutterworth much of the drink brewed was of course for sale to the throngs of people in town on market and fair days. Brewing remained, however, very much a household-based activity, so that every one of the townspeople presented at the manorial courts in connexion with brewing in the 1560s was a woman. The inventories shew that they would be brewing at home; apart from brewing vessels, several town householders, and not only gentry, had their own brew-houses. At first the rooms were called 'aling-houses'. The first distinction was in 1588, in the household of Thomas Insley, gentleman. In his brew-house he had furnaces worth £10 and in his aling-house wort leads worth £3. The townswomen brewing for sale concentrated on beer-brewing, so that by the seventeenth century there is no mention of ale in the inventories, only beer. This contrast is neatly illustrated by the occupations given in the parish registers in the 1630s; only two brewers are mentioned, a village aleman and a town beer-brewer. Out of the 18 town inventories mentioning brewing in the period 1640 to 1675 seven mention beer but none ale. This trade probably depended on imported hops. A

Lutterworth mercer, Francis Pope, had £6.14.0 worth in stock in 1626[57] A particularly significant development in the brewing trade was the general adoption of the furnace, a specialized enclosed fire which replaced the lead or copper over an open hearth. The first traced in the area were Thomas Insley's. In the 1630s a couple were listed, one in the town and one in a village; but they remained rare in the villages, while 21 were recorded in the town, all in the period from 1660 to the end of the century. The furnace, however, was not generally adopted by the innholders, who may have left the more commercial production to those who could concentrate on brewing.[58] An indication of the volume of beer brewed is the sudden increase in the numbers of cellars mentioned for its storage. Over the two centuries 45 of the town inventories mentioned cellars, but only five of these date from before 1650. From the next 50 years one quarter of the inventories included cellars.

Meanwhile in the villages, although brew-houses were becoming more common, they remained confined to the larger households of the yeomen and gentry. Twelve are listed in the inventories from the 1680s, one of them at an inn. The only active furnace noted belonged to the Swinford yeoman James Flude. Presumably the ordinary villagers were relying on the village alehouses for their drink, while any beer consumed in the area still came from the town. There are signs that the brewing of ale too was undertaken commercially in the town towards the end of the century. Out of 16 inventories mentioning brewing from 1679 to the end of the century seven mentioned ale, but only two mentioned beer. This more likely reflects a change in the use of the word 'ale' to cover light beer rather than some reversal in taste.[59] In any case it seems that the town brewers were now involved also in supplying the needs of the lower levels of local society. While brewing was the preoccupation of householders of all ranks in the town, very little brewing of any kind for general consumption appears to have been done in the villages. As might be expected in a small market town, brewing did not develop into a recognized separate occupation during this period. Nevertheless by the later seventeenth century brewing was being left more and more to people who undertook it on a commercial basis and, like malting, this was an activity very much concentrated in the town. The only distilling traced was also in the town.

Keepers of public houses

Of course a large proportion of the provisions, especially the drink, was not only prepared but also consumed in public houses of one sort or another. "Public house" is used here as a general term to cover inns, taverns and alehouses; the only relevant occupational terms used in the contemporary records are "innholder", "vintner" and "victualler". The development of the public houses and the facilities they offered both to wayfarers and to the local population has been singled out as the most important feature of the market town in these two centuries.[60] Whilst it is impossible to be certain how many of these there were at any one time, an idea of the way in which both their numbers and the scope of the facilities they offered increased may be gained from the records of houses officially recognized as licensed. In 1608 39 men and three women in the whole of Guthlaxton hundred, which includes the Lutterworth area, were actually licensed at the Quarter Sessions as victuallers or alehousekeepers. There were clearly more besides who were not; already in 1577 it was estimated that the hundred contained a round figure of 50 alehouses and four inns. The number of women presented at the manorial courts for brewing and selling ale in the 1560s suggests that two dozen of these 54 were in the town, which would leave scarcely one alehouse for each of the 36 villages in the hundred.[61]

By the early seventeenth century the numbers in the villages had almost certainly increased, especially in those villages that were to retain their common fields. The manorial court at North Kilworth cited one brewer in 1597, but two 'common brewers and tipplers' in 1607 and they were both officially licensed in the following year. At Gilmorton, however, only one was licensed then and yet at the manorial court in 1607 two other tipplers were cited along with him and up to five brewers were cited in the 1620s. In the town there were 16 men and two women who were actually licensed in 1608 and evidently several who were not. In 1630 it was estimated that there were 40 innkeepers, alehousekeepers and common bakers there.[62] It has already been shewn that there were seven common bakers; the resulting figure of over 30 public houses shews a distinct increase since the mid-sixteenth century.

In 1753 there were 105 licensed public houses in the hundred and on average about three in each village. In the villages in the Lutterworth area there were 61 and on average two in each enclosed village and three in each of the other villages.[63] This trebling in number of public houses in the villages reflects the fundamental change in the economy. No doubt nearly every village public house remained a simple alehouse and had no importance outside the village community. Meanwhile there was in every village a greatly increased proportion of the population relying on public houses for drink.

In the town the number of public houses licensed in 1753 was 31, which shews no increase since 1630. Here, however, even though the number remained static the scope of services and accommodation continued to expand. In 1686 it was estimated that 39 guests and 122 horses could be put up in the villages in the area. The common-field villages had on average two guest beds and stabling for six horses each (2 + 6), notably more than the enclosed villages (1½ + 4¼). It is clear that some villages contained main road inns, such as North Kilworth (5 + 18) and Wibtoft (6 + 16) among the former and Peatling magna (2 + 10) among the latter. The town of Lutterworth, however, had 94 guest beds and stabling for 302 horses (94 + 302), making it comparable with market centres such as Melton Mowbray (113 + 341) and Stratford-upon-Avon (105 + 309). This means that the town had two-and-a-half times the capacity of the rest of the area in, very likely, one half the number of establishments.[64]

Since the labour of keeping open house fell initially on the housewife, "innholder" was not generally adopted as an occupational designation until the mid-seventeenth century and "alehousekeeper" not at all. Previously many of the town's innholders had other occupations or else they were "new yeomen". Later many were "new gentry". It has therefore proved impossible to identify all the public houses or to classify them precisely as the households of innholders, victuallers or alehousekeepers. This particularly applies to households from the middle range of prosperity, like the yeoman and husbandman farmsteads with houses well furnished and equipped for brewing. The principal example, the Feilding family manor farm house, was certainly an inn bearing their sign, the Denbigh Arms, by the later eighteenth century. Prior to that the yeoman tenants there, the Clarke family, were specifically allowed to keep their own domestic mill. Already at the beginning of the seventeenth century they held a licence and paid tax and their household was large and very fully equipped.[65] The most productive course, therefore, is to approach the material from each end of the economic scale in turn. At the upper end the largest inns, with their inn signs, their named chambers and numerous beds, stand out above the other establishments. At the lower end it is possible to identify some of the poorer householders whose alehousekeeping appears to have been their main support.

At the beginning of the sixteenth century there were five inn signs being displayed in the town (see Map I). Of two of them there is no further trace, but the Swan, the Crown and the Bull continued to be hung throughout this period. By the 1560s they were joined by the George, making the four inns in Guthlaxton hundred, and by the end of the century by the Hind, making five again. This summary by no means solves all the problems of identifying the actual buildings. Apart from removing to different premises in mid-career there are at least three cases of an innholder taking the sign with him. Subsequently the number of establishments accepted as inns increased, apparently doubling by the 1670s. Of even more importance than the increase in numbers was the fact that during this century innholding became recognized as a separate occupation for a man and became a primary occupation too. Previously important inns were usually based on farmsteads with holdings in the common fields. By the end of this century, where an innholder was farming at all it was not as an ordinary common-field farmer.

From the last 25 years of the century nine inventories of Lutterworth innholders survive. Four had no farming stock and four had grazing stock only. One of the latter and the ninth owned crops alone, presumably either purchased direct from arable farmers or raised under contract on the holdings that went with the premises. An early instance of the latter practice was a husbandman tilling the holding going with the Crown in 1613: 'I am to dress Mr. Grene's yard land according to my covenant for which I had of him £20'.[66] In fact the upper end of the public house keeping trade came to support a group of the wealthiest of the townsmen who were independent of farming. The average inventory total among the nine was over £100, half of which was accounted for by household furnishings.

At the other end of the scale half of the two dozen households cited in the 1560s in connexion with the sale of both bread and ale seem neither to have been inns nor to have belonged to men with important or prosperous primary occupations. Thus although the majority of this business would have been confined to Thursdays and fair days, alehousekeeping may have been emerging as a possible means of livelihood. Three of these households can actually be illustrated by inventories. John Halpeny senior was a shearman and Alice Partriche and the third were both women carrying on as widows after losing their husbands. In each case there is evidence of brewing being done in the house, even though the household goods never added up to more than six pounds in value.[67] In the early seventeenth century Richard Atkins, a wheelwright with a cottage at the inner end of Ely Lane, was licensed as an alehousekeeper. Although he was able to purchase the freehold of the house in the late 1620s when the manor was split up, his goods at his death ten years later, which included 'one small brewing vessel of lead', were not quite worth five pounds.[68] The Peppercorne cottage at the end of the Spittle Row, although shewing no traces of brewing in the house, was apparently an alehouse. At two periods during the first half of the century it was being run by a widow and the household furnishings were never valued at more than £8.3.6d.[69] The surprising thing is that these households featured in the probate records at all. No equivalent inventories from the villages have been found shewing modest householders engaged in brewing. Alehousekeeping there was either a very poor occupation or, more likely, it remained a secondary one. Only in the town could the poorer householder and his widow rely on sufficient custom to provide a living.

After the middle of the seventeenth century there were distinct changes in this type of household. The 12 inventories, eight of them from the last 20 years of the century, shew them to have had furnishings worth three or four times as much as those just described, distributed around seven to nine rooms. In nearly every case the house had been adapted to the activity. Four had a brew-house, ten had cellars for drink storage and four had two parlours each. They also included nine of the 21 furnaces listed in the inventories from the last 40 years of the century. All this shews them to have grown to have much in common with the inns. These features, meanwhile, were lacking in the villages, outside the houses of the wealthy. Of the only two cellars traced outside the town, for instance, one was in the manor house at Monks Kirby.

In the town some of the alehouses contained more than the basic equipment. One of the sixteenth-century ones identified, Alice Partriche's, even had a guest chamber, the furnishings of which, including the only bed listed, amounted to half the value of her household goods. Similarly in the first half of the next century the outstanding feature of the Peppercorne household was the fact that half of the value of the furnishings was accounted for by the two main beds and their sheets. If the lower end of the public house trade had become so well established in the town, what of the rest? The inventories shew that the most spectacular development in the trade around the beginning of the seventeenth century was the lavish furnishing of the parlours and chambers at the inns for their principal guests. After the mid-century on average the number of rooms there with beds worth valuing and the value of the furnishings in them fell slightly. This does not reflect a decline in the accommodation offered so much as an increase in the number of houses recognized as inns, some of them neither so large nor so pretentious as the main ones. The inventories of the inns include on average half a dozen listed beds. If these beds are equated with the 94 official guest beds of 1686, this suggests at least 15 establishments offering such accommodation, and probably more. Throughout the public houses in the town, moreover, there would be many lodgings for wayfarers of one sort or another, other than the officially listed guest beds that stood in the parlours and chambers of the inns. A good deal of this accommodation may be listed in the inventories of the middle range of inhabitants who cannot be positively identified as public house keepers. One mid-century example is a man who occupied a house of nine rooms in which there were nine beds and 13 pairs of sheets. Five of the rooms with beds in had furnishings worth from £2 to £6.10.0. He had brewing vessels in the kitchen and cellar, but no farming stock. He was styled 'Mr' and was a victualler; in fact there is nothing to distinguish his from the inventory of an innholder.[70]

As for stabling of horses, although the largest stable buildings were attached to the inns, many horses could be accommodated at smaller establishments too. Already in 1562 the tenant of the Swan, John Johnson, had been fined for grazing up to 20 horses at a time on common meadow ground.[71] In 1607 the formal stint allowed for a total of just under 240 horses to graze in the fields. There were three dozen stable buildings listed in the town, the largest of them, one of three bays of building and one of four, belonging to inns. Stables and their fittings feature most frequently in the inventories of innholders, rather than of plain farmers. Even Alice Partriche had a stable and three of the later seventeenth-century alehousekeepers identified had two stables each; yet none of these four had a horse of their own.

The most important increase was not so much in the numbers of public houses of one sort or another as in the scope and volume of facilities provided, especially among the larger alehouses, both those that came to be accepted more or less as inns and those that continued to offer victuals and drink only. In the last 20 years of the seventeenth century the church wardens attended meetings on business, treating themselves and 'the neighbours', at the houses of about 14 different townsmen. Probably all of them kept public houses, although only half of them can be shewn to have been innholders. Hitherto public house keeping had performed two fairly distinct functions, with the inns accommodating visiting traders and the alehouses catering for the inhabitants of the area and beyond who resorted to the town on market and fair days. The expansion of the facilities would be partly a response to the demands of a wider range of wayfaring traders frequenting the town; but it also reflected the greater dependence of the local population on the town, not only for trading opportunities but also for provisions of all sorts. In other words the filling-in of the range of services was part of the progress of the town to another stage of being an integral part of the economy of the area.

So far the public house keepers have been discussed entirely in terms of the drink, victuals and lodging they provided. It must be borne in mind, however, that they owed much of their importance to the commercial business that came to be conducted within their houses.[72] Having outlined the overall development of the Lutterworth public houses during this period, therefore, it is worth asking how far the commercial connexions of these people point to the general character of the commercial activity in the town at each stage.

At the beginning of the sixteenth century, even taking into account the smallholding which amounted to about a quarter of a yard land occupied by the widow who was tenant of the Bull in Wood Market, none of the town's five inns was based on a farm holding of any importance. They were probably all primarily lodging houses for travellers and merchants. The only one at the centre of the town was the Swan, which belonged to the Hospital of Saint John and was presumably run as part of the foundation's service to poor travellers.[73] Down the High Street, opposite the Feilding family manor house, the Crown belonged to Martin Feilding, the bailiff of the principal manor. In the Wood Market both the Pannier and the Saracen's Head, which stood next door to each other, belonged to Sir Everard, Martin's elder brother and head of the family. It is tempting to see in these two signs a connexion with long-distance trading and, in view of the wool trade that was based on the town in the late fifteenth century, to say that the main role of the family's three inns was to put up visiting wool merchants. In 1515 Sir

Everard's successor sued William Parburne of Lutterworth, innkeeper, for negligence in burning down a house of his in the town.[74] Perhaps it was one of his two inns that had been destroyed. Ultimately, however, the disappearance of their two signs could best be accounted for by the removal of this wool trade from the town.

It is arguable that the main Lutterworth inns were hitherto in the nature of manorial outposts or town extensions of manorial establishments rather than independent businesses.[75] In the 1550s food and drink for people working on the Misterton estate was provided by 'Thomas Willens our host' . . . 'at the alehouse here', based on a farm in the dependent village of Walcote. He was the largest purchaser of corn, especially barley, from the estate and his wife bought a continuous supply of animals for meat. When it came, however, to securing provisions for 20 guests at the annual audit, most of the bread and drink was purchased from outside, at least half of it from the two common bakers and other public house keepers in Lutterworth. One year, however, the whole operation was catered for by John Saxton, an occupant of the estate's burgage property in the High Street. There is insufficient documentation to prove this theory; but what is clear is that the public house keepers that rose in importance in the later sixteenth century did so very much in parallel to the yeoman farmers who were concentrating on livestock-farming and livestock-dealing. In fact they were similar farmers themselves. In the 1560s the bailiff of the principal manor, Richard Johnson, had a farmstead facing onto the Beast Market.[76] He was selling meat, bread and ale and, to judge from gaming offences there ('shovelaboard' or 'showgroat', *i.e.* shuffle-board or shove-groat, now shove-halfpenny), he often entertained guests at his house, which was the George Inn. Similar activity was recorded at the house of the Lussells, one of the town's main butcher families. Their inventories shew this to have been a wine tavern that grew to function practically as an inn, although their stock-dealing and butchery business, combined with their farming in the fields, was probably of first importance to them. Another town butcher, who was not in fact farming, had a similar household, which included a 'new chamber'.[77]

The chief participant in the stock-dealing trade around the turn of the century was Thomas Farren, who resided at the Spittle. It is worth noting that his possessions listed in his will included an inn, the Crown, at Market Harborough, which could have provided a base for his business at the markets and fairs there. Much of the trade, however, was in the hands of itinerant or seasonal dealers, such as the Welsh drovers already noted. Such trading was, presumably, the background of a number of Welsh people who settled in the town towards the end of the century. One of them, Evans (or Evin) Barnard, was the tenant at the George in the 1590s. Another was David Fludd, yeoman, whose will bears his signature with this spelling but was listed under 'Flooyde or lloyd'. He occupied premises near the Drapery and the Shambles and on or next to the Lord's Headland. Soon after 1589 he moved across the High Street to the Misterton estate town property, next to the Swan. This he developed into the town's largest and most lavishly furnished inn, the Hind, for which he held a licence and paid tax. At his death in 1614 his inventory included the stock of a very small holding and he had a stable but no horse of his own. Twelve rooms and twelve beds were listed and the linen, which included 45 pairs of sheets, was valued at £26.3.4d. Sixteen of these pairs were 'fine sheets', valued at £5.12.0. Four of the six rooms with beds in were worth over £6 in furnishings, and a fifth £17. Two of the four chambers had fireplaces. The household total, £128.6.2d., was not exceeded in any other town inventory.[78]

The best lodgings offered may have been for sojourning stock-dealers, like John Hackkytt; but the association between the public house trade and the livestock trade went deeper too. The Taylor family that followed on at the George in the early seventeenth century was another family of butchers. Pursuing this connexion from the butchery trade to the leather trade, one of the alehouses traceable from the late sixteenth century belonged to the Newcombes, a family of shoemakers. Indeed half of the less prosperous alehousekeepers identified from the second half of the seventeenth century were leather-workers of one sort or another. Nor were such men only involved with the less important public houses. The victualler or innkeeper at the Crown in the 1630s was John Tarlton, who had started out as a shoemaker. He had stables, hay lofts, sheep pens and 'the herbage of two Closes', but no farming stock or horse of his own at his death in 1638. Another shoemaker died the same year leaving a very similar inventory, suggesting another public house as important as an inn, although his shoemaker's shop was still active. He was John Young, who occupied the King's Headland premises vacated by David Fludd. He too had taken out a licence in 1608 and he was one of the few craftsman to appear on the tax rolls.[79]

All this confirms that Lutterworth was the local centre of the livestock trade, not only on fair days but also on market days, and of the area's butchery trade. Indeed many of the private deals that have been described as bypassing the town's markets, such as Misterton estate purchases and sales recorded as taking place at Lutterworth, but not on Thursdays, may nevertheless have been concluded in its public houses; so that in the long run the greatest benefit to the town from the trade was an indirect one, the stimulus to its public house keeping.

The town bakers played the leading role in the local corn trade, especially in the early seventeenth century. Even in the mid-sixteenth century the households of the two common bakers were also run as public houses. Later they grew into the town's two largest inns. The Smith family evidently rebuilt their house, so that by the early 1630s they had an inn of 17 rooms. In 1634 the household was worth £70.7.4d. Ten beds were listed and 46 pairs of sheets were valued at £14.15.0. The furnishings in one of the five chambers were worth £6.12.0 and in each of the two parlours £10. Meanwhile the Billington family had taken over the Swan. The restricted corner site, however, limited the expansion of the business there and, also in the early 1630s, they transferred it to a set of premises further down the High Street. In 1607 Robert occupied small premises, technically a cottage but one of only two cottages listed in the Survey as having a separate kitchen. The location was, significantly, the Corn Market. These premises probably formed part of the new Swan, the lower end of which adjoined the Feilding family manor farm. Robert was a taxpayer in 1611/12 but at his death in 1630 he still apparently occupied the Swan on the corner site above the Hind. The new Swan was almost certainly the town's most important and lavishly furnished inn. In 1640 the household was worth £90; 16 rooms and 11 beds were listed. The furnishings in two of the five chambers were worth £14 and in one of the two parlours £24. In 1634 the £33 worth of furnishings in one of the chambers was part of a household total of £114.4.5d.[80] Later in the century this was one of the two Lutterworth inns which boasted an "ordinary", a dining room for public meals at fixed price.[81]

After the mid-century the innholders became independent of the butchery trade and of the common bakery business and for the most part relied on innholding for their livelihood. About this time, however, some of the leading inns were closely connected with retail trading. One house was occupied in turn by a vintner, George Gidley who died in 1641, and his son Matthew, a woollen draper, who died 19 years later. They were both actively trading, but the household furniture and the named chambers shew that they were running an inn, which was probably in the Beast Market. George's household goods were worth £87.8.4d. Eight beds were listed and seven chambers, including the Half Moon, the Bull Head, the White Lion and the Star, each with furnishings worth £3 or more. Matthew's household, worth nearly the same, included 15 pairs of sheets and other linen valued at £15.2.8d. The furnishings in one chamber were worth £9 and in another, which also had a fireplace, nearly £18.[82] Another man was trading later as a vintner; but on his death in 1692 his innholding was clearly his most important business and probably the reason for him being styled as 'gentleman'. His household was valued at £90.0.4d. Nine beds were listed and £12 worth of linen. Most of the eight chambers were named after their colour and all but two had furnishings worth £2.10.0 or more. This was almost certainly the George Inn.[83]

In the last ten years of the century the Justices' meetings were held at the houses of a mercer and of two apothecaries, which suggest that they were running public houses. The house most frequently used for public meetings in the 1680s, however, was that of Mr George Tilley which continued to be run for four years by his widow after his death in 1695. He was a mercer and issued trading tokens at Lutterworth as such in 1667 (see token d in Illustration 18). In that year he purchased property at the very centre of the town, next to the Drapery. He paid £200 for five bays of building on the King's Headland, together with the adjoining premises which had formerly been occupied by John Young. He soon developed the whole into the largest inn in the town, probably already under the sign of the King's Head. The inn was certainly known as the King's Head in the early eighteenth century and Tilley's token bears the king's arms. The household of 20 rooms was valued at £75.16.6d. Eight beds were listed and 12 chambers, three of them with their own grates and one with furnishings worth £13.12.6d. There is no indication, however, that he or his widow were still involved in the mercery trade.[84]

It is worth emphasizing that the original Swan, the George, the Hind and the King's Head all stood within a few yards of the High Cross at the very centre of the town, while the Crown, the new Swan premises and the Feilding manor farm, which developed into the Denbigh Arms, were not very far off down the High Street. No doubt several of the humbler public houses were crammed in amongst them. In the early eighteenth century the premises formerly run as an alehouse by Richard Atkins at the inner end of Ely Lane were flanked on each side by an 'Alehouse or common Inn', the Eagle and Child on the one side and the Wheatsheaf on the other. After the mid-sixteenth century successive stages in the development of the town economy threw into prominence a new inn as the chief one and in each case this inn, along with other public houses, reflected the general character of the main business in the town. The way that such developments were concentrated at the heart of the town shews that they were very much dependent on local trade. Moreover while at any one time the town accommodated and fed numerous wayfarers in addition to its own population, the public house trade there was also closely tied up with provisioning the inhabitants of the area and not only those who visited the town for business on Thursdays.

The regulation of middlemen

The assumption underlying the way the Tudor and Stuart administration tackled the problems of marketing was that normal conditions could be sustained, or even restored, by restricting the activities of the middleman.[85] The emergence of local middlemen of all sorts as an important factor in the national economy, however, is closely bound up with the development of the market town where, of course, they were typically based. Having examined in turn, therefore, the various types of people in the Lutterworth area concerned with the redistribution of agricultural produce, it should be asked what in general were the local responses to the growing need for marketing and how they affected the progress of the town towards a more urban economy.

The spread of the more commercial livestock farming is not easy to trace as it involved changes of ownership and location during the life of each animal. The general drift of stock, however, was towards the South East and there are also some indications that the change in farming practices was spreading through the region in a contrary direction. This boosted the importance of market towns as local exchange points, especially where they were on droving routes. Even where dealing bypassed the local fairs and markets, deals would be secured through contacts in the towns and even concluded there. And this is to say nothing of the through-trade, such as stock being bought by outsiders at the fairs and deals contracted in connexion with the droves of stock passing through. The culmination of this stage for the town of Lutterworth was during the early years of the seventeenth century. At this time, however, Thomas Farren was still able to dominate the economy of the town practically as if he were the manorial lord. It is not surprising, therefore, to find that he was the main force behind the enclosure of the adjacent village of Cotesbach. Of the 'graceless Graziers' that the elder John Moore railed against, Farren was surely the chief local representative. With the later spread of commercial livestock farming in the area further down the economic scale, the town no longer held its monopoly position and, while it no doubt remained the local stock-dealing centre, the important graziers were the farmers based on the villages.

The local butchery trade, whether in the hands of villagers or of townsmen, was centred on the town. The town butchers rose in wealth and importance and then lost their prominence in the economy of the area exactly in parallel with the livestock-dealers and grazing farmers; for indeed theirs was very much part of the same trade. After the mid-seventeenth century the majority of the meat consumed in the area would still pass through the town; but the influential butchers in the area were those who sold further afield as well, and they were some of the grazing farmers based on the villages.

To supply the corn needed to feed the rising population in the late sixteenth century involved intensifying production from existing common-field holdings. This favoured the larger farmer, who was in a better position both to increase the yield of his lands and to sell a greater proportion of his crops as surplus to his own household needs. As a result more of the population, especially in the villages where enclosure was bringing mixed husbandry to an end, came to depend on corn that had not only passed through the hands but also through the ownership of intermediaries, the millers and bakers, joined later by the maltsters. There were several village millers supplying corn, but this trade was in general concentrated in the town. Undoubtedly the largest purchasers were townspeople; for they were involved in supplying the town population, the visiting population of villagers and outsiders in the town on business and the village populations too. The practical monopoly of the town millers and bakers was also backed up by manorial restrictions and this enabled them to transfer their businesses from a customary to a commercial basis. Their importance, in fact, was not so much that they served the town community, but that they had virtual control over the greater part of the corn-redistribution trade within the area.

The men who grew to be their strongest rivals in the corn trade were the keepers of the town's public houses, buying bread-corn and quantities of barley for large-scale malting and brewing. By the late sixteenth century the manorial court was proving inadequate to keep many of these people within the framework of the customary economy. Much of their dealing would have been done in private, bypassing the open market. At times this would leave little or nothing for the small purchasers coming to buy provision for their own households only. In particular barley was a source of contention between those involved in malting it for more or less commercial purposes and those who needed it for baking their own daily bread. In the worst years too the poor had to make do with peas and beans instead of barley and this brought them into conflict with the graziers and butchers engaged in fattening animals on these crops.

As the town corn trade became more commercial, it highlighted those aspects of the customary practices that shewed them up as extortion rather than a service to the community. When prices shot up in years of dearth, so did the profits of those who were selling what they took as customary fixed tolls in kind from their customers. So long as tenants were supplying their households from off their own farm holdings, this might be no less acceptable than the tithing system; but when they were purchasing corn to be consumed by the public, the quantity surrendered could be directly valued as a cash drain on the business. Following the harvest failure of 1586 the mortality rate in Lutterworth and the area was high, as elsewhere. The situation was potentially dangerous enough to encourage the Privy Council to issue the "Book of Orders" in an attempt to restrict the activities of middlemen.[86] To deal with the lack of bread-corn in the markets in seven contiguous Midland counties, including Leicestershire, it also endeavoured to compel farmers to release some of their peas crops for the poor to buy. It can be no coincidence that this was when the first of the series of cases concerning the monopoly of the manorial mills over Lutterworth reached the court of Exchequer.[87]

The 1590s brought a widespread combination of famines and epidemics, both affecting the Lutterworth area, and elicited similar government measures. The Book of Orders was reissued three times and in 1595

Leicestershire graziers were again to release peas onto the market for the poor to buy for food. Again the Lutterworth mill monopoly was asserted in the courts. Among the offenders the greatest challenge came from Thomas Shakespeare, the Lutterworth attorney, who not only had set up a domestic malt mill but deliberately defied the monopoly by inviting others to grind there. His charge was not a toll in kind but a cash-payment at a flat rate related to the quantity ground only, one penny a strike. At this stage the practice was successfully suppressed.[88]

The sudden reversal in government attitudes to the tillage acts in the 1590s reflected the contemporary anxiety that enclosure leading to the conversion of arable to pasture was aggravating the corn shortages.[89] There were difficult years in the first two decades of the seventeenth century. The prospect of another poor harvest in 1607 was the immediate cause of the anti-enclosure riots in the Midlands. The Book of Orders was reissued in 1608 and in June that year it was thought fit in Leicester to restrain husbandmen, tradesmen and others with other means of livelihood from buying barley for malting, 'that the poor and others which buy for provision of bread may be first served' in the market. In 1615 all Leicester maltsters, some in possession of 'great store of tithe barley', were 'suppressed from buying of Barley to convert into Malt'. In the previous year official anxiety there over depopulation and decay of tillage was coupled with anxiety 'for the better suppressing of the brewing of strong Ale and beer'. In retrospect, however, these years may have seemed a period of respite; for the economic dislocation that followed after 1621 had far-reaching causes and consequences. For the smaller farmers in particular the effects of the failure of the harvest in 1622 must have been aggravated by the fact that it followed on several years of plenty and low prices. The usual measures were taken. The Book of Orders was reissued in 1622 and the Bishop of Lincoln issued regulations to restrain all sorts of people concerned with provisioning. In Leicester arrangements were made for the sale of over £500 worth of corn to the poor under the market price. This time the attempt to ensure that farmers released some of their peas and beans to make up for the absence of barley from the markets met with little success in Lutterworth as elsewhere. The Leicestershire Justices reported that 'there are some, and they (for the most part) of greatest wealth, and therefore least subject to control, who . . . will not be persuaded to forbear their old way of devouring peas with sheep and swine'. Among those named was a member of the ubiquitous family of butcher graziers, 'Thomas Sleath, *alias* Gabriel of Gilmorton'. Alehousekeepers and maltsters were blamed for the lack of bread-corn since they were buying up whole crops and tithes and not releasing any corn or malt onto the market again. It was also said that a great number of maltsters 'leave their trades wherein they were bred and only live by malting'. These complaints concerned Leicester, but 'without doubt the like wrong is done in other Market Towns within this county'.[90] It is significant, therefore, that this is the year to which the first ploughing-up of grass ground in the Lutterworth area has been traced, not only of ley ground but also of a close.

The disastrous harvest of 1630 occasioned the final and extended reissue of the Book of Orders and the final commissions of enquiry into recent enclosures. In Leicester the usual arrangements were made for the sale of barley in small quantities to the poor under the market price, which had shot up to 40/- a quarter, the highest price yet. Something similar was attempted at Lutterworth; for in April 1631 information was laid against 'one John Price a forestaller of our Market which maketh our Corn very dear that we Cannot get Corn to relieve our poor but at excessive rates and scarce to relieve our own Families'. These two years saw renewed litigation over the manorial milling monopoly. As usual the main offenders had been the public house keepers and the bakers, including Robert Billington, who was not only both but also occupied the Spittle Mills. This time, however, without the effective backing of the manorial court, the attempt to complete the monopoly of the two sets of mills over all the business in the town succeeded in theory only.[91]

It can now be seen that men like the Smiths and Billingtons were in an uniquely strong position to pioneer a new method of agricultural production. The Lutterworth bakers held a practical monopoly of the corn trade and the control of the manorial court had been swept aside. Both families took to common-field farming; but in the early 1630s Francis Billington was undertaking the first cultivation of crops on the enclosed grounds of Moorbarns. On his death in 1634 his crops were worth £150, a total not even exceeded among the village inventories from the 1680s. It was all clearly of his own growing; £100 was for 'a crop of corn upon the ground' and £20 'for the Crop in Morebarne'. He also owned the first large wagon recorded in the area, a piece of equipment dependent on the heavy horses needed for improving farming.[92]

To follow up the question of transport, the local corn trade has so far been treated as an isolated unit. No doubt local demand was satisfied from within the area. It has also been argued that the cost of transport without navigable waterways made it out of the question to export corn beyond the region. The contemporary opinions that have been quoted to support the argument, however, were expressed in 1607 and 1620, both years in which a run of several good harvests had held prices low and, ironically, just before a disastrous harvest. It should be remembered, moreover, that within the region there were sizeable urban centres to be supplied. It is hardly surprising that the Coventry authorities apparently sent out to Lutterworth 'to buy Corn for the Relief of the poor of this City' in 1596. The crop failure that year could even drive buyers to interfere with local markets in Leicestershire from as far afield as the city of York.[93]

In Leicester the experience was that if the maltsters were suppressed too effectively in a bad year, like 1608, 'the husbandmen and others that bring Corn out of other Counties where it is cheaper to our markets' chose to go elsewhere. In the winter of 1630 the Leicestershire Justices found that their efforts to hold down the price of corn throughout the county was having exactly this effect, and worse. It was causing men to 'leave the Markets of this County empty and carry it into other Counties adjoining'.[94] In other words, when the price of corn was sufficiently high, the relative cheapness in a mainly arable district outweighed the cost of long-range road transport. The corn trade was opening out into a wider arena.

These factors help to put the dispute over the activities of John Price into perspective. He was alleged to have forestalled the Lutterworth market by purchasing two quarters of barley in one day, which would have cost him about £44 in all. What did he require this corn for? He was cited as a townsman, but there is no trace of his name to suggest that he was a public house keeper or maltster there. The possibility remains that he was a local "badger" or corn-dealer purchasing for resale outside the area, which might account for the feeling against him. The motive behind the petition, however, may well have been not concern for the poor but rivalry. The petitioners, 11 in all, included men who can be identified as a baker, four keepers of substantial public houses and also a carrier. The immediate sequel was a counter-petition in his defence, signed by an impressive list of three dozen townsmen.[95] These included another baker, half a dozen public house keepers, the bailiff, the constables, the church wardens, Nathaniel Cox the curate schoolmaster and, presumably of greatest weight in the present case, the overseers of the poor. The plea as to the man's poverty need hardly be taken seriously; were these men rather defending his right to trade freely in the town? If so it is not surprising to find Francis Billington among his defenders. Billington himself was just the kind of dealer who could have been confounding the Justices by removing local corn supplies to more profitable markets. With his wagon he was uniquely equipped to do so. The only reference to the Corn Market traced was as the location of the Billington High Street "cottage" in 1607. If this was the core of the new Swan premises it is tempting to conclude that the corn market, recorded as thriving in the 1620s, was drawn off the street, through the doors of the Swan and into the corn chamber there. This might explain the need for a direction to the bailiff of the manor in 1670 to 'strive and endeavour . . . to restore and take Toll of Corn and all manner of grain as . . . hath been of late time omitted in all Fairs and Markets at Lutterworth'.[96]

Important though it was, the farming side of the Billington enterprise was in two respects only transitional. In the first place, so long as corn prices held up there was no immediate collapse of the old mixed husbandry in the face of competition from improved farming. Secondly theirs stands out as the last large common-field farm run by a commercial family in the town. In the next generation they concentrated on their other businesses, with Francis's son Thomas carrying on the baking and Robert's son Isack the innholding at the Swan. As improving farming spread through the area they could leave it to those men who were better placed to take advantage of the new practices, the larger common-field farmers in the villages. This alone, however, cannot have accounted for the fall of the town bakers from their prominent position in the economy of the area. In parallel to the earlier experience of the town livestock-dealers and butchers, what the town bakers lost was their exclusive hold on the corn market. The improving farmers in the area had, apart from the crops raised on the common fields, the heavy yields from broken-up pasture grounds to sell. With their strong horses and wagons they would no longer be restricted to the local corn markets but could seek out buyers where and when the best prices were offered. By the mid-century Moore could claim that the great benefit of the husbandry of Leicestershire and the adjacent counties to the rest of the nation was that:

> We have fed them not only with our wheat, corn, and malt, not only in plentiful years, but also in times of famine and dearth, we being the only magazine for corn in the middle of the Nation . . .[97]

One of the 'Reasons against depopulation and decay of tillage', possibly penned by Moore as part of his campaign, was that 'The Counties of Leicester and Northampton are as a Magazine for Corn, both for the North and west'.[98] By the early eighteenth century one general direction of this trade was clear. Defoe observed that the market towns of Hertfordshire were functioning as regular outposts of the metropolitan corn market and that their catchment area for wheat and barley stretched north to include Northamptonshire and the southern edge of Leicestershire. In fact he particularly noted the traffic via Bedford from Market Harborough, but it is very likely that Lutterworth was involved as well.[99]

*   *   *

Each of the two changes in the farming practice of the area, therefore, was initiated by men with businesses based on wider and more commercial connexions, which meant men based on the town. Since so much of the trade that was involved in supplying the population of the town and the villages in the area and beyond was conducted in the town, they were in the best position to adapt practices to new demands. At each stage, however, the change spread through the area and these townsmen lost their pre-eminence in the local economy as their monopoly over the exports of produce out of the area dissolved. Meanwhile at each stage the dependence of the village populations on the town as the redistribution centre was reinforced, as the farming in the area moved away from a self-sufficient peasant basis towards a commercial one. Witness to this was the continued importance of baking in the town and the concentration of malting and brewing there. Closely connected with this, of course, was the town's public house keeping trade, which expanded in more ways than one. The amount of accommodation increased and also its scope, so that the town could not only entertain more wayfaring traders of all sorts but could also provide more facilities both for the townspeople and, probably of most importance, for all the villagers who came there for business, for buying their provisions or for other shopping, activities doubtless no longer now confined to market days.

3. Craftsmen

So far the town has been represented as the trading centre of the area, the exchange point for the redistribution of agricultural produce. Two aspects of life other than farming and provisioning must now be examined. The first concerns the area's self-sufficiency with respect to the various artifacts needed by its population. The town would be functioning as the exchange point for the products of various local crafts and even, perhaps, as a collection point for their export out of the area. Some local craftsmen themselves tended to settle in the town, which also supported a few of the more specialized crafts and services that might be expected of an urban centre. The second concerns the town's role as the main distribution point for goods brought in from outside. This business was at the outset dependent on the fairs and markets. Establishing in whose hands it was conducted will shew how the town grew into a regular shopping centre for the area. Set in the context of the changes in the farming economy and in the redistribution of its products as revealed so far, the examination of these two aspects will help in assessing the urban character of the town at each stage of its development. For a start the treatment of the crafts will keep to the order already adopted, since wool was the principal material for clothing and leather-working depended on the butchery trade. Afterwards the other crafts will be covered, such as wood-working, metal-working and building.

Weavers and tailors

Before the Industrial Revolution it was a self-evident fact that, to quote Defoe, 'the woollen manufacture is the life blood of the whole nation, the soul of our trade, the top of all manufactures'.[100] The export of raw wool out of the area to supply the manufacturing districts has been discussed. Was there anything in the nature of a weaving industry in the Lutterworth area itself, or was the weaving activity there merely satisfying the needs of the local inhabitants?

In the sixteenth century a wide range of people owned sheep. While the larger farmers, like the pasture-estate owners, would have sold the greater part of their wool crops, most of the wool produced by ordinary farmers, and all of the linen and hemp that was raised on small plots, or hemp "plecks", was for home use. Spinning and winding were time-consuming tasks and if paid for would cost as much as weaving; so it was worth having them done at home by the women-folk. Witness to this were the spinning wheels, for either wool or linen, listed in the probate inventories. Linen-spinning was as common as wool-spinning, and possibly growing more common. Out of 80 wheels listed in village inventories from the 1590s 22 were specified as for wool and 23 for linen. Out of 125 from the 1630s 26 were for wool and 33 for linen. The "leases" of yarn, however, were not woven at home, but put out to local weavers; yarn or cloth 'at the weavers' was sometimes valued in an inventory, before it returned as 'new cloth'.

The cloths woven from the homespun wool were kerseys, true woollen cloths of a coarse and open texture. This reflects the fact that since only short-staple wool was grown and the best was all exported, local weaving was left dependent on the coarser wool associated with the development of sheep reared for mutton. The wool carefully sorted at Misterton one year in the 1550s for making different articles of bedding needed on the estate was only 'all our tag locks and other Refuse Woollocks'.[101] It will be recalled that the redistribution of this sort of wool was in the hands of yeomen and other villagers rather than of dealers based on the town. Weaving was similarly spread throughout the villages and was in no way concentrated in the town. It was in fact the most common non-agricultural occupation in the area, although weavers were generally far from wealthy and the 'weaver's loom' was not a very valuable piece of equipment. A few of them did indeed feature among the probate records, but on the whole only because they had some farming stock of value. An indication of the independence of the majority of them from farming may be the way that several families of weavers, such as the Smart and Iliffe families, had members in two or three parishes across the area, and beyond. The sample of inventories from the four decades include records of a dozen village weavers; yet from the whole period only one weaver based on the town appears in the probate records, William Ilive, who had £80 in money when he died in 1676.[102]

Did the town nevertheless support cloth-finishing crafts to serve the area? There was a shearman there in the mid-sixteenth century, John Halpeny senior; but he was probably only concerned with probate because his household was an alehouse. A fuller has been traced in the 1630s and another man whose occupation was given as fuller in 1664 but as shearman on his death in 1683, when his goods were worth but £6.8.9d.[103] There is no trace of a town fulling mill. Outside the town, on the other hand, village fulling may be recalled by the use of 'Fullpits' as the name of a location in the fields of two villages. There were two cloth-workers and several shearmen in the area in the mid-seventeenth century, including one of each in Broughton Astley. Another parish supported both a couple of shearmen and a dyer. The only dyer associated with the town was also connected with other market towns and was apparently based on Coventry (see token h in Illustration 18).[104] So cloth-finishing was centred on Lutterworth no more than weaving.

As for more specialized clothing crafts, there was a felt-maker in the town in the 1630s; but equally there was one in a local village too. The only references to the lace and silk crafts found concerned townspeople; but they are very slight references. Unlike the Hinckley area, the Lutterworth area did not foster an early hosiery industry of any importance, and the few references to jersey and jersey wheels shew likewise no concentration in the town. The only town inventory to mention a jersey wheel is that of Elizabeth Wood, widow, dated 1682. The village inventories from the 1680s list one each in Ullesthorpe and the parish of Broughton Astley. At the end of the century arrangements were made in South Kilworth for 'Learning the poor to spin Gersy'.[105]

In Broughton Astley, a parish already characterized as more typical of the Hinckley area and in which the hosiery industry did later thrive on a large scale, there was an unusual amount of spinning and weaving in the early seventeenth century. Of the 82 village inventories from the 1630s containing traces of one or the other, eight are from this parish. This can in fact be dated back to before the mid-sixteenth century. Of the ten inventories from the 1550s containing such traces five are from here; also two out of the six from the 1540s. By the seventeenth century, if not before, this appears to have involved weaving cloth for sale. It is significant that the only south Leicestershire carriers recorded by John Taylor in *The Carriers Cosmographie* as travelling regularly to London in the 1630s were from Broughton.[106] Two carriers are named in the parish register and one of them came from the same family as the shearman there. If they were carrying cloth for sale in London, perhaps they were also taking hand-knitted hosiery. The goods of a Leicester mercer, Robert Miller, who was known in south Leicestershire and died in 1633, included £11 worth of hose in London. Such trade might explain the introduction of the knitting-frame into the Hinckley area earlier than elsewhere. Be that as it may, this does shew that in the clothing trade, as in wool-marketing, market towns like Lutterworth were largely being bypassed.

An important change in local practices took place in the mid-seventeenth century. Up to the 1630s ordinary households often included homespun in the form of several yards of new cloth stored away. By the 1680s, however, spinning was less common. Of the 194 village inventories from the former decade 60 list a total of 125 wheels; of the 202 from the latter decade, 34 list a total of 64. Only three lengths of cloth were mentioned, all of them in villages that still retained their common fields. With the changes in the basis of the local economy, the old method of making cloth founded on the common-field farming household was dying out so that a much larger proportion of the inhabitants of both the town and the villages was becoming dependent on the town drapers and mercers for their cloths and clothing. The modest possessions of Rebecca Parbery, a widow who died in the unenclosed village of Walcote in 1687, included a wheel and 13/4d. worth of dag-lock wool. Such gleanings would have been unavailable to the inhabitants of enclosed villages other than employees.[107]

As for the final cutting and sewing of materials for use, articles like bedding and linen clothes too were no doubt made up by the women in the home. When it came to making up clothes from woollen cloths and cloths of all sorts bought in, the work would usually be entrusted to a local tailor. Throughout the villages there were very nearly the same number of tailors as weavers and although, like the weavers, most of them were far from prosperous, from the 1590s onwards in each of the decades studied three or four village tailors left inventories. All of them, however, possessed some farming stock, which may have been the main reason for their being concerned with probate.

In the town, meanwhile, there was less opportunity for such craftsmen to farm as smallholders or otherwise, so that very few tailors appeared among the probate records. Nevertheless tailors were more numerous than weavers in the town and in the 1630s tailoring was the second most common non-agricultural occupation there. This concentration of tailors was no doubt connected with the town's role as the distribution point for cloths brought into the area from outside; but it brought no great prosperity and the town tailors remained less well off than the more fortunate of the village tailors. The first town tailor traced, Richard Chapman, was relatively prosperous when he died in 1588, with goods valued at £26.8.0, including £4.6.8d. worth of cloth etc. and no farming stock.[108] Although this family produced a Lutterworth tailor in the next generation, it might more properly be called a family of village tailors from Dunton Bassett, since two members there left inventories in the 1590s and another in the 1680s. No doubt some finer work was done in the town, which boasted a girdler and a button-maker in the 1630s; but there was also a button-maker in one of the villages.

Leather-workers

Leather-working shews a complete contrast to clothing. Because the butchery business was centred on the town, shoemaking, glove-making and saddlery and also the preparation of leather were concentrated there too.

The importance of the leather trade in the town is confirmed by the presence, at least in the mid-seventeenth century, of two Leather Searchers among the manorial market officers. There was probably very much more tanning and curing being done in the town than the few references traced imply. A currier was named in the parish register in the 1630s. Another died in 1684 leaving goods worth £15.0.6d., including oil, knives etc. valued at £2.5.0. A tanner died five years earlier worth £81.5.0, his main asset being £25 in debts 'upon a Bond and other Contracts'. The preparation would formerly have been undertaken by leather-workers themselves and in the seventeenth century by those among them who could afford to keep some stock-in-trade. In 1685 a saddler had £4 worth of 'leather in the pit and shop'. On the other hand most of them probably relied on the professional tanners and curriers, like the shoemaker whose debts of £20 included money owing on 'the Curriers book'.[109]

No trace of the preparation of leather outside the town has been found from the earlier part of this period, but as the village butchery businesses rose in importance in the seventeenth century the town ceased to be the sole source of skins for leather in the area. By the 1680s several of the village inventories included leather worth valuing. In particular one yeoman had a stock of leather which may have been for sale and one improving farmer in Claybrook magna had his own tan house.[110] The town, however, provides the first indication that leather may have become an export out of the area. The early eighteenth-century representative of the Stapleton family of Lutterworth gentry owned a house there which was equipped with outhouses and tan-vats; but he himself was living in Southwark as a leather-dealer.[111]

The greater part of the leather prepared locally would have been used by local craftsmen, chiefly the shoemakers. No village shoemakers of any independent wealth have been traced from before the later seventeenth century, although shoemakers were by no means uncommon, at least in the villages that retained their common fields. In the town, on the other hand, shoemaking was the most common non-agricultural occupation and in the later sixteenth and earlier seventeenth centuries some of the shoemakers were the town's wealthiest craftsmen. Nicholas Rattclyffe, who died in 1583, had an inventory total of £91.17.3d., including £2 for two dozen shoes, two hides etc. He paid tax in 1570/1 and made pecuniary bequests amounting to £43. The Newcombe family of shoemakers also paid tax, in 1594. The inventories of this group of men shew considerable involvement in their craft and in the supply of shoes both to the town and the area. Of Rattclyffe's debts the larger ones, like the £10 owed by Thomas Shakespeare, the Lutterworth attorney, may not have been for goods supplied; but the parson of (Gil)morton owed him 16/- and also 3/4d. for pairs of shoes. Nevertheless, in each case the farming stock accounted for more than half of the inventory total. In contrast to this seven town shoemakers who left inventories during the first three quarters of the seventeenth century had no farming stock at all. On the contrary, a significant proportion of their goods consisted of stock-in-trade, such as boots, shoes, leather and lasts; and although an eighth one, who died in 1676, was farming, his shop book, shoes and leather, together valued at £30, shew the greatest commitment of all to the craft.[112]

Thus whereas in the sixteenth century the only shoemakers to rise to any prosperity – those who were possibly employing others to work for them – were based on farm holdings in the town; by the earlier years of the seventeenth century the craft had become so independent of the agricultural background of the town that it now supported men whose stock-in-trade formed as much as a sixth or a fifth of their personal goods. But although some of them were well off with large houses, it is significant that town shoemakers on the whole are very poorly represented in the probate records. Of the 14 named in the parish register in the 1630s two have been identified as alehousekeepers and a third was John Young, whose premises were almost certainly an inn. They were the only three concerned with probate. A total of 40 shoemakers have been traced in the town during the century from 1580 onwards, but only half a dozen of them were concerned with probate. The majority of them must have been far from wealthy and maybe many of them were only employees. The situation was probably aggravated by an influx of village shoemakers into the town. Several instances can be cited, including one who left Cotesbach just before the enclosure there,[113] and other family names suggest similar movements.

The situation in fact deteriorated. From the last two dozen years of the seventeenth century there is not one probate record of a shoemaker based on the town. In the villages, however, a few shoemaking businesses of some importance emerged, every one of them in villages with the mixed economy associated with open fields. From the 1680s there are three inventories of shoemakers from unenclosed villages and one from Broughton Astley. This development was no doubt connected with the increasing concentration of population in these villages and also with the rising fortunes of the butchers there. Competition from village shoemaking alone, however, can hardly have accounted for the rapid disappearance of the thriving shoemaking businesses from the town. What seems to have happened is that with the changes in the economy the local craft was now facing strong competition from outside, from places better suited to specialize in the manufacture of shoes, such as Northampton and the villages around it.[114] The Northamptonshire shoe industry had also been stimulated by the demands of the Civil War.[115]

Other leather crafts shew a similar concentration in the town. There were at least a couple of glovers in the villages in the 1630s and later; but in Lutterworth at the same time glove-making was in fact the third most common non-agricultural occupation. The first Lutterworth glover to appear in the records was also the most prosperous. He was John Ratclyfe, who died in 1568/9 and was the brother of Nicholas the first shoemaker traced. Like his brother's, his household was probably based on a common-field farm. His customers came from places within the local area and just beyond. His inventory total was £67.10.8d. Debts owed to him included 2/11d. for seven goat skins and amounted to £23, three quarters of barley and some wool. His small debtors were from Wolvey, Harborough (magna or parva) and Rugby in Warwickshire and from (North or South) Kilworth, (Husbands) Bosworth and Laughton in Leicestershire. He was also owed three larger sums, £5 by a Londoner, £6.10.0 by another man and £8 lent to a member of the Salisbury family of Ullesthorpe. Another town glover, Christopher Wood, who died in 1614, had only a very small holding in the fields. His debts, which were balanced roughly by what he owed, included money due from two other Lutterworth glovers and a village shoemaker. Perhaps he had retired from the craft but was still involved in supplying materials, like the 100 pelts he owned, to other craftsmen in the area.[116] Three other members of the Wood family were Lutterworth glovers; but after 1640 not one town glover was concerned with probate and indeed no further reference to the craft has been found.

The fact that a Lutterworth glover at the beginning of the century was concentrating on dealing in materials rather than on making gloves may reflect not his retirement so much as the changing basis of the occupation. At first glove-making in the town followed a similar development to shoemaking, with the more prosperous craftsmen emerging from their agricultural background by the early seventeenth century. Shortly afterwards, however, the craft died out completely, the remaining glovers probably trading more or less as fellmongers. This points to the decline of a local craft in the face of commercial competition from areas which specialized in the manufacture for the market.[117]

As far as can be traced there was practically nobody working as a saddler outside the town at this period. The remarkable thing about the town saddlers, moreover, is that there is no indication that the probate records under-estimate their number. Not one was mentioned in the parish register in the 1630s and yet of the half-dozen traced from other sources all but one were concerned with probate and left inventories.

Once again the earliest and wealthiest of the group, Edward Overinge, who died shortly before 1600, was also involved in farming. His goods were worth £96.9.7d. and he made pecuniary bequests amounting to £53.6.8d. Apart from three shoemakers and one glover, or rather apart from two Newcombes and the two Ratclyfes, he was the only wealthy craftsman recorded in the town before the 1630s. He traded as a chandler as well but the saddlery in his 'great shop', and his materials and finished harness, including 12 saddles, were valued at £11.7.3d., nearly three times as much as the tallow and equipment in his 'candle house'. As a member of a Leicester family of general traders he retained connexions with that town. The next Lutterworth saddler recorded also appears to have come from Leicester. He and three others from later in the century were all worth under £20, but their businesses were independent of farming and they each owned not only raw materials and buckles but also finished harness and saddles for sale.[118]

The modest success of the saddlery trade was due to more than one factor. Since the local leather crafts were very much centred on the town, it may be imagined that the town saddlers played a significant part in the growth of improving farming. The use of four-wheeled wagons, teams of large horses and heavy farm implements had, after all, spread into the area from the town. Probably of more importance to their business, however, was the town's role as a wayfaring centre, not only for visiting traders but also for through-traffic. In 1686 it was estimated that the town had stabling accommodation for 300 horses and it is likely that at times the horses in the town belonging to outsiders outnumbered those belonging to inhabitants. It is not surprising, therefore, that the town supported a few saddlers able to keep their shops stocked with harness and saddles. All but the first one recorded were independent of farming and, unlike the other leather-workers, there is no indication that their prosperity was on the decline after the mid-century; and their inventories shew that they continued working as craftsmen and were not merely retailing products brought in from outside.

At this point it is relevant to pursue the reference to candle-making because, although chandlers were becoming general traders, their craft was originally just as dependent on the butchery trade as the leather crafts. Only eight chandlers have been traced in the area, all but one of them living in parishes with the mixed economy associated with common-field farming. Of the four named in the parish registers in the 1630s two were from the parish of Broughton Astley. The first Lutterworth chandler to appear in the records, a tallow chandler, died in 1560. Like the first saddler, he almost certainly came from Leicester. He too had a second occupation; out of his goods, valued at £13.4.0, he made a bequest of 'all my instruments, looms and tools belonging unto chandler craft and Ropers craft'. At the beginning of the seventeenth century a Lutterworth man of the same surname as one of the Broughton Astley chandlers had a modest inventory, nearly half of which was accounted for by the £7.1.0 worth of tallow and candles in his 'work house'. In the mid-century one of the town's important mercers, John Almey, was a chandler as well and had a 'tallow shop', the contents of which were valued at £8.10.0. For the couple of families of chandlers traced in the town in the later part of the century, such as the Judds, general trading was probably the greater part of their business; but that they still made candles is shewn by the candles and 'chandle houses' mentioned in their inventories.[119]

To sum up, there need be no doubt that the concentration of the leather crafts in the town followed from the domination of the local butchery trade by the town butchers. The only men traced as engaged in the processing of leather before the later seventeenth century were based on the town. Important shoemakers and glovers and one saddler appeared in the records, at first supported by their farm holdings; but by the early seventeenth century they could survive off their crafts alone. But there were many more shoemakers and glovers than the probate records can shew, and the majority of them were quite poor. A couple of cases can be demonstrated of leather-working families straddling parish boundaries; but probably of more importance were the half-dozen cases of connexions between village and town. In three or four of these, it can be shewn that a craftsman moved from his village to the town. The subsequent loss by the town butchers of their pre-eminent position in the area would have affected the local leather trade and may have helped the village-based shoemaking businesses that emerged. Meanwhile the changes in the economy seem to have thrown the local crafts to the mercy of competition from outside, so that many of the town leather-workers, some of them immigrants and none with the opportunity to support themselves off the land, no doubt went to swell the numbers of potential paupers there. Of course shoemaking by no means died out; there were still 31 shoemakers working in the town in 1782.[120] A few town chandlers thrived, probably because of their general trading. Only the saddlers prospered through to the end of the seventeenth century, by supplying the demands of the improving farming and of the wayfaring community in the town.

Wood-workers and builders

Much of the timber and wood used by the inhabitants was grown locally, despite the comparative lack of trees in the region which has already been mentioned. Before dealing with the various wood-working and building crafts it is worth pursuing further one of the consequences of this scarcity, the use made of alternative fuels. The mid-seventeenth century enclosures greatly reduced the amount of fuel readily accessible to the local population. Furze in particular was used for firing baking ovens and also, apparently, for brewing. Kids of furze or gorse feature in the inventories of five town bakers and of three village bakers and also of four of the people identified as alehousekeepers in the later seventeenth century. No wonder that farmers valued the crops they took from their leys of furze. More than a quarter of the inventory total of one of the village bakers was accounted for by the £7 for 'all the furres or gosse kidds in the Little Hill Close and those that are sold and gone'.[121] On the other hand the inventories also leave no doubt that the fuel most generally used remained wood. There is in fact no evidence that there was a regular market for wood in the town, perhaps in the Wood Market. By the mid-seventeenth century, however, one town woodman had risen to a position of importance and his business may have included selling fuel. More usually, perhaps, fuel would have been sold direct by woodmen working in nearby woods. Several woodmen named Lucas recur in the church wardens' accounts; they may have worked in Newnham Woods, where the 'fall of wood' was an important source of income to the Feilding estate.[122] At all events the changes in the economy left the local population very much less self-sufficient so far as fuel was concerned. The proportion of inventories which listed stores of fuel worth valuing fell dramatically, especially in the villages: three out of every eight there did in the 1630s, but in the 1680s only one out of every seven.

This applies not only to wood and furze but also to coal; for the local supply of coal from the North Warwickshire coalfields was closely connected with the mixed husbandry system.[123] Farmers took their own teams and carts to fetch their loads of coal, so that the cash-price they paid, as the testamentary provisions which some made for their widows shew, was the price 'at the pits'. The route from this direction into a couple of the villages in the area was known as 'Coal Lane' or 'Coal Pit Way' in the seventeenth century.[124] Into Lutterworth, however, the equivalent road was already known as the 'King's road called Colespitts' at the beginning of the sixteenth. In the 1550s, and indeed earlier, coal was quite commonly listed in the inventories of villagers, all of them mixed farmers; in fact in one out of every four inventories which specified fuel. Overall, however, it occurs more frequently in the inventories of townspeople, in five out of every eight which specified fuel. The greatest change was in the villages, where the fall in the proportion of householders with their own transport must have made the population even more dependent. Inventories from the 1680s shew the local price of coal ranging from 10/- to 15/- a load, the highest priced belonging, significantly, to smallholders with no teams or carts of their own. Presumably the larger farmers with their heavy wagons were bringing in supplies to cover more than their own needs. In 1657 the Feilding estate paid a pit price of 4/6d. a load for five loads brought 'by Lutterworth teams'.[125] The inventories shew the local price in the 1640s to have been 8/- and it may already have been rising; so transport accounted for about half the cost. It is unlikely that there was any local coal-dealing independent from farming. Anthony Gore, one of the Lutterworth gentry, had a wagon and another smaller one, but at his death in 1689 was not farming. He was one of the few men with an inventory mentioning a 'coal house', but there is no indication that he was actually dealing in coal. No record of the Lutterworth Coal Market has been found from before the mid-eighteenth century.[126]

In the sixteenth century, even in an area where fuel was generally scarce, the majority of householders who required buildings and implements had farm holdings which would help furnish the materials needed. Thus the fact that no wood-workers feature among the probate records does not indicate that there were none, but that, since they worked on wood belonging to their customers employing them, they were not in a position to build up any independent wealth. Two carpenters, each with an apprentice, were frequently employed in this way on the Misterton estate in the 1550s. They probably lived in the dependent village of Walcote. Of the men with non-agricultural occupations wood-workers were in fact second in numbers only to the weavers in the 1630s. There was at least one carpenter to each village and there is no reason to suspect that this was anything new. In the seventeenth century, however, several wood-workers were concerned with probate, all but one of them based on a village that retained its common fields. Most had some farming stock, but some also had considerable amounts of timber in stock and of money in hand or owed. One of them, William Lea of Leire, who was also a mixed farmer, owned 17 elm trees, valued at one pound apiece, standing in the yards of six other men in his own and three neighbouring villages. In the town throughout the seventeenth century there was at least one carpentry business prospering. One carpenter, Peter Limber, left the village of Ashby parva some time before the final enclosure there and set up in Lutterworth.[127] Taken together these facts hardly indicate that wood-working was concentrated in the town.

As for the more specialized wood-working crafts, such traces as there are of mill-, wheel- and cart-wrighting, even for improved farming, do not appear to have been centred on the town. The only millwright traced in the area was based on a village. The one engaged to rebuild the Lodge Mills at Lutterworth was an outsider, from Earl Shilton. In the villages in the 1630s one man owned £20 worth of cart timber and William Lea of Leire, who was a wheelwright, was owed £59.8.0 and owned £20 worth of wood for plough timber, carts and wheels and his standing timber was valued at £17. Coopery, on the other hand, was mainly confined to the town, as might be expected in view of the importance of brewing and the public house trade there. A town cooper who died there in 1684 was owed £2.10.0 and possessed £14 worth of ware and £3 worth of timber. From the later sixteenth century onwards the inventories shew that joinery was of increasing importance both for the inside parts of the houses and for their furnishings. At first chamber floors did not attach to the realty but remained personal property and so were listed. To judge from the Lutterworth inventories, framed tables became common in the 1580s and joined tables and bedsteads in the 1590s. The only important joiners traced were based on the town, there being at least one very wealthy joinery business there throughout the seventeenth century. The first joiner traced became church warden and on his death in 1633 had £32 in ready money and £30 worth of 'timber in the timber houses'. In 1654 'the joiner of Lutterworth' was paid

Illustration 14. Seventeenth-century oak plate chest from Lutterworth church, possibly made by a Lutterworth turner for the five pewter church plates, which are dated 1675. The initials W W suggest William Ward, who was church warden in 1674 and was probably the predecessor of John Ward, the wealthy wood-worker who died in 1693.
   Goodacre Collection; Leicestershire Museums photograph

£1.16.0 'for the frames of 12 stools and chairs, and 2 great chairs' for the Feilding family at Newnham Paddox. He was probably the predecessor of John Ward, one of the wealthiest townsmen. On his death in 1693 Ward was owed £30.18.6d. on his debt book and £255 on bonds and mortgages and his 'Stock of board and other Timber' was valued at £58. Finally, at the end of the century one town carpenter, Elisha Newcombe, appears to have specialized in wood-turning (see Illustration 14).[128]
   There was hardly anything in the way of a building trade during the period, let alone one centred on the town. As nearly all the buildings in the

Illustration 15. Timber-framed house in Claybrook magna, from the early sixteenth century. The close-studded walls are characteristic of the period but the mouldings carved over the internal doorways and the decorative curved braces in the gable end are exceptional in this area.

Photograph: John Goodacre

area were of timber construction (see Illustration 15), the craftsman most likely to be needed in building was the carpenter, while the humbler cottages probably did not even have timber frames to their walls. Wooden hovels, commonly used for storing crops on, were probably staddle barns, reared off the ground as a protection against vermin, and they may have been rebuilt by their owners each year. Thus both hovels and hovel timber (principally the "overliggers" that formed the platform; see Illustration 11) remained personalty and feature in the inventories. All other ordinary buildings had walls of mud; but the making of clay walls never developed into a separate occupation. On the Misterton estate in the 1550s jobs like 'getting clay and making mortar with stable litter making up part of walls again that were fall down in the Rick yard' were done by regular estate employees. Straw thatching, the almost universal roof-covering, involved skills exercised every year in making stacks for storing crops. The Misterton estate was exceptional in employing a thatcher to lead the team in re-roofing some of the more important buildings; but then arable cropping was of little importance to the estate and reed suitable for thatching roofs and coping mud walls grew in the pools there.[129]

The supply of timber, boards and planks may well have been the main basis of the Lutterworth woodmen's business. In general, however, where building timber was not to hand, it was fetched for the particular job from the woodland where it grew. For a repair on the Misterton estate a local carpenter was paid for 'Cutting down and squaring an oak growing at Kimcote and putting the same in place where an other was broken'. For a new building an outside carpenter was engaged to go twice to Cannock Wood in Staffordshire 'for framing the Timber' and again 'in going thither to see the Timber at midsummer when the bargain was named to him'.[130] In 1671 the Lutterworth church wardens paid a craftsman's son 'for work and for going into the woodland to bespeak a piece of timber'. There was no need for timber to pass through any market or dealer in the town and indeed the most likely market to have been involved was the midsummer fair at Boughton Green, just north of Northampton, which drew on the resources of some of the Northamptonshire forest areas. There is a later tradition that complete frames for houses in the Lutterworth area were bought at this fair.[131]

In the sixteenth century the more specialized skills needed for grand buildings such as churches and manor houses were not available in the area so that outside craftsmen, often from Leicester, had to be called in for tiling, slating and glazing. On his death in 1523 Sir William Turpin of Knaptoft owed £2.13.4d. to an important Leicester tiler or slater, presumably for work on his Hall (see Illustration 11). At the same time the leading Ashby magna yeoman Richard Cattell owed 6/- to the same man. Outside craftsmen working on the buildings at Misterton Hall in the 1550s included two Leicester slaters, a Leicester glazier and one lead-man, each with their respective servants or apprentices. In the seventeenth century, however, some of these skills were practised locally, for the most part centred on the town. For instance a village pavior, Robert York, has been traced, but one Lutterworth pavior, John Peppercorne, featured in the probate records. The main reason could be that his house was an alehouse, but £10 owed to him may have been for work done. For more refined stonework it remained necessary to employ masons from outside, especially from where the stone was quarried. For repairs to the steeple Lutterworth church wardens engaged a man from Witherley near Atherstone and then two men from Oakham. In 1665 the paving of the great hall at Newnham Paddox was to be executed in blue stone from Bilton or Lawford Quarry in Warwickshire. Nevertheless three local village masons have been traced. Two of them, both named York, were concerned with probate, no doubt because of the farming stock they owned. Other masons, like the first Lutterworth ones identified, probably remained little more than specialized labourers. In the town there were several established families of masons at work in the seventeenth century and a couple of masons, John Kibble and William Clarke, feature among the probate records from later in the century. Kibble's 'Eight hundred of Tiles and three quarters of lime', valued at £1.4.0, shew he worked as a tiler as well. He was also a "common-field grazier", and Clarke was the baker at the manorial bakehouse, which may be the main reasons for their being concerned with probate.[132]

Among the materials supplied by the town masons to the town church wardens the most frequent, apart from quarries for floors, were bricks and mortar. The first reference to bricklaying traced is the attendance at the 1551 audit at Misterton by 'masons and bricklayers'. Towards the end of the seventeenth century it is possible that the rough masons were working mainly as bricklayers. All through this period there was a Kiln Yard in the town, which could presumably produce such quantities of bricks as were needed for chimney-stacks, ovens and malt-kilns and tiles for roofing. The Drapery and the Rectory both had tiled roofs at the beginning of the seventeenth century. At that time the Kiln Yard belonged to Thomas Gore, gentleman. The High Street house of his heir Anthony obviously stood out as being faced with brick, as it was known in the mid-century as 'the Red House'. To build a house entirely from bricks would have involved, as it did in the eighteenth century, setting up a brick-kiln for the job, as near the site as possible. George Tilley, the innholder at the King's Head, owned 'eight thousand of bricks' and three quarters of lime and 'Several other Materials belonging to the Kilnes', presumably needed for the rebuilding of his premises. He also sold some of his bricks to the church wardens in 1692. In 1726 with the Feilding manor house went 'a parcel of . . . ground . . . called the Kilne Yard and now used as a Bowling Greene' and possibly formerly used for its rebuilding as an inn. With the spread of the use of bricks for building new houses in the villages towards the end of the seventeenth century, there was no need for this section of the building trade to be centred on the town (see Illustration 16). A village yeoman also had a store of bricks and lime in 1680.[133]

The first ordinary domestic glazing traced was mentioned in 1579 in the will of Francis Peake as a fixture in his house, the Crown Inn. To judge from the Lutterworth inventories, it was not uncommon in the town in the 1580s and in the next decade even a couple of fairly modest village households had glass windows worth valuing. By the early seventeenth century the town supported a prospering firm of glaziers and by the mid-century two or three working in the 'Trade or Art of Glazier and Plumber', to quote the will of John Walton, who died in 1657. His father had died in 1621, leaving £10 to set him as apprentice and £90 at the age of 19. Meanwhile the business was run by Obediah Wightman, a colleague of his father's who was also a relation. For the last half of the sixteenth century, and until 1634, two

Illustration 16.   Brick-built house in Swinford, from the late seventeenth century. By this period bricks were used for the panels in timber-framed houses and some grander village houses were built entirely of brick. The date stone T P 1690 in the gable end suggests that this one was built by the Prowitt family of local butcher graziers.

Photograph: John Goodacre

generations of the Coleman family of painters were at work in the town, not apparently owing their wealth to their farm holding. They apparently prospered by removing their craft to Market Harborough and there is no further trace of a Lutterworth painter, so that later in the century the church wardens had to rely on outsiders for specialist work.[134] In 1652 a Lutterworth mason was good enough 'for Colouring the Canopy and Pulpit'; but at the Restoration, although a Lutterworth joiner made the Table for the King's Arms, it was taken to Coventry for another joiner to add the crest round it and for 'Stoaks the Painter' to paint the arms on it. In 1684 'Mr. Poole, the Painter', a Leicester plumber and glazier, was paid £19.3.0 for writing, colouring and gilding on the Table of Commandments and the King's Arms and Mr Heyford of Rugby 11/- for painting arms on the gallery.

To sum up, it can be said that in this period that saw only the start of the transition from timber-framed to brick buildings, there was no building trade as such and the skills needed were spread throughout the area. The town did at least, however, come to support some of the more specialized crafts needed in both town and village.

Metal-workers and other craftsmen

While village metal-workers were not quite so common as wood-workers, there had probably long been one blacksmith to each village. The only rural smiths to feature in the probate records were all based on villages with mixed economies and usually owned some farming stock. The exceptional inventory total of £469.6.10 of one who died in Gilmorton in 1678 was mainly due to the stock of his grazing and improving farm, although he also had £30 worth of iron ware and bar iron in the shop and £20 owing on 'the shop book'.[135]

A town smith could rely on a wider clientele than his village counterpart. Certainly one Lutterworth smith, Robert Mount, was well documented in the sixteenth century, perhaps partly because he was patronized as both smith and farrier by the Misterton estate to work on implements and shoe horses. Throughout the seventeenth at least one town smithy provided a good living independent of farming. One blacksmith died in 1618 with £7.7.2d. worth of tools and metal and £7 due on bond and £15 on his debt book. Later on another, George Johnson, had iron worth £4.10.0 and tools worth the same, but his brother Roger, also a blacksmith, may have been concerned with probate partly because his house was an alehouse. In 1684 George's successor was able to lend £50 to another town craftsman. In the 1630s at least four blacksmiths were at work in the town and the 1670 Hearth Tax return listed five smithies, one of them built recently. The concentration of this business here may have been connected with village blacksmiths deserting enclosing villages for the town. Roger Johnson left Ashby parva at the enclosure in 1665, although he still retained his smithy shop there.[136] Although there is no indication that the town's Iron Market would be used for supplying craftsmen with raw materials as well as for retailing metal wares, all this goes some way towards shewing that Lutterworth was functioning as the centre of the local metal-working crafts.

Better evidence of such tendency, however, is the fact that in the seventeenth century the town, unlike the villages, grew to support more specialized metal-workers. Indeed only two such specialists have been identified in the countryside during the two centuries. One was a blacksmith based on an enclosing village who changed to gunsmith just before the Civil War; though he soon removed to Leicester. The other was a nail-smith at Brockhurst in the parish of Monks Kirby in the 1660s. In the 1550s, it is true, specialists from the major urban centres, such as 'Thomas Cuttler of Coventry' and 'William Borow clockmaker', a Leicester freeman, had to be summoned to Misterton when the estate armour or the clock there required restoration, although mere repairs to the latter could be entrusted to the Lutterworth smith Robert Mount. Fifty years later, however, all these jobs might have been attended to by the Lutterworth spurrier and the Lutterworth clockmaker John Lee, upon both of whom the town of Market Harborough was relying. In the mid-seventeenth century a Lutterworth farrier was paid by the Feilding family, presumably for tending horses at Newnham Paddox. No Lutterworth pewterer has been traced, but towards the end of the century there was both a whitesmith and a brazier. That the latter was a member of the Newcombe family, moreover, suggests that the Lutterworth Newcombes were almost certainly related to the most famous of the Leicester families of bell-founders. Leicester bell-founders were, of course, called in for recasting church bells. Regular repairs to the town's church clock, however, were seen to by George Johnson or another of the town's blacksmiths. No doubt the same applied in the villages like Ashby magna, Gilmorton and Kilworth that also had church clocks. By the end of the century, finally, Lutterworth was supporting the first of its own clockmakers whose domestic clocks still survive, William Jackson and Joseph Pickering (see Illustration 17).[137]

A variety of humbler crafts made use of what materials there were available. The local cultivation of pioneer crops associated with the introduction of improving farming has been mentioned. This afforded a precarious livelihood for a few woad-workers, flax-dressers, hemp-dressers and ropers, but probably had no lasting effect on local crafts. The Shawell roper had apparently become a carrier before his death in 1665. Perhaps he had been involved in exporting the products of this local craft, which then died out on him. There were, however, other country crafts practised by independent men which relied on seasonal supplies of materials, the making of all sorts of twiggen and treen ware, such as rush and bass mats, baskets, sieves and coopery. An itinerant craftsman would keep on the road to cover his sources of materials and his accustomed markets and fairs. The chief assets of James Tomson, a sievemaker who was a cottager in Frowlesworth, were £7 in the hands of the village squire and £4 due from a basket-maker at Congerston, the other side of Hinckley. The typical itinerant craftsman, however, is the metal-worker with some special skill, such as the tinker. In 1656 two shillings were paid 'to the Tinker for mending Kettles in the Dairy' at Newnham Paddox. A tinker-errant, Nicholas Leigh, died in a barn in South Kilworth in 1632. Apart from his clothes and eightpence in his purse, he had 'one blanket to cover him and his wife in the night time as they chanced to lodge in Barns or such places' and four pounds 'left in trust with John Naseby of Swinford to be in readiness for his relief as he should chance to have need'.[138]

It is likely that the town all the time functioned as a centre for the humbler traders on the level of the itinerant craftsmen already referred to. Just beyond

Illustration 17.   Lantern clock signed by William Jackson of Lutterworth, clock-maker, from the beginning of the eighteenth century.
      Christie's

the end of the town on the Coventry road there stood the Pedlars Cross where they may have been able to sell their wares unofficially and free of market regulations.[139] The unfortunate William Banbury, who in 1676 was 'Killed by Robbers upon Over Heath near this Town', probably only features in the probate records because of his livestock as a Lutterworth "common-field grazier"; but he also had in stock 6 dozen sieves, 2½ dozen twiggen ware and 3 dozen wooden ware, all together valued at £2.10.0.[140] In the later eighteenth century an Ullesthorpe man had to cover much ground to win a living. He kept the fairs and markets of 11 of the more important places marked on Map III selling rat and mouse poison.[141]

There is some evidence of gypsies and other travellers forming part of the general vagrancy problem in the county in the early seventeenth century and further clues may emerge from a study of the names typically associated with them and their occupations, such as Lee in its various forms, Jennings and Jackson. Out of 11 Jacksons made free of Leicester in the period 1490 to 1600 two were smiths, two cutlers and one a spurrier.[142] References in the records may reflect a lack of understanding for what was in fact a well-ordered life-style. A couple named Lee had their son baptized at Misterton and buried there a year later; yet on both occasions the Rector described the parents as 'wanderers'.[143] James Tomson's four pound deposit was to go to set his son apprentice and Nicholas Leigh made sure that his two sons 'had trades whereby to get their livings'.[144]

The town was probably the local centre for these crafts, if only in providing a major source of custom. This would not have concerned the men and women employed on the more industrial crops mentioned, like the 'workers at the Woad' at Misterton. They were probably housed seasonally in cabins on the grounds where they worked and never formed part of the local communities. In the mid-sixteenth century, on the other hand, the roper's craft was being practised by a Lutterworth chandler as his secondary occupation. By the early seventeenth century the Callis family of ropers was of some importance in the town and their business can be traced through to the end of the century. By this time the church wardens were also relying on several members of another family for supplying rope. They also relied on another poor family living in the town for supplying mats. Basketry was used for a great many purposes, including the baker's panniers for carrying bread. A basket-maker had built a squatter's cottage on the common or waste at the end of the village of Gilmorton in 1598, but another of the same surname was farming as a smallholder when he died there in 1662. Two more basket-makers are recorded as having died in the town in the 1630s. Coopers bound wooden staves with hoops (not necessarily of iron) to make barrels and casks and all kinds of looms (vessels) too, such as tubs, vats, buckets, cans and churns (see Illustration 10). Of importance to the town as the centre of the drink trade were the coopers at work there. By the later seventeenth century the coopery business was well established; but the family of coopers in the town in the early part of the century look more like recently settled travellers. Christopher Ley was worth £12.5.0, including £3.6.8d. in coopery wares, but owed £6.1.8d. on his death in 1599/1600. William Lee was worth £7.11.2d. on his death in 1639. Neither left a written will.[145]

There is even clearer evidence of itinerant metal-workers having settled permanently in the town. In the 1630s a tinker, John Jennings, and a dish-mender, John Draper, both names that suggest a gypsy origin, were bringing up their large families there. There is an eighteenth century reference to 'a Piece of Ground in Tinkers Hole where — Draper's House stood', which was at the bottom of the High Street.[146] Even the first Lutterworth clockmaker traced was probably, by the very nature of his job at the beginning of the seventeenth century, more of an itinerant than a settled craftsman; and he shared the surname Lee with other travellers present in the area. Perhaps this John Lee was the ancestor of the Lee family of clockmakers prominent in Leicester and Loughborough from the late seventeenth century onwards. Other families of clockmakers practised in more than one town and there was a William Jackson, clockmaker, in Loughborough as well as in Lutterworth.[147] Thus there is reason to conclude that by the seventeenth century business in the town was building up sufficiently to attract some travellers with special skills to settle down and rely on local custom.

*   *   *

None of the crafts mentioned here was exceptional for a rural area and few of the ones based on the town were peculiarly urban. The degree of their independence from farming and of their concentration in the town, however, provides another measure of the urbanization of the town. In the sixteenth century the various basic crafts practised in the Lutterworth area were fairly evenly spread throughout the local population and craftsmen were on the whole neither dependent on farm holdings nor in a position to build up any independent wealth. The way that some families of craftsmen ranged across the area suggests that this left them more mobile. On the elimination of the mixed economy in the enclosing villages in the seventeenth century they would have been the most likely to move to places of the other type, thus reinforcing the contrast between the two economies. For some, notably the weavers, the town offered no particular attractions or advantages. In the case of the leather crafts, however, the dependence on the local butchery trade, which was concentrated in the town, meant that the town was the principal resort. The longer-term results of this would have been a great strain on the town economy, as all the leather crafts, with the single exception of the specialist saddlery trade, were soon to suffer from serious competition from outside.

With respect to the other crafts the town in general only acted as the centre in so far as it was able to support some of the more specialized skills. Here two opposing tendencies are observable. On the one hand when the leather crafts came to be practised sufficiently intensively, contributory skills, such as tanning and curing, grew up in support. On the other hand a few of the specialist craftsmen, even with quite sophisticated skills, had to practise on the road to meet a market large enough to win a livelihood; only when the business in the local centre built up in the seventeenth century was it worth their while to settle down more or less permanently. It will be seen, moreover, that the dissemination of specialist skills through an itinerant life-style and their absorption into the town community are themes very relevant to the development of retail trading there too.

4.   Retail traders

In the middle ages the main facility provided for merchants selling in the town was the Drapery. At the beginning of the seventeenth century this was one of the largest single buildings in the town, 12 bays of building, tiled and measuring 100 feet by 20½ feet. It contained 12 shops.[148] Throughout the sixteenth century these were evidently stocked with cloth and other goods that were brought in by visiting merchants to be offered for sale on market and fair days only. Just as the wool merchants travelled far in the pursuit of their trade, so the retailing merchants, whose activities overlapped theirs, would have spent much of their time on the road, very likely covering a regular weekly round of markets in the region. An Ashby-de-la-Zouch man who traded in a variety of wares, especially ironmongery and cloth, was selling also at Loughborough. A Loughborough ironmonger had ware in his shop in Leicester and a Loughborough card-maker was selling wares at Leicester and Melton Mowbray.[149] So long as this was the rule, it was not very significant where a merchant was based.

In the case of Lutterworth, after the important wool-dealing had passed out of the area it was the Paver family who continued the activities of this regional wayfaring merchant community. Their stock of mercery wares, mainly linen cloth, which they kept 'in the Warehouse and in the shop' and which was valued at £30 in 1550, was not for sale to inhabitants of the Lutterworth area alone. They joined the Leicester Chapmen's Guild so as to gain general immunity from market tolls, Robert as ironmonger in 1509–10 and Ralph as mercer in 1517–18. Alexander of Leicester, who joined in 1510–11, was also a mercer. Robert, later described as mercer too, was chosen to serve as chamberlain of the borough but, as an outsider, he expected to evade both the office and the redemption fine for not serving. He resigned, but still 'repaired to the said town on the market day with Linen cloth and other wares to be sold in the said town', so that the serving chamberlains, to enforce the fine, were able to distrain £20 worth. The family also owned property which included shops in Market Harborough and they no doubt traded elsewhere outside this triangle of south Leicestershire.[150]

A picture of the trade of a member of this travelling fraternity can be built up from the probate records of a draper who died in Lutterworth in the middle of the century and who was also possibly connected with Leicester. Judging from the three dozen sums of money owing to him, Robert Sowter's retailing was confined to Lutterworth, Rugby and Market Harborough, or even to Lutterworth alone. His debtors included five from Lutterworth and at least 12 from the area; also five from just outside the area, from Rugby, Crick, Theddingworth and Mowsley. Two thirds of his wealth was in his 'Cloth in the shop with all other stuff there', valued at £40, and his £3 worth of soap. On the other hand his debts included £12 owed to three of his 'brethren' and £27.1.0 to eight inhabitants of the town. His creditors also included two Coventry men, a Shrewsbury man, a Londoner and 'an other my chapman'. In all, three quarters of his assets were balanced by debts; and indeed he was about the last of the old-style merchants based on the town.[151]

More generally, it appears that traders tended to concentrate either on wholesale or on retail and that a more settled life-style meant that residence in a larger town brought advantages to both types of dealer. In the second half of the century it seems that most of the trade in Lutterworth was in the hands of men living in these larger centres in the region, as there were no important townsmen living off trading. There are only two inventories, of a mercer worth just under £5, 10/- of which was apparently for ware in his shop, and of a linen draper worth £12, his shop containing 6/8d. worth of fittings but no wares.[152] Meanwhile a Leicester haberdasher, trading mainly in ironmongery, kept small stocks of harness and fittings in his shops in Lutterworth and Melton Mowbray.[153] The Pratt family, the successors to the Pavers, carried on some trading. Richard had supplied tar, pitch and canvas to the Misterton estate in the 1550s and in the 1560s he was also selling fish in Lutterworth market, presumably imported dried stock-fish. He continued to be styled 'mercer' for a time and his will, in which he styled himself 'yeoman', suggests that he may still have owned £200 worth of trading stock in 1575. Nevertheless the family was abandoning the mercery trade and concentrating on their farming as local yeomen, and especially on the more commercial side of it, livestock-dealing. The Peake family, whose combined tax assessment had been the highest in the town in the 1550s, similarly moved out of local drapery. One member became a prosperous yeoman freeholder and his heir was later styled 'gentleman'. Another, Francis, became the yeoman innholder at the Crown. Most of his property passed to his first son; but the family trading interest appears to have left the town in the person of his second son. In 1598 he sold his burgage property at the top of the High Street as 'Richard Peake of London, grocer' and he was later styled as 'Richard Peake of Elbing in the province of Prussia'.[154]

By the early seventeenth century there emerged in the town two thriving families of general traders, the Popes and the Almeys. Both originated from local yeoman families and, once resident in the town, both appear to have been supported entirely by local trade. The Popes had been a leading yeoman family, first in Peatling magna and then in Arnesby, and, apart from the Pavers, had produced the only man recorded as from the area to have joined the Leicester Chapmen's Guild in the sixteenth century. On his death in 1626 Francis Pope of Lutterworth, mercer, had haberdashery and grocery worth £71.16.3d. and cloth, mainly linen, worth £50.19.3d. The Almeys, the chief yeoman family in Ashby magna, married into the squire's family and were no doubt involved in the enclosure there at the end of the sixteenth century. From 1594 onwards, however, John Almey, haberdasher or mercer, was paying tax from the town and in 1598 he bought the Peake burgage property for £100. At the time of his death in 1636 there is no sign that he was farming. The core of his wealth was his grocery, salter's ware and haberdasher's wares, which were together valued at £42.1.0. Apparently he had attempted to join the Leicester Chapmen's Guild in 1587-8 as haberdasher, but had been dismissed within two years for not complying with the requirement to reside in the borough.[155]

Since such men would not be on the road all the week they probably sold in private shops, which could be kept open for business on each weekday and so would complement the market day activities in the Drapery. These early private shops seem to have grown out of deposits of wares left at inns by merchants on their regional rounds. Thus William Chamberlain, a mercer based on Lutterworth in the early sixteenth century but probably originating from a Leicester family, was later recorded as a former occupant of the Swan, which included two shops. Two shops also went with the Bull.[156] Similarly in the mid-century a Leicester innholder had a shop in his premises stocked with ironmongery.[157] Meanwhile the greatest volume of business no doubt continued to be done on Thursdays, with much of it still in the hands of outsiders. The wealthy Leicester mercer Robert Miller, for example, not only appeared in person in Lutterworth to appraise the goods and supervise the will of Francis Pope; he also left £86.3.7d. worth of stock in a shop of his own in the town on his death in 1633, and a further £20.9.1d. worth in his shop in Melton Mowbray.[158]

The records from the later seventeenth century present a very different picture of trading in the town. Up to the Civil War period about 15 town-based traders have been traced; but from the last 40 years of the century alone another 16. None of the latter was seriously engaged in farming and nearly all had considerable trading stock, mainly cloth, which was listed in a fascinating variety of types, suggesting distant and foreign origins. Four had stock worth £100 and over. Specialized traders appeared, such as a family of hatters, a barber with £45 worth of goods to sell, a tobacconist and a couple of wealthy families of apothecaries.[159] The Iliffe family included a Lutterworth apothecary as well as mercers in two villages, and the Tant family included the apothecary Mr Mark Tant, who had the highest inventory total of any ordinary townsman for the whole period.[160] Such men kept stocks of all kinds of necessaries and luxuries, like sugar and spices. They were important figures locally; many of them served office in the town, notably as church wardens, and became the "new gentry" whose emerging fortunes are to be discussed in the next section; in fact about half of the "new gentry" for whom occupations have been traced were traders. Such men also issued seven out of the town's eight trading tokens in the years following the War (see Illustration 18).

Perhaps of most significance for the role of the town in the economy of the area was the fact that the valuable stock of these men was for sale in private shops on their own premises, so that the population of the area was no longer so dependent on weekly purchases from the Drapery. The 1607 Survey gives some clues as to the isolated shops and encroachments that highlight the importance of a foothold in the very centre of the town. A joiner had two shops next to Westminster Hall and another man had just built a little house and shop there. Similarly just before 1625 a shop or building in the Neats Market was rebuilt as two shops with a chamber over. The successor to William Chamberlain in the Swan is recorded as George Iliffe, possibly an ironmonger, who occupied a shop in the Iron Market on the Feilding freehold. This shop appears to have become the two shops, with large chamber over, which were still occupied by ironmongers in the early eighteenth century. Perhaps the Iron Market was drawn off the street into these and other ironmongers' shops nearby. As in their origin, the spread of these private shops was closely connected with the development of the town's inns. Several of the later inventories mention a 'chamber over the shop', shewing that the shop was part of the premises, as in the case of the Gidley house, which was certainly also an inn. Another inn was taxed in 1664 on seven hearths, 'one made a shop of'. In 1607 a portion of the valuable Lord's Headland adjoining the Drapery was specified as a garden with an outhouse; but the fact that it was occupied by the haberdasher or mercer John Almey suggests it was already used as commercial premises. By the mid-century it was completely built up as five shops, occupied by a baker, an ironmonger, a hatter and others, and all belonging to George Tilley as part of his King's Head Inn property. The subdivision of an inn's premises into separate retail shops may even have been one of the reasons for it being moved to a new site, as seems to have been the case with the new Swan, which belonged to a barber-surgeon at the beginning of the eighteenth

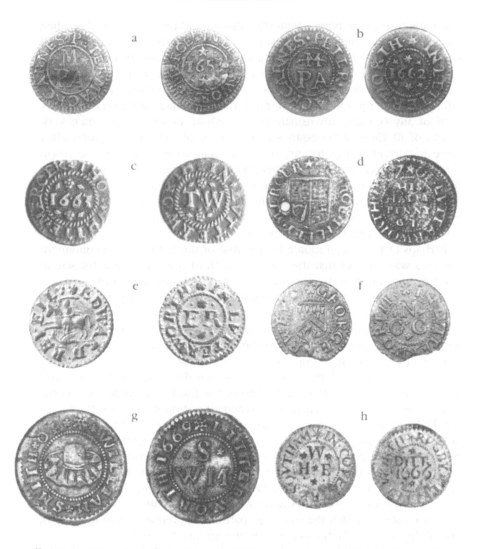

Illustration 18.   The eight Lutterworth seventeenth-century trading tokens, issued by
(a & b) Peter Mackarness mercer 1657 and 1662
(c) Thomas White mercer 1663
(d) George Tilley mercer (of the King's Head) 1667
(e) Edward Revell (of the George)
(f) George Newby (grocer)
(g) William Smith (hatter) 1669
(h) H.W. dyer 1666 also trading in Coventry, Southam and Rugby.
Shewn half again as large as actual size; apart from the two halfpennies (d & g) all are
farthings.
Leicestershire Museums (a & b); Norweb Collection (c); Birmingham Museums
(d rev. & g); Ashmolean Museum (e); Goodacre Collection, Leicestershire
Museums photographs (d obv., f & h)

century. The significant point about these private shops, however, was that the stock in them was for sale within the area and not carried round to other towns. Indeed one Lutterworth mercer even kept £2.17.5½d. worth of stock in his own branch shop in Dunton Bassett, one of the common-field villages in the area.[161]

There were also village-based traders in the area. The town parish register in the 1630s named the two established mercers already mentioned, a tradesman and two chapmen, one of them a stranger, and also a carrier and a wagoner. In the villages at the same time 13 men were recorded, mercers (but never a draper), chapmen, chandlers, carriers and a pedlar. All were based, as might be expected, on villages with mixed economies. Six of them, indeed, were from the parish of Broughton Astley. Even a Broughton Astley yeoman, who died in 1634, had £8.6.8d. worth of 'tallow, and wick yarn, and Certain linen Cloth in the house for market wares'. This suggests that, rather than keeping a regular shop in his own village, such a man was trading mainly at local markets. By the end of the century, however, a few village traders had shops in the home and built up enough independent wealth to appear in the probate records. A Bruntingthorpe chandler may be typical; he had possessions worth £7.6.6d., of which one pound's worth was in his shop. More surprisingly a chandler from the enclosed village of Ashby magna had 'in the shop a dozen pound of candles with other small mercery ware', valued at £2; but then his name was Judd, the same as one of the Lutterworth families of chandlers and as the Bruntingthorpe mercer. Another enclosed village, Peatling magna, contained a mercer; but although he had £14.1.5½d. worth of stock in his shop there, he also had £2.14.4½d. worth in his other shop in the adjacent common-field village of Arnesby. Similarly an ironmonger in Walton had general stock valued at £18.19.6d. in his shop; but he also owned a house and land in the town and 'In the shop at Lutterworth goods Amounting to £4.0.0'.[162]

While it is worth noting that such villages were eventually able to support their own village shops, it remains true that the greater part of local retail trade was concentrated in the town and indeed flourished there in a remarkable way. All this reflects an important step away from self-sufficiency in the local economy.

A key factor in the opening-out of trade into a national market was road transport. Whereas merchandise had formerly been carried round the country by merchants, the increasing volume of freight also involved common carriers, more or less professional men, some of whom ran regular services to London and back. At the end of the seventeenth century the Leicestershire Justices were regulating the rates of carriage from London to eight places in the county and *vice versa*.[163] Lutterworth was, of course, one of them and it is likely that a Lutterworth service had been running for many years; the first Lutterworth carrier traced was active in the 1620s and died in

1638.

The critical development, however, was the adoption of wagons to replace trains of pack-horses (see Illustration 6). Little is known of purely local carriers in this respect and most of the information concerns the regular lines that ran to and from the metropolis. Even for the latter, however, the wagon was still officially prohibited into the 1620s and appears not to have been adopted generally until some time after the 1630s.[164] A Melton Mowbray carrier owned a wagon in the 1620s and a Lutterworth wagoner is recòrded in 1636.[165] In 1637 John Taylor listed for every ten carriers only one wagon (or coach) service. The latter numbered 16 and 11 of them came from within only 30 miles of the capital.[166] It is very likely that the transition to wagons was accelerated by the demands of the Civil War, like the supply train of 50 wagons that passed through Leicestershire and Northamptonshire in 1643,[167] and that it was closely connected with the ensuing changes in farming practice. As has already been demonstrated, large horses and wagons were indispensable for the new improving farmer marketing his crops.

Further research is needed to ascertain how far local carriers and their teams were independent of farming. Some carriers lived in villages, which might suggest that they needed a farming base to be able to serve their local town. On the other hand some villages themselves needed the services of their own carriers, either for exporting the products of local industries or, eventually, for general purposes. The possibility that the Broughton Astley carriers exported cloth and hosiery and the Shawell carrier exported rope has been mentioned. The carrier who was paid 7/6d. for taking an orphaned apprentice to London from Walton in 1640 could well have been a village carrier too.[168] Certainly by the beginning of the eighteenth century a number of larger villages such as the former market centres of Welford and Haddon in Northamptonshire had their own carriers to London.[169] Nevertheless, even if the regular freight services were run by professional wagoners, more transport would still have been needed for particular consignments, such as loads of coal, and much of this would have been undertaken by well-equipped farmers.[170]

5.   The town transformed

Having examined the elements of the town economy separately, it is now possible to point to the characteristics of its economic and social structure that distinguished it from a village and to the ways in which these characteristics developed during the period.

Many of the villages had a squire, either an absentee or resident in his Hall or Manor House. Besides the families already named there was the Jervis

family of Peatling magna (see Illustration 9) and a branch of the Faunts of
Foston at Claybrook. The town's equivalent was the Feilding family, who let
their manor house and farm in the town and resided at Newnham Paddox.
By the late sixteenth century there were already two other families of arms-
bearing gentry, the Insleys and the Gores, based on freehold farms in the
town, whilst a third gentleman, Thomas Farren, based on the Spittle and its
grounds, came to treat the town much as if he were the manorial lord. The
town gentry tended to become county gentry based on village estates in the
neighbourhood and it is difficult to determine whether they would have
counted the town or their country houses as their main place of residence.
John Pratt, Thomas Insley, Captain William Cole, who was the subsequent
resident at the Spittle, and possibly Anthony Gore were Leicestershire
Justices in the mid-seventeenth century. John Pratt was 'of Cotesbach' in
1634, but 'of Lutterworth, esquire' in his will in 1657. The Lutterworth
house was taxed on seven hearths, the Cotesbach one on 14. William Cole
Esquire 'of Lutterworth' or 'of the Spittle' was buried in 1698 at Laughton,
where he was lord of the manor. This tendency was not in the one direction
only; a few members of the village gentry took to residing in the town. An
early instance was James Pycrofte, gentleman, who had a farm holding in
Lutterworth, where he died in 1606, but who was head of a leading yeoman
family in Ashby magna. Later examples include Mr Christopher Bradgate 'of
Wibtoft and Lutterworth' or 'of Lutterworth and Wibtoft'. Another member
of the ubiquitous Bradgate and Faunt families was 'Mary Wigley of
Lutterworth, gentlewoman', who was buried at Foston. 'William Staresmore,
late of Frowlesworth and now of Lutterworth, gentleman', was buried at
Frowlesworth.[171]

As for professional men, there were, of course, clerics throughout the area
and also a schoolmaster wherever schooling was provided beyond what the
parson himself could undertake. In the seventeenth century, besides the
school in the town, there were endowed schools at Shawell and Claybrook,
and schoolmasters recorded elsewhere.[172] Earlier on official medical men
may have been few and far between. The Pulteney family of Misterton
evidently had extreme confidence in the farrier's skills of the Lutterworth
smith Robert Mount in preparing draughts. One year he was first paid
sixpence 'for giving a drink to a young mare of my Lord's being sick at Cotes'
and then tenpence 'for his spices and labour in giving my Lord being sick a
drink'. Towards the mid-seventeenth century, at least, there was a
prospering surgeon in the town.[173] When it came to legal representation it
seems that at first a local gentleman as patron might serve as attorney.
Thomas Roos preceded Thomas Farren at the Spittle and served as steward
and then bailiff of the manor. He obtained Crown leases of properties in the
town for assignment to the occupants and frequently acted as supervisor or
overseer of wills, not only of townspeople. By the end of the sixteenth

century business in the town had grown sufficiently to attract a professional attorney to settle. This was Thomas Shakespeare, gentleman, who performed similar services for townsmen.[174] He features frequently in the probate records, where his place was taken in the 1630s by another man, who may have been a newcomer too. In the second half of the century, however, all the lawyers traced were members of the local village gentry. They include members of the Bradgate family and one Andrew Hull of Frowlesworth, who married a daughter of Jervis Bradgate of Wibtoft.[175] Clerical work for the Lutterworth church wardens was usually undertaken by tradesmen. Otherwise, apart from Mr Hull, only Mr (Richard) Stapleton (of Monks Kirby) contributed. Judging by the probate records he too may have been an attorney. He married into the Insley family and came to live in the town. It may even be that in the mid-century the town did not support an independent attorney's practice. Similarly surveying instruments, valued at ten pounds in 1632/3, belonged not to a townsman but to a gentleman grazing farmer in the enclosing village of Frowlesworth.[176]

In that they were drafted from the ranks of the gentry these professionals need hardly be accused of having usurped gentility by calling themselves 'Master'.[177] 'Thomas Bradgate of the Churchyard School', recorded at Peatling parva in 1578, was presumably a cousin of the squire there. Joseph Lee's father only became the rector at Catthorpe in 1625 after the death of his father, who was also rector there. Before that he had been 'Mr Lee, *ludimagister*' of the school at Shawell. In the 1630s Timothy Kirk was 'Clerk and Master of the freeschool in Shawell' and in the 1690s the schoolmaster was Thomas Kirke. They were related to the Elkingtons, the gentry family that had endowed the school at the beginning of the century.[178] Of more significance was the way the style was adopted by the chief commercial men in the town, notably the innholders and retail traders. This practice only became general from the 1630s onwards. Referring back to this period in 1658 former employees of the innholders at the George, the Hind and the Crown all called their former employers 'Mr'.[179] The will of William Smith, the innholder member of the family of important yeoman bakers, illustrates the turning point in 1629; the original style 'gentleman' was struck out and replaced by 'innholder'.[180] It may be significant that this was the very year in which the manor was split up. By the later part of the century the style was fairly automatic among the range of families that supplied the town officers. Of the 18 men who served as church warden in the 1680s at least 11 can be traced as styled 'Mr', but only one of these, Richard Stapleton, was of gentle descent. Out of the 60 burials inside the church in the years 1639 to 1699, 34 can be identified as from commercial families of "new gentry", but only ten as from old gentry families. Between 1675 and 1700 the pupils at Rugby School included the sons of nine families of gentry and clergy in the Lutterworth area and also of two commercial families from Lutterworth itself.[181]

A parallel development was the emergence of those who may most aptly
be termed the "new yeomen", who were typically the innholders and also
butchers and bakers. Their rise to importance was apparent a generation or
two earlier than that of the "new gentry", but for two reasons is less easy to
prove.[182] Firstly there is a possibility that a man placed in the town branch of
a manorial establishment may in any case have counted as a yeoman
attendant. John Saxton, who has been mentioned as based on the Pulteney
family's town premises and as catering for their Misterton establishment in
the 1550s, was styled locally 'of Lutterworth, yeoman'. In 1598 he was
succeeded there by Thomas Saxton 'at the earnest suit of John Saxton,
Thomas' father, a little time before his death'. Yet in 1597, when apparently
Thomas's retirement from keeping a public house there was arranged, a
property in Lilbourne was let by 'Demise by Gabriel Pulteney of Misterton,
esq., to Thomas Saxton of Lutterworth . . ., tailor, servant of the said
Gabriel'.[183]

In the second place the possession of a freeholding may in any case have
entitled such men to yeoman status. The 1607 Survey shews that the three
yard land holding of the Kirby family of butchers was freehold and that the
freehold house of the Smiths had apparently been built on part of the Kirby
freehold in the town. Of more practical importance, however, the occupier
of a freehold was in a better position to defy the controls of the manorial
court. In the sixteenth century exceptions to the suit of grist to the manorial
mills were respected in favour of the Feilding manor house, the Rectory and
one other small freehold farm house.[184] In the 1580s William Jones, one of
the town's common bakers, claimed that he never attended the Court Baron
because he was not a tenant of the manor.[185] The Misterton estate town
property was a freehold, originally burgage property and so apparently
outside the control of the manor;[186] the name Saxton is conspicuous by its
absence from the court rolls. Reading between the lines of the 1607 Survey
it can be seen that the manor was not in control over the freehold properties
and their occupants. It was just reported as a fact, for instance, that the
Insley family's freehold house in the Beast Market had been built
encroaching along all its front onto the highway. By this time, moreover,
what was still for tenurial purposes listed as a "cottage" might be substantial
premises housing one of the town's more important businesses. Out of 18
cottages for which the size was specified eight had three bays, nine had two
and only one had one. Out of 23 messuages or tenements, on the other hand,
only seven had more than three. The most conspicuous "cottages" were
Robert Billington's in the Corn Market and the original Swan, which was a
building of six bays. Several of the alehouses identified were also "cottages".
These measurements of buildings, however, were only specified for
properties let by demise; the entries for freeholds had apparently not been

brought up to date and may conceal all sorts of developments. It was presumably as the occupant of his Town Estate freehold house that Thomas Shakespeare defied the milling monopoly. In other words, during the period that yeoman farmers in the context of the area were splitting up the customary framework of farming, these men were helping split up the customary economy of the town, a process accelerated at the end of the 1620s when the manor was fragmented and the tenants by demise purchased the freeholds of their premises. In the next generation the enclosure of Ashby parva in 1665, even though it did not strictly affect the legal status of their tenure, seems to have emboldened most of the farmers in the village, who were husbandmen, to adopt the style 'yeoman'. In general, however, the most striking feature of the "new yeomen" and the "new gentry" is that both were essentially town-based phenomena. Only in the town was there an economic basis building up which necessitated cutting across the established social distinctions.

While these phenomena only affected the social status of the top layers of the community, the influence of commerce was at the same time reaching further down the economic scale; eventually Lutterworth even boasted its own Tradesmen's Benefit Society, instituted in 1747.[187] To begin with, most of the townsmen who had derived any independent wealth from non-agricultural activity had also been engaged in some traditional farming; but first their farming activities became more commercial and then, during the early seventeenth century, they were breaking away from their farming background altogether. Commercial opportunities in Lutterworth were expanding. Grown out of the area's dependence on it as the livestock-dealing centre were the butchery businesses and the leather crafts. Growing out of the area's dependence on it as the local corn market were the various businesses that involved corn-dealing. With malting and brewing concentrated there too, the town was the natural centre of all the provisioning trades, including, of course, the public house keeping trade, which helped support a whole range of substantial town households. Similarly while ordinary crafts, such as those concerned with clothing, were practised throughout the area, the town supported some of the more specialized skills already mentioned.

In those fields of activity that were centred on Lutterworth there was a tendency for the people involved to leave their villages for the town. Lutterworth was, moreover, the gateway to the world beyond. Parallel to the connexions found between the squire families and their merchants in the early sixteenth century, the area's rising yeoman families in the later part of the century had wide connexions, including members who became London traders. Needless to say some of the most significant connexions traced concerned Lutterworth-based families, like the Lussell, Kirby and Peake families.[188]

To counteract the impression that all was movement and change during this period, however, it is worth noting that there remained a core of husbandman families who continued the mixed farming of the town fields and who were also more or less involved in some of the commercial developments, such as the Taylor, Winterton and Wood families, or even, like the Woolman family, apparently not at all. To counteract the concentration on the extremes of wealth and poverty observable it is worth taking as an illustration one of the middle range of Lutterworth families, a husbandman family based in the town throughout the two centuries and thus having many connexions with other similar families there.

Members of the Newcombe family appear in the taxation rolls from the first half of the sixteenth century, presumably as occupiers of their house in the Beast Market, which they held by demise, together with its couple of yard land in the fields. William Newcombe, however, who died in 1594, provides an instance of the way in which the more commercial interests in the town were splitting up the farming interests. He had taken on extra sheep commons so as to be able to keep a larger flock in the fields than the stint of his holding allowed; but in addition to farming he was also in business as a shoemaker. The High Street cottage in which he lived, also held by demise, had with it a shop of two bays of building used as two shoemakers' shops. He left the farm to one of his sons and the shoemaking business, together with the cottage and shops, to his two other sons, who were shoemakers too. To them he also left his sheep and sheep commons; in other words he set them up as "common-field graziers".[189]

Through their connexions with the Cattle and Wightman families the Newcombes were related in the next generation to other shoemakers and to the Walton and Callis families of glaziers and rope-makers. But it was not only their crafts that supplemented the family's farming. Even at William's death the cottage in the High Street was apparently being run as an alehouse and in 1607 it was, apart from the Swan Inn, the only "cottage" listed as having a separate kitchen. In his will William specifically disposed of 'all my liquor and vessels it is in'. His grandson Elisha, who eventually carried on there some time after his own father's early death in the 1609 plague, was another shoemaker. On the sale of the manor he bought the freehold of the property, which continued as an alehouse. His son, another Elisha, moved to Leicester to make his living. He became free of the borough after his apprenticeship to Robert Cattle of Leicester, shoemaker, who was no doubt a cousin of his. Meanwhile Sarah, his widowed mother, was left running the alehouse; she was presented as one of the brewers of ale and beer at the manorial court in 1657. This is the first Lutterworth public house other than an inn for which the sign has been traced, the Black Swan.[190]

The grandson, yet another Elisha, returned to Lutterworth, where he worked as a carpenter; but presumably he concentrated on finer work, as at the end of the century he was known as a turner.[191] Meanwhile the family also included the town's brazier and a town baker, with his own oven and selling into the area as well as the town. At the same time their cousins the Wightmans included a blacksmith with his own forge and the tenant of the manorial horse mill.[192]

All this time the Newcombe, Cattle and Wightman families each continued farming on their family holdings in the fields as husbandmen and eventually as yeoman farmers, even using wagons by the end of the century. As far as can be traced, however, from the beginning of the century onwards their farming was carried on separately from their various non-agricultural activities.[193]

At the outset of this chapter the principal change in the town economy was identified as the shift in the balance of wealth from those engaged in farming to those also engaged in commercial activities of one sort or another and, eventually, to such people altogether independent of farming. It can now be seen how this shift was effected in terms, at least, of the upper layers of the community and indeed of those whose move into the town transformed their livelihood. The town must have seemed attractive as a source of employment right down the scale; but the transforming power of immigration into the town also had its negative possibilities, in that it could reduce village peasants, such as husbandmen, cottagers, labourers and craftsmen, to a new kind of wage-labourer whose former skills might be undervalued or even quite irrelevant.

In the second chapter it was suggested that towards the end of the period as many as one half of the households in the town might be considered as poor or potentially poor and that the way the additional population had been housed within the framework of the town, resulting in crowded areas like Bakehouse Lane, had also had much to do with the distinction between freehold and leasehold property. At the start of the sixteenth century there were under 40 houses but twice that number of cottages. So far the question whether the occupants of this unusual number of cottages were engaged primarily in agriculture or not has been left open. In the light of what has been found out about the status of the various non-agricultural occupations in the sixteenth century and later, it is now possible to say that, although at this time technically cottagers in that they enjoyed grazing rights in the fields, many of them formed a group of craftsmen and traders, more or less settled in the town, a feature that was unique to Lutterworth as the local market centre. It is conspicuous that nearly half of them, 36 out of 79 in 1509, were housed on the Feilding freehold, where they no doubt owed their presence to the family's patronage. As part of the manorial establishment many of them may well have been occupied in Sir Everard's wool-exporting business, so long as that lasted in the town. With the departure of both the manorial establishment and the wool trade such cottagers would have been left to their own devices. Perhaps it was awareness of this that prompted Sir William Feilding, Sir Everard's successor, to set up the stock of 120 cows, bringing in ten pounds yearly, to pay for annual distributions of clothing and alms among the poor of the town and neighbouring villages (see Illustration 19). But Lutterworth was no deserted village; it retained not only its common-field farming but also its own developing commercial life as a thriving local exchange point. These cottage properties, along with the other freeholds, remained to grow later in the century into wedges splitting apart the customary structure of the town economy.

This was particularly important with respect to the pressure for immigration into the town from the later sixteenth century onwards. Where the 1607 Survey appears to have been least comprehensive was in recording new houses or subdivisions of existing premises on freeholds. If the cases of this kind concerning tenancies by demise or at will are anything to go by, this was a problem which was getting out of hand. Far from being at the mercy of the manorial court, moreover, the few tenants at will seem to have been in the privileged position of having their encroachment or squatting officially recognized: they paid only nominal rents. Similarly the Town Estate properties which later became so crowded were also freehold and so was the Smith family's house, perhaps the one that they developed into their inn, and the three freehold cottage properties that went with it. It will be recalled that by the 1670s there were 142 households paying Hearth Tax and 106 exempted, while further poor were not counted as households. During the century the number of dwellings on the Feilding family freehold estate doubled to 70 and on the estate of the cadet branch of the family it more than quadrupled, to 31. On the Town Estate sites the half-dozen houses had multiplied to 28, including the 12 on the Cutchell which replaced a single cottage.

During the period of rapid expansion certain kinds of non-agricultural activity were drawn into the town, especially those concerned with provisioning and with leather. This effect no doubt applied right down the economic scale. Of the villagers those most ready to move would have been those least dependent on the land, like weavers and shoemakers. Contrary to the picture usually painted of rural life, it has been shewn here that the village craftsman who was also a smallholder was the exception rather than the rule by this period, even in the villages that retained their common fields. The enclosing villages in particular, where the mixed economy was being narrowed down, would be squeezing out their more skilled and independent labourers. In the short run and from the village point of view this might have looked like the town creaming off the more specialized labour. From the town point of view it may at first have played an important part in the general increase in locally based commercial activity. It would have been to

Illustration 19. Memorial effigies of Sir William Feilding and his wife, in Monks Kirby church. He died in 1547, and his wife Elizabeth, who was a daughter of Sir Thomas Pulteney of Misterton, died in 1539.
    Photograph: Wordscan, Lutterworth

the especial advantage of those townspeople who had larger households, because these were based on farm holdings and they were thus able to take in and maintain extra apprentices or servants. In the long run, however, the movement probably appeared more a case of the town being filled with under-employed labourers and such skills as some of them possessed may have proved of little use to them. In the 1630s there were numerous shoemakers, tailors and weavers in the town, taken all together, in fact, as many as the day labourers. To follow up the surnames of town labourers, there was a Smart, other Smarts being weavers in three villages and in Leicester; three Pratts, another being a tailor; and two Iliffes, others being weavers, including the one in the town. Very few of them were men of any independent wealth. Already when it came to employment there was probably little to distinguish most of them from unskilled day labourers.

Here again the break-up of the manorial control at the end of the 1620s was of crucial significance. It has already been seen that it undermined the customary basis of the milling and baking trades. It no doubt made the way easier for immigration and for multiplication of housing on sites like the Town Estate properties and elsewhere. How far the employment of labour had hitherto been subject to manorial regulation can only be guessed at; but the restriction on immigration would have functioned as a restriction on the employment of independent wage-labourers as opposed to servants in husbandry. Newcomers would have been prevented from running house-cows on the commons and in any case, to judge from the situation of the poor in villages, it probably became quite impractical for them even to contemplate the ownership of a cow. The influx of unattached labourers, whether as inmates or as precariously independent householders, opened up new possibilities for employment on a purely wage-labour basis. This contributed to the unique opportunity for town-based commercial farmers to pioneer the new methods of farming and later on the town may have been seen as a source of cheap labour for the principal employers in the area, the village-based improving farmers.[194] The main route upwards that a foothold in the town offered a labourer was to rely in addition on his wife's labour in running the household as an alehouse.

Following the established pattern of immigration into the town as the local centre, the population movements associated with the mid-century enclosures further aggravated the town's problems. There were, moreover, directions in which Lutterworth was incapable of developing to provide sufficient employment. It fostered nothing in the way of a weaving or hosiery industry. The leather crafts were a natural speciality for the town, but once the economy was thrown open onto a wider basis, even these suffered seriously in the face of outside competition. Of even more importance for the overall prosperity of the town, it lost its monopoly over the export of agricultural produce out of the area and the possibilities for further employment which its retention might have provided.

But far from being useless to the economy of the area, the town became even more essential. The release of more labourers as wage-earners only, rather than as servants receiving bed and board in their master's household, was a major factor in this step away from a peasant towards a commercial economy and made greater demands on the provisioning trades of all kinds.[195] These trades remained for the most part based on the town.

There were of course other ways in which the town continued to develop as the centre of the area. Doubtless it was for the majority the social, religious and cultural centre. In the next century there was a bowling green that went with the Denbigh Arms and horse-race meetings were held at Lutterworth, when the company would no doubt resort to one or other of the town's ordinaries; but at this stage it could hardly boast anything in the way of polite social life.[196] Moore's original pamphlet was based on 'two SERMONS, Preached at the Lecture at *Lutterworth*' in 1653, presumably to the crowds who came to the town's markets on Thursdays.[197] There are traces of popular music in the area and inventories list instruments intended for more genteel music in the hands of a few gentry and clergy. In 1643, presumably on a day when local crowds lined the High Street to watch Royal troops pass through, the church wardens paid two pounds 'to Prince Rupert's Trumpeters'; but they also paid sixpence 'to John Cartor's wife for going up and down town with a Bag-pipe'. In the town house of Anthony Gore, gentleman, however, where there was both an organ and a harpsichord, consort music in the new style could have been performed in the 1680s. The town was the business centre, even for some of the dealing in local produce that no longer passed through its open markets. The inns had become the scene for this type of business and for much else besides. In particular the development of the inns was closely connected with the emergence of important private retail shops that eventually overshadowed the weekly trading done at the Drapery.

For contemporaries approaching Lutterworth one of the surest signs that they were nearing a town with a concentration of housing and accommodation would have been the smoke rising from the many wood and coal fires that burned in domestic hearths. There were also numerous non-domestic hearths, ovens, furnaces, kilns and smithies, the extra smoke from which would have hinted at the attractions of additional employment. It has been shewn that the town did indeed offer much employment that was unique to it in the area in the second half of the seventeenth century. Yet Lutterworth still did not develop into an industrial centre which could take full advantage of the labour thrown onto the market by the mid-century changes. And indeed the greatest developments associated with this upheaval took place not in the town but in the area, where the whole farming economy moved on to a new and more commercial stage. The initiative had passed to the improving farmers in the villages. In this respect, for all its importance as the local trading centre and as a station on the national network of wayfaring trade, this town, once the base for merchants of international importance, had become an economic backwater, the chief function of which was to be the service centre for the area. The spire of its parish church was symbolic of the influence of Lutterworth in its area. Sure enough, despite the repeated sums of money laid out in repairing the stonework during the later seventeenth century, it blew down in 1703 and was never rebuilt. Indeed the church itself, which was seriously damaged by the fall of the spire, remained in a ruinous state for over 50 years afterwards.

CHAPTER FIVE

Town and Village: The Peasant Economy Transformed

The various elements of the peasant economy of the Lutterworth area as a whole, and those features of the town's economy which marked that out as an exceptional part of it at each stage during the sixteenth and seventeenth centuries, have now been examined in sufficient detail for it to be possible to conclude with a general characterization of the town's role in the transformation in both the local and wider contexts.

The early stage of enclosure in the area was almost over by the time this study begins but, by comparison with the later stages of the process, the population changes involved may be considered as the outcome more of the slow but inexorable perishing of some villages than of a deliberate policy to exterminate them in the cause of agricultural improvement. Nevertheless, when assessing the motives of the landlords, the advantages of scale on the side of extensive wool-production by the estate pasture-farms should not be underestimated; it would often have been the deciding factor in the abandonment of the more intensive mixed husbandry. At this stage, however, the town itself was not an important factor either in initiating the enclosures or in absorbing the displaced population.

These early enclosures affected only a minority of the area's population and may in a sense have been but one feature of the fifteenth-century decline in numbers, which possibly lasted into the sixteenth century. In any case there was a significant demographic set-back in the 1550s, a fact which makes the major population growth that followed stand out as even more spectacular. This involved a doubling of numbers in the area, an increase that was at first shared indifferently by each of the two types of village that have been distinguished in this study: those that were about to be enclosed and those that were to retain their common fields. By the early seventeenth century, however, contrasts between these two types of settlement were emerging. The growing divergence between livestock and arable farming interests was beginning to have an effect on local population distribution. There were, on the one hand, more enclosures around the turn of the century which involved deliberate expulsions. On the other hand, some of the common-field villages were shewing themselves to be more open to immigration and, partly because of their squatters' cottages and crowded housing, more susceptible to epidemics and disease. The evidence fully confirms Moore's alarm concerning the effects of the seventeenth-century phase of enclosure; the enclosing villages were seriously depleted in their numbers while the others continued to grow through immigration and were thus forced to face a poverty problem, which their chief inhabitants doubtless felt to be an undeserved burden. Whole areas of the Midlands were affected in this way, so that it is no surprise that John Morton's account of the consequences of this stage of enclosure in Northamptonshire, published in 1712, exactly describes what occurred here as well:

> The *Enclosures* lie dispersedly up and down the County. . . And yet far the greatest Part of the County is still open . . . And as to the Depopulation, which is so much complain'd of upon this Account; it appears by several Instances here, that as the Towns in the enclosed Lordships have been depopulated, so the neighbouring Towns that are not enclosed, and especially the Market Towns, have, since that Enclosure, been impopulated, if I may so speak, the Number of People in them much increased, and the higher the Rents of the Land and Houses; there especially where the Woollen Manufactures are encouraged.[1]

The development of the market town of Lutterworth was at each stage, in the context of its own area, exceptional even for a common-field community. Its population, whether or not it declined in the early sixteenth century, later outstripped that of any of the villages in growth, no doubt mainly because of immigration from the surrounding district. Following on this the town experienced, at least from the 1630s onwards, both periods of high mortality and a poverty problem, each of which were unparalleled in the area. Even when the populations of the remaining common-field villages shewed a new vigour towards the end of the century, the situation in the town worsened.

Turning to the advances in the local economy which must be linked with the population changes, here again the early enclosures cannot be shewn to have had any great direct impact. It was rather the penetration during the sixteenth century further down the scale among ordinary farmers of sheep farming for wool, and later for mutton, both to be sold outside the area, that broadened the base of the economy and made possible an intensification of the mixed husbandry of the common fields while still keeping the existing framework more or less intact. It was at this stage that the early enclosures did have an important indirect consequence by providing, in effect, room for territorial expansion among the yeoman farmers. They were in a position to draw greater benefits from the enclosed grounds than the loose manorial organization of the estate pasture-farms and this gave them a distinct advantage over the ordinary peasant farmers, the husbandmen confined to the common fields of their own villages. The estate farms were hampered by the customary basis of employment: the yeoman farmers were more flexible and able to make good use of wage-labour; and this was more readily available in villages where "illegal" immigration and squatting went unchecked.

The resulting imbalance in the redistribution of provisions and wealth was most keenly resented in times of dearth. Yet Moore the father was well aware of the crudity of the "population theory" of 'all wretched Atheists, who so mightily cry out and complain, supposing the earth cannot suffice them: praying still for plagues, that so they might have plenty'.[2]

The existing agrarian framework could contain this imbalance only so far; eventually it toppled. The peasant mixed husbandry in those villages that had managed to retain a more restricted economic base collapsed in the face of competition from the new production methods of the more commercial common-field farmers. The initial step taken by these deserters from the ranks of the ordinary peasants was to cultivate ancient enclosures, which brought double rewards in the form of higher grain yields and better grass quality. They then followed up with what was in effect a fresh territorial expansion, this time into the fields around living village communities. Thus the poverty problem in the remaining common-field villages was one aspect of this expansion and of the transition it involved towards wage-labour as the basis of employment. In a sense, therefore, the chief farmers there were after all themselves responsible for the expulsions from the enclosing villages that aggravated the problem. The most striking feature of these difficulties, however, is that no trace has been found of any significant alternatives to agricultural employment within the area. As Moore the son said, tillage was 'the great manufacture and trade'; but now it included tillage on a new and more efficient basis, so that the resulting redundancies were a very real problem.

Even at the beginning of the sixteenth century the town differed from a normal peasant village in its occupation structure. At first the difference was mainly at the top and bottom of the economic scale, the top being represented by a few important merchants and the bottom by a residue of petty traders and craftsmen who were more or less settled there. What employment the merchants offered, moreover, was no more deeply rooted in the town than the Feilding family's manorial establishment and the departure of both probably left the town even further enervated.

The foundation on which the town came to thrive was the expanding local economy in the later sixteenth century, as its markets became the exchange point between contrasting interests within the area. So long as the principal contrast was between the more or less self-sufficient common-field farm and the pasture estate, the role of the town was only peripheral. The former would need the markets for supplies from outside and for the sale of surplus production, but hardly at all for provisions. The latter likewise could provision its few dependants from within the manorial organization, while much of its trading bypassed the town's markets completely. With the intensification of production throughout common-field farming, however, contrasts emerged between the different village communities and, because of specialization, whether in meat, dairy or grain, between the livelihoods of individuals. The town was an integral element of this development and its body of middlemen, the people dealing in livestock and corn, were concerned not only with providing for the town and any wayfaring population there, but also with transactions of wider economic significance throughout the area.

These men were at first part of the town-based body of yeoman farmers, their distinction being that their position at the market centre enabled them to pursue more specialized farming. At the same time they were no doubt responsible for the withdrawal of more business from the open market, which had been the indispensable exchange point so long as trading was mainly direct between producer and consumer. Ultimately their peculiar power resulted from their hold not only over local trading but also over the exporting of produce out of the area. This no longer applied to wool; but the town's position as a station on main droving routes gave it unique importance for livestock-dealing. By the 1630s too, if not earlier, the town's dealers in corn were able to take advantage of their special opportunities for exporting corn out of the area. Men of this sort, or, if not the livestock-dealers, then at least the corn-dealers, may well be termed the original deserters from the ranks of the peasantry to pioneer the revolution.

As the century progressed Lutterworth suffered set-backs, some temporary, such as the plundering of the town by Royalist troops in 1644 and the losses 'by reason of a sad and fearful accident of fire happening' in 1653, claimed to be £1,038; others more serious, such as the high mortality from the 1630s onwards, and especially the 1650s.[3] After the mid-century the situation was very much an altered one. The town was no longer the "capital" of a group of basically similar village communities but the centre of an area economy, an economy sufficiently diversified and yet integrated for many of the villages to survive, albeit depleted in population, without the regular mixed husbandry of the common fields. The means to this end was a major step away from a peasant economy towards commercial farming and here the initiative was taken in the end not from within the town but within those villages that were opening out to a wider-based economy. This agrarian revolution was very much village-based. So while the town was even further integrated into the area economy as the provisioning and service centre, the major business of trading in farm produce was drawn into the hands of the more progressive of the village farmers. These were both the large-scale common-field farmers taking on enclosed grounds for cropping and improving their grazing, and the pure graziers and also, a new feature, the prospering village butchers. It is worth contrasting the inventory valuation of the village butcher and grazier William Seale, £2,286.1.8d., with the £9,300 total of all 115 of the inventories of townspeople from the last four decades of the century. Of course this does not mean that the town's markets became disused. They were still vital for the surviving peasantry of the area, as the principal outlets for the smaller producers and as the sources of provisions for the poorer sections of the populace. It was just that more of the important dealing now completely bypassed these traditional markets. The forum for the new business was no longer the open market-places but the halls, parlours, corn chambers and yards of the inns; so, while the involvement of the town manor in the economy of the area dwindled, townspeople of many sorts now derived an increasing direct benefit from it. One result of the increased proportion of the population having to purchase everyday provisions and necessities for cash was a dearth of small change. It can be no coincidence that it was in the middle of the seventeenth century that local traders took the initiative in solving this problem and made the way easier for such business in their shops by issuing their "illegal" halfpenny and farthing tokens.

What of the other non-agricultural occupations? It is easy to see that Lutterworth never became a centre of the local weaving craft. In view of the absence of a background of weaving or hosiery-knitting in the area, it is not surprising that it failed to evolve into an industrial centre. There were Iliffes engaged in weaving and trading across the area, very probably connected with the William Iliffe who introduced the stocking-frame into Hinckley. Unlike Hinckley, however, Lutterworth had no wool-dealers of the type that became the entrepreneurs in the emerging hosiery industry.

Of the various other usual village crafts the ones most clearly centred on the town were the group concerned with leather-working. This followed from the central role of the town's butchery businesses and was presumably supported entirely by local demand. So although these crafts, especially shoemaking, came nearest to an industrial concentration in the town, they had insufficient foundation for expansion into a true industry and, indeed, when faced with competition from more industrialized areas, sank in importance. Otherwise there is no evidence of the town containing suppliers or specialist craftsmen serving ordinary craftsmen in the area, with the possible exception of woodmen selling cut timber for joinery work. The town also supported several specialist craftsmen in the field of wood and metal working and building; but this was merely another aspect of its developing role as the service centre of the area.

After provisioning the most important aspect of the town's service role was the supplying of goods brought in from outside and here more than in any other field there is undeniable evidence of an intensification of activity in the town. At first it was mainly a matter of trading at fairs and the stocking of the weekly market and the Drapery, which was undertaken by a fraternity of travelling merchants. A few of these lived, only incidentally, in the town. Around the turn of the sixteenth century, however, there are clear traces of the emergence of the permanent private retail shop and a couple of prospering retail trading businesses were based on the town and relied on local custom only. By the later seventeenth century a further advance had taken place; for by then the town could boast a considerable shopping centre. Some of the shopkeepers were among the most important men in the town and they included men specializing in various cloths or other wares, or even in luxury goods. Here the town maintained an almost complete monopoly over the area and the fact that some of the chief shops grew up as part of inn premises shews this to have been closely connected with the town's importance as a point on national wayfaring trade routes.

In what sense can all these developments be said to have transformed Lutterworth into a more urban centre? The town's achievement in this direction can be sized up from two points of view: by asking firstly what immediate impact the town had on the area and secondly what kind of an urban centre the area needed or could support in the context of the increasingly diverse types of community that have now been classified within the district.

In the early sixteenth century the town made very little impression on the area; but thereafter its influence on the pace of change was considerable. During the second half of the century the town's yeoman farmers, and especially the butchers among them, rose in wealth and importance because they were able to develop their farming interests in the direction of livestock-farming and livestock-dealing. Their demand for feed for stock, because it outstripped what was available from the town fields and readily accessible pasture grounds, was a major factor in the pressure for enclosure around the turn of the century. Of these people Thomas Farren may not have been exactly typical, in that he had his own pasture grounds within the parish and also had a substantial stake in the running of the town and its markets; but his involvement in the enclosure of Cotesbach qualified him as the extreme local personification of 'the proud conceit of many graceless Graziers, and the presumptuous resolution of many greedy decayers of tillage' accused by Moore the father.[4] Pressure of this kind, like the demands which the grazing interests of Melton Mowbray farmers were making on the Wreake Valley, was spreading out from other small market centres at the same time. The 1607 riot arrived at Cotesbach from Hillmorton, the other side of Rugby. In this Warwickshire case the conflict was probably between a "close" part of the village, down by the church, and an "open" settlement up on the main road, which was the remains of a former market centre and also offered wayside accommodation. Some of the rioters at Hillmorton came from Rugby and if the recent unremitting efforts by the owner of the village's manor to secure enclosure were a response to the demands of butchers and grazing farmers centred on Rugby market, then here was a very close parallel to the relationship between Cotesbach and Lutterworth. By the 1660s, moreover, when there were few poor in the parish of Hillmorton, the inhabitants were ordered to contribute towards Rugby's poor. The widespread disturbances of the Midland Revolt were reflected in numerous more localized conflicts. There was an anti-enclosure riot at the market village of Hallaton in 1617 and in the 1630s the townspeople of Market Harborough won a victory concerning their grazing rights in the fields of the parent village of Great Bowden.[5]

For all his commercial involvement, however, Farren remained very much a magnate in the context of the manorial economy. Ultimately of more significance were the more completely commercial middlemen, especially the common bakers, whose wide-based businesses brought them into conflict with the restrictions of the manorial organization of the town. A particularly vulnerable link in the chain of redistribution at Lutterworth, as elsewhere, was the Corn Market. Here the direct conflict of interests between people at opposite ends of the economic scale was most easily seen. Competing for the same supplies of corn, especially barley, were the poor in need of weekly bread-corn and also the innholders, bakers and, a new feature, the maltsters, all of whom were buying up stocks for commercial purposes, including even export out of the area. This conflict was most serious in times of grain shortage; the authorities were then powerless to control the trade as more of the dealing was withdrawn from the open market.

The dislocations of the 1620s aggravated these problems and it can be no coincidence that the resolution originated in the crisis of the Crown.[6] The 1607 Survey of Lutterworth was evidently part of the unsuccessful attempt by the Earl of Salisbury as Treasurer to multiply the revenues from Crown leases for James I by raising entry fines rather than rents. The eventual sale of the manor by Charles I to the city of London, followed by its break-up, was a deciding factor in enabling the more commercial interests to prevail.[7] This critical step was exemplified not only by the way in which members of the town community responded to the scarcity at the beginning of the next decade, by ploughing up grass ground in the ancient enclosure of Moorbarns in order to raise crops, but also by their use of under-employed labourers in the town for that purpose.

From what has been said it is clear that Lutterworth was an essential element in the transformation of the area and it has been possible to infer a direct causal connexion between the influence and demands of the town and the enclosure movement of the mid-seventeenth century. The town provided the example and the experience of the new improving farming and it was also an important factor in the availability of the necessary labour. While parish officers throughout the area undertook their increasing duties of local administration and poor relief, those in the town fulfilled a role which extended far beyond its parish boundaries. It was the local market place, too, that was the stage for the repeated tragedy played out by the victims of Moore's "make-beggars"; and even among those husbandmen, cottagers and labourers who were not actually dislodged from their villages, Lutterworth would have functioned as a point of contact, while its fairs, markets and alehouses would have been resorted to as sources of information about possible employment in the area or beyond.

In the period leading up to the mid-century changes the town's more important commercial men, both traders and craftsmen, had been very much involved in farming and even in the changes in farming practices. The two activities had been as inseparable in the town's economy as they were in its topography. Afterwards farming no longer played such a crucial part in its economy. Symbolic of this may be the abandonment of the annual beating of the bounds of the town fields suggested by the decision in 1692 'Not to go the Perambulation to the meres'.[8] Nor did town-based farming retain any unique importance in the area. There was now little to distinguish the different types of town farmer from their village counterparts, except that, no doubt because of the continued additional demands on its fields for grazing, they remained on average less prosperous. Meanwhile the commercial section of the community at last stood separate and independent from the town's farming background. This rift may be seen in the 'several differences between the husbandmen and Tradesmen of Lutterworth', already mentioned as resolved by a Quarter Sessions order in 1693. On the ground the commercial community was also displacing farming from the centre of the town, in that the more important inn premises developed out of former farmsteads. At the same time, however, Lutterworth lost much of its influence in the area. Thus although it was in many respects a more urban community because of these changes, the new commercial power had passed to the progressive farmers. Whether enrolled from among these farmers or carrying on from surviving established families, the gentry also were able to benefit from these developments as rentiers.

The town's loss of the initiative and its failure to graduate to a new level of urban development must further be considered not only in terms of its own lack of numbers and commercial weight but also in terms of the needs and capacity of its particular area. First, however, it is worth emphasizing that no reason has been found for dismissing the Lutterworth area either as exceptional or as a backwater. On the contrary it was typical of the claylands of the Midland plain and its position on trading routes kept it very much open to outside influences. Each phase of change apparently spread up through the region from further south and this tendency may represent the growing circles of influence of London and its market demands. The early enclosures involving desertions and depopulations were a problem all over the Midlands and beyond. The anti-enclosure Midland Revolt of 1607 was concentrated in the three counties round Lutterworth. The elder Moore had his Northamptonshire counterpart in Robert Wilkinson who, in his sermon preached at the county town immediately after 'the late Rebellion and Riots in those parts committed', condemned enclosers as 'these *Anthropophagi,* these devourers of men under the name of right and property' and was at pains 'to promote the cause and complaints of the expelled, half pined, and distressed poor, that they rebel no more' (see Illustration 20).[9] And the causes for discontent, as echoed in 1607 by William Shakespeare's portrayal in *Coriolanus* of the mob rioting against withholders of corn, were widespread across the Midlands.[10] As for the main phase of enclosure in the mid-century, the contact between the local Diggers and their comrades elsewhere, the wide support for the younger Moore's campaign, the considered adoption of the cause by the Major-General for the Midland Counties and even the response to the Bill in Parliament all go to shew that this was no mere localized phenomenon. Moore's complaints against enclosure were based on 'my whole Country of *Leicester-Shire,* with most of the Inland Counties' or, more specifically, 'Leicester-shire, *and* North-hampton-shire, *and Counties adjacent'*.[11] Moore preaching at Lutterworth had his exact Northamptonshire counterpart at the market town of Kettering, also a centre of the 1607 rising.[12] Joseph Bentham preached at the Lecture there and published his attack on the effects of enclosure in the 1630s.[13] In forwarding to the Council of State one of the petitions from Leicestershire, endorsed by Warwickshire, Major-General Whalley added his own opinion that there was similar concern in the other counties in his charge, especially Nottinghamshire and Lincolnshire; and otherwise that 'the poor husbandmen . . deserve what help you can afford them'.[14]

At the outset of this study the progress of enclosure was taken as a measure of the changes in farming methods. It can now be said that what was involved was a fundamental transformation of the whole of local society. The common husbandry of the sixteenth century was but one feature of the manorially based peasant economy. The changes that culminated in the mid-seventeenth century and revolutionized agricultural production affected all levels of society and were reflected in the growth of the population and its subsequent redistribution.

While the most conspicuous deserters from the ranks of the peasantry were the people taking advantage of the new commercial opportunities, the greatest desertion in numbers was by those peasants whose uprooting from the traditional economy to become wage-labourers made the whole transformation possible. In denouncing those who profited from enclosure as 'Make-beggars, which make such swarms of Beggars in Countries, Cities, and Towns' Moore has already been quoted as identifying three different levels of society that were being displaced, namely the tenants, the cottiers and the children of both. To these he felt compelled to add a fourth type of victim of the make-beggars, namely:

A
SERMON

PREACHED
at

North-Hampton the 21. of

Iune laſt paſt, before the Lord Lieutenant of the
County, and the reſt of the Commiſſioners
there aſſembled vpon occaſion of the late
Rebellion and Riots in thoſe
parts committed.

Prou. 22. 2

The rich and the poore meete together, the Lord
is the maker of them all.

Printed at London for Io hn Flasket.
1607.

Illustration 20.   Title page of sermon delivered after the Midland Revolt of 1607.
The wheatsheaf motif symbolizes the current preoccupation with the availability of
bread-corn.
   Bodleian Library

> . . . those honest hearts, who out of a tender conscience take so *much
> care for the poor*, as they dare not comply with them in their
> uncharitable Designs, nor consent to such inclosure: Against these they
> fret and storm, and tell them in plain terms, they will undo them, and
> make them beggars; and so they do indeed, in bringing multiplicity of
> Law Suits, Actions of Trespass, for nothing, or at least for trifles, as for
> coming over their ground, &c. . . . Alas, how many amongst us are now
> persecuted in this manner, because they would keep Faith and a good
> Conscience pure, and unspotted, both before God and man . . .[15]

Evidently the passions roused by his personal involvement in the anti-
enclosure campaign were affecting his judgement at this point. Had he been
able to analyse the situation with more detachment and in the kind of detail
pursued here in the last chapter, he might well have substituted instead all
those villagers with the usual non-agricultural occupations who were
deprived of their livelihood, since it depended on the custom of a common-
field farming community.

The new commercial component of the economy was nurtured within the
local peasant economy and flourished so as to split it open and eventually to
displace it completely. At this stage it at least can be said to have deposed it
from its prime importance, as the traditional system of production ceased to
be the principal one. It is appropriate, therefore, to end the pursuit of the
question in hand with an examination of how this more commercial element
was distributed amongst the various types of community. To pursue the
matter to a logical vanishing-point is to arrive at the deserted villages that
made way for estate pasture-farming. This was indeed a form of production
for the market; but in the short run it had little direct effect on the town and
in the long run it was not structured to survive the seventeenth-century
changes.

The response to the problems of the later sixteenth century was a move
towards specialization of production, the form it took varying with the
nature of the additional resources taken in hand. In areas where the
resources had commercial possibilities the economy might take on a more
industrial character. "Industries in the countryside", however, were not
confined to areas with local industrial resources; they also flourished in areas
where a more "open" rural economy favoured the independent craftsman,
who was often also a small farmer.[16]

Developments of this kind were doubtless taking place across the
Midlands and beyond and a contemporary observation of the effect in
Northamptonshire has already been quoted. The obvious local example was
the Hinckley area where, towards the end of the seventeenth century, the
emergence of hosiery as a serious alternative employment in the villages was
transforming the town into an expanding centre of the more industrial type.
Yet this was happening under ten miles away from Lutterworth, which
remained then and has so far remained since very much a country market

town. The reasons for their having evolved into such different urban centres must be sought in the first place in the contrasting economies of their areas. Some of the contrasts have been brought to light in this study; for at each stage the first line of parishes on the Lutterworth side of the Fosse Way has been shewn as untypical of the Lutterworth area and therefore, presumably, more typical of the Hinckley area. This extends beyond their economic character to, for example, the flourishing of Nonconformity; in Sutton, in the parish of Broughton Astley, the Particular Baptist chapel reputedly dates back to a mid-seventeenth century foundation. The five places in the county chosen for recruiting meetings for Parliamentary forces in June 1642 included Broughton Astley itself, 'where appeared above 100 volunteers', an excellent response.[17] Perhaps the true boundary between the Lutterworth and Hinckley areas should after all have been drawn a couple of miles nearer to the former. In that case it would follow the division between two of the administrative bailiwicks of the mediaeval Honor of Leicester and would in fact coincide exactly with the dividing line between the two main geological formations in the region, the Trias and the Lower Lias.[18]

A basic difference was that seventeenth-century enclosure in the Hinckley area was not invariably accompanied by depopulation. This was an old "wood-pasture" area with a different settlement pattern; to quote Burton on the subject of his own manor of Lindley 'It is a kind of wood-land soil, and apt for wood, yet good pasture and corn ground'.[19] The farming speciality here tended to be pastoral, which favoured the smaller producer, and the population generally continued to grow. At the same time it may be that the larger farmers were not in a position to reap the full benefits of the kind of improving farming that has been described here and in any case the soil was probably not so suitable. Whatever the reasons, the effects in the form of a more mixed economy are traceable as far back as the mid-sixteenth century. Ultimately, however, the full potential of this type of economy was not to be exploited until the eighteenth century, when it provided the basis for rural industrialization.

Better known as typical of the Midland plain were the claylands like the Lutterworth area, where pasture was limited. This was former "wolds" landscape and here specialization threw into prominence contrasts among the surviving villages. In one type of settlement either grazing interests achieved complete enclosure around the end of the sixteenth century or the common husbandry finally collapsed in the mid-seventeenth. It has hitherto been widely assumed that the agricultural progress attested by the seventeenth-century enclosures was a triumph of enclosed ground farming and therefore a victory for the landowners in the enclosing villages; and that this victory left the peasants in the other type of village with a more primitive, with an obsolescent but inflexible means of agricultural production. It has here been shewn that, on the contrary, the farmers in the enclosing villages were faced by economic necessity that allowed them no alternative to enclosure and yet they did not themselves possess the means to achieve the improvement. Their villages became, if indeed they were not already, village communities of the "close" type. The departure of the common husbandry took with it the economic base of the whole range of village crafts and trades. As a symbol of this the elder Moore took the image of the busy village windmill, when he blamed enclosers who 'lay the earth to waste, over throwing poor mens ploughs in every place, not letting so much as a poor Mill to wag . . .' The classification here followed through is confirmed by the distribution of accommodation listed in 1686 and of alehouses licensed in 1753. It is also confirmed by the distribution in 1766 of licensed badgers and drovers (mostly the former) in the county, none of whom was based on "close" villages in the area.[20]

The final triumph of enclosed ground farming was not to come until the later eighteenth century. In the meantime the greatest achievement of the seventeenth-century agrarian revolution was based on common-field holdings. The common-field villages were "open"-type villages, containing the widest range of economic activity, from the progressive farmers, who were the largest employers, through the body of ordinary peasants, the husbandmen, down to the under-employed labourers and paupers living in pockets of rural slums.

This applied also to all kinds of non-agricultural activity, such as the usual village crafts, provisioning and trading too. The six badgers and drovers in the area in 1766 were based on the typically "open" villages of North Kilworth, Walton, Dunton Bassett, Ullesthorpe and, of course, Broughton Astley. Some of the most "open" villages, like Arnesby, were places that had once possessed market grants. A former local market centre was likely to be more susceptible to immigration and better able to respond to new influences and indeed Arnesby's Particular Baptist chapel, which dates back to the beginning of the eighteenth century, developed a more than local importance. It is of double significance, therefore, that the former market village of Welford boasted considerable wayfaring accommodation. Not only was it on droving and trading routes but it probably functioned as a local shopping centre as well. Possibly Walton and Dunton Bassett functioned similarly. The former market centre of Earl Shilton certainly had six dealers in the 1766 list, while the notoriously "open" village of Wigston magna had ten.

What of the other rural places, where the markets did survive but which failed to transform themselves into recognizably urban centres? In these cases it is likely that trading remained largely confined to their open markets and fairs, much of it in the hands of outsiders, so that they never fostered the middlemen of their own who might have made an impression on the local economy. The increase in the range of internal trade and the spread of private dealing left these intermediate centres with but desultory markets, which were probably mainly the concern of the smaller peasant producers and of the poorer people in need of weekly provisions. If this business was, apart from the annual fairs, all that remained, there was little to distinguish them from other "open" villages, especially those with the fullest economic activity. These last could doubtless be studied in terms of their role as centres, for a few purposes at least, of their own small neighbourhoods. The inhabitants of Husbands Bosworth, which is half-way between Lutterworth and Market Harborough and at the cross roads with the Welford road from Leicester, have been noted for their independence of action and the village eventually even acquired an annual fair of its own, held the week following Harborough Fair. The prime example of this type of village in the district was, of course, Broughton Astley, just off the Fosse Way and roughly twice as far from Leicester as it is from both Lutterworth and Hinckley. Any such local importance that a village had was evidently by now due less to a right to hold a weekly market in the open than to an ability to support private businesses and their premises, such as inns and shops. In the mid-seventeenth century five Leicestershire market villages had an average of two issuers of trading tokens each. By 1766, however, while Market Bosworth had three badgers, the other market villages, like Hallaton and Billesdon, did not feature at all on the list.

It is contrasts such as these that highlight the success of Lutterworth as a "simple" market town. At each stage of contemporary agrarian development it reacted to the changes differently because of its broader economic base and its wider commercial contacts. Initially its contribution to the economy of the local area was only peripheral. Later in the sixteenth century, with the expansion of trading within the area, it flourished as the local "capital". This is the period when the concept of a "local market system", as worked out by Dr Fleming for Melton Mowbray and its Wreake Valley villages, has most relevance. So long as commercial production remained subsidiary, the town had a virtual monopoly over the commercial activity involved in balancing out contrasts within the area. The confident expansion of the town's commercial economy was thus very much part of the expansion of the area's farming economy and indeed was an indispensable element in the agrarian revolution. Once the new methods prevailed throughout the area, it became an even more integral part of the local economy, which could now support a commercial community freed from its own farming background. Lutterworth was one of the six Leicestershire market towns which could boast an average of ten issuers of trading tokens each. The principal market towns on the 1766 list, Loughborough, Hinckley and Market Harborough, each had a dozen listed dealers and the smaller ones, Mountsorrel and Ashby-de-la-Zouch, had half a dozen, with Lutterworth in between, having ten. Yet although the increase in the range and volume of the country's internal trade reinforced the town's importance as a station on national droving and trading routes, these developments also deprived it of some of its prime importance in its own area.

Similar considerations no doubt affected larger urban centres at the same time, although in them the elements concerned with manufactures, wholesale and long-range trading, and various services introduced more complex differentiating factors. Granted that the influence of some towns and cities, and especially of the capital, was rising, however, it is well to bear in mind that the economy of the country as a whole remained predominantly agrarian and that the market town was the most common point of contact between rural society and something more urban. Rather than relegate it to the *lowest* category of urban classification in pre-industrial England, therefore, it should help clarify the position if the market town is concentrated on as having remained the *primary* urban unit. "The rise of the market town" was a striking feature of the period and it should not be surprising to find that, as in the case of Lutterworth, such a town was also an integral part of the development of the local economy. Many a town could doubtless be shewn to have had a parallel involvement in the Midland experience of the agrarian revolution.

This study of a single market town, by setting it in the context of the changing relationships in its area, offers four contributions to the understanding of the economy of the period. In the first place, being a local study, it has been able to identify in detail some of the causes and effects involved in the general population changes of the period. It is now well understood that the apparent stagnation of numbers in the later seventeenth century, which followed the phenomenal growth of the sixteenth, concealed a considerable redistribution of population, notably into the capital and urban centres of various types and between areas with differing economies. What has so far escaped attention is the effect this same process might have even within a local area, within which such movements took place between contrasting types of community. Secondly, and in the light of this, an examination of the various phases of enclosure and of the economy of the area as a whole has shewn that, whatever the progress made in the sixteenth century, only the fundamental changes around the mid-seventeenth should be counted as an agrarian revolution which affected the whole of rural society. The crisis of the Crown was resolved by the Civil War. At the same time the crisis of the local economy was resolved. Private property and profit were freed sufficiently from monopolistic restraints and manorial controls, typified by the Book of Orders, to allow the new capitalist farming to flourish and this helped to make way for the capitalist mode to become the dominant mode of production. Thirdly the various social and economic elements involved in this revolution have been thrown into prominence, and principally the progressive farmers and the wage-labourers, both of whom emerged from the background of the peasant economy of common-field farming. Joseph Lee could write with optimism that the new techniques of production, then being adopted by improving farmers, would sweep away the problems that had been piling up since the 1620s. He was blind to the fact that these techniques would, on the other hand, also help to exacerbate the problems simply because for their "success" they would depend on exploiting the poverty of labourers who had been severed from their peasant roots. In his turn John Moore's pessimistic forebodings of the extinction of traditional arable husbandry blinded him to the fact that the changes were, on the contrary, to be a victory for common-field farming, albeit in its new capitalist guise. It is these findings, then, that have prompted a rearrangement of the lower end of the classification of communities so that it now matches the presence or absence of the new commercial activity of all sorts. At the same time such a reclassification matches the distinction to be made between "open" and "close" villages which is usually reserved for later periods, after the final enclosures of the eighteenth century; a distinction, indeed, which is still observable among the same villages to this day. It is now clear that this contrast may be carried back to the time of the seventeenth-century agrarian revolution and this suggests that the terms themselves may even have originated in the distinction between open and enclosed fields. Finally the study as a whole has shewn that the rise of the market town was central to the emergence of this contrast. The town's wider role as the exchange point between its area and the world beyond reinforced its more local role as the meeting place for contrasting interests within the area itself. It was only such a combination of these two functions that was able to provide the commercial links necessary for the economic revolution which transformed society during the seventeenth century.

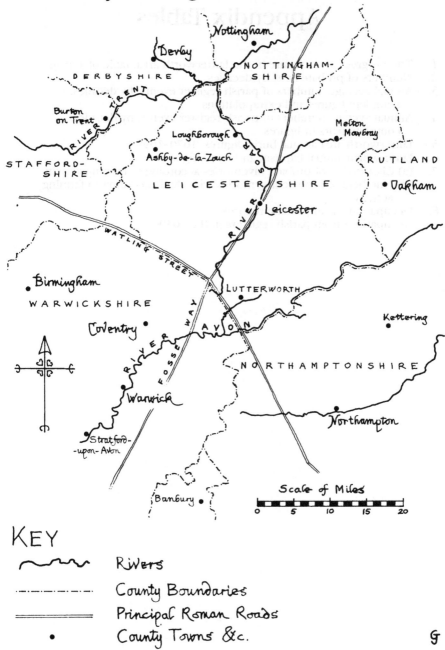

MAP IX

THE CENTRAL MIDLANDS OF ENGLAND

Nottingham

Derby

DERBYSHIRE

NOTTINGHAM-
SHIRE

Burton
on Trent

RIVER TRENT

Loughborough

Melton
Mowbray

STAFFORD-
SHIRE

Ashby-de-la-Zouch

RIVER SOAR

LEICESTERSHIRE

RUTLAND

Oakham

RIVER

Leicester

WATLING STREET

Birmingham

Lutterworth

WARWICKSHIRE

Kettering

Coventry

RIVER AVON

FOSSE WAY

NORTHAMPTONSHIRE

Warwick

Northampton

Stratford-
-upon-Avon

Banbury

Scale of Miles

0   5   10   15   20

KEY

〜〜〜   Rivers

—·—·—   County Boundaries

=====   Principal Roman Roads

•   County Towns &c.

G

Appendix Tables

Appendix Table 1 The progress of enclosure in the Lutterworth area: table of acreages (displayed on Map IV)

Leicestershire villages	acres	acres	percentage	Parish of Lutterworth	acres	acres	Total percentage
Early enclosure:							
8 whole townships							
by 1507	6,727 ⎫	7,547	16½	Moorbarns	564½ ⎫	664½	17
3 Hall Farms	820 ⎭			Spittle Grounds	100 ⎭		
Late sixteenth-century enclosure:							
Cotesbach final	1,007½ ⎫	1,166½	2½				2½
2 farms	159 ⎭						
c. 1620–1665 enclosure:							
11 townships final	12,944	12,944	28				26½
1681–1725 enclosure:							
Claybrook, 3 townships							
final	2,725 ⎫	3,410½	7½				7
Leire partial	685½ ⎭						
1762–1797 enclosure:							
13 townships final	21,033	21,033	45½	Final		1,749	47
Total acreage:		46,101	100			2,413½	100

Source: J. Goodacre, 'Lutterworth', Appendix A

Appendix Table 2 Numbers of probate acts, by decades (displayed in Figure I)

Decades	1500	'10	'20	'30	'40	'50	'60	'70	'80	'90	1600	'10	'20	'30	'40	'50
Town of Lutterworth	1	3	14	6	2	6	8	14	18	14	19	23	19	44	7	9
Lutterworth area:																
Enclosing villages	4	11	28	17	10	35	23	30	37	42	49	57	48	45	12	14
Open-field villages	5	18	49	38	36	88	53	62	89	76	84	149	154	143	67	28
Lutterworth area including town	10	32	91	61	48	129	84	106	144	132	152	229	221	232	86	51
Leicestershire including Leicester	12	380	802	608	679	1,242	976	1,323	1,366	1,764	1,715	2,537	2,195	3,035	1,207	–

Source: indexes of probate acts at L.R.O. and P.R.O.; see J. Goodacre, 'Lutterworth', Appendix B

Appendix Table 3 Annual average numbers of parish register events, by decades: complete figures and extrapolations (displayed in Figure II)

Decades	1560s	'70s	'80s	'90s	1600s	'10s	'20s	'30s	'40s	'50s	'60s	'70s	'80s	'90s
Baptisms:														
Number of complete figures	9	12	15	17	17	18	18	21	16	14	19	21	21	21
Total of complete figures	41.1	84.3	104.1	109.9	123.3	128.5	129.2	158.6	111.9	96.5	118.0	135.5	144.8	122.7
Total including extrapolations	104.7	151.7	149.5	140.9	161.9	152.4	149.3	158.6	154.0 150.2	136.4 136.1	132.2	135.5	144.8	122.7
Burials:														
Number of complete figures	9	13	14	17	17	17	18	21	13	13	18	21	21	21
Total of complete figures	21.9	39.4	45.5	70.0	64.3	82.2	95.7	111.6	60.2	77.7	77.9	97.5	112.1	84.9
Total including extrapolations	64.4	72.1	70.1	90.4	82.3	103.0	108.9	111.6	96.7 110.3	115.3 120.3	89.9	97.5	112.1	84.9
Excess of baptisms over burials as percentage of baptisms	39½	52½	53	36	49	32½	27	29½	37½ 25½	15½ 11½	32	28	22½	31

Source: to render the figures from the parish registers and transcripts comparable over the decades they have been completed by a system of extrapolation backwards, based on averages from the succeeding three decades, starting with the 1670s to 1690s, for which the records are complete. The alternative calculations for the defective 1640s and 1650s are based on a similar system working forwards, as the records from the preceding three decades are fairly complete; see J. Goodacre, 'Lutterworth', Appendix C

Appendix Table 4 Annual average numbers of parish register events, by decades: complete pairs of figures (displayed in Figure III)

Decades	1560s	'70s	'80s	'90s	1600s	'10s	'20s	'30s	'40s	'50s	'60s	'70s	'80s	'90s
12 open-field parishes:														
Number of complete figures	6	6	8	9	9	9	11	12	7	7	10	12	12	12
Baptisms	31.8	55.3	75.0	76.1	86.8	82.6	101.3	115.8	73.7	72.8	82.2	102.9	115.0	95.9
Burials	16.5	21.7	31.6	45.4	44.5	61.1	77.2	84.8	46.9	54.9	58.4	75.3	86.7	60.8
Excess of baptisms over burials as percentage of baptisms	48	61	58	40½	48½	26	24	27	36½	24½	29	27	24½	36½
9 enclosing parishes:														
Number of complete figures	3	6	6	8	8	8	7	9	5	5	8	9	9	9
Baptisms	9.3	29.0	24.0	33.8	36.5	35.8	27.9	42.8	20.8	18.2	32.5	32.6	29.8	26.8
Burials	5.3	13.6	13.9	24.6	19.8	21.1	18.5	26.8	11.3	14.7	19.5	22.2	25.4	24.1
Excess of baptisms over burials as percentage of baptisms	43	53	42	27	45½	41	33½	37½	45½	10	40	32	15	10
All 21 parishes:														
Number of complete figures	9	12	14	17	17	17	18	21	12	12	18	21	21	21
Baptisms	41.1	84.3	99.0	109.9	123.3	118.4	129.2	158.6	94.5	91.0	114.7	135.5	144.8	122.7
Burials	21.8	35.3	45.5	70.0	64.3	82.2	95.7	111.6	58.2	69.6	77.9	97.5	112.1	84.9
Excess of baptisms over burials as percentage of baptisms	47	58	54	36	48	30½	26	29½	38½	23½	32	28	22½	31

Source: to compare the excess baptisms between the two types of village decade by decade the extrapolations have here been omitted; see J. Goodacre, 'Lutterworth', Appendix C

Appendix Table 5 Lutterworth area annual burial figures, 1670–1699 (displayed in Figure IV)

Decade				1670s						
Year	0	1	2	3	4	5	6	7	8	9
12 open-field parishes	93	85	67	66	68	84	81	68	71	69
9 enclosing parishes	23	19	25	26	25	20	23	17	22	24
Total of 21 parishes	116	104	92	92	93	104	104	85	93	93

Decade				1680s						
Year	0	1	2	3	4	5	6	7	8	9
12 open-field parishes	112	87	104	79	110	68	123	63	60	58
9 enclosing parishes	36	35	21	21	34	17	26	24	25	22
Total of 21 parishes	148	122	125	100	144	85	149	87	85	80

Decade				1690s						
Year	0	1	2	3	4	5	6	7	8	9
12 open-field parishes	56	48	56	52	64	72	50	47	92	69
9 enclosing parishes	22	16	25	16	35	24	29	27	23	24
Total of 21 parishes	78	64	81	68	99	96	79	74	115	93

Source: parish registers and transcripts at L.R.O. and registers in the parishes

Appendix Table 6 Lutterworth annual baptism and burial figures (incomplete figures in brackets) (displayed in Figure V)

Year in decade	16th century Bap.	16th century Bur.	1610s Bap.	1610s Bur.	1630s Bap.	1630s Bur.	1660s Bap.	1660s Bur.	1680s Bap.	1680s Bur.
0			22	16	44	23	49	47	36	47
1					42	24	46	38	50	28
2			(4)		50	31	37	25	41	35
3	(20) [1564]	(12)			44	73	40	23	40	35
4							40	(8)	49	39
5					38	29	(14)		35	28
6	(9) [1566]	(8)			32	22	(13)		46	30
7			32	(4)	28	46	33	(13)	44	34
8	22 [1578/9]	7			39	30	47	22	52	31
9							43	36	40	46

Year in decade	1600s Bap.	1600s Bur.	1620s Bap.	1620s Bur.	1650s Bap.	1650s Bur.	1670s Bap.	1670s Bur.	1690s Bap.	1690s Bur.
0			(32)	21			38	45	34	17
1			(12)	16			47	22	42	24
2							47	20	32	34
3		(1)	43	23	(18)	(20)	47	38	34	32
4	35	24			37	26	37	22	29	34
5	25				42	27	43	44	27	40
6	(26)	(3)			44	30	42	35	37	36
7	26	11	41		43	59	42	47	31	37
8		15			47	40	46	27	39	36
9	22	10+32	43	33	(13)	37	40	25	33	36

Source: Parish Register and Bishops Transcripts at L.R.O.

Appendix Table 7

(a) Classification of probate inventories according to farming activity.

1 Mixed farming:
   (a) Mixed farmer:
   Farmer with arable crops and equipped for cultivation with a team of horses and a plough, cart and harrow
   (b) Smallholder:
   Farmer with arable crops but no team or implements for cultivation

2 Grazing farming:
   (a) Grazing farming with mixed farming:
   (i) Grazing farmer with mixed farm:
   Mixed farmer whose arable crops, excluding hay, were worth not more than one fifth of the livestock
   (ii) Grazing farmer with smallholding:
   Smallholder whose arable crops, excluding hay, were worth not more than one fifth of the livestock
   (b) Pure grazing farming:
   (i) Grazing farmer:
   Livestock farmer with no crops other than hay
   (ii) Small grazing farmer:
   Livestock farmer with no crops other than hay and no more than 5 beasts or 15 sheep

3 Non-farming:
   (a) Cottager:
   Owner of 1 or 2, but no more than 3, cows or of up to 5 sheep, but with no crops other than a little hay
   (b) Non-farmer:
   Owner of no farming stock, including owner of a horse as a personal mount or of domestic swine

(b) Numbers of probate inventories, classified according to farming activity

V = 29 villages ⎰ E = 12 enclosing villages
⎱ O = 17 open-field villages

L = town of Lutterworth

	1530s and 1540s				1550s				1590s				1630s				1680s				Total of sample decades			
	E	O	V	L	E	O	V	L	E	O	V	L	E	O	V	L	E	O	V	L	E	O	V	L
1 Mixed farming:																								
(a) Mixed farmers	12	30	42	1	46	60	106	3	27	30	57	8	25	45	70	8	1	54	55	5	111	219	330	25
(b) Smallholders	2	6	8	–	3	3	6	1	9	10	19	3	4	39	43	2	6	40	46	1	24	98	122	7
2 Grazing farming:																								
(a) Grazing farming with mixed farming																								
(i) Grazing farmers with mixed farms	–	–	–	–	–	–	–	–	–	–	–	1	–	–	–	3	5	1	6	–	5	1	6	4
(ii) Grazing farmers with smallholdings	–	–	–	–	–	1	1	–	–	–	–	–	6	1	7	1	2	3	5	2	8	5	13	3
(b) Pure grazing farming																								
(i) Grazing farmers	–	2	2	1	–	7	7	–	2	3	5	1	1	7	8	–	11	–	11	3	14	19	33	5
(ii) Small grazing farmers	2	–	2	–	–	2	2	1	2	5	7	–	5	2	7	3	5	3	8	–	14	12	26	4
3 Non-farming:																								
(a) Cottagers	–	2	2	–	–	2	2	–	1	15	16	6	11	16	27	8	14	16	30	2	26	51	77	16
(b) Non-farmers	2	2	4	2	1	1	2	1	5	5	10	3	6	26	32	16	14	27	41	15	28	61	89	37
Total	18	42	60	4	50	76	126	6	46	68	114	22	58	136	194	41	58	144	202	28	230	466	696	101

Source: Leicester Archdeaconry Court probate records at L.R.O. All the files have been searched for records concerning the Lutterworth area. The four decades have been chosen to obtain the largest samples and each includes 11 years, chosen so as to avoid gaps in the series, as follows: 1550–1560; 1586, 1588–91, 1594–97, 1599–1600; 1631–1641; 1680–1690: see J. Goodacre, 'Lutterworth', Appendix D. In addition all the inventories from before 1550, mostly dating from the 1530s and 1540s, have been studied, together with all those from the early enclosed townships, most of those from the enclosing townships throughout the period and any others traced for people with non-agricultural occupations. The result is that although the main sample covers only 44 years out of 180, this study is based on over half of the surviving village inventories.

Appendix Table 8 Occupations from probate records (summarized in Table 4.3)

V = 23 villages { E = 9 enclosing villages } Numbers of inventories from four decades
{ O = 14 open-field villages }
L = town of Lutterworth Numbers of probate records divided into four periods

	1550s (L 1530–79)				1590s (L 1580–1619)				1630s (L 1620–59)				1680s (L 1660–99)				Total of four decades (L 1530–1699)			
	E	O	V	L	E	O	V	L	E	O	V	L	E	O	V	L	E	O	V	L
Gentry and clergy	2	3	5	1	2	1	3	5	2	6	8	2	8	5	13	15	14	15	29	23
Yeoman, husbandmen etc.	23	39	62	13	24	30	54	21	26	67	93	19	15	71	86	19	88	207	295	72
Labourers, cottiers, servants etc.	-	-	-	2	-	7	7	5	4	19	23	6	4	10	14	5	8	36	44	18
Sub-total, agricultural	25	42	67	16	26	38	64	31	32	92	124	27	27	86	113	39	110	258	368	113
Food																				
butcher	-	-	-	2	-	-	-	1	1	-	1	-	-	3	3	2	1	3	4	5
miller	-	1	1	1	-	3	3	1	-	2	2	-	-	1	1	-	-	7	7	2
baker	-	-	-	2	-	-	-	-	1	-	1	3	1	-	-	3	2	-	2	8
maltster	-	-	-	-	-	-	-	-	-	-	-	1	-	-	-	3	-	-	-	4
vintner	-	-	-	-	-	-	-	-	-	-	-	1	-	-	-	1	-	-	-	1
victualler	-	-	-	-	-	-	-	-	-	-	-	2	-	-	-	-	-	-	-	3
innholder (-keeper)	-	-	-	-	-	-	-	-	-	-	-	2	1	1	2	8	1	1	2	10
Total	0	1	1	5	0	3	3	2	2	2	4	9	2	5	7	17	4	11	15	33

continued

Appendix Table 8 (continued)

	1550s				1590s				1630s				1680s				Total			
	E	O	V	L	E	O	V	L	E	O	V	L	E	O	V	L	E	O	V	L
Clothing																				
wool-winder	-	-	-	-	-	-	-	-	1	-	1	-	-	-	-	-	1	-	1	-
weaver	-	-	-	-	1	2	3	-	-	4	4	-	1	3	4	1	2	9	11	1
shearman	-	-	-	1	-	-	-	-	-	-	-	-	-	-	-	1	-	-	-	2
cloth-worker	-	-	-	-	-	-	-	-	-	-	-	-	-	1	1	-	-	1	1	-
dyer	-	-	-	-	-	-	-	-	-	-	-	-	-	1	1	-	-	1	1	-
tailor	-	-	-	-	2	2	4	1	-	3	3	1	2	1	3	2	4	6	10	4
Total	0	0	0	1	3	4	7	1	1	7	8	1	3	6	9	4	7	17	24	7
Leather																				
fellmonger	-	-	-	-	-	-	-	-	-	-	-	-	-	1	1	-	-	1	1	-
tanner	-	-	-	-	-	-	-	-	-	-	-	-	-	-	-	1	-	-	-	1
currier	-	-	-	-	-	-	-	-	-	-	-	-	-	-	-	1	-	-	-	1
shoemaker	-	-	-	-	-	-	-	6	-	-	-	5	-	4	4	4	-	4	4	15
glover	-	-	-	1	-	-	-	1	-	-	-	1	-	-	-	-	-	-	-	3
saddler	-	-	-	-	-	-	-	1	-	-	-	1	-	-	-	3	-	-	-	5
Total	0	0	0	1	0	0	0	8	0	0	0	7	0	5	5	9	0	5	5	25

continued

Appendix Table 8 (continued)

	1550s				1590s				1630s				1680s				Total			
	E	O	V	L	E	O	V	L	E	O	V	L	E	O	V	L	E	O	V	L
Crafts																				
blacksmith	-	-	-	-	-	-	-	1	-	1	1	-	-	2	2	2	-	3	3	3
smith	-	1	1	-	-	-	-	1	-	-	-	-	-	1	-	-	-	2	1	1
brazier	-	-	-	-	-	-	-	-	-	-	-	-	-	-	-	1	-	-	-	1
painter	-	-	-	-	-	-	-	1	-	-	-	1	-	-	-	-	-	-	-	2
glazier	-	-	-	-	-	-	-	-	-	-	-	2	-	-	-	-	-	-	-	2
mason	-	-	-	-	-	-	-	-	-	-	-	-	1	-	1	2	1	-	1	2
pavior	-	-	-	-	-	-	-	-	-	-	-	1	-	-	-	-	-	-	-	1
carpenter	-	-	-	-	-	-	-	1	-	1	1	1	-	4	4	1	-	5	5	3
joiner	-	-	-	-	-	-	-	-	-	-	1	1	-	-	1	1	-	-	2	2
wheelwright	-	-	-	-	-	-	-	-	-	2	2	1	-	-	1	1	-	2	3	2
(craftsman?)	-	-	-	-	-	-	-	-	-	-	-	-	-	1	-	-	-	1	-	-
cooper	-	-	-	-	-	-	-	1	-	-	-	1	-	-	-	1	-	-	-	3
rope-maker (roper)	-	-	-	-	-	-	-	-	1	-	-	2	-	-	-	-	1	-	-	2
sieve-maker	-	-	-	-	-	-	-	-	-	-	-	-	-	-	-	-	-	-	-	-
Total	0	1	1	0	0	0	0	5	1	4	5	10	1	8	9	9	2	13	15	24

continued

Appendix Table 8 (concluded)

	1550s				1590s				1630s				1680s				Total			
	E	O	V	L	E	O	V	L	E	O	V	L	E	O	V	L	E	O	V	L
Trading etc.																				
mercer	-	-	-	2	-	-	-	-	-	-	-	2	-	-	-	4	-	-	-	8
mercer and chandler	-	-	-	-	-	-	-	-	-	-	-	-	-	-	-	1	-	-	-	1
draper	-	-	-	1	-	-	-	-	-	-	-	-	-	-	-	-	-	-	-	1
woollen draper	-	-	-	-	-	-	-	-	-	-	-	-	-	-	-	2	-	-	-	2
linen draper	-	-	-	-	-	-	-	1	-	-	-	-	-	-	-	-	-	-	-	1
chandler	-	-	-	-	-	-	-	-	-	-	-	-	-	-	-	3	-	-	-	3
tallow chandler	-	-	-	1	-	-	-	1	-	-	-	-	-	-	-	-	-	-	-	2
chapman	-	-	-	-	-	-	-	-	-	1	1	-	-	-	-	-	-	1	1	-
tinker errant	-	-	-	-	-	-	-	-	-	1	1	-	-	-	-	-	-	1	1	-
(dealer in wares)	-	-	-	-	-	-	-	-	-	-	-	-	-	-	-	1	-	-	-	1
barber	-	-	-	-	-	-	-	-	-	-	-	-	-	-	-	1	-	-	-	1
apothecary	-	-	-	-	-	-	-	-	-	-	-	-	-	-	-	1	-	-	-	1
surgeon	-	-	-	-	-	-	-	-	-	-	-	-	-	-	-	-	-	-	-	-
schoolmaster	-	-	-	-	-	-	-	-	-	-	-	1	-	-	-	1	-	-	-	2
Total	0	0	0	4	0	0	0	2	0	2	2	3	0	0	0	14	0	2	2	23
Sub-total, non-agricultural	0	2	2	11	3	7	10	18	4	15	19	30	6	24	30	53	13	48	61	112
Sub-total, all occupations	25	44	69	27	29	45	74	49	36	107	143	57	33	110	143	92	123	306	429	225
Widows etc.	2	9	11	6	2	8	10	8	5	22	27	11	5	26	31	32	14	65	79	57
Occupation unspecified	15	31	46	7	8	22	30	16	3	21	24	13	8	20	28	12	34	94	128	48
Total	42	84	126	40	39	75	114	73	44	150	194	81	46	156	202	136	171	465	636	330

Source: for the villages, the same sample decades of inventories as defined on Appendix Table 7; for the town, all the probate records at L.R.O. and P.R.O., divided into the four periods shewn; see J. Goodacre, 'Lutterworth', Appendix E

Appendix Table 9   Occupations from parish registers in the 1630s: numbers of people with occupations given (summarized in Table 4.3)

V = 23 village parishes   { E = 9 enclosing parishes
                             { O = 14 open-field parishes

L = town of Lutterworth

	E	O	V	L
Gentry and clergy	20	33	53	7
Yeomen, husbandmen etc.	84	214	298	24
Labourers, cottiers, servants etc.	51	155	206	34
Sub-total, agricultural	155	402	557	65
Food				
butcher	2	6	8	3
miller	4	8	12	1
baker	1	5	6	5
maltster	1	–	1	1
aleman	1	–	1	–
beer-brewer	–	–	–	1
victualler	–	2	2	1
innkeeper	–	–	–	1
Total	9	21	30	13
Clothing				
wool-winder	–	2	2	–
weaver	4	21	25	5
felt-maker	–	1	1	1
fuller	–	–	–	1
shearman	–	1	1	–
cloth-worker	–	1	1	–
hatter	–	1	1	–
tailor	5	19	24	8
button-maker	–	1	1	1
girdler	–	–	–	1
Total	9	47	56	17
Leather				
fellmonger	1	–	1	–
currier	–	–	–	1
shoemaker	1	7	8	14
cobbler	–	–	–	1
glover	1	1	2	7
Total	3	8	11	23

Appendix Table 9 (concluded)

	E	O	V	L
Crafts				
blacksmith	5	13	18	4
smith	-	-	-	1
metal-man	-	1	1	-
tinker	-	-	-	1
dishmender	-	-	-	1
painter	-	-	-	1
glazier	-	-	-	2
plasterer	-	1	1	-
mason	-	-	-	3
pavior	1	-	1	-
carpenter	5	18	23	4
wheelwright	-	2	2	2
cooper	-	1	1	2
roper	1	-	1	1
basket-maker	-	-	-	2
Total	12	36	48	24
Trading etc.				
mercer	-	2	2	2
chandler	-	4	4	1
tradesman	-	-	-	1
chapman	-	3	3	2
pedlar	-	1	1	-
woodman	-	-	-	1
carrier	-	2	2	1
wagoner	-	-	-	1
surgeon	-	-	-	1
schoolmaster	-	-	-	1
bearward	-	-	-	1
Total	0	12	12	12
Sub-total, non-agricultural	33	124	157	89
Sub-total, all occupations	188	526	714	154
Vagrants, poor etc.	3	15	18	1
Total	191	541	732	155

Source: for a few years in the 1630s, starting in 1636, the parish clergy, apparently following an archdeaconry direction, entered occupations in the parish registers and transcripts. For the coverage of this sample in the area, see J. Goodacre, 'Lutterworth', Appendix F. In Lutterworth the details were meticulously entered by the curate schoolmaster Nathaniel Cox.

Notes

List of abbreviations

A.A.S.R.P.	*Associated Architectural Societies' Reports and Papers*
A.H.E.W., IV	*The Agrarian History of England and Wales, IV, 1500-1640*
A.H.E.W., V ii	*The Agrarian History of England and Wales, V ii, 1640-1750 Agrarian Change*
Ag.H.R.	*The Agricultural History Review*
B.M.	The British Library
Ec.H.R.	*The Economic History Review*
L.R.O.	Leicestershire Record Office
J. Goodacre, 'Lutterworth'	J. Goodacre, 'Lutterworth in the sixteenth and seventeenth centuries: a market town and its area' (Ph.D. thesis, University of Leicester, 1977)
J. Nichols, *Leics.*	J. Nichols, *The History and Antiquities of the County of Leicester*
P.R.O.	The Public Record Office
S.R.O.	Staffordshire Record Office
T.L.A.S.	*Transactions of the Leicestershire (Architectural and) Archaeological (and Historical) Society*
V.C.H.,	*The Victoria History of the Counties of England,*
Leics.	*Leicestershire*
Warwicks.	*Warwickshire*
W.R.O.	Warwickshire Record Office

Notes to Preface

1. J. Nichols, *The History and Antiquities of the County of Leicester*, 4 vols in 8 parts (1795-1815); W. G. Hoskins, *The Midland Peasant: The Economic and Social History of a Leicestershire Village* (1957); A. H. Dyson (ed. H. Goodacre), *Lutterworth: John Wycliffe's Town* (1913).
2. J. Nichols, *Leics.*, IV i (1810), 263 & 47; W. Burton, *The Description of Leicester Shire, Containing Matters of Antiquitye, Historye, Armorye, and Genealogy* (1622), 187.
3. Presented as subject for a local history group project in the town;

Lutterworth Town Study Group, 'Lutterworth in 1509', *Leicestershire Historian*, II vii (1976), 17-25.

4. G. E. Fussell, *The Classical Tradition in West European Farming* (1972) and *The Old English Farming Books from Fitzherbert to Tull, 1523 to 1730* (1947).

5. R. Williams, *The Country and the City* (1973): cf. a later classical appreciation of the romantic potential of one local prospect in two passages in A. Macaulay, *The History and Antiquities of Claybrook, in the County of Leicester; including The Hamlets of Bittesby, Ullesthorpe, Wibtoft, and Little Wigston* (1791), 43-4 & 123; the latter refers to the engraving of it to be published in J. Throsby, *Select Views in Leicestershire, From Original Drawings: Containing Seats of the Nobility and Gentry, Town Views and Ruins, Accompanied with Descriptive and Historical Relations*, I (Leicester, 1789), pl. XXXIV, no. 4.

6. J. Goodacre, 'Wyclif in Lutterworth: Myths and Monuments', *Leicestershire Historian*, III ii (1983/4), 25-34.

Notes to Introduction

1. A. Macfarlane, *The Origins of English Individualism: The Family, Property and Social Transition* (1978); reviewed by R. Hilton, 'Individualism and the English Peasantry', *New Left Review*, CXX (March-April 1980), 109-11.

2. Based on R. H. Hilton, 'The Peasantry as a Class', in his *The English Peasantry in the Later Middle Ages* (1975), 13.

3. R. Hilton, 'The Manor', *Journal of Peasant Studies*, I i (1973), 107-9.

4. R. H. Tawney, *The Agrarian Problem in the Sixteenth Century* (1912); E. Kerridge, *The Agricultural Revolution* (1967); C. Dyer, *Warwickshire Farming 1349-c. 1520: Preparations for Agricultural Revolution*, Dugdale Society Occasional Papers, XXVII (1981); J. Thirsk, *Economic Policy and Projects: The Development of a Consumer Society in Early Modern England* (1978).

5. C. Hill, *The English Revolution*, 1640 (1940).

6. J. Thirsk (ed.), *The Agrarian History of England and Wales*, IV, 1500-1640 (1967).

7. R. H. Hilton, *A Medieval Society: The West Midlands at the End of the Thirteenth Century* (1966) and *The English Peasantry in the Later Middle Ages* (1975).

8. R. H. Hilton (introduction), *The Transition from Feudalism to Capitalism* (1978).

9. J. E. Martin, *Feudalism to Capitalism: Peasant and Landlord in English Agrarian Development* (1983).

10. R. Hilton, 'Towns in English Feudal Society', in his *Class Conflict and the Crisis of Feudalism: Essays in Medieval Social History* (1985), 180.

11. D. Fleming, 'A local market system: Melton Mowbray and the Wreake Valley 1549-1720' (Ph.D. thesis, University of Leicester, 1980), 1-9.

12. This study is based on J. Goodacre, 'Lutterworth in the sixteenth and seventeenth centuries: a market town and its area' (Ph.D. thesis, University of Leicester, 1977).

Notes to Chapter I

1. General appraisal of the market town by A. Everitt, 'The Marketing of Agricultural Produce', in *A.H.E.W.*, ed. J. Thirsk, IV (1967), 466–90.
2. A. Everitt, 'The Primary Towns of England', *Local Historian*, XI v (1975), 263–77.
3. A. White, *A History of Loughborough Endowed Schools* (Loughborough, 1969), 17.
4. A. Everitt, 'The Marketing of Agricultural Produce', *loc. cit.*, 478–9; triple classification proposed by P. Clark and P. Slack in their introduction in *Crisis and order in English towns 1500-1700: Essays in urban history*, ed. P. Clark and P. Slack (1972), 4–6.
5. W. G. Hoskins, 'English Provincial Towns in the Early Sixteenth Century', in his *Provincial England: Essays in Social and Economic History* (1963), 79–80.
6. A. Everitt, 'The English Urban Inn, 1560-1760', in *Perspectives in English Urban History*, ed. A. Everitt (1973), 96; D. Defoe, *A Tour through England and Wales* (Everyman edn, 1928), II, 86–7.
7. V.C.H. Leics., IV (1958), 156–7 & 168.
8. W. G. Hoskins, 'English Provincial Towns in the Early Sixteenth Century', *loc. cit.*, 82; C. Phythian-Adams, *Desolation of a City: Coventry and the Urban Crisis of the Late Middle Ages*, Past and Present Publications (1979); *V.C.H. Warwicks.*, VIII (1969), 4–5 & 156.
9. M. Bateson (ed.), *Records of the Borough of Leicester, 1509-1603* (1905), 43–4.
10. This characterization is based on the four characteristics of the pre-industrial town proposed by P. Clark and P. Slack and illustrated throughout their introduction, *loc. cit.*, 4 & 1–41; together with A. Everitt, 'The Marketing of Agricultural Produce', *loc. cit.*, 467–506.
11. *V.C.H. Leics.*, III (1955), 166–7. The Lay Subsidy rolls from the 1520s are of little help in contrasting the size of towns and villages, there being a higher proportion of townspeople not worth taxing.
12. The figures for Melton Mowbray, 80, and for Ashby-de-la-Zouch, 64, have been demonstrated to be too low; *v. infra*, cap. II n. 51.
13. *The Itinerary of John Leland in or about the year 1535-1543*, ed. L. Toulmin Smith, I (1964), 19.
14. *V.C.H. Leics.*, III, 170–2; the order partly corrected by reference to the original exemption certificates; P.R.O., E 179, Box 332 (unsorted).
15. Market Harborough: M. Beresford, *New Towns of the Middle Ages: Town Plantation in England, Wales and Gascony* (1967), 462. Ashby-de-la-Zouch: *V.C.H. Leics.*, II (1954), 177.
16. Source for Map I: W.R.O., CR 2017/E42.
17. Walton by Kimcote: J. Nichols, *Leics.*, IV i (1810), 215. Clifton-upon-Dunsmore and Dunchurch: W. O. Wait, *Rugby Past and Present with an Historical Account of Neighbouring Parishes* (Rugby, 1893), 197.
18. Hillmorton: W. O. Wait, *op. cit.*, 269. Welford: A. W. Gibbons (ed.), *Early Lincoln Wills: An Abstract of all the Wills & Administrations recorded in the Episcopal Registers of the old Diocese of Lincoln, 1280-1547* (Lincoln, 1888), 64. Naseby: R. L. Greenall (ed.), *Naseby: A Parish History*, Leicester University Vaughan Papers in Adult Education, no. 19 (1974), 4–5.

19.   Banbury: *V.C.H. Oxfordshire*, X (1972), 7-8. Market Harborough: J. E. Stocks, *Market Harborough Parish Records 1531 to 1837* (1926), 135. Lutterworth: A. P. Moore, 'The Metropolitical Visitation of Archdeacon Laud, with an appendix containing transcripts of documents in ecclesiastical suits of the period, and other papers', *A.A.S.R.P.*, XXIX ii (1908), 524-5.

20.   Lutterworth: W.R.O., CR 2017/E42. Market Harborough: J. E. Stocks and W. B. Bragg, *Market Harborough Parish Records to A.D. 1530* (1890), 166 & 168-9. Coventry: *V.C.H. Warwicks.*, VIII, 151.

21.   J. Nichols, *Leics.*, II ii (1795), 599.

22.   Rugby: *V.C.H. Warwicks.*, VI (1951), 202. Lutterworth: P.R.O., SC 6, 1146/17; W.R.O., CR 2017/E42; P.R.O., LR 2, 255, f. 161; W.R.O., CR 2017/E115, 40 & 79.

23.   P.R.O., C 93, 2/4, mm. 2-3.

24.   *Ibid.*

25.   W.R.O., CR 2017/E42; L.R.O., 35'29/379; W.R.O., CR 2017/M42-6 & E3; L.R.O., DE 66 (Box 2225).

26.   F. W. Bottrill, *An Illustrated Hand Book of Lutterworth with Notes on the Neighbouring Villages* (Lutterworth, 3rd edn 1890), 11.

27.   A. Everitt, 'The Marketing of Agricultural Produce', *loc. cit.*, 480.

28.   Market areas named in P.R.O., LR 2, 255, ff. 117-72; *cf.* W. Burton, *The Description of Leicester Shire, Containing Matters of Antiquitye, Historye, Armorye, and Genealogy* (1622), 187.

29.   G. H. Tupling, 'Lancashire Markets in the Sixteenth and Seventeenth Centuries', *Transactions of the Lancashire and Cheshire Antiquarian Society*, LVIII (1945-6), 20-5; T. S. Willan, *Elizabethan Manchester*, Chetham Society, 3rd ser. XXVII (1980), 67.

30.   W. O. Wait, *op. cit.*, 110 & 113; D. Fleming, 'A local market system: Melton Mowbray and the Wreake Valley 1549-1720' (Ph.D. thesis, University of Leicester, 1980), 13; C. J. M. Moxon, 'Ashby-de-la-Zouch - a social and economic survey of a market town - 1570-1720' (D.Phil. thesis, University of Oxford, 1971), 204-8.

31.   The officers were specified in a Court Roll of 1657; W.R.O., CR 2017/M34. In the Court Rolls of the 1560s only the Ale Tasters were specified but the division of the business shows that there were equivalent officers; P.R.O., SC 2, 183/83-4.

32.   J. Nichols, *Leics.*, IV i, 259 & 247-8.

33.   *Ibid.*, 249-51 & 252.

34.   L.R.O., 5 D 33/189, *sub nomine* Lutterworth (1445).

35.   *Ibid.*, *sub nomine* Lutterworth (1548); W.R.O., CR 2017/E42; P.R.O., LR 2, 255, ff. 121-4.

36.   L.R.O., 35'29/379.

37.   J. Nichols, *Leics.*, IV i, 252.

38.   W.R.O., CR 2017/D172-94.

39.   J. Nichols, *Leics.*, IV i, 280.

40.   R. H. Hilton, *A Medieval Society: The West Midlands at the End of the Thirteenth Century* (1966), 187-93 and 'Medieval Market Towns and Simple Commodity Production', *Past & Present*, CIX (1985), 15.

41.   Lutterworth: P.R.O., SC 12, 10/7, m. 3v; *v. infra*, pp. 209-10. Hinckley and Ashby-de-la-Zouch: *V.C.H. Leics.*, II, 177.

42.   J. Thompson (of Leicester), *An Essay on English Municipal History* (printed in Leicester, 1867), 41-2 & 47; *V.C.H. Leics.*, IV, 36-7.

43. Loughborough: W. G. Dimmock Fletcher, *Chapters in the History of Loughborough* (Loughborough, 1883), 9. Stratford-upon-Avon: *V.C.H. Warwicks.*, III (1945), 239-41. Market Harborough: *V.C.H. Leics.*, V (1965), 145. Hinckley: H. J. Francis, *A History of Hinckley* (Hinckley, 1930), 63. Hallaton: L.R.O., Will Transcripts 1535, no. 30.
44. L.R.O., Wills R.B. 1533, f. 95 and 1523, f. 179.
45. Wills of Robert Hadarwood of Broughton (Astley) and Thomas Caball of Ashby parva, L.R.O., Wills & Invv. 1534.
46. Wills at P.R.O. and L.R.O.; Chantry Certificate concerning Guild, J. Nichols, *Leics.*, IV i, 264.
47. J. Thompson, *op. cit.*, 146-62.
48. D. Pockley, 'The Origins and Early Records of the Melton Mowbray Town Estate', *T.L.A.S.*, XLV (1969-70), 22-4 & 31.
49. W.R.O., CR 2017/E42; P.R.O., LR 2, 255, f. 160.
50. P.R.O., PROB 11, 31 (49 Alen).
51. L.R.O., Wills R.B. 1520, f. 374.
52. J. Nichols, *Leics.*, IV i, 254-6.
53. L.R.O., BR II/18/9/79. The attorney was Thomas Shakespeare; W. Kelly, *Notices Illustrative of the Drama, and other popular amusements, chiefly in the sixteenth and seventeenth centuries, incidentally illustrating Shakespeare and his contemporaries; extracted from the Chamberlains' Accounts and other manuscripts of the Borough of Leicester* (1865), 279-82.
54. *V. infra*, p. 185.
55. W.R.O., CR 2017/L5 (no. 6).
56. *V. infra*, p. 70.
57. P.R.O., E 179, 133/122; W.R.O., CR 2017/E42.
58. W. G. Hoskins, 'English Provincial Towns in the Early Sixteenth Century', *loc. cit.*, 73; W. G. Dimmock Fletcher, *op. cit.*, 37.
59. C. J. M. Moxon, *op. cit.*, 37, 90, 113 & 173.
60. J. Young, 'The Token Coinage of Leicestershire and Rutland in the XVII. Century', *T.L.A.S.*, XI i & ii (1913-14), 115-31; W. J. Davis, *The Token Coinage of Warwickshire, with Descriptive and Historical Notes* (Birmingham, 1895).
61. A. Everitt, 'The Marketing of Agricultural Produce', *loc. cit.*, 489.
62. D. Fleming, *op. cit.*, Table VII; C. J. M. Moxon, *op. cit.*, 69-71.
63. P.R.O., C 93, 2/4, m. 3.
64. D. Fleming, *op. cit.*, 213; C. J. M. Moxon, *op. cit.*, 94-7.
65. P.R.O., E 179, Box 332 (unsorted).
66. *V.C.H. Leics.*, III, 170-2.
67. R. H. Hilton, 'The Small Town as Part of Peasant Society', in his *The English Peasantry in the Later Middle Ages* (1975), 76-94.
68. Market Harborough: J. E. Stocks and W. B. Bragg, *op. cit.*, 119-20. Ashby-de-la-Zouch: C. J. M. Moxon, *op. cit.*, 147-8. Lutterworth: Will of John Fildyng, 1403; A. W. Gibbons (ed.), *op. cit.*, 99.
69. (R. Blome), *Britannia, or a Geographical Description of the Kingdomes of England, Scotland, and Ireland . . .* (1673), 138-9, 231 & 177.
70. Sturbridge: A. Everitt, 'The Marketing of Agricultural Produce', *loc. cit.*, 535-6. Boughton Green: F. Whellan & Co., *History, Topography, and Directory of Northamptonshire* (1874), 226 & 228. Harborough: A. Everitt, 'The Marketing of Agricultural Produce', *loc. cit.*, 539. Atherstone: *v. infra*, p. 26.

262

71. Northamptonshire Record Office, I.(L), 1491, f. 28v.
72. A. P. Moore, *loc. cit.*, 529.
73. L.R.O., Wills of John Turner of Walcote, Wills & Invv. 1558 (P-Z); of Robert Hill of Ashby parva, Wills 1599, no. 58; of John Marriatt sen. of Lutterworth, Wills 1613, no. 81.
74. L.R.O., DE 40/40; *cf.* L.R.O., DE 147/15.
75. W. Camden, *Britain, or a Chorographical Description of the most flourishing Kingdomes, England, Scotland, and Ireland* . . . (1610 edn), 510.
76. R. L. Greenall (ed.), *op. cit.*, 10; *cf.* J. Mastin, *The History and Antiquities of Naseby, in the County of Northampton* (1792), 77-8.
77. *V.C.H. Leics.*, II, 175.
78. M. Bateson (ed.), *Records of the Borough of Leicester*, 1103-1327 (1899), 123.
79. *V.C.H. Leics.*, I (1907), 329; G. F. Farnham, *Leicestershire Medieval Village Notes*, III (Leicester, 1929), 52-3, V (1931), 404 & VI (1933), 169.
80. *V.C.H. Leics.*, IV, 40; D. Fleming, *op. cit.*, 93; G. H. Green and M. W. Green, *Loughborough Markets and Fairs (through 7½ Centuries)* (Loughborough, 1964), 18-19.
81. *Calendar of Patent Rolls*, Edward IV, Henry VI, 1467-1477 (1900), 212-3; J. Nichols, *Leics.*, IV i, 265.
82. W. G. Hoskins, 'English Provincial Towns in the Early Sixteenth Century', *loc. cit.*, 73. Wigston: A. Hamilton Thompson, *A Calendar of Charters and other Documents belonging to the Hospital of William Wyggeston at Leicester* (Leicester, 1933), 39-46. Burton: W. G. Dimmock Fletcher, *op. cit.*, 37. Paver: P.R.O., E 179, 133/122 & /121.
83. *V.C.H. Leics.*, III, 75-6; *V.C.H. Warwicks.*, VIII, 34.
84. *V.C.H. Nottinghamshire*, I (1906), 248.
85. W. G. Hoskins, 'The Origin and Rise of Market Harborough', in his *Provincial England: Essays in Social and Economic History* (1963), 54-6.
86. (R. Blome), *op. cit.*, 138 & 139.
87. I. D. Margary, *Roman Roads in Britain* (1967), 217.
88. *V.C.H. Leics.*, II, 42-4.
89. *V.C.H. Leics.*, III, 69; *v. supra*, n. 68.
90. W. Camden, *op. cit.*, 562; D. Defoe, *A Tour through England and Wales*, II, 86.
91. S.R.O., D 1734/4/1/9, ff. 5v & 22v.
92. *The Itinerary of John Leland in or about the year 1535-1543*, ed. L. Toulmin Smith, I, 10.
93. Will of William Palley of Lutterworth, P.R.O., PROB 11, 1507 (23 Adeane).
94. K. J. Bonser, *The Drovers: who they were and how they went: an epic of the English Countryside* (1970), 193: J. Thirsk, 'Enclosing and Engrossing', in *A.H.E.W.*, ed. J. Thirsk, IV (1967), 229-30; *cf.* B.M., Cotton MSS, Titus F.IV, f. 323.
95. *V.C.H. Leics.*, III, 80.
96. W. Burton, *op. cit.*, 187.
97. R. J. Colyer, 'A Nineteenth Century Welsh Cattle Dealer in Northamptonshire', *Northamptonshire Past and Present*, V ii (1974), 122-3.
98. S.R.O., D 1734/4/1/6-9, especially /9, ff. 13v & 14r and /6, f. 24v.
99. *Ibid.*, /9, ff. 6r & 14r.
100. D. Defoe, *A Tour through England and Wales*, II, 88 & 131 and *The Complete English Tradesman* (1745, 1841 edn), II, 174.

101. D. Defoe, *A Tour through England and Wales*, I, 83; S.R.O., D 1734/4/1/6, f. 38r. & /9, f. 22v.

102. W.R.O., CR 2017/L5 (no. 6).

103. *E.g.* S.R.O., D 1734/4/1/6, ff. 9r & 18v.

104. Weedon: F. Whellan & Co., *op. cit.*, 436. Fosters Booth: A. Everitt, 'The English Urban Inn, 1560-1760', in *Perspectives in English Urban History*, ed. A. Everitt, 96. *Cf.* P.R.O., WO 30, 48.

105. Caves Inn: A. P. Moore, *loc. cit.*, 534; J. Nichols, *Leics.*, I i (1795), cli; Shawell Enclosure Agreement, L.R.O., DE 66 (Box 2504); *sub nomine* Cave under date 1719 in Shawell Parish Register Transcripts at L.R.O. High Cross: J. Nichols, *Leics.*, IV i, pl.XXII; inventory of Nathaniel Reeve of Claybrook magna, innholder, L.R.O., Invv. 1690, no. 147. Smockington: W.R.O., CR 2017/E115, 61; *The Journeys of Celia Fiennes*, ed. C. Morris (1947), 333.

106. J. Taylor, *The Carriers Cosmographie* (1637, 1873 edn).

107. A. Everitt, 'The Marketing of Agricultural Produce', *loc. cit.*, 552-65.

108. D. Defoe, *A Tour through England and Wales*, I, 43 & 141 and *The Complete English Tradesman*, II, 181-3.

109. D. Defoe, *A Tour through England and Wales*, I, 43.

110. H. Stocks (ed.), *Records of the Borough of Leicester, 1603-1688* (1923), 536.

111. J. Nichols, *Leics.*, IV ii (1811), 679.

112. Inventories of two wool-combers and one hosier, all of Hinckley, L.R.O., Invv. 1674, no. 13, 1690, no. 63 and 1689, no. 49.

113. A. Everitt, 'The Marketing of Agricultural Produce', *loc. cit.*, 467.

114. Sources for Map II: *Royal Commission on Market Rights and Tolls First Report*, I (1889), Appendices xix & xxi; R. H. Hilton, 'Medieval Agrarian History', *V.C.H. Leics.*, II (1954), 175 and *A Medieval Society: The West Midlands at the End of the Thirteenth Century*, 173; W. A. Barker, 'Warwickshire Markets', *Warwickshire History*, VI v (1986), 161-75; *v. supra*, p. 22.

115. *Cf.* R. H. Britnell, 'The Proliferation of Markets in England, 1200-1349', *Ec.H.R.*, 2nd ser. XXXIX ii (1981), 221.

116. Loughborough: *V.C.H. Leics.*, III, 132. Lutterworth: N. S. B. Gras, *The Evolution of the English Corn Market from the Twelfth to the Eighteenth Century* (1926), 20. Monks Kirby: *V.C.H. Warwicks.*, II (1908), 130-1.

117. W. O. Wait, *op. cit.*, 9-10 & 109.

118. *V.C.H. Warwicks.*, VI, 202; W. Camden, *op. cit.*, 562.

119. *V.C.H. Warwicks.*, VI, 109 & 79; P.R.O., WO 30, 48; D. Defoe, *A Tour through England and Wales*, II, 118.

120. *V. supra*, n. 104.

121. Source for accommodation shewn on Map III: P.R.O., WO 30, 48.

122. Billesdon: *V.C.H. Leics.*, V, 6 & 10-11. Dunchurch: *V.C.H. Warwicks.*, VI, 79; D. Defoe, *A Tour through England and Wales*, II, 118. *Cf.* P.R.O., WO 33, 48.

123. D. Davis, *A History of Shopping* (1966), 145-9; T. S. Willan, *The inland trade: Studies in English internal trade in the sixteenth and seventeenth centuries* (1976), 83-9; *cf.* J. Thirsk and J. P. Cooper (eds), *Seventeenth-Century Economic Documents* (1972), 397: *v. supra*, n. 60.

124. A. Everitt, 'The Marketing of Agricultural Produce', *loc. cit.*, 496-502.

125. C. Phythian-Adams, *Re-thinking English Local History*, Leicester University Department of English Local History Occasional Papers, 4th ser. no. 1 (1987), 37-42.

126. Guthlaxton hundred: *V.C.H. Leics.*, III, 211. Lutterworth Poor Law Union: W. White, *History, Gazetteer and Directory of the Counties of Leicester and Rutland* (2nd edn, Sheffield, 1863), 721 & 758.

127. H. Hartopp, *Register of the Freemen of Leicester 1196-1770* (Leicester, 1927), 369-82.

128. P.R.O., RG 4, 507.58.

129. Sources for Map IV: *v. infra*, n. 132 and Appendix Table 1.

130. W. Burton, *op. cit.*, 44, 109, 187 & 192.

131. J. Thirsk, 'The Farming Regions of England', in *A.H.E.W.*, ed. J. Thirsk, IV (1967), 3-4 & 89-99.

132. R. H. Hilton, 'Medieval Agrarian History', *loc. cit.*, 189-95; W. G. Hoskins, 'The Deserted Villages of Leicestershire', in his *Essays in Leicestershire History* (1950), 67-107; Deserted Medieval Village Research Group, 'Provisional List of Deserted Medieval Villages in Leicestershire', *T.L.A.S.*, XXXIX (1963-4), 24-33; L. A. Parker, 'Enclosure in Leicestershire, 1485-1607' (Ph.D. thesis, University of London, 1948); L. A. Parker, 'The Depopulation Returns for Leicestershire in 1607', *T.L.A.S.*, XXIII (1947), 231-89; M. W. Beresford, 'Glebe Terriers and Open-Field Leicestershire', in *Studies in Leicestershire Agrarian History*, ed. W. G. Hoskins, *T.L.A.S.*, XXIV (1949), 77-126; J. Thirsk, 'Agrarian History, 1540-1950', *V.C.H. Leics.*, II (1954), 199-245; J. Thirsk, 'Inclosure in Leicestershire without Parliamentary Act', *ibid.*, 254-9; J. Thirsk, 'List of Parliamentary Inclosure Acts and Awards for Leicestershire', *ibid.*, 260-4. Further general references listed in J. Goodacre, 'Lutterworth', 39 nn. 1-4. Additional sources for Lutterworth area and adjacent parts of Warwickshire listed, *ibid.*, Appendix A.

133. Lilinge identified by elimination and on the evidence of the ownership of adjacent Domesday manors; *V.C.H. Leics.*, I, 330. Cotes de Val may have survived some time as a common-field farming community: H. L. Gray, *English Field Systems* (1915). 470; R. E. Glasscock (ed.), *The Lay Subsidy of 1334*, British Academy Records of Social and Economic History, new ser. II (1975), 160 n. 3.

134. E. Kerridge, 'The Returns of the Inquisitions of Depopulation', *English Historical Review*, LXX (1955), 212-28; the original returns published in I. S. Leadam, *The Domesday of Inclosures 1517-1518* (2 vols, 1897).

135. L. A. Parker, 'Enclosure in Leicestershire, 1485-1607', *op. cit.*

136. M. W. Beresford and J. G. Hurst (eds), *Deserted Medieval Villages* (1971), 11.

137. L. A. Parker, 'Enclosure in Leicestershire, 1485-1607', *op. cit.*, 149.

138. E. F. Gay, 'The Midland Revolt and the Inquisitions of Depopulation of 1607', *Transactions of the Royal Historical Society*, n.s. XVIII (1904), 195-244; J. E. Martin, *Feudalism to Capitalism: Peasant and Landlord in English Agrarian Development* (1983). 'The rising of the commons for inclosures': Bodleian Library, Gough Add. Leic. 8vo 16; printed in R. Hazlewood, 'William Davy, of Leicester', *Leicestershire and Rutland Notes and Queries*, II (1893), 194. Account of exposure and execution of Captain Pouch: E. Howes, *The Annales, or Generall Chronicle of England, begun first by maister John Stow, and after him continued and augmented* . . . (1615), 889. 'The Diggers or Delvers of Warwickshire, to all other Diggers: or a Declaration of the Mobile, against the increase of Pasturage, by Inclosures': B.M., Harl. MS 787, f.9v; printed in J. O. Halliwell (ed.), *The Marriage of Wit and Wisdom, an Ancient Interlude. to which are added Illustrations of Shakespeare and the Early English Drama* (1846), 140-1. Recent enclosing: M. E. Finch, *The*

Wealth of Five Northamptonshire Families, 1540-1640, Publications of the Northamptonshire Record Society, XIX (1956), 17, 66, 74 & 87-8.

139. L. A. Parker, 'The Agrarian Revolution at Cotesbach, 1501-1612', in *Studies in Leicestershire Agrarian History*, ed. W. G. Hoskins, *T.L.A.S.*, XXIV (1949), 41-76.

140. E. Howes, *op. cit.*, 889.

141. L.R.O., BR II/18/9/103-15.

142. J. Moore, *A Target for Tillage, briefly containing the most necessary, pretious, and profitable use thereof both for king and state* (1612), Epistle Dedicatory.

143. M. Beresford, 'Habitation versus Improvement: The Debate on Enclosure by Agreement', in *Essays in the Economic and Social History of Tudor and Stuart England in honour of R. H. Tawney*, ed. F. J. Fisher (1961), 40-69.

144. Extent acknowledged at the beginning of this century by E. M. Leonard, 'The Inclosure of Common Fields in the Seventeenth Century', *Transactions of the Royal Historical Society*, n.s. XIX (1905), 101-46; J. R. Wordie, 'The Chronology of English Enclosure, 1500-1914', *Ec.H.R.*, 2nd ser. XXXVI iv (1983), 483-505.

145. The first two counties cited in J. Moore, *A Scripture-Word against Inclosure* (1656), Advertisement; the last three cited in the 1607 MS 'A consideration concerning the cause in question before the Lords touchinge depopulation', B.M., Cotton MS Titus F.IV, ff. 322-3; printed in W. Cunningham, *The Growth of English Industry and Commerce in modern times*, II (1917), Appendix B, 897-9.

146. J. Thirsk, 'Agrarian History, 1540-1950', *loc. cit.*, 218-9; J. Thirsk, 'Enclosing and Engrossing', *loc. cit.*, 238; M. Beresford, 'Habitation versus Improvement: The Debate on Enclosure by Agreement', *loc. cit.*; E. Kerridge, *Agrarian Problems in the Sixteenth Century and After* (1969), 125-7; J. Thirsk, 'Agricultural Policy: Public Debate and Legislation', in *A.H.E.W.*, ed. J. Thirsk, V ii (1985), 317-21.

147. J. Nichols, *Leics.*, IV i, 222 & 265.

148. 'Crying sin', like 'caterpillars of the commonwealth', was a current phrase; *v. infra*, n. 157. Although the first two replies to Moore were published under a pseudonym which has confused scholars, there is no reason to doubt the traditional ascription to Lee, who only came out into the open by stages; J. Nichols, *Leics.*, IV i, 85. To remove confusion all the local pamphlets are listed in the Bibliography giving dates of composition so as to establish the order in which they should be read.

149. J. Moore, *A Scripture-Word against Inclosure*, 9; *cf. ibid.*, Advertisement.

150. J. Thirsk, 'Enclosing and Engrossing', *loc. cit.*, 238.

151. J. Lee, *A Vindication of A Regulated Inclosure* (1656), 5 & 8.

152. J. Moore, *A Scripture-Word against Inclosure*, 10. Source for Map VII: J. Lee, *A Vindication of A Regulated Inclosure*, 8.

153. (J. Lee), *A Vindication of the Considerations concerning Common-fields and Inclosures* (1656), 46; J. Lee, *A Vindication of A Regulated Inclosure*, 5; *cf.* J. Moore, *A Scripture-Word against Inclosure*, Advertisement. The fact that this, together with his confusion between the two pamphleteers, dislodges the corner-stone of Beresford's argument may be of no great significance; for he was clearly preoccupied with deserted villages and not aware of a more subtle form of depopulation; M. Beresford, 'Habitation versus Improvement: The Debate on Enclosure by Agreement', *loc. cit.*, 43-4.

154. J. Thirsk, 'Enclosing and Engrossing', *loc. cit.*, 238; E. Kerridge, *Agrarian Problems in the Sixteenth Century and After*, 127.
155. Much evidence obligingly collected together by Beresford, even though it undermines his argument; M. Beresford, 'Habitation versus Improvement: The Debate on Enclosure by Agreement', *loc. cit.*
156. K. Thomas, 'Another Digger Broadside', *Past & Present*, XLII (1969), 65; L. A. Parker, 'Enclosure in Leicestershire, 1485-1607', *op. cit.*, 48-50 & 209-14.
157. Shakespearean commonplace quoted in J. Lee, *A Vindication of A Regulated Inclosure*, 14.
158. First Petition, 1651: H. Stocks (ed.), *op. cit.*, 412. Second Petition 1653: *ibid.*, 414. These two petitions, if kept, would have perished in the Houses of Parliament fire of 1834. A signed original, damaged and undated, but probably from 1653, bears about 175 signatures; L.R.O., BR II/18/27/605. Third Petition, 1656: *Journals of the House of Commons*, VII, 1651-1659, Index *sub voce* Petitions; H. Stocks (ed.), *op. cit.*, 428; *Calendar of State Papers, Domestic Series*, 1655-6 (1882), 9 & 21. A draft petition, undated but datable to 1655-6; L.R.O., BR II/18/28/89.
159. H. Stocks (ed.), *op. cit.*, 412, 414 & 428; *v. supra*, n. 147.
160. L.R.O., BR II/18/28/59 & 64; M. James, *Social Problems and Policy during the Puritan Revolution 1640-1660* (1930), 123-4.
161. *Journals of the House of Commons*, VII, 1651-1659, 470; *The Dictionary of National Biography* (1885-1900), *sub nomine*. The original of Whalley's Bill would also have perished in the fire of 1834.
162. E. M. Leonard, *loc. cit.*, 130; J. Thirsk, 'Agrarian History, 1540-1950', *loc. cit.*, 219; W. E. Tate, *The English Village Community and the Enclosure Movements* (1967), 127.
163. *Journals of the House of Commons*, VII, 1651-1659, 358.
164. *Diary of Thomas Burton, Esq. Member of the Parliaments of Oliver and Richard Cromwell from 1656 to 1659*, ed. J. T. Rutt, I (1828), 175-6; M. James, *op. cit.*, 120-1; *cf.* R. H. Tawney, *The Agrarian Problem in the Sixteenth Century* (1912), 394. Beresford's apparently complete account of Parliamentary and Government action fails to mention this campaign and the Bill it launched; M. Beresford, 'Habitation versus Improvement: The Debate on Enclosure by Agreement', *loc. cit.*
165. *V. infra*, p. 55.
166. *Ibid.*
167. E. Kerridge, *Agrarian Problems in the Sixteenth Century and After*, 127. Kerridge's assertion is not supported by the references he cites; J. Goodacre, *op. cit.*, 50.
168. J. Lee, *A Vindication of A Regulated Inclosure*, 3-4.
169. J. Moore, *A Scripture-Word against Inclosure*, Advertisement.
170. (J. Lee), *Considerations concerning Common Fields, and Inclosures* (1653), 11-12.
171. J. Lee, *A Vindication of A Regulated Inclosure*, 8.

Notes to Chapter II

1. The statistical sources and methods used in this chapter, especially the aggregate analysis of parish register figures, are discussed more fully in J. Goodacre, 'Lutterworth', 55-102 and Appendices B & C.

2.   C. T. Smith, 'Population', *V.C.H. Leics.*, III (1955), 129-55.
3.   This study has not employed the sophisticated techniques applied to the national sample in E. A. Wrigley and R. S. Schofield, *The Population History of England 1541-1871: A Reconstruction*, Studies in Social and Demographic History (1981). Direct comparative analysis has sufficed to bring out the contrasts and the overall trends are confirmed by the probate figures. For another possible reason for the increase in the latter, however, *v. infra*, p. 142.
4.   J. Lee, A *Vindication of A Regulated Inclosure* (1656), 5.
5.   J. Moore, *A Scripture-Word against Inclosure* (1656), 9-10.
6.   *Cf.* W. G. Hoskins, *Provincial England: Essays in Social and Economic History* (1963), 185-7.
7.   C. T. Smith, *loc. cit.*, 138.
8.   P.R.O., E 179, 133/122 & /121.
9.   Figures entered at various times in the *Speculum Dioeceseos Lincolniensis sub Episcopis Gul. Wake et Ed. Gibson, 1705-23* printed in W. G. Dimmock Fletcher, 'Documents relating to Leicestershire, preserved in the Episcopal Registry at Lincoln', *A.A.S.R.P.*, XXII ii (1894), 227-365; compared with the original replies of 1718-23, St Paul's Cathedral Library, 17 D 20-1.
10.   The deficiencies of the series of figures and the possibility that they are affected by under-registration due to Nonconformity are dealt with in J. Goodacre, *op. cit.*, Appendix C; *v. infra*, n. 23.
11.   J. D. Chambers, *Population, Economy, and Society in Pre-Industrial England* (1972), 91-2.
12.   W. G. Hoskins, 'Harvest Fluctuations and English Economic History, 1620-1759', *Ag.H.R.*, XVI i (1968), 22.
13.   J. D. Chambers, *op. cit.*, 22-3, 141 *et seqq.*; E. A. Wrigley and R. S. Schofield, *op. cit.*, 179.
14.   W. G. Hoskins, 'Harvest Fluctuations and English Economic History, 1480-1619', *Ag.H.R.*, XII i (1964), 36; C. J. Harrison, 'Grain Price Analysis and Harvest Qualities, 1465-1634', *Ag.H.R.*, XIX ii (1971), 153; (T. Staveley), 'The History and Antiquities of the Antient Towne and once Citty of Leicester', MS including chronicle at Leicester City Reference Library.
15.   F. J. Fisher, 'Influenza and Inflation in Tudor England', *Ec.H.R.*, 2nd ser. XVIII i (1965), 120-9.
16.   1587: C. J. Harrison, *loc. cit.*, 154; *v. infra*, p. 182; W. G. Hoskins, 'Harvest Fluctuations and English Economic History, 1480-1619', *loc. cit.*, 37. 1590s: *ibid.*, 38.
17.   *Ibid.*, 39.
18.   L. A. Parker, 'The Agrarian Revolution at Cotesbach, 1501-1612', in *Studies in Leicestershire Agrarian History*, ed. W. G. Hoskins, *T.L.A.S.*, XXIV (1949), 66.
19.   W. G. Hoskins, 'Harvest Fluctuations and English Economic History, 1620-1759', *loc. cit.*, 20.
20.   L.R.O., DE 1941/1.
21.   J. E. O. Wilshere, 'Plague in Leicester 1558-1665', *T.L.A.S.*, XLIV (1968-9), 63.
22.   Phrase used under date 1645 in Broughton Astley Parish Register, L.R.O., DE 3319/1.
23.   It is also possible that the registration of baptisms was less thorough in the open-field villages; *v. infra*, p. 56.
24.   L.R.O., BR II/18/27/605 (MS defective); *v. supra*, cap. I n. 158.

25. J. Moore, *A Scripture-Word against Inclosure*, 14.
26. J. Moore, *The Crying Sin of England, Of not Caring for the Poor* (1653), 11.
27. P.R.O., E 179, Box 332 (unsorted); *cf.* J. Patten, 'The Hearth Taxes, 1662-1689', *Local Population Studies*, VII (1971), 19-21.
28. *Cf.* (J. Lee), *Considerations concerning Common Fields, and Inclosures* (1653), 23.
29. J. Patten, *loc. cit.*, 18.
30. Wills of Richard Smith of Broughton Astley and Thomas Sumpter of Ashby magna, L.R.O., Wills & Invv. 1546 and 1558 (P-Z).
31. *V. infra*, n. 54.
32. L.R.O., Wills 1604, no. 21, Wills R.B. 1573, f. 9, Wills 1633, no. 20; MS Enclosure Award at Ashby parva.
33. A. P. Moore, 'Leicestershire Churches in the Time of Charles I.', in *Memorials of Old Leicestershire*, ed. A. Dryden (1911), 148.
34. Shawell Enclosure Agreement, L.R.O., DE 66 (Box 2504).
35. J. Lee, *A Vindication of A Regulated Inclosure*, 3-6.
36. Shawell Parish Accounts, L.R.O., DE 734/6; L.R.O., Invv. 1676, no. 111.
37. J. Thirsk, 'Enclosing and Engrossing', in *A.H.E.W.*, ed. J. Thirsk, IV (1967), 254-5 and 'Agricultural Policy: Public Debate and Legislation', in *A.H.E.W.*, ed. J. Thirsk, V ii (1985), 317-21; E. Kerridge, *Agrarian Problems in the Sixteenth Century and After* (1969), 108.
38. Peatling parva Enclosure Agreement, L.R.O., EN/251/4; J. Moore, *A Scripture-Word against Inclosure*, 9.
39. Shawell and Peatling parva Enclosure Agreements.
40. L.R.O., 35'29/411.
41. Peatling magna Parish Register, L.R.O., DE 437/2/1.
42. J. Moore, *The Crying Sin of England, Of not Caring for the Poor*, 11.
43. (J. Lee), *Considerations concerning Common Fields, and Inclosures*, 15; *e.g.* Shawell Parish Accounts, L.R.O., DE 734/6.
44. L.R.O., QS.6/1/3, *sub nomine* Knaptoft; QS.6/1/2/1 & 2, *sub nominibus* Bittesby, Claybrook and Mowsley.
45. Bruntingthorpe Parish Register, L.R.O., DE 765/1.
46. K. D. M. Snell, *Annals of the Labouring Poor: Social Change and Agrarian England*, 1660-1900, Cambridge Studies in Population, Economy and Society in Past Time (1985), 138-227.
47. W.R.O., CR 2017/E42.
48. *E.g.* W. G. Hoskins, 'English Provincial Towns in the Early Sixteenth Century', in his *Provincial England: Essays in Social and Economic History* (1963), 68-85; J. Cornwall, 'English Country Towns in the Fifteen Twenties', *Ec.H.R.*, 2nd ser. XV i (1962), 54-69; D. Charman, 'Wealth and Trade in Leicester in the Early Sixteenth Century', *T.L.A.S.*, XXV (1949), 69-97.
49. P.R.O., E 179, 133/122.
50. C. Phythian-Adams, *Desolation of a City: Coventry and the Urban Crisis of the Late Middle Ages*, Past and Present Publications (1979), 35 n. 8.
51. *Cf.* C. J. M. Moxon, 'Ashby-de-la-Zouch - a social and economic survey of a market town - 1570-1720' (D.Phil. thesis, University of Oxford, 1971), 26-7 and D. Fleming, 'A local market system: Melton Mowbray and the Wreake Valley 1549-1720' (Ph.D. thesis, University of Leicester, 1980), 24 n. 5.
52. P.R.O., E 179, 240/279 & Box 332 (unsorted).
53. Phrases in Church Wardens' Accounts, L.R.O., DE 2559/18.
54. A. Whiteman (ed.), *The Compton Census of 1676: A Critical Edition*, British

Academy Records of Social and Economic History, new ser. X (1986), xxix-xxxi & 295-301; A. P. Moore, 'Leicestershire Livings in the Reign of James I.', *A.A.S.R.P.*, XXIX i (1907), 158-60.

55. P.R.O., E 134, Chas. I, Mich. 39.
56. P.R.O., E 134, 1658-9, Hil. 16, m. 5r.
57. (J. Goodacre ed.), 'Letters from a Seventeenth Century Rector of Lutterworth: Nathaniel Tovey as Marriage Agent', *Leicestershire Historian*, III ii (1983/4), 14.
58. L.R.O., Parish·Register, DE 2094/1 and Parish Register Transcripts.
59. It is unlikely that the presence of an Independent congregation in the town seriously reduced the registration of baptisms; J. Goodacre, *op. cit.*, 86 n. 1.
60. Sources for Map V: P.R.O., E 179, 240/279; *v. infra*, pp. 69-71.
61. J. Nichols, *Leics.*, IV i (1810), 43.
62. *E.g. V.C.H. Nottinghamshire*, II (1910), 282.
63. J. Thirsk. 'Agrarian History, 1540-1950', *V.C.H. Leics.*, II (1954), 204. 1597: J. Thompson, *The History of Leicester, from the Time of the Romans to the End of the Seventeenth Century* (Leicester, 1849), 299-301. 1607: *v. supra*, p. 37; J. E. Martin, *Feudalism to Capitalism: Peasant and Landlord in English Agrarian Development* (1983), 191-7. 1614: L.R.O., BR II/5/130. 1650s: *v. supra*, p. 41.
64. L.R.O., BR II/18/28/89.
65. J. Moore, *A Scripture-Word against Inclosure*, 11.
66. T. A. North, 'Melton Mowbray Town Records', *T.L.A.S.*, IV (1878), 353-4.
67. P.R.O., E 179, 133/122 & 192/121.
68. P.R.O., C 93, 2/4; will of Thomas Gore, L.R.O., Wills 1634, no. 28.
69. Will of John Wheteley, L.R.O., Wills R.B. 1564, f. 1.
70. *V. infra*, p. 184.
71. Church Wardens' Accounts, L.R.O., DE 2559/18.
72. Overseers of the Poor Accounts, L.R.O., DE 2559/35 & 36.
73. Constables' Accounts, L.R.O., DE 2559/24; Shawell Parish Accounts, L.R.O., DE 734/6.
74. Order of 1628: under date 1663 in Church Wardens' Accounts, L.R.O., DE 2559/18. Order of 1693: L.R.O., QS.6/1/2/1, f. 157r.
75. W.R.O., CR 2017/E42; P.R.O., LR 2, 255, ff. 117-72; phrase used in Inclosure Award, L.R.O., EN/AX/211/1.
76. W.R.O., CR 2017/D244.
77. *V. supra*, n. 56.
78. W.R.O., CR 2017/D174.
79. W.R.O., CR 2017, Classes D, E, & M; L.R.O., 35'29/379 & /382.
80. W.R.O., CR 2017/D181.
81. B.M., Sloane MSS, 2728B, f. 224.
82. W.R.O., CR 2017/D163.
83. P.R.O., LR 2, 255, f. 164 and SC 12, 32/7.29.38.ii.
84. J. Nichols, *Leics.*, IV i, 256.
85. L.R.O., DE 914/1.
86. Vestry Book, L.R.O., DE 1463/6.
87. Source for Map VI: 'Plan of the Premises situate at Lutterworth belonging to the Town Masters', at Ashby parva; *cf.* under date 1811 in Vestry Book.
88. L.R.O., Ti/211/1.
89. W.R.O., CR 2017/D215.
90. Glebe Terrier 1606 at Lincolnshire Archives Office; Glebe Terrier 1679,

L.R.O., 1 D 41/2/431.

91. *V. supra*, n. 78; L.R.O., DE 66 (Box 2503).

92. *Cf.* D. Fleming, *op. cit.*, 202.

93. Based on a comparison of the Inclosure Award and the Tithe Award, L.R.O., EN/AX/211/1 & Ti/211/14.

94. *Ex inf.* Dr R. S. Schofield; E. A. Wrigley and R. S. Schofield, *op. cit.*, 165–6.

Notes to Chapter III

1. W. G. Hoskins, 'The Leicestershire Farmer in the Sixteenth Century', *T.L.A.S.*, XXII i (1941-2), 34-94, revised and republished in his *Essays in Leicestershire History* (1950), 123-83.

2. W. G. Hoskins, 'The Leicestershire Farmer in the Seventeenth Century', in his *Provincial England: Essays in Social and Economic History* (1963), 149-69.

3. W. G. Hoskins, 'The Leicestershire Farmer in the Sixteenth Century', *loc. cit.*, 146-59.

4. Note dated 1611 in Claybrook Parish Register, L.R.O., DE 732/1 (numbers added).

5. They are of gentry and yeomen known to have been engaged in pasture ground farming and having exceptional livestock figures; *v. infra*, pp. 101-2.

6. P. Bowden, Statistical Appendix to *A.H.E.W.*, ed. J. Thirsk, IV (1967), 860 & 857.

7. W. G. Hoskins, 'The Leicestershire Farmer in the Sixteenth Century', *loc. cit.*, 168.

8. *E.g.* (J. Lee), *Considerations concerning Common Fields, and Inclosures* (1653), 10, 12 & 13.

9. *Cf.* J. Thirsk, 'Farming Techniques', in *A.H.E.W.*, ed. J. Thirsk, IV (1967), 164-5.

10. *V.C.H. Leics.*, II (1954), 104; W. G. Hoskins, 'The Leicestershire Farmer in the Sixteenth Century', *loc. cit.*, 149.

11. For shares in a plough *v. supra*, p. 56.

12. P. Bowden, Statistical Appendix, *loc. cit.*, 860.

13. *Pace* Thirsk, who evidently misunderstood Hoskins's treatment of grazing winter corn (based on the Wymeswold regulations, which do not, however, prove this practice) to have meant feeding stock with grain: J. Thirsk, 'Agrarian History, 1540-1950', *V.C.H. Leics.*, II (1954), 313; W. G. Hoskins, 'The Leicestershire Farmer in the Sixteenth Century', *loc. cit.*, 174.

14. Inventory of Richard Cattell of Ashby magna 1521/2, L.R.O., Inv. file 2, no. 169/11 & /91; will of Richard Colles of South Kilworth, L.R.O., Wills & Invv. 1556.

15. *Cf.* P. J. Bowden, *The Wool Trade in Tudor and Stuart England* (1962), 27.

16. P. Bowden, Statistical Appendix, *loc. cit.*, 860-1.

17. W.R.O., CR 2017/M39.

18. Fitzherbert, *Surveyenge*, 1767 reprint of 1539 edn quoted in R. H. Tawney and E. Power (eds), *Tudor Economic Documents: being select documents illustrating the economic and social history of Tudor England* III (1924), 22 (numbers added).

19. W.R.O., CR 2017/E42; P.R.O., LR 2, 255, ff. 117-72; L.R.O., EN/AX/211/1; L.R.O., Ti/211/14.

20. *Cf.* R. H. Hilton, 'Medieval Agrarian History', *V.C.H. Leics.*, II (1954), 159-60.

21. E. Kerridge, *The Agricultural Revolution* (1967), 100-7; *pace* W. G. Hoskins, 'The Leicestershire Farmer in the Sixteenth Century', *loc. cit.* 139-44.

22. P. Bowden, 'Agricultural Prices, Farm Profits, and Rents', in *A.H.E.W.*, ed. J. Thirsk, IV (1967), 615 & 626-7.

23. W. G. Hoskins, 'Harvest Fluctuations and English Economic History, 1480-1619', *Ag.H.R.*, XII i (1964), 38-9.

24. G. F. Farnham, *Leicestershire Medieval Village Notes*, II (Leicester, 1929), 102.

25. Historical Manuscripts Commission, *Report on the Manuscripts of Lord Middleton* (1911), 106-9.

26. P.R.O., LR 2, 255, f. 125.

27. S.R.O., D 1734/4/1/7, f. 25v & /9 f. 24v.

28. H. S. A. Fox, 'The People of the Wolds in English Settlement History', in *The Rural Settlements of Medieval England: Studies dedicated to M. Beresford and J. Hurst*, ed. M. Aston, D. Austin and C. Dyer (1989), 79-81.

29. Inventory of Robert Cotton of Kimcote, L.R.O., Wills & Invv. 1539.

30. P.R.O., PROB 11, 31 (49 Alen).

31. S.R.O., D 1734/4/1/6-11 & /3/4/18.

32. L.R.O., Wills & Invv. 1550.

33. S.R.O., D 1734/4/1/8, f. 4v.

34. L.R.O., Inv. file 6b, no. T22.

35. P. L. Hughes and J. F. Larkin (eds), *Tudor Royal Proclamations*, I (1964), 530-1 & III (1969), 283; S.R.O., D 1734/4/1/6, ff. 10v & 39r.

36. *Ibid.*, f. 8v.

37. *Ibid.*, f. 5r.

38. G. F. Farnham, *op. cit.*, V (1931), 396.

39. S.R.O., D 1734/4/1/6-9, especially /6, f. 38r.

40. W. Burton, *The Description of Leicester Shire, Containing Matters of Antiquitye, Historye, Armorye, and Genealogy* (1622), 192 (punctuation corrected from 2nd edn (Lynn, 1777), 174).

41. P.R.O., E 134, 12 Chas. I, East. 24, mm. 6v & 8 and 30 Eliz., Hil. 5, m.(5)r.

42. E. F. Gay, 'The Rise of an English Country Family', *Huntington Library Quarterly*, I iv (1938), 367-90; P.R.O., SC 12, 32/7.19; N. W. Alcock, *Warwickshire Grazier and London Skinner 1532-1555: The account book of Peter Temple and Thomas Heritage*, British Academy Records of Social and Economic History, new ser. IV (1981), 220 & 233-5; P.R.O., LR 2, 255, f. 160.

43. L.R.O., DE 1012/1/1; S.R.O., D 1734/4/1/6-9.

44. Historical Manuscripts Commission, *Report on the Manuscripts of the Duke of Buccleuch and Queensberry*, III (1926), 55; P.R.O., C 2, Eliz., K.2, 54; P.R.O., PROB 11, 122 (100 Capell).

45. M. E. Finch, *The Wealth of Five Northamptonshire Families 1540-1640*, Publications of the Northamptonshire Record Society, XIX (1956), 38-46.

46. L.R.O., Inv. file 6b, no. T22.

47. L. A. Parker, 'The Agrarian Revolution at Cotesbach, 1501-1612', in *Studies in Leicestershire Agrarian History*, ed. W. G. Hoskins, *T.L.A.S.*, XXIV (1949), 43-5.

48. S.R.O., D 1734/4/1/6-9, especially /9, f. 15r & /8, f. 20v.

49. I. S. Leadam, *The Domesday of Inclosures 1517-1518*, II (1897), 432; L. A. Parker, 'Enclosure in Leicestershire, 1485-1607' (Ph.D. thesis, University of London, 1948), 36-8.

50.   S.R.O., D 1734/4/1/6-9, especially /9, f. 28r & v.
51.   L.R.O., Inv. file 25, no. 89; P.R.O., E 134, 12 Chas. I, East. 24, m. 3v.
52.   S.R.O., D 1734/4/1/6-9, especially /6, f. 41r.
53.   Inventory of Thomas Bent of Walcote, L.R.O., Inv. file 12, no. 106.
54.   P.R.O., LR 2, 255, f. 148.
55.   W. G. Hoskins, *Essays in Leicestershire History* (1950), 128; wills and inventories of Thomas and Richard Bradgate, L.R.O., Wills & Invv. 1539 and 1572.
56.   L. A. Parker, 'Enclosure in Leicestershire, 1485-1607', *op. cit.*, 56; inventory of Richard Cattell of Ashby magna 1521/2, L.R.O., Inv. file 2, no. 169/11 & 91.
57.   *Ibid.*; A. Hamilton Thompson, *A Calendar of Charters and other Documents belonging to the Hospital of William Wyggeston at Leicester* (Leicester, 1933), 34, 45, 85 & 292-5.
58.   L. A. Parker, 'The Agrarian Revolution at Cotesbach, 1501-1612', *loc. cit.*, 51 & 70.
59.   S.R.O., D 1734/4/1/9, f. 4v; wills of Hugh Lussell senior, yeoman, 1564 and Richard Pratt, yeoman, 1574/5, P.R.O., PROB 11, 47 (21 Stevenson) and 57 (34 Pyckering).
60.   Inventories of Thomas Insley 1588 and Thomas Gore 1633/4, L.R.O., Inv. file 9, no. 205 and file 37, no. 119.
61.   P.R.O., E 134, 42 Eliz., Trin. 8.
62.   Inventory of Sir William Turpin 1617, L.R.O., filed separately.
63.   S.R.O., D 1734/4/1/6-9, especially /8, f. 22r.
64.   Inventory of Richard Bradgate, L.R.O., Wills & Invv. 1572.
65.   W. Burton, *op. cit.*, 44, 78, (110), 192 & 273; *ibid.*, 2 & 192.
66.   L. A. Parker, 'The Agrarian Revolution at Cotesbach, 1501-1612', *loc. cit.*, 63-4 & 71.
67.   J. Nichols, *Leics.*, IV i (1810), 221.
68.   J. Moore, *A Target for Tillage, briefly containing the most necessary, pretious, and profitable use thereof both for king and state* (1612), Epistle Dedicatory & 51-2 (dated 1611, but written earlier).
69.   L. A. Parker, 'The Agrarian Revolution at Cotesbach, 1501-1612', *loc. cit.*, 41-76, especially 61, 71 & 73.
70.   Lutterworth: P.R.O., LR 2, 255, f. 160; inventory of Robert Car of Moorbarns, L.R.O., Inv. file 25, no. 89; P.R.O., E 134, 12 Chas. I, East. 24, m.3v. Clifton-upon-Dunsmore: A. Gooder, *Plague and Enclosure: A Warwickshire Village in the Seventeenth Century*, Coventry & North Warwickshire History Pamphlets, no. 2 (1965), 13. Primethorpe: will of John Hyll of Primethorpe, L.R.O., Wills 1558 (G-O). Monks Kirby: W.R.O., CR 2017/D1.8-11.
71.   J. Nichols, *Leics.*, IV ii (1811), 604-5.
72.   S.R.O., D 1734/4/1/6, f. 21r; *ibid.*, /6, f. 19r & v, /7, f. 30v & /9, f. 27r.
73.   W. Burton, *op. cit.*, 2.
74.   P. J. Bowden, *The Wool Trade in Tudor and Stuart England*, xviii; P. Bowden, 'Agricultural Prices, Farm Profits, and Rents', *loc. cit.*, 635; P. J. Bowden, Statistics in Appendices to *A.H.E.W.*, ed. J. Thirsk, V ii (1985), 855.
75.   *Ibid.*, 641.
76.   J. Lee, *A Vindication of A Regulated Inclosure* (1656), 15; *V.C.H. Leics.*, II (1954), 110.
77.   Pulteney: J. Nichols, *Leics.*, IV i, 310; G. F. Farnham, *op. cit.*, III (1929), 232-4. Turpin: *ibid.*, V, 396-7. Staresmore: J. Nichols, *Leics.*, IV i, 183; G. F. Farnham, 'Frolesworth - Notes on the Descent of the Manor', *T.L.A.S.*, XII ii

(1922), 191-2.

78. *V.C.H. Leics.*, II, 110. Feilding: J. Nichols, *Leics.*, IV i, 290 & 291; W.R.O., CR 2017/A1. Cave: J. Nichols, *Leics.*, IV i, 352 & 372. Temple: E. F. Gay, 'The Temples of Stowe and Their Debts: Sir Thomas and Sir Peter Temple, 1603-1653', *Huntington Library Quarterly*, II iv (1939), 430.

79. Will of Thomas Gore, L.R.O., Wills 1634, no. 28; J. Nichols, *Leics.*, IV i, 118 & 128.

80. Bittesby: L.R.O., 23 D 63/1. Moorbarns: L.R.O., 35'29/382.

81. J. Lee, *A Vindication of A Regulated Inclosure*, 8.

82. W. G. Hoskins, 'Harvest Fluctuations and English Economic History, 1620-1759', *Ag.H.R.*, XVI i (1968), 28-9; P. J. Bowden, Statistics in Appendices, *loc. cit.*, 827-8; Bodleian Library, Gough Add. Leic. 8vo 16; J. Lee, *A Vindication of A Regulated Inclosure*, 8-9.

83. *V. infra*, pp. 113 & 143.

84. W. Burton, *op. cit.*, 221, 44 & 273.

85. L.R.O., 23 D 63/1.

86. G. F. Farnham, *op. cit.*, III, 234; J. Nichols, *Leics.*, IV i, 311.

87. L.R.O., Invv. 1684, no. 254 and Wills 1684, no. 213.

88. J. Moore, *The Crying Sin of England, Of not Caring for the Poor* (1653), 12; (J. Lee), *Considerations concerning Common Fields, and Inclosures*, 10.

89. L.R.O., DE 66 (Box 2529).

90. *Cf.* W. H. Hosford, 'An Eye-Witness's Account of a Seventeenth-Century Enclosure', *Ec.H.R.*, 2nd ser. IV (1951-2), 216-20.

91. Sources for Map VIII: MS Enclosure Award and Deeds at Ashby parva.

92. J. Nichols, *Leics.*, IV i, 47.

93. Under date 1624 in Swinford Parish Register, L.R.O., DE 1630/1; *cf.* J. Nichols, *Leics.*, IV i, 363.

94. E. F. Gay, 'The Temples of Stowe and Their Debts: Sir Thomas and Sir Peter Temple, 1603-1653', *Huntington Library Quarterly*, II iv (1939), 409, 412-14 & 430; E. F. Gay, 'The Rise of an English Country Family', *ibid.*, I iv (1938), 377; order of 1628 under date 1663 in Church Wardens' Accounts, L.R.O., DE 2559/18; P.R.O., E 134, 12 Chas. I, East. 24. *Cf.* the Feilding family in 1635 forbidding the ploughing of Denmark, a ten-acre close of demesne pasture adjoining the Monks Kirby manor house: Historical Manuscripts Commission, *Report on the Manuscripts of the Earl of Denbigh, preserved at Newnham Paddox, Warwickshire* V (1911), 14; Bradford Central Library, Cunliffe Lister Collection, Manorial Records Box 5.

95. Inventory of Francis Billington 1634, L.R.O., Inv. file 36, no. 80.

96. L.R.O., 35'29/382.

97. J. Lee, *A Vindication of A Regulated Inclosure*, 8-9; J. Moore, *A Scripture-Word against Inclosure* (1656), 10.

98. *Ibid.*; G. F. Farnham, *op. cit.*, I (1929), 73; M. W. Beresford, 'Glebe Terriers and Open-Field Leicestershire', in *Studies in Leicestershire Agrarian History*, ed. W. G. Hoskins, *T.L.A.S.*, XXIV (1949), 102.

99. L. A. Parker, 'The Agrarian Revolution at Cotesbach, 1501-1612', *loc. cit.*, 74; J. Nichols, *Leics.*, IV i, 148 & 149.

100. L. A. Parker, 'The Agrarian Revolution at Cotesbach, 1501-1612', *loc. cit.*, 66-8.

101. 'Pasture-men': term used in R. W(ilkinson), *A Sermon preached at North-Hampton the 21, of June last past, before the Lord Lieutenant of the County, and the rest of the Commissioners there assembled upon occasion*

of the late Rebellion and Riots in those parts committed (1607), F1(v). 'You gentlemen that rack your rents, and throw down Land for corn': first line of verse libel from 1607 entitled 'The poor mans Joy: & the Gentlemens plague', Rutland MSS at Belvoir Castle, Letters etc. XV, f. 41. J. Moore, *A Target for Tillage* . . ., 'To the Conscionable Reader' & 54.

102. Frolesworth: J. Nichols, *Leics.*, IV i, 183. Leicester Forest: *ibid.*, IV ii, 785-95; B. Sharp, *In Contempt of All Authority: Rural Artisans and Riot in the West of England, 1586-1660* (1980), 149-50. Willoughby Waterless: L.R.O., DE 66 (Box 2529).

103. J. Lee, *A Vindication of A Regulated Inclosure*, 4.

104. (J. Lee), *Considerations concerning Common Fields, and Inclosures*, 8-9; *cf.* J. Moore, *A Scripture-Word against Inclosure*, 14 with G. Slater, *The English Peasantry and the Enclosure of Common Fields* (1907), 51.

105. J. Lee, *A Vindication of A Regulated Inclosure*, 16-18.

106. *Cf.* Fitzherbert, *Surveyenge*, quoted in R. H. Tawney and E. Power (eds), *op. cit.*, III, 24-5.

107. *V. supra*, pp. 44-6.

108. (J. Lee), *A Vindication of the Considerations concerning Common-fields and Inclosures* (1656), 23.

109. *V. supra*, p. 53.

110. J. Moore, *A Scripture-Word against Inclosure*, 14.

111. J. Moore, *The Crying Sin of England, Of not Caring for the Poor*, 12; (J. Lee), *Considerations concerning Common Fields, and Inclosures*, 10; *cf.* E. Kerridge, *op. cit.*, 102 & 108.

112. *Cf.* J. Lee, *A Vindication of A Regulated Inclosure*, 9.

113. *Ibid.*, 22.

114. *Ibid.*; J. Moore (sen.), *A Target for Tillage* . . ., 40; J. Moore (jun.), *A Reply to a Pamphlet intituled Considerations concerning Common fields and Inclosures, &c.* (1653), (4); (J. Lee), *A Vindication of the Considerations concerning Common-fields and Inclosures*, 23.

115. J. Nichols, *Leics.*, IV i, 352-3.

116. E. Kerridge. *op. cit.*, 196; J. Thirsk, 'Seventeenth-Century Agriculture and Social Change', in *Land, Church, and People: Essays presented to Professor H. P. R. Finberg*, ed. J. Thirsk, *Ag.H.R.*, XVIII Supplement (1970), 158 *et seqq*.

117. J. Lee, *A Vindication of A Regulated Inclosure*, 8. Woad: P.R.O., E 134, 12 Chas. I, East. 24; *v. infra*, p. 206; J. Moore, *A Scripture-Word against Inclosure*, 10. Flax: under date 1642 onwards in Catthorpe Parish Register, L.R.O., DE 1453/1. Hops: W.R.O., CR 2017/E115 (1694); *cf.* L.R.O., DE 1221/59.

118. J. Lee, *A Vindication of A Regulated Inclosure*, 8; *cf.* J. Thirsk, 'Seventeenth-Century Agriculture and Social Change', *loc. cit.*, 155.

119. *Ibid.*, 162-4.

120. L.R.O., 35'29/382.

121. D. Defoe, *The Complete English Tradesman* (1745, 1841 edn), II, 97; *cf.* P. J. Bowden, Statistics in Appendices, *loc. cit.*, 855.

122. Bittesby: W.R.O., CR 2017/E3. Moorbarns: L.R.O., 35'29/382. Peatling magna: L.R.O., 35'29/404.

123. J. Lee, *A Vindication of A Regulated Inclosure*, 8; (J. Lee), *Considerations concerning Common Fields, and Inclosures*, 10: P.R.O., LR 2, 255, f. 160; L.R.O., 35'29/382.

124. Monks Kirby: *cf.* Bradford Central Library, Cunliffe Lister Collection, Manorial

Records Box 5 with W.R.O., CR 2017/E115. Peatling magna: *cf.* L.R.O., 35'29/73 with /403-5.
125. W.R.O., CR 2017/E115.
126. (J. Lee), *Considerations concerning Common Fields, and Inclosures*, 12; J. Moore, *A Reply to a Pamphlet intituled Considerations concerning Common fields and Inclosures, &c.*, (4); J. Lee, *A Vindication of A Regulated Inclosure*, 24.
127. (J. Lee), *Considerations concerning Common Fields, and Inclosures*, 19; J. Lee, *A Vindication of A Regulated Inclosure*, 16 & 22.
128. Named horses in S.R.O., D 1734/4/1/6-9; inventory of Sir William Turpin 1617, L.R.O., filed separately; inventory of Rector of Misterton, L.R.O., Invv. 1684, no. 190. *Cf.* J. Thirsk, *Horses in early modern England: for Service, for Pleasure, for Power*, University of Reading, The Stenton Lecture 1977 (1978).
129. J. Lee, *A Vindication of A Regulated Inclosure*, 30.
130. W. Burton, *op. cit.*, (2nd edn, Lynn, 1777), 174; this edition evidently based on seventeenth-century revision, although not his 1642 MS, S.R.O., D 649/4/3.
131. "Follows" was the local form of the term; in quoting *verbatim* Moore's passage on tilths, Lee copied his 'following tilth' but, perhaps intending to eliminate this vulgarism, corrected it to 'fallowing tilth' in his Errata: *v. infra*, p. 130; (J. Lee), *Considerations concerning Common Fields, and Inclosures*, 22 & Errata.
132. J. Lee, *A Vindication of A Regulated Inclosure*, 30; (J. Lee), *Considerations concerning Common Fields, and Inclosures*, 11.
133. J. Thirsk, 'Agrarian History, 1540-1950', *loc. cit.*, 221-2.
134. W. G. Hoskins, *Provincial England*, 160.
135. *V. infra*, p. 159.
136. Inventory of Nathaniel Reeve of Claybrook magna, innholder, L.R.O., Invv. 1690, no. 147; W.R.O., CR 2017/E115 (1685).
137. L.R.O., Wills 1639 & 1640, no. 72.
138. These terms contrasted in (J. Lee), *Considerations concerning Common Fields, and Inclosures*, 13.
139. Description of small and nimble fine-woolled sheep surviving in rocky northern parts of the county; J. Throsby, *The Memoirs of the Town and County of Leicester: . . . To which is added, A Brief Supplimentary Account of the present state of Leicestershire*, VI (Leicester, 1777), 3.
140. J. Lee, *A Vindication of A Regulated Inclosure*, 30; J. Moore, *A Scripture-Word against Inclosure*, 7; *cf.* J. Moore, *The Crying Sin of England, Of not Caring for the Poor*, 9.
141. J. Moore, *A Reply to a Pamphlet intituled Considerations concerning Common fields and Inclosures, &c.*, (4).
142. J. Moore, *A Scripture-Word against Inclosure*, 7.
143. J. Lee, *A Vindication of A Regulated Inclosure*, 22.
144. (J. Lee), *Considerations concerning Common Fields, and Inclosures*, 11.
145. W. Burton, *op. cit.*, 134.
146. Ullesthorpe: L.R.O., DE 40/40 (1686). Gilmorton: L.R.O., DE 147/17.
147. *E.g.* L.R.O., DE 40/40 (1686).
148. (J. Lee), *A Vindication of the Considerations concerning Common-fields and Inclosures*, 44 & 45.
149. J. Lee, *A Vindication of A Regulated Inclosure*, 25.
150. *Ibid.*, 5 & 4.

151.   (J. Lee), *Considerations concerning Common Fields, and Inclosures*, 7.
152.   L.R.O., DE 147/16-17, *cf.* /14.
153.   (J. Lee), *ibid.*
154.   *Ibid.*, 10.
155.   *Ibid.*, 10-12; (J. Lee), *A Vindication of the Considerations concerning Common-fields and Inclosures*, 44; J. Lee, *A Vindication of A Regulated Inclosure*, 24.
156.   (J. Lee), *Considerations concerning Common Fields, and Inclosures*, 11 & 14.
157.   (J. Lee), *A Vindication of the Considerations concerning Common-fields and Inclosures*, 42.
158.   (J. Lee), *Considerations concerning Common Fields, and Inclosures*, 14.
159.   Ullesthorpe: L.R.O., DE 40/40 (1685). *Cf.* Wigston magna: W. G. Hoskins, *The Midland Peasant: The Economic and Social History of a Leicestershire Village* (1957), 238.
160.   L.R.O., DE 40/40 (1684); *cf.* (J. Lee), *Considerations concerning Common Fields, and Inclosures*, 4.
161.   J. Moore, *The Crying Sin of England, Of not Caring for the Poor*, 10; (J. Lee), *A Vindication of the Considerations concerning Common-fields and Inclosures*, 43.
162.   *V. infra*, p. 146.
163.   (J. Lee), *Considerations concerning Common Fields, and Inclosures*, 13.
164.   (J. Lee), *A Vindication of the Considerations concerning Common-fields and Inclosures*, 45.
165.   L.R.O., DE 40/40 (1690).
166.   (J. Lee), *Considerations concerning Common Fields, and Inclosures*, 10-11; *cf.* J. Lee, *A Vindication of A Regulated Inclosure*, 24.
167.   (J. Lee), *A Vindication of the Considerations concerning Common-fields and Inclosures*, 43.
168.   L.R.O., DE 147/15 & /17.
169.   J. Thirsk, *English Peasant Farming: The Agrarian History of Lincolnshire from Tudor to Recent Times* (1957), 89 & 97; B. K. Roberts, 'Field Systems of the West Midlands', in *Studies in Field Systems in the British Isles*, ed. A. R. H. Baker and R. A. Butlin (1973), 203.
170.   *E.g.* the 'neats pasture' at Wymeswold; *v. supra*, p. 92.
171.   *Cf* map of 1587 with map of 1727 at Kettering Manor House Museum; F. W. Bull, *Supplement to the History of the Town of Kettering, together with a further account of its Worthies* (Kettering, 1908), *cf.* Frontispiece with 7.
172.   Monks Kirby: W.R.O., CR 2017/E115, 38 & 50. Stoneleigh: N. W. Alcock, *Stoneleigh Villagers 1597-1650*, University of Warwick Open Studies (1975), 25 & 4.
173.   *Cf.* J. Thirsk, *English Peasant Farming . . .*, 89.
174.   Leicester: H. Stocks (ed.), *Records of the Borough of Leicester, 1603-1688* (1923), 214; W. G. Hoskins, 'The Leicestershire Farmer in the Sixteenth Century', *loc. cit.*, 143-4 misrepresented in his 'The Leicestershire Farmer in the Seventeenth Century', *loc. cit.*, 161. Gilmorton: L.R.O., DE 147/15.
175.   W. G. Hoskins, *The Midland Peasant*, 160-1.
176.   Ashby parva: Glebe Terriers; 1625 & 1601, at Lincolnshire Archives Office and L.R.O., 1 D 41/2/28b (n.d. but datable to 1638). Leire, L.R.O., Wills 1589, no. 60. Shawell: L.R.O., DE 66 (Box 2504); *v. infra*, p. 204. Catthorpe: *v. supra*, p. 116.

177. Ashby parva: MS Enclosure Award and Deeds at Ashby parva, especially Reserve Bundle A, Class IV, 3. Wigston magna: W. G. Hoskins, *The Midland Peasant*, 161-2.
178. Deeds at Ashby parva, Box 2, Bundle 16.
179. L.R.O., BR II/18/28/89.
180. Cotesbach: W. G. Hoskins, *Essays in Leicestershire History*, 144. Monks Kirby: Bradford Central Library, Cunliffe Lister Collection, Manorial Records Box 5. Bitteswell: W.R.O., CR 2017/M39.
181. Shawẹll: L.R.O., DE 734/6, 17. Wigston magna: W. G. Hoskins, *The Midland Peasant*, 236-8. Ullesthorpe: L.R.O., DE 40/40 (1684-90).
182. (J. Lee), *Considerations concerning Common Fields, and Inclosures*, 14.
183. L.R.O., DE 734/6, f. 112v.
184. (J. Lee), *Considerations concerning Common Fields, and Inclosures*, 4.
185. Wigston magna: W. G. Hoskins, *The Midland Peasant*, 245. Ashby parva: L.R.O., 9 D 43/47.
186. J. Nichols, *Leics.*, II ii (1795), 599-600.
187. (J. Lee), *Considerations concerning Common Fields, and Inclosures*, 4; (J. Lee), *A Vindication of the Considerations concerning Common-fields and Inclosures*, 45.
188. L.R.O., Inv. file 34, no. 76; Inv. file 33, no. 181; Invv. 1660 Commiss., no. 33.
189. (J. Lee), *Considerations concerning Common Fields, and Inclosures*, 11.
190. J. Moore, *A Reply to a Pamphlet intituled Considerations concerning Common fields and Inclosures, &c.*, (4).
191. L.R.O., DE 40/40 (1685), (1686) & (1690).
192. J. Moore, *ibid*.
193. (J. Lee), *A Vindication of the Considerations concerning Common-fields and Inclosures*, 43.
194. *Ibid*.
195. J. Lee, *A Vindication of A Regulated Inclosure*, 10.
196. (J. Lee), *A Vindication of the Considerations concerning Common-fields and Inclosures*, 45.
197. L.R.O., BR II/18/28/89; *v. supra*, p. 41.
198. *E.g.* W. Burton, *op. cit.*, 2.
199. *Ibid.*; (J. Lee), *Considerations concerning Common Fields, and Inclosures*, 11; *The Journeys of Celia Fiennes*, ed. C. Morris (1947), 162; L.R.O., DE 40/40 (1686).
200. 'A consideration concerning the cause in question before the Lords touchinge depopulation', *v. supra*, cap. I n. 145.
201. Cotesbach: L. A. Parker, 'Enclosure in Leicestershire, 1485-1607', *op. cit.*, 209-14. Lutterworth: P.R.O., LR 2, 255, ff. 170-1.
202. (J. Lee), *Considerations concerning Common Fields, and Inclosures*, 11.
203. *V. supra*, p. 105.
204. Bittesby: L.R.O., 23 D 63/1. Ullesthorpe: L.R.O., DE 40/40 (1686).
205. Haines: L.R.O., Invv. 1687, no. 137; under dates 1638 & 1639 in Misterton Parish Register, L.R.O., DE 452/1. Wigfall: L.R.O., Invv. 1685, no. 201.
206. Lutterworth: P.R.O., E 134, 12 Chas. I, East. 24, m. 7r; *cf.* J. Lee, *A Vindication of A Regulated Inclosure*, 9. Peatling parva: L.R.O., EN/251/4.
207. J. Thirsk, 'Plough and Pen: Agricultural Writers in the Seventeenth Century', in *Social Relations and Ideas: essays in honour of R. H. Hilton*, ed. T. H. Aston *et al.* (1983), 311.
208. J. W(orlidge), *Systema Agriculturae, The Mystery of Husbandry Discovered*

(1669), Catalogue.

209. Moore: J. Nichols, *Leics.*, IV i, 222. Lee: R. H. Evans, 'Nonconformists in Leicestershire in 1669', *T.L.A.S.*, XXV (1949), 134. P.R.O., PROB 11, 420, f. 130; this source *ex inf.* Dr Joan Thirsk.

210. L.R.O., Invv. 1682, no. 175; L.R.O., 35'29/403; under date 1682 in Peatling magna Parish Register, L.R.O., DE 437/2/1.

211. L.R.O., Invv. 1686, no. 85; H. Hartopp, *Register of the Freemen of Leicester 1196-1770* (Leicester, 1927), 216; L.R.O., Invv. 1688, no. 176.

212. L.R.O., Invv. 1683, no. 17.

213. Northamptonshire: J. Mastin, *The History and Antiquities of Naseby, in the County of Northampton* (Cambridge, 1792), 25. Wiltshire: J. Aubrey, printed in J. Thirsk and J. P. Cooper (eds), *Seventeenth-Century Economic Documents* (1972), 179. Oxfordshire: R. P(lot), *The Natural History of Oxford-shire, Being an Essay toward the Natural History of England* (Oxford, 1677), 257.

214. L.R.O., Inv. file 36, no. 80.

215. J. Moore, *The Crying Sin of England, Of not Caring for the Poor*, 9.

216. *Ibid.*, 10.

217. (J. Lee), *Considerations concerning Common Fields, and Inclosures*, 21.

218. (J. Lee), *A Vindication of the Considerations concerning Common-fields and Inclosures*, 40.

219. J. Moore, *The Crying Sin of England, Of not Caring for the Poor*, 9-11.

220. J. Moore, *A Scripture-Word against Inclosure*, 7-8.

Notes to Chapter IV

1. The area covered by this study is the same as for the previous two chapters. Here, however, since its population trends and economy are more typical of the open-field villages, the compound parish of Broughton Astley has been restored to that classification.

2. Sixteenth century: 1509 Terrier of town and fields, W.R.O., CR 2017/£42; Crown leases in Patent Rolls, P.R.O., C 66 and in Augmentation Office, P.R.O., E 309, boxes 1-6 & E 310, 16/70-4; 1607 Survey, P.R.O., L.R.2, 255, ff. 117-72; other survey material, P.R.O., SC 12, 27/46 & 32/7. Seventeenth century: Feilding family purchase of principal manor and sub-sales, W.R.O., CR 2017/D172 & 173-94; Rent Rolls etc. 1656-87, W.R.O., CR 2017/M40, D195, L.R.O., 35'29/379, W.R.O., CR 2017/M42-6 & E3. Eighteenth century: Feilding family recitals of property, W.R.O., CR 2017/D163 & 24, and leases, D210-64; 1790 Inclosure Award, L.R.O., EN/AX/211/1. Also various seventeenth- and eighteenth-century title deeds at L.R.O.

3. Under date 1666 in Church Wardens' Accounts, L.R.O., DE 1559/18.

4. Based on a comparison of the wills and inventories with Lay Subsidy rolls of 1545 to 1611; P.R.O., E 179, 133/147, /154, 134/171, /173, /176, /205, /214, /245, /251, /254, /280 & /284.

5. W. G. Hoskins, *The Midland Peasant: The Economic and Social History of a Leicestershire Village* (1957), 167.

6. L.R.O., Admm. 1589, no. 12; BR II/18/12/230 & /15/264; Inv. file 32A, no. 121; L.R.O., Parish Register Transcript 1638; P.R.O., E 134, 12 Chas. I, East. 24, m.2v.

7. Wigston: D. Charman, 'Wealth and Trade in Leicester in the Early Sixteenth

Century', *T.L.A.S.*, XXV (1949), 79-82, 88-9 & 90. Reynolds: J. Nichols, *Leics.*, IV i (1810), 265; H. Hartopp, *Roll of the Mayors of the Borough of Leicester and Lord Mayors of the City of Leicester 1209 to 1935* (Leicester, 1935), 272; C. Phythian-Adams, *Desolation of a City: Coventry and the Urban Crisis of the Late Middle Ages*, Past and Present Publications (1979), 258. Saxby: J. Nichols, *ibid.*, 356; *cf.* B. Winchester, *Tudor Family Portrait* (1955), 17. Cave: *ibid.*, 371; the Stanford estate straddled the county boundary even before the Norman Conquest and was doubtless the reason for foreign wool-dealers trading at Lilbourne in the thirteenth century; *V.C.H. Leics.*, I (1907), 327-8 & 294, *v.* Map II. Pulteney: A. Hamilton Thompson, *A Calendar of Charters and other Documents belonging to the Hospital of William Wyggeston at Leicester* (Leicester, 1933), xii. Temple: E. F. Gay, 'The Rise of an English Country Family', *Huntington Library Quarterly*, I iv (1938), 383.

8. *Calendar of Patent Rolls*, Henry VII, II, 1494-1509 (1916), 447; P.R.O., PROB 11, 18 (5 Holder).

9. Feilding: *ibid.*; *cf.* A. Hamilton Thompson, *op. cit.*, 529. Paver: H. Hartopp, *Register of the Freemen of Leicester 1196-1770* (Leicester, 1927), *sub nomine* Lutterworth; *cf.* Robert Porver, whose £80 assessment on goods in 1524 was the highest in Melton Mowbray, D. Fleming, 'A local market system: Melton Mowbray and the Wreake Valley 1549-1720' (Ph.D. thesis, University of Leicester, 1980), 94-5; inventories of Margaret and Ralph Paver, L.R.O., Wills & Invv. 1550 and Inv. file 1, no. 30. Wigston: D. Charman, *loc. cit.*, 82 & 94.

10. Paver: inventory of Margaret Paver, L.R.O., Wills & Invv. 1550. Feilding manor farm (Clarke family): L.R.O., Inv. file 21, no. 80 and file 27, no. 20. Gore: L.R.O., Inv. file 37, no. 119 and Invv. 1689, no. 45. Billington: L.R.O., Inv. file 36, no. 80 and file 42, no. 70. Newcombe: will and inventory of William Newcombe, shoemaker, L.R.O., Wills 1594, no. 64 and Inv. file 13, no. 87; P.R.O., LR 2, 255, f. 155.

11. L.R.O., Invv. 1683, no. 17 and Invv. 1684, no. 198.

12. S.R.O., D 1734/4/1/6, f. 6r, /9, f. 5v & /8, f. 4v; will of Margaret Paver, L.R.O., Wills & Invv. 1550.

13. *Cf.* P. J. Bowden, *The Wool Trade in Tudor and Stuart England* (1962), 79-80.

14. *V. infra*, p. 193.

15. L.R.O., DE 147/15.

16. L.R.O., Invv. 1684, no. 14.

17. P. J. Bowden, *op. cit.*, 72-3.

18. Will and inventory of Clement Stretton, L.R.O., Wills & Invv. 1597, no. 90 and Wills 1597, no. 38.

19. H. Hartopp, *op. cit.*, *sub nominibus*. Dowell: P.R.O., C 3, 464/77; L.R.O., Peculiar of St Margaret's, Wills 1642, no. 97; Frowlesworth Parish Register, first volume, at Frowlesworth. Pougher: W. G. Hoskins, *The Midland Peasant*, 258.

20. A. Everitt, 'The Marketing of Agricultural Produce', in *A.H.E.W.*, ed. J. Thirsk, IV (1967), 492.

21. Market Bosworth: Folger Shakespeare Library, MS.V.b.165; *ex inf.* Dr P. Edwards. Lutterworth: P.R.O., LR 2, 255, f. 161. Leicester: L.R.O., BR II/8/41. *Cf.* D. Fleming, *op. cit.*, 16.

22. Stratford-upon-Avon: Shakespeare Birthplace Trust, Misc. Docts. XIV, 1 & 2;

ex inf. Dr P. Edwards. Lutterworth: W.R.O., CR 2017/A1, 66 & 24; P. Russell and O. Price (eds), *England Displayed being a New, Complete, and Accurate Survey and Description of the Kingdom of England and Principality of Wales*, II (1769), 5.

23.   S.R.O., D 1734/4/1/9, f. 12v.

24.   S.R.O., D 1734/4/1/8, ff. 5r, 6r & 4v; inventory of John Ryggly, L.R.O., Inv. file 5; L.R.O., 23 D 63/5.

25.   P.R.O., LR 2, 255, f. 161; P.R.O., SC 2, 183/83-4.

26.   S.R.O., D 1734/4/1/7, ff. 13v-14v; will and inventory of Thomas Lussell of Dunton Bassett, L.R.O., Wills & Invv. 1564 and Wills R.B. 1564, f. 35.

27.   Inventory of Nicholas Ratclyffe, L.R.O., Wills & Invv. 1583, no. 9; P.R.O., SC 2, 183/84, m. 1; L.R.O., inventories of Edward Overing, Francis Pope and John Hackkytt, Inv. file 16, no. 149 & *ulto*, file 32A, no. 121 and file 26, no. 187(189).

28.   L.R.O., DE 147/14-17.

29.   H. Hartopp, *op. cit.*, 122-83 & 536-7; *cf.* H. Stocks (ed.), *Records of the Borough of Leicester, 1603-1688* (1923), 322.

30.   Inventories of John Taylor and William Winterton, L.R.O., Invv. 1660 Commiss., nos. 41 and 121.

31.   P.R.O., SC 2, 183/83-4.

32.   W. Burton, *The Description of Leicester Shire, Containing Matters of Antiquitye, Historye, Armorye, and Genealogy* (1622), 187.

33.   1557: L.R.O., Wills & Invv. 1557, no. 39; *cf.* bequest by the town baker John Wheteley, *v. supra*, p. 67. 1591: L.R.O., Inv. file 12, no. 92. 1598/9: L.R.O., Inv. file 14, no. 59(A.60).

34.   P.R.O., E 134, 6 Chas. I, Mich. 39.

35.   L.R.O., Wills R.B. 1571, f. 5; P.R.O., E 134, 7 Chas. I, East. 26, m. 3v; L.R.O., DE 1012/2-3; P.R.O., E 134, 6 Chas. I, Mich. 39, m. 7r.

36.   Swancote: P.R.O., E 134, 30 Eliz., Hil. 5, m. (4)r; L.R.O., Inv. file 31, no. 86 and Wills 1625, no. 92. Chamberlaine: P.R.O., E 134, 7 Chas. I, East. 26, m. 3r; L.R.O., Inv. file 26, no. 53. Engrossing: J. Nichols, *Leics.*, IV i, 300. Complaint: P.R.O., E 134, 30 Eliz., Hil. 5, m. (5)r. Billington: Huntington Library, STT Manorial Box 19 (August 24, 1622); this source *ex inf.* Professor P. Clark.

37.   P.R.O., E 134, 6 Chas. I, Mich. 39, m. 4r & 7 Chas. I, East. 26, m. 3v.

38   J. Nichols, *Leics.*, IV i, 253-4.

39.   P.R.O., E 134, 6 Chas. I, Mich. 39, m. 7r.

40.   Huntington Library, STT Manorial Box 19 (1667).

41.   *Cf.* J. A. Chartres, 'The Marketing of Agricultural Produce', in *A.H.E.W.*, ed. J. Thirsk, V ii, *1640-1750 Agrarian Change* (1985), 415-6.

42.   W.R.O., CR 2017/D266.

43.   P.R.O., E 152, 129.

44.   1562: P.R.O., SC 2, 183/83, m. 4. 1590s: P.R.O., E 134, 40 Eliz., East. 12, m. (4)r.

45.   Saunders: L.R.O., Wills R.B. 1569, f. 76. Wheteley: L.R.O., Wills & Invv. 1564.

46.   L.R.O., DE 147/5, /7, /11 & /14.

47.   Cotesbach: *ibid., sub nomine* William Heele; L.R.O., BR II/18/12/230; P.R.O., LR 2, 255, f. 125. Sutton: inventory of Richard Bosse, L.R.O., Invv. 1675, no. 48. Frowlesworth: L.R.O., Inv. file 41, no. 92 and Invv. 1686 V.G., no. 31. Lutterworth: W.R.O., CR 2017/M34; P.R.O., E 134, 1658-9, Hil. 16, mm. 5r, 4r & 6r; L.R.O., DE 147/24 & /12/2.

48. H. Hartopp, *op. cit.*, 149, 160 etc. (Allsopp) and 82 etc. (Hallam).
49. Will of William Haywoode 1594, P.R.O., PROB 11, 84 (79 Dixy).
50. P.R.O., E 134, 1658-9, Hil. 16, mm. 6r & 5r.
51. L.R.O., Invv. 1680, no. 214 and Invv. 1698, no. 36.
52. P.R.O., E 134, 6 Chas. I, Mich. 39, mm. 7r & 3r.
53. Billington: L.R.O., Inv. file 36, no. 80. Flude: L.R.O., Parish Register Transcript 1639. Goodacre: W.R.O., CR 2017/D196. Grazier: L.R.O., Invv. 1696, no. 44. Swinford: L.R.O., Invv. 1680, no. 22s.
54. S.R.O., D 1734/4/1/9, f. 16r; inventory of Sir William Turpin 1617, filed separately; Bradford Central Library, Cunliffe Lister Collection, Manorial Records Box 5.
55. S.R.O., D 1734/4/1/8, f. 35r & /9, f. 37r.
56. Hops: L.R.O., Inv. file 9, no. 82. Hop-yards: G. F. Farnham, *Leicestershire Medieval Village Notes*, II (Leicester, 1929), 243; L.R.O., DE 1012/12; *v. supra*, p. 116.
57. Insley: L.R.O., Inv. file 9, no. 205. Pope: L.R.O., Inv. file 32A, no. 121.
58. *Cf.* J. Thirsk, *Economic Policy and Projects: The Development of a Consumer Society in Early Modern England* (1978), 54-5.
59. P. Clark, *The English Alehouse: a social history 1200-1830* (1983), 97.
60. A. Everitt, 'The English Urban Inn, 1560-1760', in *Perspectives in English Urban History*, ed. A. Everitt (1973), 91-137.
61. 1608: P.R.O., SP 14, 32.72; *cf.* P. Clark, *op. cit.*, 173. 1577: P.R.O., SP 12, 118.15.
62. North Kilworth: L.R.O., DE 147/5 & /11. Gilmorton: *ibid.*, /14-17. Lutterworth: P.R.O., E 134, 6 Chas. I, Mich. 39, m. 7r.
63. L.R.O., QS.36/2/1.
64. P.R.O., WO 30, 48.
65. W.R.O., CR 2017/D235; *v. supra*, n. 10.
66. L.R.O., Wills 1613, no. 81.
67. L.R.O., Wills & Invv. 1567, Inv. file 9, no. 100 and Inv. file 14, no. 14(A.11).
68. P.R.O., LR 2, 255, f. 158; L.R.O., DE 66 (Boxes 2217, 2540 & 4342): L.R.O., Inv. file 40, no. 355.
69. *V. supra*, p. 74; W.R.O., CR 2017/D190; L.R.O., Inv. file 32C, no. 50, Inv. file 36, no. 140 and Inv. file 42, no. 75.
70. L.R.O., Invv. 1664 C. & O., no. 99.
71. P.R.O., SC 2, 183/83, m. 1.
72. A. Everitt, 'The Marketing of Agricultural Produce', *loc. cit.*, 559-61.
73. J. Nichols, *Leics.*, IV i, 260.
74. L.R.O., 5 D 33/189, *sub nomine* Lutterworth (1515).
75. J. Goodacre, 'Occupations and Status in a Midland Market Town', unpublished paper contributed to Urban History Group Annual Conference, Canterbury (1983).
76. W.R.O., CR 2017/M48; P.R.O., LR 2, 255, f. 137.
77. L.R.O., Inv. file 8, no. 46(49) and Inv. file 12, no. 54; inventory of John Wallis, L.R.O., Admm. 1572.
78. Barnard: P.R.O., E 134, 40 Eliz., East. 12, m. (6)r; P.R.O., LR 2, 255, f. 143. Fludd: *ibid.*, ff. 136, 147 & 119; L.R.O., Wills 1614, no. 43 and Inv. file 25, no. 151.
79. Tarlton: *v. supra*, n. 6; L.R.O., Inv. file 40, no. 87. Young: *ibid.*, no. 157; P.R.O., LR 2, 255, f. 153.
80. Smith: L.R.O., Inv. file 36, no. 174. Billington: L.R.O., Wills R.B. 1630, 172,

Inv. file 42, no. 70 and Inv. file 36, no. 80.

81. Inventory of Isack Billington, innholder, L.R.O., Invv. 1676, no. 121; L.R.O., Invv. 1678, no. 44.

82. L.R.O., Inv. file 43, no. 158 and Invv. 1660 Commiss., no. 122.

83. L.R.O., Invv. 1692, no. 85.

84. L.R.O., DE 66 (Boxes 4310, 4318 & 2217); W.R.O., CR 2017/D221; L.R.O., Invv. 1695, no. 163 and Invv. 1699, no. 81.

85. A. Everitt, 'The Marketing of Agricultural Produce', *loc. cit.*, 577-86.

86. Successive issues of the Book of Orders: N. S. B. Gras, *The Evolution of the English Corn Market from the Twelfth to the Eighteenth Century* (1926), 236-42; P. Slack, 'Books of Orders: the Making of English Social Policy, 1577-1631', *Transactions of the Royal Historical Society*, 5th ser. XXX (1980), 1-22; B. Sharp, *In Contempt of All Authority: Rural Artisans and Riot in the West of England*, 1586-1660 (1980), 50-80.

87. *Acts of the Privy Council of England*, new ser. XIV, 1586-1587 (1897), 248; P.R.O., E 134, 30 Eliz., Hil. 5.

88. M. Bateson (ed.), *Records of the Borough of Leicester, 1509-1603* (1905), 321; P.R.O., E 134, 40 Eliz., East. 12.

89. J. Thirsk, 'Enclosing and Engrossing', in *A.H.E.W.*, ed. J. Thirsk, IV (1967), 228-32.

90. 1607: J. E. Martin, *Feudalism to Capitalism: Peasant and Landlord in English Agrarian Development* (1983), 161-3. 1608: H. Stocks (ed.), *op. cit.*, 74. 1615: *ibid.*, 152-3. 1614: L.R.O., BR II/5/130; *v. supra*, p. 66. 1622: P. Bowden, 'Agricultural Prices, Farm Profits, and Rents', in *A.H.E.W.*, ed. J. Thirsk, IV (1967), 631-2; L.R.O., BR II/18/14/108 & /107; H. Stocks (ed.), *op. cit.*, 204 & 206-7; P.R.O., SP 14, 140.81; *v. supra*, pp. 113 & 133.

91. H. Stocks (ed.), *op. cit.*, 254 & 262; P.R.O., SP 16, 176.56 & 188.59; P.R.O., E 134, 6 Chas. I, Mich. 39 & 7 Chas. I, East. 26.

92. L.R.O., Inv. file 36, no. 80.

93. J. Thirsk, 'Enclosing and Engrossing', *loc. cit.*, 248. 1607: 'A consideration concerning the cause in question before the Lords touchinge depopulation', *v. supra*, cap. I n. 145. 1620: P.R.O., SP 14, 112.91. 1596: Coventry Record Office, A 14(a), f. 132; D. M. Palliser, 'York under the Tudors: The Trading Life of the Northern Capital', in *Perspectives in English Urban History*, ed. A. Everitt (1973), 49.

94. 1608; H. Stocks (ed.), *op. cit.*, 74. 1630: P.R.O., SP 16, 176.56.

95. P.R.O., SP 16, 191.24.

96. W.R.O., CR 2017/E115, 40. *Cf.* J. A. Chartres, 'The Marketing of Agricultural Produce', *loc. cit.*, 416-8.

97. J. Moore, *A Scripture-Word against Inclosure* (1656), 7.

98. H. Stocks (ed.), *op. cit.*, 396.

99. D. Defoe, *A Tour through England and Wales* (Everyman edn, 1928), II, 123 and *The Complete English Tradesman* (1745, 1841 edn), II, 175.

100. (D. Defoe), *A Humble Proposal to the People of England, For the Increase of their Trade, And encouragement of their Manufactures . . .* (1729, 1841 edn), 50.

101. S.R.O., D 1734/4/1/8, f. 38v.

102. L.R.O., Invv. 1676, no. 163.

103. P.R.O., E 179, 251/4; inventory of William Clarke, L.R.O., Invv. 1683, no. 110.

104. J. Nichols, *Leics.*, IV i, pl. XXXVIII, no. 35.

105. L.R.O., Invv. 1682, no. 110; J. Nichols, *ibid.*, 205.

106. J. Taylor, *The Carriers Cosmographie* (1637, 1873 edn), 9; L.R.O., Inv. file 35, no. 140.

107. L.R.O., Invv. 1687, no. 154.

108. L.R.O., Inv. file 9, no. 175.

109. L.R.O., Invv. 1684, no. 194, 1679, no. 31, 1685, no. 5 and 1673, no. 21.

110. L.R.O., Invv. 1687, no. 190; inventory of Nathaniel Reeve of Claybrook magna, innholder, L.R.O., Invv. 1690, no. 147.

111. L.R.O., DE 66 (Box 2217).

112. Inventories of Nicholas Ratclyffe and John Clark, shoemakers, L.R.O., Wills & Invv. 1583, no. 9 and Invv. 1676, no. 87.

113. Probate papers of William Nucombe, L.R.O., Wills 1609, no. 3.

114. Similar experience of towns of Market Harborough and Banbury: J. Nichols, *Leics.*, II ii (1795), 500; *V.C.H. Oxfordshire*, X (1972), 64.

115. *V.C.H. Northamptonshire*, II (1906), 319–20.

116. Ratclyfe: L.R.O., Wills R.B. 1568, f. 14 and Wills & Invv. 1568. Wood: L.R.O., Inv. file 25, no. 76.

117. Similar experience of Leicester and Stratford-upon-Avon: *V.C.H. Leics.*, IV (1958), 86; *V.C.H. Warwicks.*, III (1945), 25.

118. L.R.O., Wills 1597, no. 109 & Inv. file 16, no. 149 & *ulto*; L.R.O., Inv. file 37, no. 77; H. Hartopp, *op. cit.*, *sub nominibus* Overend, Overing and Hutchwitt.

119. Will and inventory of William Parker, L.R.O., Wills & Invv. 1560; inventory of Gilbert Ward, L.R.O., Invv. 1666, no. 14.

120. J. Nichols, *Leics.*, IV i, 257.

121. L.R.O., Invv. 1660 Commiss., no. 42.

122. W.R.O., CR 2017/E3.

123. *The Journeys of Celia Fiennes* ed. C. Morris (1947), 162; *cf.* A. Macaulay, *The History and Antiquities of Claybrook, in the County of Leicester; including The Hamlets of Bittesby, Ullesthorpe, Wibtoft, and Little Wigston* (1791), 112.

124. Claybrook parva: *ibid.*, 87. Ashby parva: MS Enclosure Award at Ashby parva. Shawell: Enclosure Award, L.R.O., DE 66 (Box 2504).

125. W.R.O., CR 2017/A1, 165.

126. L.R.O., Invv. 1689, no. 45; W.R.O., CR 2017/D238.

127. L.R.O., Wills 1640, no. 91.

128. 1630s: L.R.O., Inv. file 37, no. 203 and Inv. file 41, no. 94. Cooper: L.R.O., Invv. 1684, no. 230. Joiners: L.R.O., Inv. file 35, no. 29; W.R.O., CR 2017/A1, 10; L.R.O., Invv. 1693, no. 51. Turner: *v. infra*, p. 219.

129. Hovels: when no longer needed they could, being personalty, be dismantled and the timber re-used; hence their rare survival. In the northern provinces of Spain the *horreo* (a granary likewise belonging to the farmer), even where obsolete, is preserved as a symbol of the independent peasant mixed farm. Walling: S.R.O., D 1734/4/1/9, f. 18r. Thatching: *ibid.*, /7, f. 19r, /8, f. 12r & /7, f. 17r.

130. *Ibid.*, /9, ff. 16r & 36v.

131. F. Whellan & Co., *History, Topography, and Directory of Northamptonshire* (1874), 226 & 228; A. E. Treen, *The History and Antiquities of the Vicinity of Rugby, Written and Printed on the hand-press*, I (Rugby, 1909), 195.

132. Tilers etc.: L.R.O., Inv. file 6b, no. T22; H. Hartopp, *op. cit.*, *sub nomine* Westoes; L.R.O., Inv. file 2, no. 169/11 & /91. Pavior: L.R.O., Inv. file 32C, no. 50. Masons: W.R.O., CR 2017/E115, 5; L.R.O., Invv. 1680, no. 214 and Invv. 1686 V.G., no. 41.

133. Bricklayers: S.R.O., D 1734/4/1/6, f. 24r. Kiln yard: P.R.O., LR 2, 255, f. 126. Tiled roofs: *ibid.*, f. 161; Glebe Terrier 1606 at Lincolnshire Archives Office. Red house: L.R.O., DE 66 (Box 2225). Bricks: W.R.O., CR 2017/D163; L.R.O., Invv. 1680, no. 153.

134. Glass: P.R.O., PROB 11, 62 (8 Arundell). Glaziers: P.R.O., PROB 11, 267, f. 356; L.R.O., Wills 1621, no. 139. Painters: L.R.O., Inv. file 9, no. 174 and Inv. file 38, no. 127; under dates 1634/5-41 in Market Harborough Parish Register, L.R.O., DE 1587/1.

135. L.R.O., Invv. 1678, no. 153.

136. L.R.O., Inv. file 28, no. 183; inventories of George and Roger Johnson, L.R.O., Invv. 1664 C. & A., no. 112 and Invv. 1679, no. 133; loan to Elisha Newcombe, carpenter, L.R.O., DE 66 (Box 2483); P.R.O., E 179, 240/279.

137. Gunsmith: under dates 1636-40 in Catthorpe Parish Register, L.R.O., DE 1453/1; H. Hartopp, *op. cit., sub nomine* Daniel Smith. Nail-smith: W.R.O., CR 2017/E115, 16. Cutler: S.R.O., D 1734/4/1/9, f. 17r. Leicester clockmaker: *ibid.*, /8, f.12r; H. Hartopp, *op. cit.*, 67. This is now the earliest reference to a Leicestershire clockmaker; the only earlier clock recorded, also tended by him, was in the county town: J. Daniell, *Leicestershire Clockmakers: Directory of Watch and Clock Makers working in Leicestershire before 1900* (Leicester, 1975), 5-6. Lutterworth spurrier and clockmaker: J. E. Stocks, *Market Harborough Parish Records 1531 to 1837* (1926), 123, 135 & 253; R. Rouse, *A Collection of the Charities and Donations, given for any Religious or other Public Use to the Town of Market-Harborough In the County of Leicester. . .* (Market-Harborough, 1768), 103. Bell-founders: T. North, *The Church Bells of Leicestershire: Their Inscriptions, Traditions, and Peculiar Uses; with Chapters on Bells and the Leicester Bell Founders* (Leicester, 1876), *sub nominibus* Newcombe and Watts. Church clocks: A. P. Moore, 'Leicestershire Churches in the Time of Charles I.', in *Memorials of Old Leicestershire*, ed. A. Dryden (1911), 144 n. 2.

138. Roper: *sub nomine* Samuel Dunkley in Shawell Parish Register Transcripts at L.R.O.; *v. supra*, p. 133. Sieve-maker: L.R.O., Inv. file 43, no. 159. Tinkers: W.R.O., CR 2017/A1, 97; L.R.O., Inv. file 34, no. 80.

139. W.R.O., CR 2017/E42 & D171.

140. L.R.O., Invv. 1677, no. 29.

141. A. Macaulay, *op. cit.*, 45.

142. J. E. Stocks, *op. cit.*, 53-111; H. Hartopp, *op. cit., sub nomine* Jackson.

143. Under dates 1678/9 and 1679/80 in Misterton Parish Register, L.R.O., DE 452/1.

144. L.R.O., Wills 1641, no. 135 and Wills 1632, no. 105.

145. Woad-workers: under dates 1646-65 in Misterton Parish Register, L.R.O., DE 452/1; *cf.* E. Kerridge, *The Agricultural Revolution* (1967), 194 & 210. Basket-makers: L.R.O., DE 147/14; L.R.O., Invv. 1662 V.G., no. 39. Coopers: L.R.O., Admm. 1600 (missing) and Inv. file 14, no. 25(A.23); inventory (filed with nuncupatory will), L.R.O., Wills 1639, no. 149.

146. L.R.O., DE 914/1.

147. H. Hartopp, *op. cit., sub nomine* Lee; J. Daniell, *op. cit., sub nominibus* Lee, Jackson and Wilkins.

148. P.R.O., LR 2, 255, f. 161.

149. L.R.O., Inv. file 4, no. 144; inventories of Clement Sutton and Thomas Hallyman, L.R.O., Inv. file 5.

150. H. Hartopp, *op. cit., sub nomine* Pauer, Pavyer, Payver, Poer, Poryr, Power;

P.R.O., C 1, 665/39; will and inventory of Margaret Paver, L.R.O., Wills & Invv. 1550; *cf.* Robert Porver in Melton Mowbray, *v. supra*, n. 9, and Ralph Power of Atherstone, who joined Leicester Chapmen's Guild in 1492-3.

151.   Will and inventory of Robert Sowter, L.R.O., Wills & Invv. 1551; H. Hartopp, *op. cit.*, *sub nomine* Shewter, Sutor.

152.   Inventory of Thomas Clerke, L.R.O., Admm. 1576; L.R.O., Inv. file 14, no. 44(A.44).

153.   Inventory of Richard Billing, L.R.O., Wills & Invv. 1560-1.

154.   Pratt: S.R.O., D 1734/4/1/8, ff. 39v & 40r; P.R.O., PROB 11, 57 (34 Pyckering). Peake: L.R.O., Wills 1591, no. 102; P.R.O., LR 2, 255, f. 118; P.R.O., PROB 11, 62 (8 Arundell); L.R.O., DE 66 (Box 3517); *v. infra*, n. 188.

155.   Pope: G. F. Farnham, *op. cit.*, III (1929), 315 & I (1929), 41-2; L.R.O., Wills R.B. 1626, 111 and Inv. file 32A, no.121; for his exceptional farming stock *v. supra*, p. 161. Almey: G. F. Farnham, *op. cit.*, I, 72; L.R.O., Wills 1600, no. 14 and Inv. file 18, no. 141; L.R.O., Inv. file 38, no. 143; H. Hartopp, *op. cit.*, 88.

156.   P.R.O., LR 2, 255, ff. 155 & 150.

157.   L.R.O., Inv. file 1, no. 32.

158.   L.R.O., Inv. file 35, no. 140.

159.   Barber: L.R.O., Invv. 1694, no. 102. Tobacconist: J. Farrell, 'Lutterworth Pauper Children and Apprenticeship, 1673-1856', *Leicestershire Historian*, III ii (1983/4), 21.

160.   L.R.O., Invv. 1672, no. 136.

161.   Town centre shops: P.R.O., LR 2, 255, ff. 117, 138 & 163. Neats Market shops: L.R.O., DE 1012/5. Iron Market shops: P.R.O., SC 12, 32/7.29/38.ii and LR 2, 255, f. 124; W.R.O., CR 2017/D163 & 221. King's Headland shops: P.R.O., LR 2, 255, f. 147; L.R.O., DE 66 (Boxes 2217, 4318 & 4310); W.R.O., CR 2017/D221; *v. supra*, p. 180. Shops in former Swan Inn: L.R.O., DE 66 (Box 3510). Branch shop in village: L.R.O., Invv. 1695, no. 97.

162.   Broughton Astley: L.R.O., Inv. file 36, no. 106. Bruntingthorpe: L.R.O., Invv. 1695, no. 60. Ashby magna: L.R.O., Invv. 1694, no. 96. Peatling magna: L.R.O., Invv. 1675, no. 169. Walton: L.R.O., Wills 1694, no. 8 and Invv. 1694, no. 8.

163.   L.R.O., QS.6/1/2/1, f. 153r.

164.   J. F. Larkin and P. L. Hughes (eds), *Stuart Royal Proclamations*, I (1973), 396-7 & 551-3.

165.   D. Fleming, *op. cit.*, 184.

166.   J. Taylor, *op. cit.*; *cf.* J. A. Chartres, 'Road Carrying in England in the Seventeenth Century: Myth and Reality', *Ec.H.R.*, 2nd ser. XXX i (1977), 81-7.

167.   E. W. Hensman, 'Henry Hastings, Lord Loughborough, and the Great Civil War', in *Memorials of Old Leicestershire*, ed. A. Dryden (1911), 210.

168.   L.R.O., Inv. file 41A, no. 43.

169.   J. A. Chartres, *loc. cit.*, 88-94.

170.   *V. supra*, p. 196; *cf.* D. Defoe, *The Complete English Tradesman*, II, 175-6.

171.   Pratt: L.R.O., Wills 1634, no. 28; P.R.O., PROB 11, 270 (Ruthen f. 473). Cole: P.R.O., PROB 11, 445, f. 118 (204); J. Nichols, *Leics.*, II ii, 696. Pycrofte: P.R.O., LR 2, 255, f. 159; G. F. Farnham, *op. cit.*, I, 72; will of Robert Pycrofte of Ashby magna, L.R.O., Wills & Invv. 1558 (P-Z). Bradgate: P.R.O., E 179, 251/9; J. Nichols, *Leics.*, IV i, 79 & 122. Wigley: *ibid.*, 119, 122 & 175; L.R.O., Wills 1696, no. 44. Staresmore: L.R.O., Wills 1699, no. 117.

172.   J. Simon, 'Town Estates and Schools in the Sixteenth and Early Seventeenth Centuries' and 'Post-Restoration Developments: Schools in the County

1669-1700', in *Education in Leicestershire 1540-1940: A regional study*, ed. B. Simon (Leicester, 1968), 15, 41, 227 & 230.

173. S.R.O., D 1734/4/1/9, ff. 25r & 38r; inventory of Mr Joseph Squire 1659, L.R.O., Invv. 1662 Commiss., no. 128.

174. Roos: P.R.O., E 134, 30 Eliz., Hil. 5, m. (3)r; P.R.O., E 310, 16/72.2, .8 & .45. Shakespeare: P.R.O., E 310, 16/73.18 & .27-9.

175. J. Nichols, *Leics.*, IV i, 119, 122, 156, 201 & 330.

176. L.R.O., Inv. file 34, no. 183.

177. *Cf.* "pseudo-gentry" in A. Everitt, 'Social Mobility in Early Modern England', *Past & Present*, XXXIII (1966), 69-70.

178. Bradgate: under date 1578 in Peatling parva Parish Register, L.R.O., Misc. 14; J. Nichols, *Leics.*, IV i, 122. Lee: under dates 1619, 1624 & 1625 in Catthorpe Parish Register, L.R.O., DE 1453/1; J. Simon, *loc. cit.*, 15. Kirke: under dates 1638 and 1695 in Shawell Parish Register Transcripts at L.R.O. and date 1659 in Catthorpe Parish Register; *v. supra*, p. 110.

179. P.R.O., E 134, 1658-9, Hil. 16, m. 4r.

180. L.R.O., Wills R.B. 1629, 261.

181. *Rugby School Register. From 1675 to 1874 inclusive. With alphabetical index* (Rugby, 1886).

182. J. Goodacre, 'Occupations and Status in a Midland Market Town', unpublished paper contributed to Urban History Group Annual Conference, Canterbury (1983).

183. Inventory of Thomas Towars of Claybrook, L.R.O., Wills & Invv. 1557 (K-Y); *A Descriptive Catalogue of Ancient Deeds in the Public Record Office*, V (1906), no. 13460 and III (1900), no. 5612.

184. P.R.O., E 134, 40 Eliz., East. 12, m. (6)r.

185. *Ibid.*, 30 Eliz., Hil. 5, m. (4)r.

186. P.R.O., SC 12, 10/7, m. 3v and L.R.2, 255, f. 199.

187. L.R.O., DE 66 (Box 2217).

188. Lussell (yeoman butchers): will of Hugh Lussell, senior, 1564, P.R.O., PROB 11, 47 (21 Stevenson); *cf.* will of an ordinary yeoman usher of the Queen's Great Chamber 1579, *ibid.*, 62 (11 Arundell). Kirby (yeoman butchers) and Peake (draper and yeomen): will of Humphrey Kirby, citizen and butcher of London, 1579, *ibid.*, 61 (31 Bakon); W. F. Carter and E. A. Barnard (eds), *The Records of King Edward's School Birmingham*, III, Publications of the Dugdale Society, XII (1933), *sub nominibus* Kirby, Peake (and Freher).

189. P.R.O., LR 2, 255, ff. 154 & 155; L.R.O., Wills 1594, no. 64 and Inv. file 13, no. 87; for his wool house, *v. supra*, pp. 155-6.

190. Elisha i: probate papers of William Nucombe, L.R.O., Wills 1609, no. 3; W.R.O., CR 2017/D175 & 188. Elisha ii: H. Hartopp, *op. cit.*, 141, 376, 540 & 115. Widow: W.R.O., CR 2017/M34; L.R.O., DE 66 (Box 2483).

191. Elisha iii (carpenter in 1684 but turner in 1697): *ibid.*

192. Brazier: will of Ralph Newcombe, L.R.O., Wills 1688, no. 3. The Leicester branch of the family also embraced both leather and metal crafts, as tanners and notable bell-founders; *V.C.H. Leics.*, III (1955), 47-9; W. G. Hoskins, *Provincial England: Essays in Social and Economic History* (1963), 97. Baker: *v. supra*, p. 167. Blacksmith: P.R.O., E 179, 240/279. Miller: J. Nichols, *Leics.*, IV i, 301.

193. *E.g.* L.R.O., Invv. 1685, no. 223, 1687, no. 46 and 1693, no. 82.

194. *Cf.* B. A. Holderness, ''Open' and 'Close' Parishes in England in the Eighteenth and Nineteenth Centuries', *Ag.H.R.*, XX ii (1972), 133.

195.   *Cf.* A. Everitt, 'Farm Labourers', in *A.H.E.W.*, ed. J. Thirsk, IV (1967), 437–42.
196.   P. Borsay, *The English Urban Renaissance: Culture and Society in The Provincial Town, 1660–1770* (1989), 360–1.
197.   J. Moore, *The Crying Sin of England, Of not Caring for the Poor* (1653), title page.

Notes to Chapter V

1.   J. Morton, *The Natural History of Northamptonshire; with Some Account of the Antiquities.* . . (1712), 15.
2.   J. Moore, *A Target for Tillage, briefly containing the most necessary, pretious, and profitable use thereof both for king and state* (1612), 15.
3.   Plundering: E. W. Hensman, 'Henry Hastings, Lord Loughborough, and the Great Civil War', in *Memorials of Old Leicestershire*, ed. A. Dryden (1911), 211. Fire: S. C. Ratcliff and H. C. Johnson (eds), *Warwick County Records*, III (Warwick, 1937), 215; the Lutterworth Constables paid out 8/- 'for the beer which the watchers drank who watched when the fire was', L.R.O., DE 2559/24; Leicester contributed £10 towards the loss, J. Nichols, *Leics.*, I ii (1815), 429.
4.   J. Moore, *A Target for Tillage* . . ., 51. It was to Lutterworth that Leicester aldermen went 'to admonish the people of the town of Leicester, who were gone to Cotesbach to help or see the unlawful assembly'; H. Stocks (ed.), *Records of the Borough of Leicester, 1603–1688* (1923), 71: a later account of the riot located it 'about Lutterworth', omitting all reference to Cotesbach; quoted in J. Throsby, *The Memoirs of the Town and County of Leicester: Displayed under an Epitome of the Reign of each Sovereign in the English History: containing, The Antiquities of each, and the Historical and Biographical Relations at Large.* . ., IV (Leicester, 1777), 41–3.
5.   Melton Mowbray: D. Fleming, 'A local market system: Melton Mowbray and the Wreake Valley 1549–1720' (Ph.D. thesis, University of Leicester, 1980), 44 & 70. Hillmorton: *V.C.H. Warwicks.*, VI (1951), 108–9; J. E. Martin, *Feudalism to Capitalism: Peasant and Landlord in English Agrarian Development* (1983), 188–9. Hallaton: *V.C.H. Leics.*, V (1965), 126. Market Harborough: R. Rouse, *A Collection of the Charities and Donations, given for any Religious or other Public Use to the Town of Market-Harborough In the County of Leicester. To which is added The Decree issued out of the High Court of Chancery, 13th. of Charles I. confirming the Proprietors of certain ancient Cottages in Harborough in their Right of Commons, Acre-Hades, &c. in the Common Fields of Great-Bowden* . . . (Market-Harborough, 1768), 113–29.
6.   *Cf.* P. A. J. Pettit, *The Royal Forests of Northamptonshire: a Study in their Economy, 1558–1714*, Publications of the Northamptonshire Record Society, XXIII (1968); B. Sharp, *In Contempt of All Authority: Rural Artisans and Riot in the West of England, 1586–1660* (1980).
7.   J. Thirsk (ed.), *A.H.E.W.*, IV (1968), 268–72, 691, & 273. A petition to correct an error in a new lease was addressed direct to Salisbury; P.R.O., SP 14, 37.59.
8.   Church Wardens' Accounts, L.R.O., DE 2559/18.
9.   R. W(ilkinson), *A Sermon preached at North-Hampton the 21, of June last past, before the Lord Lieutenant of the County, and the rest of the Commissioners there assembled upon occasion of the late Rebellion and*

Riots in those parts committed (1607), title page, D(1r) and (A2r).

10.   E. C. Pettet, 'Coriolanus and the Midlands Insurrection of 1607', *Shakespeare Survey*, III (1950), 34–42; *cf.* J. Lee, *A Vindication of A Regulated Inclosure* (1656), 10–12.

11.   J. Moore, *The Crying Sin of England, Of not Caring for the Poor* (1653), 8 and *A Scripture-Word against Inclosure* (1656), 5.

12.   Historical Manuscripts Commission, *Report on the Manuscripts of the Duke of Buccleuch and Queensberry*, III (1926), 117–18.

13.   J. Bentham, *The Christian Conflict: A Treatise, Shewing the Difficulties and Duties of this Conflict, with the Armour, and speciall Graces to be exercised by Christian Souldiers . . . The case of Usury and Depopulation, and the errours of Antinomists occasionally also discussed . . .* (1635); cited in (J. Lee), *Considerations concerning Common Fields, and Inclosures* (1653), 40.

14.   *A Collection of the state papers of John Thurloe, Esq.*, ed. T. Birch, IV (1742), 686; *cf.* 'The Poor Husbandman's Advocate to Rich Racking Landlords' (1691) printed in 'The Reverend Richard Baxter's Last Treatise', ed. F. J. Powicke, *Bulletin of the John Rylands Library Manchester*, X i (1926), 175–218, especially 179–187.

15.   J. Moore, *The Crying Sin of England, Of not Caring for the Poor*, 7 & 13–14.

16.   J. Thirsk, 'Industries in the countryside', in *Essays in the Economic and Social History of Tudor and Stuart England in honour of R. H. Tawney*, ed. F. J. Fisher (1961), 70–88.

17.   J. Nichols, *Leics.*, III ii (1804), Appendix iv, 22–3.

18.   L. Fox, *The Administration of the Honor of Leicester in the Fourteenth Century* (Leicester, 1940), 74–6; *V.C.H. Leics.*, I (1907), 1.

19.   W. Burton, *The Description of Leicester Shire, Containing Matters of Antiquitye, Historye, Armorye, and Genealogy* (1622), 174.

20.   J. Moore, *A Target for Tillage . . .*, 47–8; P.R.O., WO 30, 48; L.R.O., QS.36/2/1 and QS.37/1.

Bibliography

(Place of publication generally London and only given otherwise for local books)

A   PRIMARY SOURCES
    I   Manuscript
        (i)   National
        (ii)   Local
    II   Published
        (i)   National
        (ii)   General
        (iii) Local
        (iv) Contemporary local pamphlets
B   SECONDARY SOURCES
    I   Population
        (i)   General
        (ii)   Regional and local
    II   Agrarian and enclosure history
        (i)   General
        (ii)   Regional and local
    III Industry and trade
        (i)   General
            (a) Industry
            (b) Trade
        (ii)   Regional and local
    IV Economic and social history
        (i)   General studies
        (ii)   Regional and local studies
            (a) Regions and counties
            (b) Villages
            (c) Towns
        (iii) Urban studies

A Primary Sources

I Manuscript

(i) National

Public Record Office
Chancery

C 1	Early Proceedings	
C 2	,, ,,	Series I
C 3	,, ,,	Series II
C 66	Patent Rolls	
C 93	Proceedings of Commissioners for Charitable Uses	

Exchequer

E 134	King's Remembrancer	Depositions taken by Commission
E 152	,, ,,	Inquisitions *post mortem*
E 179	,, ,,	Subsidy Rolls etc.
E 309	Augmentations	Enrolments of Leases
E 310	,,	Particulars for Leases
LR 2	Land Revenue	Miscellaneous Books

Prerogative Court of Canterbury
    PROB 11   Registered Copy Wills

Registrar General's Office
    RG 4   Authenticated Registers, Main Series

Special Collections
    SC 2   Court Rolls
    SC 6   Ministers' Accounts
    SC 12   Rentals and Surveys

State Papers Domestic
    SP 12   Elizabeth I
    SP 14   James I
    SP 16   Charles I

War Office
    WO 30   Miscellanea

(ii) Local

Leicestershire Record Office

1 D 41/2	Leicester Archdeaconry Glebe Terriers
1 D 41/3	,, ,, Parish Register Transcripts
5 D 33	Farnham
9 D 43	Harris, Watts and Bouskell
18 D 67	Bretherton, Turpin and Pell
23 D 63	Reverend H. V. Atkinson, Claybrook Vicarage
35'29	Clayton
BR	Borough of Leicester
DE 40/40	Andrew Hull Esq.
DE 66	Bray and Bray
DE 73	Leicester Archdeaconry Wills, Administrations and Probate Inventories
DE 147	Packe
DE 914	Lutterworth Town Estate
DE 1012	Waterhouse and Company
DE 1221	H. V. Jackson and Company
DE 1941	Leicester City Council
EN	Enclosure Awards
QS	Quarter Sessions
Ti	Tithe awards
DE	Deposited Parish Records

Leicester City Reference Library

(T. Staveley)   'The History and Antiquities of the Antient Towne and once Citty of Leicester'

Belvoir Castle
Rutland MSS

Bodleian Library
Gough MSS

Bradford Central Library
Cunliffe Lister Collection

British Library
Cotton MSS
Harleian MSS
Sloane MSS

Coventry Record Office
A 14(a)   Council Book

Folger Shakespeare Library, Washington DC
MS.Vb.165

Huntington Library, San Marino, California
STT Manorial

Lincolnshire Archives Office
Lincoln Diocese Glebe Terriers

Northamptonshire Record Office
I.(L)   Isham of Lamport

Saint Paul's Cathedral Library
17 D   Bishop's Parochial Enquiry

Shakespeare Birthplace Trust, Stratford-upon-Avon
Misc. Docts. XIV

Staffordshire Record Office
D 649   Shrewsbury Collection
D 1734   Anglesey Collection

Warwickshire Record Office
CR 2017   Feilding of Newnham Paddox

at Ashby parva
Goodacre family Deeds and Manuscripts

II   Published

(i)   National
Acts of the Privy Council of England, new ser. XIV, 1586–1587 (1897)
Calendar of Patent Rolls, Edward IV, Henry VI, 1467–1477 (1900)
Calendar of Patent Rolls, Henry VII, II, 1494–1509 (1916)
Calendar of State Papers, Domestic Series, 1655–6 (1882)
A Descriptive Catalogue of Ancient Deeds in the Public Record Office, 6 vols
      (1890–1915)
Journals of the House of Commons, VII, 1651–1659
Royal Commission on Market Rights and Tolls First Report, I (1889)

(ii)   General

R. Baxter, 'The Reverend Richard Baxter's Last Treatise', ed. F. J. Powicke, *Bulletin of the John Rylands Library, Manchester*, X i (1926), 163-218

W. Blyth, *The English Improver, or a New Survey of Husbandry* (1649)

W. Blith, *The English Improver Improved or the Survey of Husbandry Surveyed* (1653)

(R. Blome), *Britannia, or a Geographical Description of the Kingdomes of England, Scotland, and Ireland . . .* (1673)

P. Bowden, Statistical Appendix to *A.H.E.W.*, ed. J. Thirsk, IV (1967), 814-70

P. J. Bowden, Statistics in Appendices to *A.H.E.W.*, ed. J. Thirsk, V ii (1985)

T. Burton, *Diary of Thomas Burton, Esq. Member of the Parliaments of Oliver and Richard Cromwell from 1656 to 1659*, ed. J. T. Rutt, 4 vols (1828)

W. Camden, *Britain, or a Chorographical Description of the most flourishing Kingdomes, England, Scotland, and Ireland . . .* (1610 edn)

D. Defoe, *The Complete English Tradesman* (1745, 1841 edn), II

(D. Defoe), *A Humble Proposal to the People of England, For the Increase of their Trade, And encouragement of their Manufactures . . .* (1729, 1841 edn)

D. Defoe, *A Tour through England and Wales* (Everyman edn, 1928)

The Dictionary of National Biography (1885-1900)

C. Fiennes, *The Journeys of Celia Fiennes*, ed. C. Morris (1947)

R. E. Glasscock (ed.), *The Lay Subsidy of 1334*, British Academy Records of Social and Economic History, new ser. II (1975)

H. Halhead, *Inclosure Thrown Open: or, Depopulation Depopulated. Not By Spades and Mattocks; but, By the Word of God, the Laws of the Land, and Solid Arguments. And the most material pleas that can be brought for it, considered and answered* (1650)

J. O. Halliwell (ed.), *The Marriage of Wit and Wisdom, an Ancient Interlude. to which are added Illustrations of Shakespeare and the Early English Drama* (1846)

Historical Manuscripts Commission, *Report on the Manuscripts of the Duke of Buccleuch and Queensberry*, III (1926)

Historical Manuscripts Commission, *Report on the Manuscripts of the Earl of Denbigh, preserved at Newnham Paddox, Warwickshire*, V (1911)

Historical Manuscripts Commission, *Report on the Manuscripts of Lord Middleton* (1911)

E. Howes, *The Annales, or Generall Chronicle of England, begun first by maister John Stow, and after him continued and augmented . . .* (1615)

P. L. Hughes and J. F. Larkin (eds), *Tudor Royal Proclamations*, 3 vols (1964-9)

J. F. Larkin and P. L. Hughes (eds), *Stuart Royal Proclamations*, 2 vols (1973-83)

I. S. Leadam, *The Domesday of Inclosures* 1517–1518, 2 vols (1897)

J. Leland, *The Itinerary of John Leland in or about the year 1535–1543*, ed. L. Toulmin Smith, I (1964)

R. P(owell), *Depopulation arraigned, convicted and condemned, by the laws of God and man, with a decree 7 Chas I against the ingrossing of corne. A Treatise necessary in these times* (1636)

P. Russell and O. Price (eds), *England Displayed being a New, Complete, and Accurate Survey and Description of the Kingdom of England and Principality of Wales*, 2 vols (1769)

A. Standish, *The Commons Complaint. Wherein is contained two Speciall Grievances. Foure remedies for the same* (1611)

W. E. Tate, *A Domesday of English enclosure acts and awards*, edited with an introduction by M. E. Turner (1978)

R. H. Tawney and E. Power (eds), *Tudor Economic Documents: being select documents illustrating the economic and social history of Tudor England*, 3 vols (1924)

J. Taylor, *The Carriers Cosmographie. or A Briefe Relation of The Innes, Ordinaries, Hosteries, and other lodgings in, and neere London, where the Carriers, Waggons, Foote-posts and Higglers, doe usually come . . .* (1637, 1873 edn)

S. T(aylor), *Common-Good: or, the Improvement of Commons, Forrests, and Chases, by Inclosure. Wherein The Advantage of the Poor, the Common Plenty of All, and The Increase and Preservation of Timber, With other things of common concernment, Are Considered* (1652)

J. Thirsk and J. P. Cooper (eds), *Seventeenth-Century Economic Documents* (1972)

K. Thomas, 'Another Digger Broadside', *Past & Present*, XLII (1969), 57–68

(J. Thurloe), *A Collection of the state papers of John Thurloe*, Esq., ed. T. Birch, IV (1742)

A. Whiteman (ed.), *The Compton Census of 1676: A Critical Edition*, British Academy Records of Social and Economic History, new ser. X (1986)

G. C. Williamson, *Trade Tokens Issued in the Seventeenth Century in England, Wales, and Ireland by Corporations, Merchants, Tradesmen, &c.: A New and Revised Edition of William Boyne's Work* (1889–91)

J. W(orlidge), *Systema Agriculturae, The Mystery of Husbandry Discovered* (1669)

(iii)   Local

N. W. Alcock, *Warwickshire Grazier and London Skinner 1532–1555: The account book of Peter Temple and Thomas Heritage*, British Academy Records of Social and Economic History, new ser. IV (1981)

M. Bateson (ed.), *Records of the Borough of Leicester, 1103–1327* (1899)

M. Bateson (ed.), *Records of the Borough of Leicester, 1509–1603* (1905)

R. K. Baum, *Antique Maps of Leicestershire* (Loughborough, 1972)

M. W. Beresford, 'Glebe Terriers and Open-Field Leicestershire', in *Studies in Leicestershire Agrarian History*, ed. W. G. Hoskins, *T.L.A.S.*, XXIV (1949), 77-126

W. Burton, *The Description of Leicester Shire, Containing Matters of Antiquitye, Historye, Armorye, and Genealogy* (1622 and 2nd edn, Lynn, 1777)

W. F. Carter and E. A. Barnard (eds), *The Records of King Edward's School Birmingham*, III, Publications of the Dugdale Society, XII (1933)

A. B. Clarke, 'Leicestershire Uncalendared Wills 1489-1538', Leicestershire Archaeological Society duplicated leaflet (1951)

J. Curtis, *A Topographical History of the County of Leicester, the ancient part compiled from parliamentary and other documents, and the modern from actual survey* (Ashby-de-la-Zouch, 1831)

W. Dugdale, *The Antiquities of Warwickshire illustrated; From Records, Leiger-Books, Manuscripts, Charters, Evidences, Tombes, and Armes; Beautified With Maps, Prospects and Portraictures* (1656)

G. F. Farnham, *Leicestershire Medieval Village Notes*, 6 vols (privately printed, Leicester, 1929-33)

W. G. Dimmock Fletcher, 'Documents relating to Leicestershire, preserved in the Episcopal Registry at Lincoln', *A.A.S.R.P.*, XXII ii (1894), 227-365

W. G. Dimmock Fletcher, 'A Religious Census of Leicestershire in 1676', *T.L.A.S.*, VI (1888), 296-306

A. W. Gibbons (ed.), *Early Lincoln Wills: An Abstract of all the Wills & Administrations recorded in the Episcopal Registers of the old Diocese of Lincoln, 1280-1547* (Lincoln, 1888)

B. L. Gimson and P. Russell, *Leicestershire Maps: a Brief Survey* (Leicester, 1947)

(J. Goodacre ed.), 'Letters from a Seventeenth Century Rector of Lutterworth: Nathaniel Tovey as Marriage Agent', *Leicestershire Historian*, III ii (1983/4), 9-16

W. Harrod, *The History of Market-Harborough, In Leicestershire, and it's Vicinity* (Market-Harborough, 1808)

H. Hartopp, *Leicestershire Marriage Licenses, 1570-1729*, The Index Library, XXXVIII (1910)

H. Hartopp, *Leicestershire Wills and Administrations, 1495-1649*, The Index Library, XXVII (1902)

H. Hartopp, *Leicestershire Wills and Administrations, 1660-1750*, The Index Library, LI (1920)

H. Hartopp, *Register of the Freemen of Leicester 1196-1770* (Leicester, 1927)

H. Hartopp, *Roll of the Mayors of the Borough of Leicester and Lord Mayors of the City of Leicester 1209 to 1935* (Leicester, 1935)

P. D. A. Harvey and H. Thorpe, *The Printed Maps of Warwickshire 1576-1800*, Warwick County Occasional Series, I (1959)

R. Hazlewood, 'William Davy, of Leicester', *Leicestershire and Rutland Notes and Queries*, II (1893), 193-6

W. Kelly, *Notices Illustrative of the Drama, and other popular amusements, chiefly in the sixteenth and seventeenth centuries, incidentally illustrating Shakespeare and his contemporaries; extracted from the Chamberlains' Accounts and other manuscripts of the Borough of Leicester* (1865)

A. Macaulay, *The History and Antiquities of Claybrook, in the County of Leicester; including The Hamlets of Bittesby, Ullesthorpe, Wibtoft, and Little Wigston* (1791)

J. Mastin, *The History and Antiquities of Naseby, in the County of Northampton* (Cambridge, 1792)

A. P. Moore, 'Leicestershire Churches in the Time of Charles I.', in *Memorials of Old Leicestershire*, ed. A. Dryden (1911), 142-72

A. P. Moore, 'Leicestershire Livings in the Reign of James I.', *A.A.S.R.P.*, XXIX i (1907), 129-82

A. P. Moore, 'The Metropolitical Visitation of Archdeacon Laud, with an appendix containing transcripts of documents in ecclesiastical suits of the period, and other papers', *A.A.S.R.P.*, XXIX ii (1908), 479-534

J. Morton, *The Natural History of Northamptonshire; with Some Account of the Antiquities. . .* (1712)

J. Nichols, *The History and Antiquities of the County of Leicester*, 4 vols in 8 parts (1795-1815)

T. North, *The Church Bells of Leicestershire: Their Inscriptions, Traditions, and Peculiar Uses; with Chapters on Bells and the Leicester Bell Founders* (Leicester, 1876)

T. A. North, 'Melton Mowbray Town Records', *T.L.A.S.*, IV (1878), 329-84

L. A. Parker, 'The Depopulation Returns for Leicestershire in 1607', *T.L.A.S.*, XXIII (1947), 231-89

R. P(lot), *The Natural History of Oxford-shire, Being an Essay toward the Natural History of England* (Oxford, 1677)

D. Pockley, 'The Origins and Early Records of the Melton Mowbray Town Estate', *T.L.A.S.*, XLV (1969-70), 20-38

S. C. Ratcliff, H. C. Johnson and N. J. Williams (eds), *Warwick County Records*, 9 vols (Warwick, 1937)

R. Rouse, *A Collection of the Charities and Donations, given for any Religious or other Public Use to the Town of Market-Harborough In the County of Leicester* (Market-Harborough, 1768)

Rugby School Register. From 1675 to 1874 inclusive. With alphabetical index (Rugby, 1886)

H. Stocks (ed.), *Records of the Borough of Leicester, 1603-1688* (1923)

J. E. Stocks, *Market Harborough Parish Records 1531 to 1837* (1926)

J. E. Stocks and W. B. Bragg, *Market Harborough Parish Records to A.D. 1530* (1890)

J. Thirsk, 'Inclosure in Leicestershire without Parliamentary Act', *V.C.H. Leics.*, II (1954), 254-9

J. Thirsk, 'List of Parliamentary Inclosure Acts and Awards for Leicestershire', *V.C.H. Leics.*, II (1954), 260-4

A. Hamilton Thompson, *A Calendar of Charters and other Documents belonging to the Hospital of William Wyggeston at Leicester* (Leicester, 1933)

J. Throsby, *The Memoirs of the Town and County of Leicester: Displayed under an Epitome of the Reign of each Sovereign in the English History: containing The Antiquities of each, and the Historical and Biographical Relations at Large. To which is added, A Brief Supplimentary Account of the present state of Leicestershire*, 6 vols (Leicester, 1777)

J. Throsby, *Select Views in Leicestershire, From Original Drawings: Containing Seats of the Nobility and Gentry, Town Views and Ruins, Accompanied with Descriptive and Historical Relations* 2 vols (Leicester, 1789-90)

A. Trollope, *An Inventory of the Church Plate of Leicestershire, with Some Account of The Donors* 2 vols (Leicester, 1890)

J. L. Wetton and N. L. Wetton, 'The Seventeenth Century Trade Tokens of Leicestershire' (typescript at L.R.O., 1967)

F. Whellan & Co., *History, Topography, and Directory of Northamptonshire* (1874)

H. Whitaker, *A Descriptive List of the Printed Maps of Northamptonshire A.D. 1576-1900*, Publications of the Northamptonshire Record Society, XIV (1948)

W. White, *History, Gazetteer and Directory of the Counties of Leicester and Rutland* (2nd edn, Sheffield, 1863)

J. Wright, *The History and Antiquities of the County of Rutland: Collected From Records, Ancient Manuscripts, Monuments on the Place, and other authorities. Illustrated with Sculptures* (1684)

J. Young, 'The Token Coinage of Leicestershire and Rutland in the XVII. Century', *T.L.A.S.*, XI i & ii (1913-14), 115-31

(iv)   Contemporary local pamphlets

R. W(ilkinson), *A Sermon preached at North-Hampton the 21, of June last past, before the Lord Lieutenant of the County, and the rest of the Commissioners there assembled upon occasion of the late Rebellion and Riots in those parts committed* (1607)

J. Moore, *A Target for Tillage, briefly containing the most necessary, pretious, and profitable use thereof both for king and state* (1612)

J. Bentham, *The Christian Conflict: A Treatise, Shewing the Difficulties and Duties of this Conflict, with the Armour, and speciall Graces to be exercised by Christian Souldiers . . . The case of Usury and Depopulation, and the errours of Antinomists occasionally also discussed . . .* (1635)

1. May 1653
   J. Moore, *The Crying Sin of England, of not Caring for the Poor. Wherein Inclosure, viz. such as doth unpeople Townes, and uncorn Fields, is Arraigned, Convicted, and Condemned by the Word of God. Being the chief Heads of two Sermons, Preached at the Lecture at Lutterworth in Leicester-Shire in May last, and now published in love to Christ, his Country, and the Poor* (1653)

2. (November) 1653
   (J. Lee), *Considerations concerning Common Fields, and Inclosures, dialoguewise, Digested into deliberative Discourse between two supposed Friends, Philopeustus and Parrhesiastes. And tending Partly to state and determine the question of lawfulnesse or unlawfulnesse between Inclosures, and Common Fields, Partly to answer some passages, which may be thought to make against Inclosure in general, in another discourse lately published by Mr John Moore, under this Title, The crying sinne of England, of not caring for the poor* (1653)

3. 1653
   J. Moore, *A Reply to a Pamphlet intituled Considerations concerning Common fields and Inclosures, &c. Being partly an Answer to some passages which may be thought to make against Inclosure in generall, in an other discourse lately published by Mr. John Moore, under this title, The Crying sin of England of not careing for the poore* (1653)

4. 7th March 1653/4
   (J. Lee), *A Vindication of the Considerations concerning Common-fields and Inclosures: or, A Rejoynder unto that Reply which Mr. Moore hath pretended to make unto those Considerations* (1656)

5. 12th November 1656
   J. Lee, Ἐυταξία τοῦ ᾿Αγροῦ: *or A Vindication of A Regulated Inclosure. Wherein is plainly proved, that Inclosure of Commons in general and the Inclosure of Catthorp in the County of Leicester in particular, are both lawful and laudable. As also that those evils which too usually accompany Inclosure of Commons, are not the faults of Inclosure, but of some Inclosers only* (1656)

6. 1656
   J. Moore, *A Scripture-Word against Inclosure; viz: Such as doe Un-People Townes, and Un-Corne Fields. As also, Against all such, that daub over this black Sinne with untempered morter* (1656)

B Secondary sources

I Population

(i) General

M. Beresford, *The Lost Villages of England* (1954)

M. W. Beresford and J. G. Hurst (eds), *Deserted Medieval Villages* (1971)

I. Blanchard, 'Population Change, Enclosure, and the Early Tudor Economy', *Ec.H.R.*, 2nd ser. XXIII iii (1970), 427-45

J. D. Chambers, *Population, Economy, and Society in Pre-Industrial England* (1972)

F. J. Fisher, 'Influenza and Inflation in Tudor England', *Ec.H.R.*, 2nd ser. XVIII i (1965), 120-9

J. D. Gould, 'Mr. Beresford and the Lost Villages: a Comment', *Ag.H.R.*, III ii (1955), 107-13

D. M. Palliser, 'Tawney's Century: Brave New World or Malthusian Trap?', *Ec.H.R.*, 2nd ser. XXXV iii (1982), 339-53

J. Patten, 'The Hearth Taxes, 1662-1689', *Local Population Studies*, VII (1971), 14-27

P. Slack, 'Mortality crises and epidemic disease in England 1485-1610', in *Health, medicine and mortality in the sixteenth century*, ed. C. Webster (1979)

E. A. Wrigley and R. S. Schofield, *The Population History of England 1541-1871: A Reconstruction*, Studies in Social and Demographic History (1981)

(ii) Regional and local

K. J. Allison, M. W. Beresford, J. G. Hurst, *The Deserted Villages of Northamptonshire*, Leicester University Department of English Local History Occasional Papers, 1st ser. no. 18 (1966)

M. W. Beresford, 'The Deserted Villages of Warwickshire', *Birmingham Archaeological Society Transactions and Proceedings*, LXVI (1945-6), 49-106

C. J. Bond, 'Deserted medieval villages in Warwickshire and Worcestershire', in *Field and Forest: An historical geography of Warwickshire and Worcestershire*, eds T. R. Slater and P. J. Jarvis (1982), 147-71

J. Cornwall, 'The People of Rutland', *T.L.A.S.*, XXXVII (1961-2), 7-28

Deserted Medieval Village Research Group, 'Provisional List of Deserted Medieval Villages in Leicestershire', *T.L.A.S.*, XXXIX (1963-4), 24-33

N. Griffin, 'Epidemics in Loughborough', *T.L.A.S.*, XLIII (1967-8), 24-34

W. G. Hoskins, 'The Deserted Villages of Leicestershire', in his *Essays in Leicestershire History* (1950), 67-107

W. Kelly, *Visitations of the Plague at Leicester: A Paper read before the*

Royal Historical Society of Great Britain, July 12, 1877 (privately printed, Edinburgh, 1877)

C. T. Smith, 'Population', *V.C.H. Leics.*, III (1955), 129-75

J. E. O. Wilshere, 'Plague in Leicester 1558-1665', *T.L.A.S.*, XLIV (1968-9), 45-71

II Agrarian and enclosure history

(i) General

M. Beresford, 'Habitation versus Improvement: The Debate on Enclosure by Agreement', in *Essays in the Economic and Social History of Tudor and Stuart England in honour of R. H. Tawney*, ed. F. J. Fisher (1961), 40-69

M. W. Beresford, *Time and Place: Collected Essays* (1985)

P. Bowden, 'Agricultural Prices, Farm Profits, and Rents', in *A.H.E.W.*, ed. J. Thirsk, IV (1967), 593-695

A. R. Bridbury, 'Sixteenth-Century Farming', *Ec.H.R.*, 2nd ser. XXVII iv (1974), 538-56

C. Clay, 'The Price of Freehold Land in the later Seventeenth and Eighteenth Centuries', *Ec.H.R.*, 2nd ser. XXVII ii (1974), 173-89

A. Everitt, 'Farm Labourers', in *A.H.E.W.*, ed. J. Thirsk, IV (1967), 396-465

G. E. Fussell, *The Classical Tradition in West European Farming* (1972)

G. E. Fussell, *The Old English Farming Books from Fitzherbert to Tull, 1523 to 1730* (1947)

E. F. Gay, 'Inclosures in England in the Sixteenth Century', *Quarterly Journal of Economics*, XVII (1903), 576-97

E. F. Gay and I. S. Leadam, 'The Inquisitions of Depopulation in 1517 and the 'Domesday of inclosures'', *Transactions of the Royal Historical Society*, n.s. XIV (1900), 231-303

E. C. K. Gonner, 'The progress of Inclosure during the Seventeenth Century', *English Historical Review*, XXIII (1908), 477-501

H. L. Gray, *English Field Systems* (1915)

C. J. Harrison, 'Grain Price Analysis and Harvest Qualities, 1465-1634', *Ag.H.R.*, XIX ii (1971), 135-55

W. G. Hoskins, 'Harvest Fluctuations and English Economic History, 1480-1619', *Ag.H.R.*, XII i (1964), 28-46

W. G. Hoskins, 'Harvest Fluctuations and English Economic History, 1620-1759', *Ag.H.R.*, XVI i (1968), 15-31

G. Geraint Jenkins, *The English Farm Wagon: Origins and Structure* (1961)

E. Kerridge, *Agrarian Problems in the Sixteenth Century and After* (1969)

E. Kerridge, *The Agricultural Revolution* (1967)

E. Kerridge, 'The Movement of Rent, 1540-1640', *Ec.H.R.*, 2nd ser. VI i (1953-4), 16-34

E. Kerridge, 'The Returns of the Inquisitions of Depopulation', *English*

Historical Review, LXX (1955), 212-28

C. Lane, 'The Development of Pastures and Meadows During the Sixteenth and Seventeenth Centuries', *Ag.H.R.*, XXVIII i (1980), 18-30

J. Langdon, 'The Economics of Horses and Oxen in Medieval England', *Ag.H.R.*, XXX i (1982), 31-40

E. M. Leonard, 'The Inclosure of Common Fields in the Seventeenth Century', *Transactions of the Royal Historical Society*, n.s. XIX (1905), 101-46

J. Martin, 'Enclosure and the Inquisitions of 1607: An Examination of Dr Kerridge's Article 'The Returns of the Inquisitions of Depopulation'', *Ag.H.R.*, XXX i (1982), 41-8

A. R. Michell, 'Sir Richard Weston and the Spread of Clover Cultivation', *Ag.H.R.*, XXII ii (1974), 160-1

R. B. Outhwaite, 'Progress and Backwardness in English Agriculture, 1500-1650', *Ec.H.R.*, 2nd ser. XXXIX i (1986), 1-18

O. Rackham, *Trees and Woodland in the British Landscape* (1976)

M. L. Ryder, 'The History of Sheep Breeds in Britain', *Ag.H.R.*, XII i & ii (1964), 1-12 & 65-82

G. Slater, *The English Peasantry and the Enclosure of Common Fields* (1907)

W. E. Tate, *The English Village Community and the Enclosure Movements* (1967)

R. H. Tawney, *The Agrarian Problem in the Sixteenth Century* (1912)

E. G. R. Taylor, 'The Surveyor', *Ec.H.R.*, XVII ii (1947), 121-33

J. Thirsk (ed.), *The Agrarian History of England and Wales*, IV, 1500-1640 (1967)

J. Thirsk (ed.), *The Agrarian History of England and Wales*, V ii, *1640-1750 Agrarian Change* (1985)

J. Thirsk, 'Agricultural Policy: Public Debate and Legislation', in *A.H.E.W.*, ed. J. Thirsk, V ii (1985)

J. Thirsk, 'Enclosing and Engrossing', in *A.H.E.W.*, ed. J. Thirsk, IV (1967)

J. Thirsk, *England's Agricultural Regions and Agrarian History, 1500-1750*, Studies in Economic and Social History (1987)

J. Thirsk, 'The Farming Regions of England', in *A.H.E.W.*, ed. J. Thirsk, IV (1967), 1-112

J. Thirsk, 'Farming Techniques', in *A.H.E.W.*, ed. J. Thirsk, IV (1967), 161-99

J. Thirsk, *Horses in early modern England: for Service, for Pleasure, for Power*, University of Reading, The Stenton Lecture 1977 (1978)

J. Thirsk, *Land, Church, and People: Essays presented to Professor H. P. R. Finberg*, *Ag.H.R.*, XVIII Supplement (1970)

J. Thirsk, 'Plough and Pen: Agricultural Writers in the Seventeenth Century', in *Social Relations and Ideas: essays in honour of R. H. Hilton*, ed. T. H. Aston *et al.* (1983)

J. Thirsk, *The Rural Economy of England: Collected Essays* (1984)

J. Thirsk, 'Seventeenth-Century Agriculture and Social Change', in *Land, Church, and People: Essays presented to Professor H. P. R. Finberg*, ed. J. Thirsk, *Ag.H.R.*, XVIII Supplement (1970), 148–75

J. R. Wordie, 'The Chronology of English Enclosure, 1500–1914', *Ec.H.R.*, 2nd ser. XXXVI iv (1983), 483–505

(ii)   Regional and local

K. J. Allison, 'Flock Management in the Sixteenth and Seventeenth Centuries', *Ec.H.R.*, 2nd ser. XI i (1958), 98–112

J. Broad, 'Alternate Husbandry and Permanent Pasture in the Midlands, 1650–1800', *Ag.H.R.*, XXVIII ii (1980), 77–89

C. Dyer, *Warwickshire Farming 1349–c. 1520: Preparations for Agricultural Revolution*, Dugdale Society Occasional Papers, XXVII (1981)

M. E. Finch, *The Wealth of Five Northamptonshire Families, 1540–1640*, Publications of the Northamptonshire Record Society, XIX (1956)

L. Fox and P. Russell, *Leicester Forest* (Leicester, 1948)

E. F. Gay, 'The Midland Revolt and the Inquisitions of Depopulation of 1607', *Transactions of the Royal Historical Society*, n.s. XVIII (1904), 195–244

E. F. Gay, 'The Rise of an English Country Family', *Huntington Library Quarterly*, I iv (1938), 367–90

E. F. Gay, 'The Temples of Stowe and Their Debts: Sir Thomas and Sir Peter Temple, 1603–1653', *Huntington Library Quarterly*, II iv (1939), 399–438

R. H. Hilton, *The Economic Development of Some Leicestershire Estates in the Fourteenth and Fifteenth Centuries* (1947)

R. H. Hilton, 'Medieval Agrarian History', *V.C.H. Leics.*, II (1954), 145–98

W. H. Hosford, 'An Eye-Witness's Account of a Seventeenth-Century Enclosure', *Ec.H.R.*, 2nd ser. IV (1951–2), 216–20

W. G. Hoskins, 'The Leicestershire Farmer in the Seventeenth Century', in his *Provincial England: Essays in Social and Economic History* (1963), 149–69

W. G. Hoskins, 'The Leicestershire Farmer in the Sixteenth Century', *T.L.A.S.*, XXII i (1941–2), 34–94, revised and republished in his *Essays in Leicestershire History* (1950), 123–83

W. G. Hoskins (ed.), *Studies in Leicestershire Agrarian History*, *T.L.A.S.*, XXIV (1949)

L. A. Parker, 'The Agrarian Revolution at Cotesbach, 1501–1612', in *Studies in Leicestershire Agrarian History*, ed. W. G. Hoskins, *T.L.A.S.*, XXIV (1949), 41–76

L. A. Parker, 'Enclosure in Leicestershire, 1485–1607' (Ph.D. thesis, University of London, 1948)

P. A. J. Pettit, *The Royal Forests of Northamptonshire: a Study in their*

Economy, 1558-1714, Publications of the Northamptonshire Record Society, XXIII (1968)

B. K. Roberts, 'Field Systems of the West Midlands', in *Studies in Field Systems in the British Isles*, eds A. R. H. Baker and R. A. Butlin (1973)

J. Thirsk, 'Agrarian History, 1540-1950', *V.C.H. Leics.*, II (1954), 199-264

J. Thirsk, *English Peasant Farming: The Agrarian History of Lincolnshire from Tudor to Recent Times* (1957)

III Industry and trade

(i) General

(a) Industry

S. D. Chapman, 'The Genesis of the British Hosiery Industry 1600-1750', *Textile History*, III (1972), 7-50

L. A. Clarkson, 'The Leather Crafts in Tudor and Stuart England', *Ag.H.R.*, XIV i (1966), 25-39

D. C. Coleman, 'An Innovation and its Diffusion: the "New Draperies"', *Ec.H.R.*, 2nd ser. XXII iii (1969), 417-29

W. Felkin, *History of the Machine-Wrought Hosiery and Lace Manufactures* (1867, Centenary edn 1967)

G. Henson, *The Civil, Political, and Mechanical History of the Framework-Knitters in Europe and America* (1831, 1970 edn)

J. U. Nef, *The Rise of the British Coal Industry*, 2 vols (1932)

J. Thirsk, *Economic Policy and Projects: The Development of a Consumer Society in Early Modern England* (1978)

J. Thirsk, 'Industries in the countryside', in *Essays in the Economic and Social History of Tudor and Stuart England in honour of R. H. Tawney*, ed. F. J. Fisher (1961), 70-88

(b) Trade

K. J. Bonser, *The Drovers: who they were and how they went: an epic of the English Countryside* (1970)

P. J. Bowden, *The Wool Trade in Tudor and Stuart England* (1962)

R. H. Britnell, 'The Proliferation of Markets in England, 1200-1349', *Ec.H.R.*, 2nd ser. XXXIX ii (1981), 209-21

J. A. Chartres, 'The Marketing of Agricultural Produce', in *A.H.E.W.*, ed. J. Thirsk, V ii, *1640-1750 Agrarian Change* (1985)

J. A. Chartres, 'Road Carrying in England in the Seventeenth Century: Myth and Reality', *Ec.H.R.*, 2nd ser. XXX i (1977), 73-94

W. Cunningham, *The Growth of English Industry and Commerce in modern times*, 2 vols (1917-21)

D. Davis, *A History of Shopping* (1966)

P. Edwards, *The Horse Trade of Tudor and Stuart England* (1988)

A. Everitt, 'The Marketing of Agricultural Produce', in *A.H.E.W.*, ed. J. Thirsk, IV (1967)

F. J. Fisher, 'The Development of the London Food Market, 1540-1640', *Ec.H.R.*, V ii (1934-5), 46-64

N. S. B. Gras, *The Evolution of the English Corn Market from the Twelfth to the Eighteenth Century* (1926)

M. J. Hodgen, 'Fairs of Elizabethan England', *Economic Geography*, XVIII (1942), 389-400

I. D. Margary, *Roman Roads in Britain* (1967)

T. S. Willan, *The inland trade: Studies in English internal trade in the sixteenth and seventeenth centuries* (1976)

(ii)   Regional and local

W. A. Barker, 'Warwickshire Markets', *Warwickshire History*, VI v (1986), 161-75

R. J. Colyer, 'A Nineteenth Century Welsh Cattle Dealer in Northamptonshire', *Northamptonshire Past and Present*, V ii (1974), 121-6

J. Daniell, *Leicestershire Clockmakers: Directory of Watch and Clock Makers working in Leicestershire before 1900* (Leicester, 1975)

W. J. Davis, *The Token Coinage of Warwickshire, with Descriptive and Historical Notes* (Birmingham, 1895)

R. F. Dennington, 'Sale of Horses at Leicester, 1598', *Northamptonshire Past & Present*, IV v (1970-71), 268

R. A. Foster, 'Domestic Architecture of the Lutterworth District 1500-1840' (M.A. dissertation, University of Manchester, 1968)

M. J. Kingman, 'Markets and Marketing in Tudor Warwickshire; The Evidence of John Fisher of Warwick and the Crisis of 1586-87', *Warwickshire History*, IV i (1978), 16-28

D. R. Mills, 'Rural Industries and Social Structure: Framework Knitters in Leicestershire', *Textile History*, XIII ii (1982), 183-203

P. R. Mounfield, 'The footwear industry in the East Midlands', *East Midlands Geographer*, XXII (1964), 293-306, XXIII (1965), 394-413, XXIV (1965), 434-53, XXV (1965), 8-23

G. H. Tupling, 'Lancashire Markets in the Sixteenth and Seventeenth Centuries', *Transactions of the Lancashire and Cheshire Antiquarian Society*, LVIII (1945-6), 1-34

B. Winchester, *Tudor Family Portrait* (1955)

IV Economic and social history

(i) General studies

A. B. Appleby, 'Grain prices and subsistence crises in England and France, 1590-1740', *Journal of Economic History*, XXXIX (1979), 865-87

A. R. Bridbury, *Economic Growth: England in the Later Middle Ages* (1962)

M. Campbell, *The English Yeoman Under Elizabeth and the Early Stuarts* (1942)

P. Clark, *The English Alehouse: a social history 1200-1830* (1983)

D. C. Coleman, 'Labour in the English Economy of the Seventeenth Century', *Ec.H.R.*, 2nd ser. VIII iii (1956), 280-95

C. S. L. Davies, 'Peasant Revolt in France and England: a Comparison', *Ag.H.R.*, XXI ii (1973), 122-34

A. Everitt, *Change in the Provinces: the Seventeenth Century*, Leicester University Department of English Local History Occasional Papers, 2nd ser. no. 1 (1969)

A. Everitt, *Landscape and Community in England* (1985)

A. Everitt, 'Social Mobility in Early Modern England', *Past & Present*, XXXIII (1966), 56-73

F. J. Fisher (ed.), *Essays in the Economic and Social History of Tudor and Stuart England in honour of R. H. Tawney* (1961)

H. S. A. Fox, 'The People of the Wolds in English Settlement History', in *The Rural Settlements of Medieval England: Studies dedicated to M. Beresford and J. Hurst*, ed. M. Aston, D. Austin and C. Dyer (1989), 77-101

C. Hill, *The English Revolution*, 1640 (1940)

R. Hilton, *Class Conflict and the Crisis of Feudalism: Essays in Medieval Social History* (1985)

R. H. Hilton, *The English Peasantry in the Later Middle Ages* (1975)

R. Hilton, 'Individualism and the English Peasantry', *New Left Review*, CXX (March-April 1980), 109-11

R. Hilton, 'The Manor', *Journal of Peasant Studies*, I i (1973), 107-9

R. H. Hilton, 'The Peasantry as a Class', in his *The English Peasantry in the Later Middle Ages* (1975), 3-19

R. H. Hilton (introduction), *The Transition from Feudalism to Capitalism* (1978)

B. A. Holderness, ' 'Open' and 'Close' Parishes in England in the Eighteenth and Nineteenth Centuries', *Ag.H.R.*, XX ii (1972), 126-39

M. James, *Social Problems and Policy during the Puritan Revolution 1640-1660* (1930)

E. M. Leonard, *The Early History of English Poor Relief* (1900)

A. Macfarlane, *The Origins of English Individualism: The Family, Property and Social Transition* (1978)

R. B. Outhwaite, 'Dearth and Government Intervention in the English Grain Markets, 1590-1700', *Ec.H.R.*, 2nd ser. XXXIV iii (1981), 389-406

J. Saville, 'Primitive Accumulation and Early Industrialization in Britain', *Socialist Register* (1969), 247-71

P. Slack, 'Books of Orders: the Making of English Social Policy, 1577-1631', *Transactions of the Royal Historical Society*, 5th ser. XXX (1980), 1-22

P. Slack, *Poverty and Policy in Tudor and Stuart England* (1988)

K. D. M. Snell, *Annals of the Labouring Poor: Social Change and Agrarian England, 1660-1900*, Cambridge Studies in Population, Economy and Society in Past Time (1985)

P. Styles, 'The evolution of the law of settlement', in his *Studies in Seventeenth Century West Midlands History* (Kineton, 1978), 175-204

E. P. Thompson, 'The Moral Economy of the English Crowd in the eighteenth century', *Past & Present*, L (1971), 76-136

J. Walter and K. Wrightson, 'Dearth and Social Order in Early Modern England', *Past & Present*, LXXI (1976), 22-42

R. Williams, *The Country and the City* (1973)

K. Wrightson, 'Aspects of Social Differentiation in Rural England, c.1589-1660', *Journal of Peasant Studies*, V i (1977), 33-47

(ii)   Regional and local studies

(a)   Regions and counties

A. Dryden (ed.), *Memorials of Old Leicestershire* (1911)

R. H. Evans, 'Nonconformists in Leicestershire in 1669', *T.L.A.S.*, XXV (1949), 98-143

R. H. Evans, 'The Quakers of Leicestershire, 1660-1714', *T.L.A.S.*, XXVIII (1952), 63-83

L. Fox, *The Administration of the Honor of Leicester in the Fourteenth Century* (Leicester, 1940)

E. W. Hensman, 'Henry Hastings, Lord Loughborough, and the Great Civil War', in *Memorials of Old Leicestershire*, ed. A. Dryden (1911), 201-27

R. H. Hilton, *A Medieval Society: The West Midlands at the End of the Thirteenth Century* (1966)

W. G. Hoskins, *Essays in Leicestershire History* (1950)

W. G. Hoskins, *Provincial England: Essays in Social and Economic History* (1963)

J. E. Martin, *Feudalism to Capitalism: Peasant and Landlord in English Agrarian Development* (1983)

E. C. Pettet, 'Coriolanus and the Midlands Insurrection of 1607', *Shakespeare Survey*, III (1950), 34-42

C. Phythian-Adams, *Re-thinking English Local History*, Leicester University Department of English Local History Occasional Papers, 4th ser. no. 1

(1987)

B. Sharp, *In Contempt of All Authority: Rural Artisans and Riot in the West of England, 1586-1660* (1980)

J. Simon, 'Town Estates and Schools in the Sixteenth and Early Seventeenth Centuries' and 'Post-Restoration Developments: Schools in the County 1669-1700', in *Education in Leicestershire 1540-1940: A regional study*, ed. B. Simon (Leicester, 1968), 3-26 & 27-54

Victoria History of the County of Leicester, 5 vols (1907-65)

Victoria Histories of the Counties of Northampton, Nottingham, Oxford and Warwick

C. E. Welch, 'Early Nonconformity in Leicestershire', *T.L.A.S.*, XXXVII (1961-2), 29-43

(b)   Villages

N. W. Alcock, *Stoneleigh Villagers 1597-1650*, University of Warwick Open Studies (1975)

M. Bloxsom, *A History of the Parish of Gilmorton, in the County of Leicester* (Lincoln, 1918)

G. F. Farnham, 'Frolesworth - Notes on the Descent of the Manor', *T.L.A.S.*, XII ii (1922), 189-95

H. Goodacre, *Ashby Parva, Leicestershire* (privately printed, Lutterworth, n.d.)

A. Gooder, *Plague and Enclosure: A Warwickshire Village in the Seventeenth Century*, Coventry & North Warwickshire History Pamphlets, no. 2 (1965)

R. L. Greenall (ed.), *Naseby: A Parish History*, Leicester University Vaughan Papers in Adult Education, no. 19 (1974)

C. Holme, *A History of the Midland Counties (Guthlaxton Deaneries and adjacent Parishes), together with An Account of the Condition of the People During the Middle Ages* (Rugby, 1891)

W. G. Hoskins, *The Midland Peasant: The Economic and Social History of a Leicestershire Village* (1957)

A. E. Treen, *The History and Antiquities of the Vicinity of Rugby, Written and Printed on the hand-press*, I (Rugby, 1909)

A. Wood, 'Lancelot Brown and Newnham Paddox', *Warwickshire History*, I i (1969), 3-17

(c)   Towns

M. W. Beresford, 'The Origins of Medieval Boroughs of Warwickshire', *Warwickshire History*, I ii (1969), 2-14, I iii (1970), 29-30, I iv (1970), 28-9

C. J. Billson, *Medieval Leicester* (Leicester, 1920)

F. W. Bottrill, *An Illustrated Hand Book of Lutterworth with Notes on the*

Neighbouring Villages (Lutterworth, 3rd edn 1890)

F. W. Bull, *A Sketch of the History of the Town of Kettering together with some account of its Worthies* (Kettering, 1891)

F. W. Bull, *Supplement to the History of the Town of Kettering, together with a further account of its Worthies* (Kettering, 1908)

D. Charman, 'Leicester in 1525', *T.L.A.S.*, XXVII (1951), 19–29

D. Charman, 'Wealth and Trade in Leicester in the Early Sixteenth Century', *T.L.A.S.*, XXV (1949), 69–97

A. Dyer, 'Warwickshire Towns under the Tudors and Stuarts', *Warwickshire History*, III iv (1976–7), 122–35

A. H. Dyson (ed. H. Goodacre), *Lutterworth: John Wycliffe's Town* (1913)

J. Farrell, 'Lutterworth Pauper Children and Apprenticeship, 1673–1856', *Leicestershire Historian*, III ii (1983/4), 17–24

D. Fleming, 'A local market system: Melton Mowbray and the Wreake Valley 1549–1720' (Ph.D. thesis, University of Leicester, 1980)

W. G. Dimmock Fletcher, *Chapters in the History of Loughborough* (Loughborough, 1883)

W. G. Dimmock Fletcher, *Historical Handbook to Loughborough* (Loughborough, 1881)

H. J. Francis, *A History of Hinckley* (Hinckley, 1930)

J. Goodacre, 'Lutterworth in the sixteenth and seventeenth centuries: a market town and its area' (Ph.D. thesis, University of Leicester, 1977)

J. Goodacre, 'Occupations and Status in a Midland Market Town', unpublished paper contributed to Urban History Group Annual Conference, Canterbury (1983)

J. Goodacre, 'Wyclif in Lutterworth: Myths and Monuments', *Leicestershire Historian*, III ii (1983/4), 25–34

G. H. Green and M. W. Green, *Loughborough Markets and Fairs (through 7½ Centuries)* (Loughborough, 1964)

R. H. Hilton, 'The Small Town and Urbanisation - Evesham in the Middle Ages', *Midland History*, VII (1982), 1–8

J. F. Hollings, *The History of Leicester during the Great Civil War; a Lecture, delivered to the Members of the Leicester Mechanics' Institute, November 4, 1839* (Leicester, 1840)

W. G. Hoskins, 'English Provincial Towns in the Early Sixteenth Century', in his *Provincial England: Essays in Social and Economic History* (1963), 68–85

W. G. Hoskins, 'The Origin and Rise of Market Harborough', in his *Provincial England: Essays in Social and Economic History* (1963)

G. Irving, *Lutterworth Grammar School* (Leicester, 1956)

Lutterworth Town Study Group, 'Lutterworth in 1509', *Leicestershire Historian*, II vii (1976), 17–25

C. J. M. Moxon, 'Ashby-de-la-Zouch - a social and economic survey of a market town - 1570-1720' (D.Phil. thesis, University of Oxford, 1971)

D. M. Palliser, 'York under the Tudors: The Trading Life of the Northern Capital', in *Perspectives in English Urban History*, ed. A. Everitt (1973), 39-59

C. Phythian-Adams, *Desolation of a City: Coventry and the Urban Crisis of the Late Middle Ages*, Past and Present Publications (1979)

A. J. Pickering (ed. H. W. Chandler), *The Cradle and Home of the Hosiery Trade* (Hinckley, 1940)

T. R. Slater, 'Urban genesis and medieval town plans in Warwickshire and Worcestershire', in *Field and Forest: An historical geography of Warwickshire and Worcestershire*, eds T. R. Slater and P. J. Jarvis (1982), 173-202

J. Thompson, *The History of Leicester, from the Time of the Romans to the End of the Seventeenth Century* (Leicester, 1849)

J. Thompson, 'The Secular History of Lutterworth', *T.L.A.S.*, IV 1869-74 (1878), 159-70

A. E. Treen, *Historical Memorials of Lutterworth* (Rugby, 1911)

W. O. Wait, *Rugby Past and Present with an Historical Account of Neighbouring Parishes* (Rugby, 1893)

A. White, *A History of Loughborough Endowed Schools* (Loughborough, 1969)

T. S. Willan, *Elizabethan Manchester*, Chetham Society, 3rd ser. XXVII (1980)

(iii)   Urban studies

M. Beresford, *New Towns of the Middle Ages: Town Plantation in England, Wales and Gascony* (1967)

M. W. Beresford and H. P. R. Finberg, *English Medieval Boroughs: a hand-list* (1973)

P. Borsay, *The English Urban Renaissance: Culture and Society in The Provincial Town*, 1660-1770 (1989)

P. Clark (ed.), *The Transformation of English Provincial Towns 1600-1800* (1984)

P. Clark and P. Slack (eds), *Crisis and order in English towns 1500-1700: Essays in urban history* (1972)

J. Cornwall, 'English Country Towns in the Fifteen Twenties', *Ec.H.R.*, 2nd ser. XV i (1962), 54-69

A. Everitt, 'The English Urban Inn, 1560-1760', in *Perspectives in English Urban History*, ed. A. Everitt (1973), 91-137

A. Everitt (ed.), *Perspectives in English Urban History* (1973)

A. Everitt, 'The Primary Towns of England', *Local Historian*, XI v (1975), 263-77

R. H. Hilton, 'Small Town Society in England before the Black Death', *Past &*

Present, CV (1984), 53-78

R. H. Hilton, 'Lords, Burgesses and Hucksters', *Past & Present*, XCVII (1982), 3-15

R. H. Hilton, 'Medieval Market Towns and Simple Commodity Production', *Past & Present*, CIX (1985), 3-23

R. H. Hilton, 'The Small Town as Part of Peasant Society', in his *The English Peasantry in the Later Middle Ages* (1975), 76-94

R. Hilton, 'Towns in English Feudal Society', in his *Class Conflict and the Crisis of Feudalism: Essays in Medieval Social History* (1985), 175-86

J. Merrington, 'Town and Country in the Transition to Capitalism', in *The Transition from Feudalism to Capitalism*, ed. R. Hilton (1976), 170-95

C. V. Phythian-Adams, 'Urban Decay in Late Medieval England', in *Towns in Societies: Essays in Economic History and Sociology*, eds P. Abrams and E. A Wrigley (1978), 159-83

J. Thompson (of Leicester), *An Essay on English Municipal History* (printed in Leicester, 1867)

Index

The index incorporates a glossary. A figure in double quotation marks refers to the initial or defining occurrence of an unfamiliar term or of a word used as a special term. For weights and measures see the list on pp. xii–xiii.

The names of people mentioned in the text have been indexed, with explanatory details added to the entries for some local people.

Figures in italics refer to the appearances of names of places on the maps. Entries in capitals are the names of the villages in the Leicestershire part of the Lutterworth area.

For Product Safety Concerns and Information please contact our
EU representative GPSR@taylorandfrancis.com Taylor & Francis
Verlag GmbH, Kaufingerstraße 24, 80331 München, Germany